THE POLITICAL ECONOMY OF CHINESE FINANCE

INTERNATIONAL FINANCE REVIEW

Series Editor: J. Jay Choi

International Finance Review publishes theme-oriented volumes on various issues in international finance, such as international business finance, international investment and capital markets, global risk management, international corporate governance and institution, currency markets, emerging market finance, international economic integration, and related issues in international financial economics.

INTERNATIONAL FINANCE REVIEW   VOLUME 17

THE POLITICAL ECONOMY OF CHINESE FINANCE

EDITED BY

J. JAY CHOI
Temple University, Philadelphia, PA, USA

MICHAEL R. POWERS
Tsinghua University, Beijing, China

XIAOTIAN TINA ZHANG
Saint Mary's College of California, Moraga, CA, USA

United Kingdom – North America – Japan
India – Malaysia – China

Emerald Group Publishing Limited
Howard House, Wagon Lane, Bingley BD16 1WA, UK

First edition 2016

Copyright © 2016 Emerald Group Publishing Limited

Reprints and permissions service
Contact: permissions@emeraldinsight.com

British Library Cataloguing in Publication Data
A catalogue record for this book is available from the British Library

ISBN: 978-1-78560-958-9
ISSN: 1569-3767 (Series)

Printed and bound by CPI Group (UK) Ltd, Croydon, CR0 4YY

ISOQAR certified
Management System,
awarded to Emerald
for adherence to
Environmental
standard
ISO 14001:2004.

Certificate Number 1985
ISO 14001

INVESTOR IN PEOPLE

CONTENTS

PART III
CONTROL AND OWNERSHIP IN THE CORPORATE SECTOR

PART IV
RISK, REGULATION, AND FINANCIAL MARKETS

PART V
THE POLITICAL ECONOMY IN THE EXTERNAL SECTOR

LIST OF CONTRIBUTORS

C. Bülent Aybar	Southern New Hampshire University, Hooksett, NH, USA
Agyenim Boateng	Glasgow Caledonian University, Glasgow, UK
Hanwen Chen	University of International Business and Economics, Beijing, China
Zhirong Cheng	Xiamen International Bank, Xiamem, Fujian, China
Jongmoo Jay Choi	Temple University, Philadelphia, PA, USA
Bo Fan	Southern New Hampshire University, Hooksett, NH, USA
Aysun Ficici	Southern New Hampshire University, Hooksett, NH, USA
Ping He	Tsinghua University, Xiamem, Fujian, China
Qihao He	University of Connecticut, Storrs, CT, USA
Weijing He	University of Jinan, Jinan, Shandong, China; Glasgow Caledonian University, Glasgow, UK
Doohoi Heo	SK Research Institute for SUPEX Management, Seoul, Korea
Fang Hu	Griffith University, Nathan, QLD, Australia
Zsuzsa R. Huszár	National University of Singapore, Singapore, Singapore

Byung Jin Kang	Soongsil University, Seoul, Korea
Masaaki Kotabe	Temple University, Philadelphia, PA, USA
Seong-Bong Lee	Seoul Women's University, Seoul, Korea
Hao Liang	Singapore Management University, Singapore, Singapore
Artie W. Ng	Hong Kong Polytechnic University, Hong Kong, China
Michael R. Powers	Tsinghua University, Beijing, China
Luc Renneboog	Tilburg University, Tilburg, The Netherlands
Patrick Ring	Glasgow Caledonian University, Glasgow, UK
W. Travis Selmier, II	Indiana University, Bloomington, IN, USA
Robert Keith Shaw	Guangdong University of Foreign Studies, Guangzhou, Guangdong, China
Sunny Li Sun	University of Missouri at Kansas City, Kansas City, MO, USA
Ruth S. K. Tan	National University of Singapore, Singapore, Singapore
Wallace Tang	Saint Mary's College of California, Moraga, CA, USA
Kun Wang	Tsinghua University, Beijing, China
Lingling Wang	Worcester State University, Worcester, MA, USA
Xing Xiao	Tsinghua University, Beijing, China
Albert H. Yoon	US Bureau of Economic Analysis, Washington, DC, USA
Falin Zhang	Peking University, Beijing, China
Weina Zhang	National University of Singapore, Singapore, Singapore

Xiaotian Tina Zhang   Saint Mary's College of California, Moraga, CA, USA

Yahua Zhang   University of Southern Queensland, Toowoomba, QLD, Australia

Haiyan Zhou   University of Texas at Rio Grande Valley, Edinburg, TX, USA

PART I
AN OVERVIEW AND CONCEPTUAL FOUNDATIONS

MARKET SOCIALISM WITH "CHINESE CHARACTERISTICS"

Jongmoo Jay Choi, Michael R. Powers and
Xiaotian Tina Zhang

ABSTRACT

Purpose — *The paper provides an overview of material helpful in placing the subsequent papers in context, as well as a summary of the research contributions made by the individual papers themselves.*

Methodology/approach — *We begin with a timeline of China's Economic Reform, including both major events that permitted the opening and expansion of the nation's economy, and important milestones of the historical movement. We then consider the impact of philosophy and culture (particularly, Confucianism and socialism) on China's society and government, which leads naturally to certain observations regarding the political-economic model in which state-owned enterprises play a central role. In the final section, we briefly summarize the contents of the remaining papers.*

Keywords: China's economic reform; Confucianism; socialism; market forces; state-owned enterprises

The Political Economy of Chinese Finance
International Finance Review, Volume 17, 3–13
Copyright © 2016 by Emerald Group Publishing Limited
ISSN: 1569-3767/doi:10.1108/S1569-376720160000017007

INTRODUCTION

The opening and expansion of China's economy is arguably the most important economic story of the inter-millennium period. Identifying a comparable predecessor is difficult, but America's great Westward Expansion of the nineteenth century – with its unprecedented national economic growth – is an obvious candidate. Just as America's Westward Expansion was a period of dramatic political change for the United States, both domestically and internationally, so too China's Economic Reform has led to significant internal political reform and the emergence of China as a global superpower. In the present volume, we focus on those aspects of China's political economy impacting domestic and international financial markets during the Economic Reform period.

Political economy refers broadly to the collection of beliefs, practices, and laws underlying the creation and evolution of a nation's distribution of goods and services, but often is limited to relationships between government, through its decision makers and institutions, and the operation of various markets under its direct or indirect control. In the context of editing the present volume, we have employed the latter (more restrictive) definition, recognizing that individual papers may use the term more expansively. Thus, the book's title refers specifically to the relationships between China's government and firms and financial markets, primarily through the common economic mechanisms of monetary policy, fiscal policy, taxation, regulation, foreign trade, and commercial ownership. As will be seen, the last item in this list forms the most distinctive aspect of China's economic development.

The present paper provides a concise overview of background material helpful in placing the subsequent papers in context, as well as a summary of the research contributions made by the individual papers themselves. We begin with a timeline of China's Economic Reform, including both major events that permitted the opening and expansion of the nation's economy, and important milestones of the historical movement. We then consider the impact of philosophy and culture (particularly, Confucianism and socialism) on China's society and government, which leads naturally to certain observations regarding the political-economic model in which state-owned enterprises (SOEs) play a central role. In the final section, we briefly summarize the contents of the remaining papers.

TIMELINE OF CHINA'S ECONOMIC REFORM

The beginning of China's period of Economic Reform is often dated from the death of Chinese Communist Party (CCP) Chairman Mao Zedong in

1976. In Table 1, we provide a timeline of the major events and milestones of this period, from the implementation of Deng Xiaoping's first economic reforms to the present day. During this period, the CCP has had five official leaders: Hua Guofeng (1976–1981), Hu Yaobang (1981–1986), Zhao Ziyang (1986–1989), Jiang Zemin (1989–2002), Hu Jintao (2002–2012), and Xi Jinping (2012–present). However, from 1978 to his death in 1997, Deng Xiaoping – who never assumed the formal title of head of state or General Secretary of CCP – retained principal control of the government, and was known as the "paramount leader." Thus, Deng had many years in which to shape and guide his economic legacy.

Major economic changes of the reform period have included steps to: encourage private ownership of property and means of production; enhance foreign trade and investment; reduce regulation of the yuan and financial markets; and infuse capital into the economy. One crucial mechanism for introducing market forces was the creation and funding of SOEs (to be discussed in the following section), which often compete with one another within the same markets. Other important channels of reform have included domestic legal/regulatory changes necessary to support the new property and financial components of the developing economy and major diplomatic initiatives throughout the world.

As previously mentioned, China's Economic Reform has led to significant internal political change, most notably the formal recognition of private enterprise by the CCP. Indeed, the admission of private entrepreneurs to membership in the CCP would seem to have turned Karl Marx' scientific socialism on its head, but has been justified within Marxist theory by Deng and his successors (to be discussed in the next section). Moreover, the pattern of political change has not always been smooth, as can be seen from the abrupt dismissal of both Hu Yaobang (in 1986) and Zhao Ziyang (in 1989) following episodes of domestic unrest. Internationally, the growth of China's economy has led to a rising national self-confidence, boosted further by the country's achievements in space exploration and hosting of the 2008 Beijing Olympics. Although hinted at by only one event in Table 1 (the commissioning of the country's first aircraft carrier in 2012), China also has begun to use its growing economic might to project an enhanced military presence throughout Asia.

To offer a quantitative perspective on the period of Economic Reform, we present Figs. 1 and 2, which show how China's rapidly growing GDP has accompanied the events and milestones of Table 1. In Fig. 1, the size of China's economy is compared to the world's five other largest economies (the United States of America, Japan, Germany, the United Kingdom, and France), whereas in Fig. 2, it is compared to the four other "BRICS" economies (Brazil, Russia, India, and South Africa). Interestingly, China is something of an outlier in both plots.

6   JONGMOO JAY CHOI ET AL.

Table 1. Major Events and Milestones of China's Economic Reform.

Year	Event/Milestone
1976	• *Death of Mao Zedong (succeeded by Hua Guofeng as Chairman of the CCP).*
1978	• Implementation of economic reforms backed by *Deng Xiaoping*, including: opening trade with other nations; establishing "household-responsibility system," allowing farmers to sell surplus crops on the open market; and creation of "town village enterprises."
1979	• Normalization of diplomatic relations with the United States. • Enactment of law to allow domestic–foreign joint ventures. • Beginning of one-child policy.
1980	• Membership in the International Monetary Fund and World Bank. • Establishment of special economic zones in Shenzhen, Xiamen, Zhuhai, and Shantou to experiment with competitive market practices.
1981	• *Appointment of Hu Yaobang as Chairman of the CCP (whose title becomes "General Secretary" in 1982).* • Reform of household-responsibility system, permitting individual farmers (rather than collectives) to retain profits from surplus crops.
1984	• Creation of "open areas" in coastal regions to attract foreign investment.
1986	• Statement of basic legal principles underlying the market economy. • Anti-corruption protests in some major cities. • *Dismissal of Hu Yaobang as General Secretary of the CCP (replaced by Zhao Ziyang).*
1987	• CCP recognition of the need for a private sector.
1988	• Regulations for sole proprietorships, partnerships, and limited liability corporations.
1989	• Anti-government protests in some major cities, including Tiananmen Square events. • *Dismissal of Zhao Ziyang as General Secretary of the CCP (replaced by Jiang Zemin).*
1990	• Opening of Shanghai and Shenzhen stock exchanges.
1992	• *Deng Xiaoping*'s publicized tour of southern China, intended to encourage market liberalization. • CCP endorsement of "socialist market economy."
1993	• Period of high inflation; government response of controlling and restructuring loans.
1994	• Setting of official yuan exchange rate. • Creation of tax payment and auditing system. • Major economic cooperation with ASEAN. • Expansion of foreign-investment "open areas" to entire country.
1996	• Convertibility of yuan on current account, permitting the free flow of funds for imports and exports.
1997	• *Death of Deng Xiaoping.* • Handover of Hong Kong by the United Kingdom. • Reforms in response to the Asian financial crisis. • Chinese aid of more than 4 billion USD to Thailand and other Asian nations. • Enactment of law to allow market-based prices, with government oversight.

Table 1.   (*Continued*)

Year	Event/Milestone
1998	• Major (500 billion USD) government bailout of China's banks, necessary to address bad loans made early in the reform period.
1999	• Enactment of securities law.
2001	• Membership in the World Trade Organization, eliminating protectionist price controls and export subsidies.
	• Trading of B-share stocks by Chinese citizens.
2002	• Opening of CCP membership to private entrepreneurs.
	• *Appointment of Hu Jintao as General Secretary of the CCP.*
2003	• Trading of A-share stocks by foreign investors.
	• First manned space flight.
2004	• Formal constitutional recognition of private property.
	• Open-market agreement with 10 Southeast Asian nations.
2005	• Floating of yuan within managed band.
	• First Sino-US Strategic Economic Dialogue (SED).
2006	• Accumulation of 1 trillion USD in foreign currency reserves.
	• Completion of Three Gorges Dam and Tibet railway projects.
2007	• Second and Third SEDs.
2008	• Fourth SED.
	• Major government stimulus package to boost various economic sectors.
	• Hosting of Beijing Olympic Games.
2009	• Major oil purchase (25 billion USD over 20 years) from Russia.
2011	• World's second largest economy (surpassing Japan).
2012	• *Appointment of Xi Jinping as General Secretary of the CCP.*
	• Commissioning of first aircraft carrier.
2013	• Launch of anti-corruption drive by *Xi Jinping.*
	• Soft landing of robotic rover on the moon.
2014	• Majority ownership by foreign companies of some telecom services in Shanghai.
2015	• End of one-child policy.

In Fig. 1, China surpasses one major nation after another beginning in 2005, establishing itself as the world's second largest economy in 2011. If and when China eventually catches United States in GDP is a matter for soothsayers to debate; but if recent history is a reasonable guide, then this event is likely to occur within the next two decades.

In Fig. 2, China stands out as having the only economy that has not stagnated in recent years. Given this period of flat growth for Brazil, Russia, and India, and the much lower GDP of South Africa, it seems clear that (1) China has little in common with the other "BRICS" nations, and (2) the entire concept of "BRICS" nations as a cohesive international force is rather questionable.

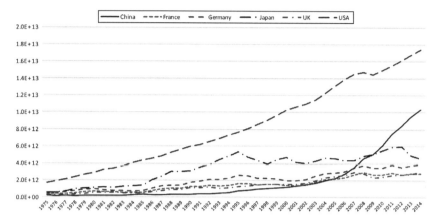

Fig. 1. National GDP (in 2014 USD) – China versus Other Largest Economies.
Source: World Bank.

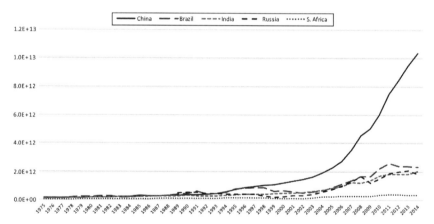

Fig. 2. National GDP (in 2014 USD) – China versus Other BRICS Economies.
Source: World Bank.

CONFUCIANISM, SOCIALISM, AND SOES

At the beginning of this paper, we compared China's Economic Reform to America's Westward Expansion. Interestingly, this comparison is consistent with a rough, and somewhat stereotypical, cultural dichotomy: that Western philosophy tends to encourage *individual* achievement, through overcoming challenges of the *external* world, whereas Eastern philosophies tend to encourage *group* (community) success through *local* (personal) social adaptation. Without asserting the broad applicability of this distinction, we do believe it provides a reasonable starting point for understanding China's approach to economic reform. Indeed, the Eastern half of the dichotomy, involving community success and personal adaptation, is more easily justified than the Western half of uncompromised individualism. This is because the ancient and enduring philosophy of Confucianism specifically promotes both ideas through its exhortation to create a harmonious society through each member's fitting well into his or her preordained role in the social hierarchy.[1]

Since 1949, Mainland China has been ruled by the CCP, which even today recognizes the political and economic theory of Karl Marx' scientific socialism as foundational. Although clearly a Western philosophy, socialism does value a preeminent concept of *group* success: the dictatorship of the proletariat.[2] Thus, it is not difficult to find similarities between certain critical elements of socialism − in particular, the concept of social progress through acceptance of a central political authority − and China's underlying Confucianism.

The political and economic views of Mao Zedong began to deviate from those of Soviet Marxists prior to 1949. Given the preindustrial economy of China, Mao advocated a form of revolution that skipped the conventional Marxist dialectic between proletariat (working class) and bourgeoisie (capitalist class), jumping directly from a postfeudal agrarian society to peasant-based socialism. Several decades later, Mao's adaptation would redound to the very different adaptation of Deng Xiaoping, which asserted that preindustrial China had entered only the "primary stage of socialism," and that a fully industrial economy − with competitive markets setting prices − would have to be developed before Marx' vision of socialism could be achieved. Deng's pragmatic approach is often described as socialism with "Chinese characteristics"; but given its emphasis on both social harmony and pragmatic adaptation to circumstances, one might argue that the term "Confucian characteristics" is equally fitting.

As noted in section "Timeline of China's Economic Reform," Deng's reforms took an innovative path of agricultural, commercial, and financial developments that dramatically changed China's national economy, with significant ramifications for the country's political system as well. A core innovation − and possibly the most important feature of the reform movement − has been the use of SOEs. Although government-owned corporations are reasonably common in Western market economies, they differ greatly from the Chinese model in that they tend to exist primarily as natural monopolies (in sectors such as transportation, telecommunications, energy, etc.), and rely on government regulation, rather than market forces, to set prices.

In China, SOEs appear in all major sectors of the economy, and often compete with one another in the same markets. In this way, they have played a major role in introducing the benefits of market forces to China's economy. The use of competition among SOEs to set market prices is entirely consistent with the CCP's theory that China is currently within the primary stage of socialism, and therefore needs the state to assume the role of the capitalist class in industrializing the nation. SOEs also frequently serve as an arm of the government in executing its fiscal policy (i.e., by directing funds to sectors in need of expansion through investments in relevant SOEs).

Although the market shares of SOEs in some sectors, such as manufacturing, have declined markedly over time, they remain strong in the financial sector, where banking is dominated by the "Big Four" SOEs (Industrial and Commercial Bank of China, China Construction Bank, Agricultural Bank of China, and Bank of China) and insurance by the "Big Five" SOEs (China Life Insurance Company, Ping An Insurance, China Pacific Insurance, People's Insurance Company of China, and New China Life Insurance). Most major SOEs are partially privatized and listed on domestic and/or foreign stock markets, in an effort both to raise capital and encourage operational transparency. One critical challenge remaining for China's SOEs is the potential for corruption caused by paying SOE executives substantially less than their private-sector counterparts. For this reason, SOEs have been an important focus of Xi Jinping's ongoing anti-corruption campaign.

FORTHCOMING PAPERS

The present volume is divided into five parts:

   I. An overview and conceptual foundations (to which this introductory paper belongs).
  II. State and corporate governance
 III. Control and ownership in the corporate sector
 IV. Risk, regulation, and financial markets
  V. The political economy in the external sector

In terms of the relationships between China's government and various financial markets, these five parts will specifically address the mechanisms of state versus private ownership (Parts II and III), regulation (Part IV), monetary and exchange rate policy (Part V), and foreign trade and investment (also Part V). Although the book touches only lightly on the specific topics of fiscal policy and taxation, we would note that: (1) as discussed in section "Confucianism, Socialism, and SOEs," China's fiscal policy often is carried out through investments in SOEs; and (2) taxation has played a relatively minor role in the Economic Reform, and is used primarily as a fine-tuning mechanism for heating/cooling economic activity.

The second (and remaining) paper of Part I — "The metaphysical foundations of political economy in China and the West," by Robert Keith Shaw — explores the fundamental differences between the political economy of China and that of the West through the metaphysical systems extant in the two respective cultures.

Part II covers fundamental governance issues within China's SOEs through the following papers:

- "A state-stewardship view on executive compensation," by Hao Liang, Luc Renneboog, and Sunny Li Sun, studies the level and structure of Chinese executive compensation, and finds that it fails to satisfy principal-agent model expectations.
- "Netizens and private monitoring in Chinese banking," by W. Travis Selmier, II, investigates whether a confluence of factors (including the social obligations embedded in the Chinese system of *guanxi*, information dynamics released through the Internet and other media, and certain unique aspects of Chinese banking and finance) lead to a better-functioning, better-governed banking system.
- "CEO promotion, relative performance measures and institutions in an emerging market: Evidence from China's listed state-owned enterprises," by Fang Hu and Yahua Zhang, studies the nature, motivation, and effectiveness of incentive schemes in SOEs.

Part III peers more deeply into the realm of SOEs and their nongovernment competitors, with an emphasis on the relationship between state ownership and firm value:

- "Does government control always reduce firm value? Theory and evidence from China," by Ping He, Kun Wang, and Xing Xiao, assesses both benefits and costs of government control, and demonstrates, both theoretically and empirically, that the government likely chooses a suboptimal level of control with respect to maximizing firm value.

- "Internal control, corporate life cycle and firm performance," by Haiyan Zhou, Hanwen Chen, and Zhirong Cheng, explores whether the impact of internal control on Chinese firm performance varies across a firm's life cycle stages.
- "The effect of privatization processes and the split-share structure reform on the market reaction to the announcements of transitional non-traditional shares," by Bo Fan, Aysun Ficici, Lingling Wang, and C. Bülent Aybar, considers the relationship between the split-share structure reform and privatization in light of the interplay between listing announcements of nontraditional shares within the steel industry and market reaction to these shares, and analyzes the value gained by firms as a result of privatization.

Part IV addresses the roles of government, banking, and insurance in regulating and mitigating financial risks:

- "Regulatory risks and strategic controls in the global financial center of China," by Artie W. Ng and Wallace Tang, examines the experiences of Hong Kong's financial institutions exposed to global systemic risk, and explores the underlying regulatory risk controls that have been emphasized and implemented within the developmental experience of Hong Kong's financial regulatory system.
- "Bank internationalization: An examination of the role of government and home institutions in emerging economies," by Weijing He, Patrick Ring, and Agyenim Boateng, studies the role of government and home institutions in bank internationalization through an analysis of the effect of government policy on Chinese commercial banks' international expansion.
- "Climate change, catastrophe risk, and government stimulation of the insurance market: A study of transitional China," by Qihao He, introduces the impact of climate change, assesses the Chinese government's responsibilities under the "whole-nation system" with regard to catastrophe risks, and then proposes a catastrophe insurance market to combine the merits of both government and private markets.

Finally, Part V embarks on a review of the international impacts of China's Economic Reform through both the nation's monetary and exchange rate policy and foreign trade and investment:

- "Determinants and fluctuations of China's exchange rate policy: National interests and decision-making processes," by Falin Zhang, offers a two-pronged explanation of the determinants and fluctuation of

China's exchange rate policy in the past decade, arguing that China's exchange rate policy is essentially driven by the country's national interests in the long run, with specific decision-making processes conforming to or violating these interests in the short and medium term.

- "Efficiency of regulated and unregulated FOREX markets: An analysis of onshore and offshore renminbi forward markets," by Zsuzsa R. Huszar, Ruth S. K. Tan, and Weina Zhang, argues that, despite China's growing importance in global trade, its financial markets, including the Chinese foreign exchange (FOREX) market, are hindered by both a lack of foreign participants and excessive government intervention.
- "Do sectoral and locational factors of foreign direct investment from emerging countries matter for firm performance? The case of Korean firms' FDI in China's service sector," by Seong-Bong Lee, Masaaki Kotabe, Doohoi Heo, Byung Jin Kang, and Albert H. Yoon, addresses a new pattern of foreign direct investment in which multinational enterprises from growing economies actively search for investment opportunities abroad, and explores this phenomenon from the perspective of Korean firms seeking to invest in China.

It is our view that the state of academic research on the political-economic dimensions of Chinese finance is in early flux, as is the state of political economy of China that is in transition and evolution. We have collected 13 unpublished individual scholarly research papers that examine specific conceptual and empirical issues pertaining to various dimensions of the political economy of Chinese finance. Together, it is hoped that this volume provides a broader perspective on the state of the political economy of Chinese financial markets and systems, and thereby assists scholars and practitioners alike.

NOTES

1. For example, in *Analects* XII, 11, Confucius states: "There is government, when the prince is prince, and the minister is minister; when the father is father, and the son is son."
2. Of course, Marx did not propose achieving this objective through social adaptation, but rather by the (very Western and likely violent) resolution of a social/political dialectic.

THE METAPHYSICAL FOUNDATIONS OF POLITICAL ECONOMY IN CHINA AND THE WEST

Robert Keith Shaw

ABSTRACT

Purpose − *This paper extends our understanding of the concept and global practice of political economy.*

Approach − *The paper sets out the limits of conceptual analysis regarding political economy. It then applies Heidegger's theory of metaphysics to the cultures of China and the West.*

Findings − *It is possible to construct an account of Confucianism metaphysics which contrasts with modern western metaphysics. The paper suggests some implications of the contrast.*

Research limitations − *The paper is exploratory and broad-brush. It suggests the potential of further systematic enquiries.*

Practical implications − *National and business leaders seek to understand the global business environment. This requires insights into the*

The Political Economy of Chinese Finance
International Finance Review, Volume 17, 15−35
Copyright © 2016 by Emerald Group Publishing Limited
ISSN: 1569-3767/doi:10.1108/S1569-376720160000017008

nature of culture and the foundations of cultures. The paper provides a way to make sense of national aspirations and global political/business responses to changed circumstances.

Originality — *The paper continues a research programme which seeks to explicate Chinese decision-making and relate it to the western decision-making. It is the first paper to use Heidegger's concept of metaphysics in relation to Confucianism.*

Keywords: Phenomenology; ontology; Heidegger; management; Confucianism; modernity

INTRODUCTION

This paper argues that the difference between the political economy of China and that of the West is profound in a very fundamental way. It is more than an expression of history or culture. There are deeper, hidden forces at work which ensure the two worlds remain apart. This hidden underpinning of culture and political economy is metaphysics.

Chinese metaphysics, or more accurately Confucian metaphysics, is distinct from Western metaphysics. If you are Chinese and you live in China then Chinese metaphysics permeates your every thought and action — but it is hidden from you, not something which becomes a part of your conscious deliberations. Likewise, if you are from a Western country you engage with the world in accordance with your western metaphysical presuppositions. Neither the Chinese person nor the Western person has the ability to shake-off metaphysics. Your metaphysical strictures are not like culture. You can adapt your thinking and your actions to accommodate cultural differences.

Chinese political leadership proclaims that China wants to learn and borrow from the West but China wants to remain distinctly Chinese. This paper argues that the Chinese leadership has nothing to fear regarding this matter: it is not possible for the Chinese to lose their metaphysical heritage — to cease to be Confucian. Chinese metaphysics will remain regardless of what Western practices people adopt in mainland China. Culture, however, is subject to flux.

One of the goals of this paper is to discuss examples which enable us to see the influence of metaphysics. This may lead to an appreciation of the profound differences between metaphysical groupings of peoples and how it can be unwarranted to judge the actions of others who are so profoundly different from yourself, and whom you cannot possibly understand. Our situation is somewhat like the fish in the goldfish bowl. The fish cannot see the water, nor can the fish imagine a world of life above the water.

Each of us is the "victim" of our own metaphysics. In our everyday living metaphysics is transparent − it is not experienced, it is the background upon which experience occurs. In the history of philosophy there is a famous article entitled "What it is like to be a bat" (Nagel, 1974). This discusses what it is like to be a bat, not what it is like to be human and act like a bat, or to pretend to be a bat. All we can do is to imagine hanging upside down in the dark and receiving some sort of stimulus from a sensory apparatus which human beings do not have. We might liken the sensory experience to hearing or to seeing or to smelling. But, is the experience of hearing the same as the experience of seeing and the same as the experience of smelling? Not really at our level of sophistication. Likewise, the sensory input to the bat is beyond human experience in the sense of beyond human knowing. You can never experience what a bat experiences. You cannot abide with the metaphysical world other than that which is yours.

Another aspect of the bat discussion relates to language. This concerns us because Western metaphysics entails many of the limitations of modern science and some of these relate to language. We cannot reliably and accurately describe colours, tastes and smells. Isaac Newton, a major figure in the establishment of modern science, confronted this when he used a prism to divide white light into colours. Newton makes many attempts to describe his experiments and the "seemingly innumerable variants from the first" (Newton, 1984b, p. 51). As Newton says of his work in optics when he came to indicate the colours:

> But to present my idea more distinctly: First, I find that to differently refrangible rays there correspond different colors. To the most refrangible ones there corresponds purple or violet, and to the least refrangible red, and the intermediate ones green, or rather the boundary of green and greenish blue. Blue, however, falls between purple and green, and yellow between green and red. Hence, as the rays are more and more refrangible, they are disposed to generate these colours in order: red, yellow, green, blue, and violet, together with all of their successive gradations and intermediate colors. (Newton, 1984a, p. 437)

There were not words available to describe all the colours Newton saw nor was there a way to indicate colours without showing them to people. Newton asserts that modern science could not be accurate in human terms. Scientists have overcome the limitations of the human sensory apparatus through the use of transducers. A colour is now described as a wavelength of light. In doing this, science has taken a step away from human reality. You and I have never seen a wavelength of light. We do not see any *length* when we see red or blue. Likewise, we cannot describe the sensory input that a bat receives. We can see that modern science — from its origins — entails uncertainties and limitations. We can see in Newton's dilemma the difference between the human phenomenology of experience and the scientific rendition of a limited reality (the word "phenomenology" has come to have all manner of meanings, but here it is used in the sense that shows in the work of Husserl and Heidegger).

The approach taken below is to set out Heidegger's ontic concept of "political economy" and relate that to a few of the issues that appear in the literature about China and the West. Heidegger did not consider the notion of political economy as such, but we can construct what he might have said from the examples he gave, primarily those of the physical sciences. Then, Heidegger's theory of metaphysics is introduced and used to address issues that relate to China and the West. Western metaphysics rests upon a construct of understanding which is less than 500 years old. It arose with the rise of modern science. It holds the West firmly in its grip.

POLITICAL ECONOMY

'Political economy' as an intellectual discipline originated in the West. It is a construct of Western culture(s). What is the ontological status of the *concept* of 'political economy'? According to Heidegger, it is an ontic construct. The word "ontic" derives from the Greek ὄν, genitive ὄντος and refers to that which is, or which exists for us. Early in *Being and Time*, Heidegger refers to the "ontical sciences" and contrasts research in these sciences with research in ontology.

The Phenomenology of Political Economy

Political economy is an example of an ontical science. Inquiry, in such a science, "is concerned primarily with *entities* and the facts about them" (Heidegger, 1927/1962, p. 31). Ontic beings are discrete objects or concepts, with physical, real or factual existence. 'Political economy' is an ontic construct generated from within a particular calculating, intellectual discipline. The origins of the concept reside within the works of its founding scholars.

It is phenomenological but its phenomenology shows us that 'political economy' is to be found in our human deliberations and not as an identifiable object in any physical world we inhabit. Business people, for example, may function perfectly well within the political economy of a country without that abstract construct engaging them in any way. Metaphysics, in contrast, engages the business practitioner, all be it without it being an object of consciousness.

The phenomenology of the concept 'political economy' is located within the practices and engagement of those involved in the intellectual discipline of political economy. 'Political economy' is a part of what Heidegger describes as a regional ontology. The concept only makes sense within an association of other concepts and with the adoption of a particular way of thinking about identifiable phenomena. Below we relate this to the "tree analogy" of metaphysics.

The tellers in an old-fashioned bank are not engaged with the concept of 'political economy' nor the discipline of political economy. The reality they encounter is a world of rules, computers, program outputs and inputs (not the programs themselves), customers and managers. These objects, involvements and purposes are (in Heidegger's creative terminology) *ready-to-hand*. Tellers deal with situations competently and completely, but at the end of the day they cannot recall each action, or even the particular customers who were cleared. The more busy the bank branch and the more demanding the tellers' work, the easier it is for us to observe these phenomena. The actual processing undertaken by tellers – the physical and mental work, but strictly we should avoid confusing this ontological account of the human being with one that involves the psychologists' mental and physical dualism – is "invisible" to them. They do not dwell upon each action or decision; it is just advanced in a smooth flow of work. When tellers cope easily with tasks in familiar circumstances, they deal with ready-to-hand beings. Everything encountered in this way is of practical use and there is no reflective involvement with things. Everything the tellers encounter appears as equipment and it is dealt with as equipment. Heidegger describes this in his seminal work *Being and Time*:

> Only because equipment has *this* 'Being-in-itself' and does not merely occur, is it manipulable in the broadest sense and at our disposal. No matter how sharply we just look...
> at the outward appearance of Things, in whatever form this takes, we cannot discover anything ready-to-hand. (Heidegger, 1927/1962, p. 98)

The tellers manipulate equipment – that which is there to be dealt with – but they do not deliberate or consciously think. The tellers themselves become a part of the equipment. They are in the world of equipment. Ontologically their status is that they are ready-to-hand beings or in the mode of ready-to-hand beings (a Heideggerian phenomenologist might debate these assertions).

Modern psychologists may say the tellers' actions are undertaken in the subconscious or in "memory", but that is to confuse the present ontological description with a description from within the scientific discipline of psychology. Tellers classify the paper they hold and place it in the correct receptacle without any awareness of the receptacle. Or, they type the customer's name without any awareness of the individual letters or keys they must identify and hit on the keyboard. If after a teller's shift you ask them what they did they will construct the details for you. People asked about what occurs as they engage with ready-to-hand beings often "fill in the gaps" − they will create an account about what happened. Those asked about particular classifications of documents or keys hit, admit, "I did not pay attention" "it did not seem important" or "I did not notice". The use of the word "attention" takes us to the foundations of an ontic discipline, the modern discipline of psychology, and specifically to the pioneering work of William James (James, 1950, pp. 402−458). As an empirical discipline, psychology must explain what occurs with reference to that which it objectifies. The inability of people to detail ready-to-hand involvements, which a psychologist might describe as a lapse of self-consciousness or self-awareness, is explained by reference to a lapse in attention.

It is when something goes wrong, there is a problem of some kind, that the work of the teller becomes "visible" and things take on a different kind of significance. It is then that different ontic beings (or the same beings in a different mode) appear with their significance. The teller confronts equipment which has failed and become unusable:

> When its unusability is thus discovered, equipment becomes conspicuous. This conspicuousness presents the ready-to-hand equipment as in a certain un-readiness-to hand. (Heidegger, 1927/1962, pp. 102−103)

In *Being and Time*, Heidegger considers this to have been something understood by the pre-Socratic philosophers, such as Parmenides:

> ... that simple awareness of something present-at-hand in its sheer presence-at-hand, which Parmenides had already taken to guide him in his own interpretation of Being − has the Temporal structure of a pure 'making-present' of something. (Heidegger, 1927/1962, p. 48)

The involvement of the truth of disclosure in the human way of being relates to both ready-to-hand and present-at-hand. About the time when he writes *Being and Time*, Heidegger proffers to his students:

> For Parmenides, the most proper possibility of truth presupposes untruth. Not change and becoming, but *doxa itself as belonging to truth.* More precision in the actual interpretation. Truth-Being: The most intimate connection. Being and knowledge, Being and consciousness. ... *Through and in the one truth, the one Being; and only in Being, truth.* (Heidegger, 1926/2008, p. 53, his emphasis)

Thus, there are two modes of being which can involve political economy.

The scholar who works in a Finance, Economics or Political Science department may engage with the concept 'political economy' as an ontic concept but with a phenomenology distinct from that of the teller — in each case the ontic beings are a part of the real world that involves them, which is to say, in the case of the teller the world within the bank and in the case of the scholar the world we associate with the library.

The Concept of Political Economy

A direct relationship to familiar human activities is established, along with the liberal use of analogies, at the founding of the discipline, political economy. When Jean-Jacques Rousseau wrote *A Discourse on Political Economy* for Diderot and d'Alembert's *Encyclopedia* in the mid-eighteenth century he began with these words:

> The word Economy, or OEconomy, is derived from *oikos*, a *house*, and *nomos*, *law*, and meant originally only the wise and legitimate government of the house for the common good of the whole family. The meaning of the term was then extended to the government of that great family, the State. To distinguish these two senses of the word, the latter is called general or political economy, and the former domestic or particular economy. The first only is discussed in the present discourse. (Rousseau, 1755, p. 1)

His discussion of the family, authority, strength and convention sets out a model for the analysis of modern States. Rousseau develops a notion of a "general will" (akin to various forms of the "common/universal wealth or good") which stands in contrast to the many constructs of individual inclination, self-interest, rights and prerogatives. Thus, the discipline of political economy is set on a path which involves moral principles and phenomenological observations, in the main understood by reference to the grand analogy with the family.

Alfred Marshall, another significant figure in the establishment of the discipline of political economy, reinforces the human perspective in his introductory *Principles of Economics*. He establishes the relationship between the intellectual discipline and human activity from the outset:

> Political Economy or Economics is a study of mankind in the ordinary business of life; it examines that part of individual and social action which is most closely connected with the attainment and with the use of the material requisites of wellbeing. (Marshall, 1890, p. 6)

The ethical prerogative enters this opening paragraph with "ordinary business of life" and "wellbeing". Marshall then asserts that "study of man" is the most important "side" of the discipline:

> Thus it is on the one side a study of wealth; and on the other, and more important side, a part of the study of man. For man's character has been moulded by his every-day work, and the material resources which he thereby procures, more than by any other influence unless it be that of his religious ideals; and the two great forming agencies of the world's history have been the religious and the economic. (Marshall, 1890, p. 6)

Marshall begins his work with assumptions about the nature and human character of people as well as assumptions about the kind of lives people lead. These are assumptions about culture.

It is easy to forget the origins of intellectual disciplines when they come to involve us. Theorists and commentators become entrapped in the presuppositions of their disciplines. The foundational presuppositions remain embedded in the discipline as the theory and the practice evolves. The pathways towards the creation of wealth have altered radically in the last half-century. The West moved beyond the nineteenth century phase of capitalism when globalisation created wealth through hard-structure technology and colonialism. Knowledge about technology and the flow of information, we are told, now govern the differential growth patterns of individual corporations and nation states. Corporate and national innovation is critical. Universities, reconstructed, must align to serve the knowledge economy for they are the principal drivers of the modern economy (Peters & Besley, 2006). All this is premised on the received view of political economy which privileges individualism and competition. This organic description of wealth creation asserts that "economic progress" is the outcome of human initiative, but not of global human design. The organic paradigm (prominent theorists include Hayek, Smith, Marx and Desai) has largely overcome the mechanistic paradigm.

The same presuppositions enter into English language enquiries into the modern development of China. For example, Wong and Bo applaud

Deng Xiaoping's "pragmatic policies" and detail how China embarked on "a journey of economic reform and development, learning and adapting from its neighbours and former socialist countries as well as from the West" (Wong & Bo, 2010, p. 1). China, in its engagement with former socialist countries and the West, encounters the economic paradigm which is loosely called "neoliberalism". Many authors debate the power within modernity and neoliberalism (e.g., DeMartino, 2000; Harris & Seid, 2000; Marttila, 2013; Peters, 2002; Toulmin, 1990). The relationship between 'neoliberalism' and concepts such as 'ideology' and 'capitalism' are discernable in Flew's taxonomy of the uses of the word "neoliberalism". According to Flew the word "neoliberalism" may refer to:

1. An all-purpose denunciatory category;
2. The way things are;
3. A particular institutional framework characterizing Anglo-American forms of national capitalism;
4. A dominant ideology of global capitalism;
5. A form of governmentality and hegemony; and
6. A variant within the broad framework of liberalism as both theory and policy discourse. (Flew, 2014, p. 49)

Flew draws attention to how "this sprawling set of definitions are not mutually compatible" (in other words, 'neoliberalism' is a concept), and suggests that some authors use the term for "anything and everything ... [they] find objectionable" (Flew, 2014, p. 49). The sprawling uses of the word do not, nevertheless, preclude our recognising the Eurocentric character of the whole.

We might ask if the same constructs are in use in discussions of political economy in China. One ongoing study raises questions, at least in the mind of the present author, about the concepts at work in Chinese business. An international research team, coordinated by Professor Xiaoming Huang at Victoria University of Wellington (New Zealand), investigates the institutional dynamics of China's great transformation (New Zealand China Contemporary Research Centre Political Economy Research Cluster, 2015). Their case studies reveal a persistent tension between two sets of dynamic forces and interests in the shaping of the institutional setting. These are, on the one hand, the state and its associated agencies, and on the other, the existing and emergent forces in society which have the capacity to shape and influence the formation of institutions. The team asserts:

The findings in these case studies clearly defy the conventional wisdom that sees the process of institutional formation and change in China as driven primarily by the state, a view ironically shared by both China scholars with a state centric view about the Chinese system, and conventional institutional theorists who tend to see institutional formation and change as primarily about state-sanctioned formal institutions. (New Zealand China Contemporary Research Centre Political Economy Research Cluster, 2015)

This challenge to the conventional view of Chinese business development opens for scholars several questions. We wish to know more of the "forces" and "processes" that the researchers mention — but we also ask, is it possible for European scholars to achieve an adequate understanding of Chinese business formation.

The concepts of the discipline of political economy are historical, interrelated and evolving. Nevertheless, they reflect their origins and the phenomenology which relates to their origins. Wittgenstein suggests we should heed the use of words to discern concepts (e.g., as opposed to dictionary definitions). The phenomenology of political economy was in its origins homely or domestic. Now the intellectual discipline proceeds in many dimensions without its contributors engaging the domestic origins. Heidegger would say it has become "calculating", meaning that its phenomenology now primarily involves people sitting at their desks. And, further, the concepts of a Western discipline, much bound by culture and their generative forces, are being taken into enquires in China.

METAPHYSICS

This section introduces the concept of metaphysics and then sets out Heidegger's unique rendition of that concept, which involves the concept of historical metaphysical periods. The section concludes with a description of Western metaphysics and Confucian metaphysics.

An Historical Perspective on the Concept of 'Metaphysics'

The concept 'metaphysics' has a long and disputatious history. Alexandrians in the first century gave the term "metaphysics" to the works written by Aristotle that appeared after those on physics. The diverse content of those books renders them as a poor guide to the subject of metaphysics itself. Aristotle's work *Metaphysics* discusses "first causes", that which founds all the disciplines of human enquiry (e.g., ethics, mathematics, physics and politics), that which is of most generality or most foundational for human beings. It enquires into beings *qua* beings.

Immanuel Kant draws upon both Aristotle and Newton in his account of metaphysics. Kant seeks to explain the success of Newton's physics, which is to say, the ability of modern science to predict and to contribute to technological advancement. This success of modern science is not merely theoretical for acclaimed discoveries are frequent in Kant's city. For example, Knutzen predicts the return of a comet in 1744 (Kuehn, 2001, p. 83). The association of modern science with technological innovation began with Galileo and continued with Newton and many other early experimental scientists. Kant requires for modern science a foundation that is as credible as the science itself:

> Metaphysical thinking is not in the least entitled to be an invention; it is not prospective as in geometry, in which new conclusions are successively formed from an original definition, but rather retrospective, so that given a state of affairs it seeks out the conditions from which that state results; for a total phenomenon it seeks the possible "grounds of explanation". (Cassirer, 1981, p. 71)

The determinacy and evidence associated with Newton's physics need to be associated with metaphysics. Thus for Kant, metaphysics became the study of appearances and ultimate or foundational reality to the extent that humankind may know these things. Heidegger largely concurs with Kant on the nature of metaphysics although he gives the subject a new dimension. For Heidegger, metaphysics is also about appearances and reality — as rendered in the study of beings and beings in their totality, which equates to the study of what exists, ontology. This, of course, includes all human economic activity as phenomena and the theorising of political economy.

Heidegger's Concept of Metaphysics

A concept of metaphysics, in Heidegger's sense, must provide an account of human beings which integrates our understanding of several things. First, it must indicate how the distinctive periods of human existence relate to each other (thus, it must consider what must be for there to be different periods of human history); and second it must indicate how the individual human being is maintained within the metaphysical era (how the business practitioner and the scholar are equally held as creatures of their age).

The concept which enables these apparently dispirit objectives to be achieved is 'truth'. The "mechanisms of metaphysics" depend on a particular concept of truth, *alētheia* (Ancient Greek ἀλήθεια, truth as disclosure).

Although the notion of *alētheia* develops in Heidegger's work, it generally refers to that which enables ontic beings to be intelligible to us. We commonly think of truth as being about the dichotomy true-false. But ask yourself what is necessary for there to be such a dualism. At work in all our judgements about what is true (or real or exists) is this foundational understanding of what we consider as possible. In Heidegger's terminology, it is what enables us to abide with our ontological world. Heidegger likens *alētheia* to the sap within a tree:

> As the root of the tree, it sends all nourishment and all strength into the trunk and its branches. The root branches out into the soil and ground to enable the tree to grow out of the ground and thus to leave it. The tree of philosophy grows out of the soil in which metaphysics is rooted. The ground and soil is the element in which the root of the tree lives, but the growth of the tree is never able to absorb this soil in such a way that it disappears in the tree as part of the tree. (Heidegger, 1949/1998, p. 278)

This analogy enables our access to several ideas. Below the ground, hidden from us, is the reserve of truth. This is a foundation of understanding upon which rests all human thought and action. The constructs of disclosed truth (*alētheia*) flow through all human being (existence) as the sap rises and flows throughout the tree. The primordial truths (from below the ground) are enduringly with you and (always to a significant extent, but not exclusively) determine what you can think and what you can do. The judgements you make about what is true or real are based on this foundation. Truth as the soil or the ground of things that can be true, *alētheia*, which is a "self-evident determination of truth" and "it settles into an openness already holding sway and does so, as it were, each time anew" (Heidegger, 1938/ 1994, pp. 22–23).

Heidegger's Metaphysical Eras

Heidegger did not develop a notion of Confucian metaphysics. He did however describe in great detail several metaphysical eras: the Pre-Socratic Greek metaphysics, Western Medieval metaphysics and Western metaphysics. Metaphysics is the foundation of an "age" or historical era. The characteristic of each age is determined by a particular comprehension of disclosed truth (*alētheia*) which determines how the people of that age comprehend whatever they do comprehend and however they act. For each era there is a primordial truth construct of the people, which, if we can discern it, offers an explication of both the individual human way of being and distinct cultures.

In *The Age of the World Picture*, Heidegger says metaphysics is the "ground plan" and the "sphere opened up". By this he means that the metaphysical constructs of truth are the human beings most primeval constructs and they set the parameters within which all understanding of an action must occur. This is akin to the subconscious world picture or world view that the human being is given by virtue of their heritage and the circumstances into which they are born.

This tree analogy is in the tradition of those theory-building philosophers who distinguish between structure (ground, foundations and form) and content (the West, Confucianism, intellectual disciplines and the way ordinary human beings exist day-by-day). Consider the structure of a tree. Some of the "large branches" are analogous to constructs such as Ancient Greek metaphysics, Western metaphysics and Confucian metaphysics. Cultures and intellectual disciplines are towards the end of the major branches. Modern science gives rise to Western metaphysics and the neoliberal way of business. Historians trouble about why modern science appeared in the West and not in Islamic or Confucian cultures which were comprehensive and sophisticated (Huff, 1995). There are other questions to ask, such as how the different cultures and metaphysical groups temporally maintain themselves.

The small branches that sprout from the trunk that is Western metaphysics represent the intellectual disciplines which began in the West. They have hidden within them the presuppositions of *alētheia* (disclosed truth) that accord with Western metaphysics.

Western Metaphysics

The word "modernity" roughly equates to the notion of Western metaphysics. That comparison is helpful when students build their ideas about metaphysics but "modernity" lacks precision and there is not an established, systematic literature which can facilitate enquires into the relationship between Confucian and modernism/modernity. To facilitate the project of the present paper we need an articulated concept of metaphysics − one which systematically addresses all the aspects of our subject of enquiry. Heidegger provides that concept. An advantage of Heidegger's concept is

that it describes the mechanism whereby Confucianism and Western metaphysics come to be present in the thoughts and actions of their respective
peoples.

As said above, in the tree analogy for metaphysics, a major branch
carries Western metaphysics. What is characteristic of the modern western way of being? How do western people think and act now that is so
distinctly different from all other metaphysical traditions, including the
contemporary Confucian tradition? Heidegger's answer to these questions
is, as we must expect, about *alētheia*. The carrier of truth in modern
society is primarily the innerness of science and technology. Modern
science began in a struggle to discern truth. Galileo and Newton (nonetheless Heisenberg and Einstein) were consumed in the struggle about
truth. Einstein in his 1935 essay, "The World As I See It", nominates
"Truth" as an ideal that "lit" his way (Einstein, 1954, p. 9). Heidegger
observes how scientists today have lost sight of truth:

> Contemporary natural scientists, in contrast to scientists working on the level of
> Galileo and Newton, have abandoned vigorous philosophical reflection and no longer
> know what the great thinkers thought. (Heidegger, 1959−1969/2001, p. 57)

The current physicists' lack of self-critique is not a consequence of their
"negligence or laziness" but is "due to the blindness determined by the des-
tiny of the present age" (Heidegger, 1959−69/2001, p. 60).

For Heidegger, the essence of "what we today call science is research",
and he explains that the essence of research is found in three interrelated
characteristics (Heidegger, 1938/1977, p. 118). Each of these characteristics
is apparent in Western thinking about business and the intellectual discipline of political economy. The three characteristics are: restrict reality,
force revelations and specialisation.

Whist modern scientists (mere researchers, for Heidegger) came to forget
their engagement with truth, the new constructs of disclosed truth came to
take hold and be expressed through the everyday thinking of Western
peoples. The Medieval Age, with its engagement with God and humility,
was overcome by a new Scientific Age. Nietzsche in 1882 declared God
is dead, and we killed him (Nietzsche, 1882/2001). He meant that the
Medieval Era was over because people had come to believe in themselves,
progress and modern science. The Medievals encountered things as the
work of God and thus saw inevitability in events. They had a sense of awe
which is not profound in current Western metaphysics.

Heidegger provides an example of how our understanding of wealth
altered in the transition to Western metaphysics. For Medieval peoples,

money was gold coin. In the fourteenth century riches entailed gold and gold shone. It could be touched and viewed with awe and satisfaction. Western people today encounter their wealth as a number on a screen. Money is abstract. The stock market rises and you feel pleased but you are in no way engaged as you would be if you held the gold in your hand. The two experiences are different. There is now a disjunction between you and your wealth. In an effort to overcome the yearning for the experience that was formerly the experience of wealth, people may adopt symbols to indicate their wealth. The luxury markets cater to these needs. Executives do not need a $5,000 watch to tell the time. They need the watch to see and to hold their gold and to tell others about it. Heidegger quotes correspondence from the German poet Rilke, who in 1912 writes:

> The world draws into itself; for things, too, do the same in their turn, by shifting their existence more and more over into the vibrations of money, and developing there for themselves a kind of spirituality, which even now already surpasses their palpable reality. (Heidegger, 1946/2001, p. 111)

Wealth has become the vibrations of money and thus an aspect of an especial spirituality (the spirituality of Western metaphysics) — but wealth has lost its earlier, palpable human reality.

In another example, Heidegger considers accommodation and homes and he draws upon his concept of 'dwelling'. Houses have become for many in the West "accommodation resources" (Young, 2002, p. 55). People are not involved in the practical building of their own houses. Thus, people come to occupy or inhabit houses which they achieve in exchange for money. People no longer dwell in their houses. Dwelling involves connecting and belonging. Dwelling and building are now separated.

> These buildings house man. He inhabits them and yet does not dwell in them, when to dwell means merely that we take shelter in them. In today's housing shortage even this much is reassuring and to the good; residential buildings do indeed provide shelter; today's houses may even be well planned, easy to keep, attractively cheap, open to air, light, and sun, but—do the houses in themselves hold any guarantee that *dwelling* occurs in them? Yet those buildings that are not dwelling places remain in turn determined by dwelling in so far as they serve man's dwelling. (Heidegger, 1946/2001, p. 144)

People are entrapped by *Ge-stell*, the arrangement, or the set-up. The mechanism which does this is disclosed truth working in accordance with the tree analogy. Those in Western metaphysics, Medieval people, and those with Confucian metaphysics encounter the world in their own way.

Confucian Metaphysics

Investigations into Confucian metaphysics appear in the context of a
Chinese engagement with western philosophy. Chinese philosophers
attempt to interrogate western philosophy and relate Chinese philosophy
to western philosophy. Some seek to bring about a Confucian revival with
the help of the resources of the West (Part I: Pioneering New Thought
from the West; Cheng & Bunnin, 2002, pp. 15–124; Ci, 2002, p. 201). He
Lin seeks to strengthen both Western and Confucian philosophy:

> Our own spirit? Our own Reason? Such incoherence, if it is that, expressed a deep ten-
> sion between He's universalistic aspirations and his deep sense of rootedness in the
> Chinese cultural and philosophical tradition. It is this coherence or tension that allowed
> He Lin to attach great importance to ta revival of Confucianism. But even as he tried
> to inject new life into Confucianism as Chinese Spirit, he sought to reinterpret
> Confucianism in a universalistic spirit. Behind this universalism lurked, in turn, his
> deep admiration for Western philosophy, which He Lin saw as a substance of the tech-
> nological and military might of the West. (Ci, 2002, p. 200)

The appealing substance of western philosophy which he discerns is
western metaphysics and its expression is found in science and practical
knowhow.

The word "metaphysics" shows as diverse and contradictory use in relation to the Chinese as it does in relation to the West. Over about the last
two decades scholars have begun to explore concepts of Confucian metaphysics. Each adopts the theoretical framework they believe appropriate
for their work (Allinson, 1990; Fang, 1964; Rapoza, 2012; Shen & Shun,
2007; Shun, 1997; Shun & Wong, 2004).

Zhao, for example, discerns in the recent work of scholars two contrasting approaches to ancient Chinese metaphysics:

> There are two tendencies in the arguments of the legitimacy of metaphysics in ancient
> China: the tendency to argue that there was no metaphysics in ancient China and
> the tendency to argue that ancient Chinese metaphysics is totally different from that of
> the West. (Zhao, 2006, p. 22)

He then adopts a hermeneutic strategy which Heidegger would approve,
and asks about *origins*:

> ... the author [Zhao] counters these tendencies [towards a dichotomy] and argues that
> Chinese and western metaphysics both originated from a dynamic cosmology and
> shared objects of investigation and characteristics of thinking in terms of Becoming.
> However, in their later development, due to the difference in the problems of their

focus, traditions of "moral metaphysics" and "(natural) metaphysics of Being" were formed in China and in the West, respectively. (Zhao, 2006, p. 22)

Whilst this account is not inconsistent with many of Heidegger's notions, there is a need to focus on the mechanisms by which such developments could be achieved. Heidegger's account of truth provides this. Incidentally, Heidegger engaged with Eastern texts and scholars (Hirsch, 1970; Kolb, 2009; Ma, 2008).

Western people cannot shake-off their metaphysical heritage, even though they can adapt to new cultures. Their understanding of cultures must always come through Western eyes. The observations which Western people make about Confucian people often include reference to the same group personality and existential factors. A psychotherapist outlines a "basket of concepts" under the heading "Cultural factors and psychotherapy in China", based in mainly on his work with educated Chinese women who speak good English (Myler & Tong, 2015). A selection of examples indicates similarities and contrasts with Western cultural givens:

1. Many Chinese people see their own problems as coming last compared to the welfare of others. The Chinese client often thinks they are troubling the counsellor with trifles and are more concerned about the therapist's welfare than their own well-being.
2. There is a great mistrust among Chinese people toward authorities in general. Most people do not discuss their emotional turmoil with anyone, as they will lose face. In China there is a high degree of anxiety about judgement, criticism and evaluation by the state and other people.
3. A crucial thing for the Western therapist to understand is that the Chinese client before them is not going to tell the truth in a direct manner due to the issue of face. Face means not being put in a position of shame. The awareness of shame is very high and controls the daily aspects of business, government and personal behaviour.
4. In China the word relationship carries with it the factor of favour — that is, a relationship is about what you do for each other. Often, it is to one's advantage that a person does a favour for you. In return, at some future point, you will return that favour — often many times bigger than the original favour. This system of relationships works through government, business and in daily life.
5. Family has always been strong in China and from an early age, family loyalty is seen as crucial to survival in the future, as one generation relies on the next for support in old age or infirmity (Myler & Tong, 2015, edited and numbered).

When asked about the things which appear in Myler and Tong's list, Confucian people may construct an account of themselves in accordance with their understanding of what Western people might understand. This will be different from the account that Confucian people might give in discussions among themselves. The difference is not just a matter of culture. It derives from that which initiates culture and is universal among Confucian cultures.

CONCLUSION

Reflection on the inner significance of the origins of political economy enables us to take a new perspective on the discipline. The insights of continental philosophers, such as Martin Heidegger, provide us with access to ideas which we can incorporate into our own thought.

The origins of the concepts of political economy relate to a domestic or home-front phenomenology. This is explicit in the work of the Rousseau and Marshall. Much of the development that follows from the origins of the discipline relates to a different phenomenology, one which involves present-at-hand objects and is "calculating" (to use Heidegger's terminology). The "present-at-hand" concepts of the discipline are expressions of a hidden Western metaphysics. Managers and academics recognise and work with cultures, but they do not engage with that which is foundational of all cultures.

The machinations of business, essentially a part of culture, are expressions of a hidden metaphysics. Western metaphysics is new and dates from the advent of modern science – just over 400 years ago. With modern science came a new way to understand the world. The West entails inalienable presuppositions about the nature of humankind. Humankind has the ability to manipulate and progress, and, most critically, everything that exists is available for human use as humankind works towards progress. The West invented the concept of "resource" – that which is available for use. That concept is now hegemonic in the Western understanding of the environment. One example (elaborated above) which shows this is the Western approach to housing.

China abides with a different metaphysics from that of the West. Confucian metaphysics has a tradition of at least 7,000 years and is expressed by many cultures, and more recently by modern nations. The recent openness of China to western cultural artefacts, including the mechanisms of markets, trade and justice, represents a pragmatism that accords with Confucian metaphysics. It does not represent an overthrowing of Confucian metaphysics. The grounding distinction between Western and Confucian societies is beyond manipulation.

Commentators and scholars who argue that China is becoming like the West see only the artefacts of culture. Chinese young people may follow fashion and appear to be westernised, but they remain grounded in their metaphysical era. Youth culture changes whilst the foundations of the Confucian human being endure. The adoption of western justice systems and laws does not alter fundamentally the nature of the Confucian person. China's progress now depends on China being able to build upon the true inner character of the Chinese.

Western metaphysics is essentially a European phenomenon. In the South Pacific, for example, Maori people and Pacific Island peoples share a heritage which has them understanding their relationship to the natural world in a harmonious way. Similar notions of harmony and peacefulness which are in the Pacific resonate in Confucian societies. Perhaps we may speculate that the South East Asian origins of mid-Pacific and south-Pacific peoples have something to do with the accordance we observe.

Western peoples made a rapid transition from a Medieval metaphysics to modern Western metaphysics. Science was disruptive of human nature itself over a period of (say) about 200 years. When Nietzsche declared God was dead and that we killed him, he pointed to the transition. We can pose the question: will Confucian metaphysics be assailed by the same invisible forces which were at work in Europe? Heidegger's theory of metaphysics, on balance, suggests this will not occur.

REFERENCES

Allinson, R. E. (Ed.). (1990). *Understanding the Chinese mind: The philosophical roots.* Oxford: Oxford University Press.

Cassirer, E. (1981). *Kant's life and thought* (J. Haden, Trans.). New Haven, CT: Yale University.

Cheng, C.-Y., & Bunnin, N. (Eds.). (2002). *Contemporary Chinese philosophy.* Malden, MA: Blackwell Publishers.

Ci, J. (2002). He Lin's sinification of idealism. In C.-Y. Cheng & N. Bunnin (Eds.), *Contemporary Chinese philosophy* (pp. 188–210). Malden, MA: Blackwell Publishers.

DeMartino, G. (2000). *Global economy, global justice: Theoretical objections and policy alternatives to neoliberalism.* London: Routledge.

Einstein, A. (1954). *Ideas and opinions. Based on Mein Weltbild* (C. Seelig, Ed. & S. Bargmann, Trans.). New York, NY: Crown Publishers.

Fang, T. H. (1964). The world and the individual in Chinese metaphysics. *Philosophy East and West, 14*(2), 101–130.

Flew, T. (2014). Six theories of neoliberalism. *Thesis Eleven, 122*(1), 49–71.

Harris, R. L., & Seid, M. (2000). *Critical perspectives on globalization and neoliberalism in the developing countries.* Boston, MA: Brill.

Heidegger, M. (1926/2008). *Basic concepts of ancient philosophy* (R. Rojcewicz, Trans.). Bloomington, IN: Indiana University Press.

Heidegger, M. (1938/1994). *Basic questions of philosophy: Selected "problems" of "logic"* (R. Rojcewicz & A. Schuwer, Trans.). Bloomington, IN: Indiana University Press.

Heidegger, M. (1938/1977). The age of the world picture. In W. Lovitt (Trans.), *The question concerning technology, and other essays* (pp. 115–154). New York, NY: Harper & Row.

Heidegger, M. (1946/2001). Building dwelling thinking. In A. Hofstadter (Ed. & Trans.), *Poetry, language, thought … Translations and introduction by Albert Hofstadter* (pp. 141–160). New York, NY: Harper & Row.

Heidegger, M. (1949/1998). Introduction to "What is metaphysics?" (W. Kaufmann, Trans.). In W. McNeill (Ed.), *Pathmarks* (pp. 277–290). Cambridge: Cambridge University Press.

Heidegger, M. (1959–1969/2001). *Zollikon seminars: Protocols, conversations, letters* (M. Boss, Ed. & F. Mayr & R. Askay, Trans.). Evanston, IL: Northwestern University Press.

Heidegger, M. (1927/1962). *Being and time* (J. Macquarrie & E. Robinson, Trans.). Oxford: Blackwell.

Hirsch, E. F. (1970). Martin Heidegger and the east. *Philosophy East and West, 20*(3), 247–263.

Huff, T. E. (1995). *The rise of early modern science: Islam, China, and the West.* Cambridge: Cambridge University Press.

James, W. (1950). *The principles of psychology* (Vol. 1). New York, NY: Dover.

Kolb, D. (2009). Heidegger on East-West dialogue. *American Catholic Philosophical Quarterly, 83*(1), 164–167.

Kuehn, M. (2001). *Kant: A biography.* New York, NY: Cambridge University Press.

Ma, L. (2008). *Heidegger on East-West dialogue: Anticipating the event.* New York, NY: Routledge.

Marshall, A. (1890). *Principles of economics.* London: Macmillan.

Marttila, T. (2013). *The culture of enterprise in neoliberalism: Specters of entrepreneurship.* New York, NY: Routledge.

Myler, S. F., & Tong, H. Q. (2015). *Psychotherapy in China: Western and Eastern perspectives.* psychotherapy.net: resources to inspire therapists. Retrieved from https://www.psychotherapy.net/article/psychotherapy-in-china#section-getting-a-feel-for-chinese-culture. Accessed on August 5, 2015.

Nagel, T. (1974). What is it like to be a bat? *The Philosophical Review, 83,* 435–450.

New Zealand China Contemporary Research Centre Political Economy Research Cluster. (2015). *Political economy.* Retrieved from http://www.victoria.ac.nz/chinaresearchcentre/research-and-fellowships/research-clusters/political-economy. Accessed on October 4, 2015.

Newton, I. (1984a). Optica (the Optical Lectures, deposited version). A. E. Shapiro (Ed.), *The optical papers of Isaac Newton* (Vol. 1, pp. 280–603). Cambridge: Cambridge University Press.

Newton, I. (1984b). In A. E. Shapiro (Ed.), *The optical papers of Isaac Newton* (Vol. 1). Cambridge: Cambridge University Press.

Nietzsche, F. W. (1882/2001). *The gay science: With a prelude in German rhymes and an appendix of songs* (B. A. O. Williams, J. Nauckhoff, & A. Del Caro, Eds. & J. Nauckhoff, Trans.). Cambridge: Cambridge University Press.

Peters, M. A. (Ed.). (2002). *Heidegger, education, and modernity*. Lanham, MD: Rowman & Littlefield.

Peters, M. A., & Besley, T. (2006). *Building knowledge cultures: Education and development in the age of knowledge capitalism*. Lanham, MD: Rowman & Littlefield.

Rapoza, K. (2012). *In China, why piracy is here to stay*. Retrieved from http://www.forbes.com/sites/kenrapoza/2012/07/22/in-china-why-piracy-is-here-to-stay/

Rousseau, J.-J. (1755). *A discourse on political economy*. Retrieved from www.constitution.org/jjr/polecon.htm

Shen, Q., & Shun, K.-l. (2007). *Confucian ethics in retrospect and prospect*. Washington, DC: Council for Research in Values and Philosophy.

Shun, K.-L. (1997). *Mencius and early Chinese thought*. Stanford, CA: Stanford University Press.

Shun, K.-L., & Wong, D. B. (2004). *Confucian ethics: A comparative study of self, autonomy, and community*. New York, NY: Cambridge.

Toulmin, S. E. (1990). *Cosmopolis: The hidden agenda of modernity*. New York, NY: Free Press.

Wong, J., & Bo, Z. (2010). *China's reform in global perspective*. Hackensack, NJ: World Scientific.

Young, J. (2002). *Heidegger's later philosophy*. Cambridge: Cambridge University Press.

Zhao, D. (2006). Metaphysics in China and in the west: Common origin and later divergence. *Frontiers of Philosophy in China, 1*(1), 22−32.

PART II
STATE AND CORPORATE
GOVERNANCE

A STATE-STEWARDSHIP VIEW ON EXECUTIVE COMPENSATION

Hao Liang, Luc Renneboog and Sunny Li Sun

ABSTRACT

Purpose — *We take a state-stewardship view on corporate governance and executive compensation in economies with strong political involvement, where state-appointed managers act as responsible "stewards" rather than "agents" of the state.*

Methodology/approach — *We test this view on China and find that Chinese managers are remunerated not for maximizing equity value but for increasing the value of state-owned assets.*

Findings — *Managerial compensation depends on political connections and prestige, and on the firms' contribution to political goals. These effects were attenuated since the market-oriented governance reform.*

Research limitations/implications — *Economic reform without reforming the human resources policies at the executive level enables the autocratic state to exert political power on corporate decision making, so as to ensure that firms' business activities fulfill the state's political objectives.*

The Political Economy of Chinese Finance
International Finance Review, Volume 17, 39–91
Copyright © 2016 by Emerald Group Publishing Limited
All rights of reproduction in any form reserved
ISSN: 1569-3767/doi:10.1108/S1569-376720160000017009

Practical implications – *As a powerful social elite, the state-steward managers in China have the same interests as the state (the government), namely extracting rents that should adhere to the nation (which stands for the society at large or the collective private citizens).*

Social implications – *As China has been a communist country with a single ruling party for decades, the ideas of socialism still have a strong impact on how companies are run. The legitimacy of the elite's privileged rights over private sectors is central to our question.*

Originality/value – *Chinese executive compensation stimulates not only the maximization of shareholder value but also the preservation of the state's interests.*

Keywords: State-stewardship view; agency theory; executive compensation; political connections

JEL classifications: G34; H70; M12; P26; P31

INTRODUCTION

The executive compensation policies in emerging economies puzzle researchers as the seemingly low registered pay and the other-than-performance pay for managers running large internationally active corporations located in those economies challenge the standard economic theories on corporate governance.[1] Conyon and He (2011) document that the executive pay (salary and bonus) of US top managers is about 17 times higher than that in China. When stock options and equity compensation are considered, the difference augments to approximately 42 times. The majority of the extant literature on corporate governance resorts to agency theory to explain executive compensation policies (e.g., Core, Holthausen, & Larcker, 1999; Garen, 1994; Jensen & Murphy, 1990). The interests of the managers (the agent) and shareholders (the principal) can be in conflict, and agency problems may arise if managers abuse their power. Consequently, the compensation scheme should be designed in such a way as to elicit effort from the management while avoiding the above conflicts of interest (Bebchuk & Fried, 2004; Jensen, Murphy, & Wruck, 2004). However, is this agency logic valid for emerging economies? The answer is negative because in countries undergoing political and institutional transition such as China, the state and the political authorities own significant equity stakes and their political influence extends beyond ownership. The use of non-cash compensation is very rare and, if it is used at all, disclosure is incomplete, but perquisite consumption may be more prevalent (Adithipyangkul, Alon, & Zhang, 2009).[2] Business activities are heavily influenced by the government and other political powers through the government's deliberate policies on resource allocation, as well as the vast presence of government ownership and managers' political connections. In Russia, for example, politically connected firms represent over 85% of the market capitalization (Faccio, 2006; Shleifer, 1998). It is reasonable to believe that such strong political influence on business activities results in relatively less market-based managerial compensation schemes.

Several papers have examined executive compensation in emerging economies, in particular, China (e.g., Chen, Ezzamel, & Cai, 2011; Chen, Liu, & Li, 2010; Conyon & He, 2011; Firth, Fung, & Rui, 2006), but their focus was mainly on testing western corporate governance theories, such as pay-for-performance sensitivity or managerial power theory (Bebchuk, Fried, & Walker, 2002; Grabke-Rundell & Gomez-Mejia, 2002), in the Chinese context. Unsurprisingly, the validity of the agency theory in the Chinese corporate world is weak. An alternative theoretical framework incorporating the broader political and institutional determinants of China's corporate governance system is needed (Buck, Liu, & Skovoroda, 2008; Van Essen, Heugens, Otten, & Van Oosterhout, 2012). It is also important to take an institutional perspective as significant shifts of state powers in the economy and businesses have arisen over the last decade. Therefore, in the context of compensation contracting in China, two main research questions emerge: (1) What roles (other than "agents") do managers play and how are they remunerated? (2) How do such roles and compensation evolve over time?

In this paper, we find that the level and structure of Chinese executive compensation does not tie in with the principal-agent's predications on pay-for-performance. The low compensation of Chinese managers (relative to their international peers) is prevalent in firms with stronger state control, and when self-dealing opportunities are larger. Managers are also rewarded more for maximizing the value of state-owned assets (rather than for maximizing shareholder value). Furthermore, their compensation is not closely linked to ability, but to their political connections and prestige, as well as to their firms' contribution to the local officials' political goals. All these effects have evolved over time, whereby especially the major privatization effort of 2006 (the split-share structure reform) has had a big influence on the roles of managers and their compensation contracts. Some of these findings were also documented in other studies, most recently in Cao, Lemmon, Pan, Qian, and Tian (2011), although they have not housed them in a consistent theoretical framework. In our analysis, we take a *state-stewardship view* to explain these unique governance and compensation contracting patterns. For a clear understanding of some key concepts, we make the following two definitional distinctions. First, the "state" is not necessarily the "nation": the former refers in the context of this paper to the interest of the ruling political elites, while the latter represents the interest of the public masses (citizens). Therefore, by calling Chinese managers the state's stewards we mean that their interests are in line with those of the politicians, but not necessarily with the public interest. Second, "state-stewardship" is different from "stewardship": the former describes a state-manager relationship that is institutionalized by coercive or normative political forces (the manager can still be self-interested), while the latter describes a pro-organizational behavior based on human altruism assumptions. A comparison between the traditional principal-agent perspective and our state-stewardship perspective is offered in Table 1, and will be further illustrated in the following sections.

Our work makes the following contributions. First, as the traditional agency theory is not able to explain the level, composition, and evolution of executive compensation in China (e.g., Conyon & He, 2011; Firth et al., 2006, 2007), we focus on state influence and managers' political connections from a state-stewardship view on Chinese corporations. This institutional perspective has stronger explanatory power as it incorporates the organizing principle, incentive structures, and enforcement mechanisms of firms and managers within China's authoritarian political system after the economic reform and incomplete privatization. Second, we take an institutional perspective with a focus on institutional change to study how the Chinese state controls the economy – by means of ownership stakes and political connections with the 2006 split-share reform as a watershed. Such institutional change also implies a shift of wealth from the state (the government) to the nation (the private citizens), while the authoritarian state still maintains tight control over (corporate) employees (Xu, 2011). Third, the state-manager relationship has broader implications for China's economic and political development. Economic reform without reforming the human resources policies at the executive level enables the autocratic state to exert political power on corporate decision making, so as to ensure that firms' business activities fulfill the state's political objectives. Therefore, this study also has some welfare implications.

Table 1. Comparing Principal-Agent and State-Stewardship Perspectives.

	Principal-Agent Perspective	State-Stewardship Perspective
Key idea	Owner-manager relationship should reflect the efficient organization of information and risk-bearing costs.	Owner-manager relationship reflects a high degree of loyalty and effective interaction skills in order to reach multiple (economic, social, and political) high performance goals.
Human assumptions	• Self-interest; • Bounded rationality; • Risk aversion.	• Bounded rationality; • Mutual and voluntary acceptability of bargains; • Human ambivalence.
Context	• Separation of ownership and control	• Partial separation of ownership and control (e.g., split-share reform)
Problem domain	• Owner and manager have conflicts of (1) goal alignment and (2) risk-sharing	• Multiple economic, social, and political goals could conflict; • Interdependence of these interests.
Problem issue	• Information asymmetry between owner and manager; • Agency (moral hazard and adverse selection); • Risk-sharing between owner and manager.	• Company's economic interests are in conflict with the government's political and social interests and agenda. • State's direct intervention could be in conflict with market-based principles and damage other shareholder's interests.
Solutions	• Comprehensive contract formation; • Incentives compensation policy for managers. • Controlling agency costs: (1) behavior and (2) outcome observations.	• Two-way communication and influences under an administrative orders (e.g., political connections serve as a major channel); • Formal contracts are incomplete; social and psychological informal contracts are required; • Ex post allocation of power is important (such as turnover/promotion mechanisms); • Ownership and voting rights become state's major tools of control after the split-share reform.
Decision making	• An aggregative process between the interests of owners and agents; • Leadership involves the brokerage of coalitions among different interests.	• An integrating process among multiple interests of multiple stakeholders; • Leadership involves a trusteeship.
Organization evolvement	• Instantaneous response to owner/agent interests.	• A slow adaptation of the system with institutionalization.

INSTITUTIONAL BACKGROUND

Privatization and the Split-Share Structure Reform

When China started its economic reform in 1978, one of the key elements was the privatization (or "corporatization"; Clarke, 2003) of the formerly state-owned enterprises (SOEs). Two stock exchanges, in Shanghai and Shenzhen, were established in 1990 for privatization. The managerial resource allocation system has been improved since the modern industrial and corporate reforms were initiated in 1978 and continued throughout the 1980s and 1990s (Groves, Hong, McMillan, & Naughton, 1994, 1995). Initially, a dual share structure was established for all listed companies: approximately two-thirds of domestically listed shares (A-shares) were not tradable on the market and were usually owned by the government and state agencies, which hindered the privatization process considerably. Chinese government reformed the split-share structure at April 2005 (effective from 2006), changing non-tradable shares into tradable ones for all public firms. More than 1,400 public firms turned their tradable shares. The owners of non-tradable shares[3] negotiated and compensated the owners of tradable shares (Liang, Ren, & Sun, 2015). Even after the split-share structural reform, the state is still playing a major role in regulating companies' strategic decision making, developing corporate governance regulation, and setting executive compensation schemes through retaining the executive-level employees as state-appointees, maintaining a stake in privatized firms, and supervising firms via the China Securities Regulatory Commission (CSRC). In many firms, especially those within the electronics, automobile manufacturing, steel, natural resource exploitation, and extraction industries, the state has kept majority control while foreign share stakes are restricted. The managers, the board's chairperson, the political secretary of the firm (the Communist Party representative), and other managers are usually directly appointed by the state, and their compensation contracts are directly determined by the Organization Department of the Communist Party and the State Council, rather than by the board of directors. As a consequence, corporate governance and executive compensation contracting in China's state-oriented economy exhibit unique patterns not present in Western economies. The change of state ownership over our sample period for different industries is exhibited in Fig. 1. Fig. 1(a) shows the evolution of the state ownership in the top five industries ranked by market capitalization. Fig. 1(b) depicts the industry-average state

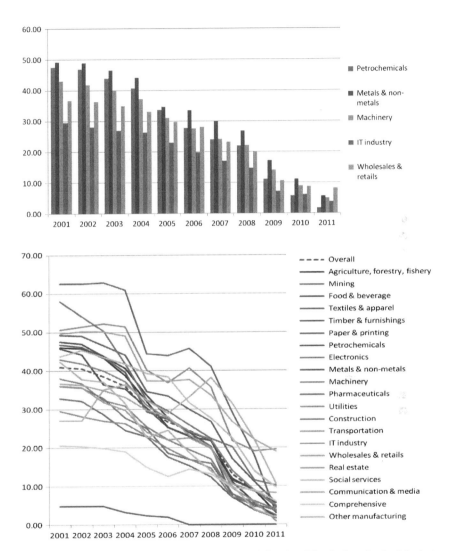

Fig. 1. (a) Change of Mean State Ownership of the Top Five Industries by Market Capitalization and (b) Change of Mean State Ownership of All Sample Industries. *Note*: The vertical axis denotes the percentage of industry-average state ownership. The figure comprises all industries included in our sample (based on the CSRC Industry Code).

ownership of all industries included in our sample. The split-share reform is visible from 2005 to 2006; the decline of state ownership has continued in all subsequent years.

Corporate Governance Structure and Executive Compensation Structure

China's corporate governance structure has been set up since the privatization in the early 1990s[4] and is based on western governance codes and corporate law, although China's Socialist-featured company law and related codes (in particular, the CSRC Codes) comprise some singularities. For instance, the Chinese corporate board structure combines some aspects of the Anglo-American one-tier board model and the German two-tier one.[5] In principle, it is loosely based on the two-tier structure, but in practice more like a muddled one-tier Anglo-American board (IIF, 2006) whereby the board[6] (i) consists of several independent directors (CSRC requires the independent director ratio of the board to be above one-third), (ii) is the main decision-making authority within the firm, and (iii) oversees and aids management practice. In practice, the Chinese supervisory board has only a symbolic function and hence does not play an effective governance role (Tam, 2002; Tenev & Zhang, 2002).

In SOEs[7] which still account for over 80% of market capitalization in China, the dominant shareholder is the state, and their boards of directors usually consist of members directly appointed by the central or local government to serve on, for example, the strategy committee (which makes the strategic investment and development decisions) or the compensation committee. At the same level with the board of directors are a supervisory board and a representative Party committee led by the Party Secretary who vouches for the ideological influence over the board and the entire firm. It is clear that this board(s) structure(s) can lead to confusion and induce some ambiguity about the board member duties (*Financial Times*, April 2, 2008). The counterpart of the Western CEO of a Chinese SOE is usually called "general manager" who does not own shares of the company. In many cases, especially in large SOEs, the functions of general manager (CEO) and chairperson of the board are combined by one person, a phenomenon which is usually termed as *managerial duality*. Fig. 2 illustrates the unique internal governance structure of Chinese companies (especially of SOEs).

Under such special corporate governance arrangements, executive compensation schemes in SOEs have been based on the highly structured civil service pay scale which mainly reflects the differences in region, industry,

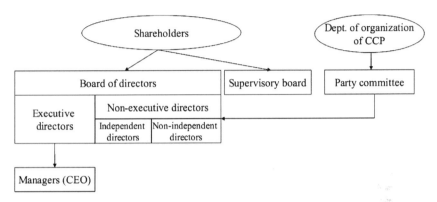

Fig. 2. China's Corporate Governance Structure after Privatization. This figure illustrates a conceptual internal governance structure of a typical Chinese company since the privatization. The two-tier board structure (the board of directors and the supervisory board) is similar to the German model but the combination of executive and non-executive directors within the board of directors is similar to the US/UK model. The Chinese Communist Party (CCP) usually assigns a Party committee to ensure ideological control. Members of the Party committee usually also sit on the board of directors.

and seniority. Even in private firms which account for less than 20% market capitalization, the influence of the state is still salient, usually through government policies and politically connected executives (*Economist*, September 3, 2011). Moreover, the communist tenets advocating similarity in pay across all ranks of members of society also put regulatory ceilings on their registered compensation (including cash salaries and bonuses).[8] In addition, stock options and equity-based pay are very rare in Chinese companies. Despite these caps, managers are often compensated by perquisites such as free housing and gray income which is not recorded on the balance sheets, and bribery and self-dealing are not exceptional (Adithipyangkul et al., 2009; Jiang, Lee, & Yeung, 2010).

A STATE-STEWARDSHIP VIEW

Since the ground-breaking paper by Donaldson and Davis (1991), scholars have resorted to the management stewardship theory as a basis for managers' and shareholders' interest alignment. This theory, a sociological and psychological approach to governance, hinges on the assumption that executives have a strong psychological ownership of their firms, and hence are more likely to serve the firm as stewards. These "organizationally centered" executives (Davis, Schoorman, & Donaldson, 1997, p. 25) would accept lower cash compensation with higher levels of "psychic income" (Gimeno, Folta, Cooper, & Woo, 1997). This perspective stands in marked contrast with agency theory in which managers are assumed to act in their own interest at the expense of shareholders. We adapt this stewardship concept to the Chinese context, and use this term to describe the fact that Chinese managers are in principle (required to be) accountable to the state. Chinese managers are usually appointed by the state, and maintain close political connections with the government. As a result they actually act like the stewards of the state, and work towards fulfilling both the economic objectives of the firm and the political ones of the state. Different from the stewardship theory which makes a human managerial altruism assumption on the manager, our perspective admits that Chinese managers can still be self-interested. However, the institutionalization of state-stewardship ensures that acting in the interest of the state is also in managers' own interest. We illustrate the formation and institutionalization of state-stewardship from three angles: (a) the organizing principles of the company, (b) the incentive structures of the manager, and (c) the enforcement mechanisms imposed by the state.

In terms of the organizing principle, the state is involved in every level of activity of the firm, both at the political and economic one. The political organizing principle requires that firms' business activities be fundamentally state-driven, be aligned with goals such as safeguarding the political power/social demand, and be conformed to the ideological requirements. The economic organizing principle requires that firms' business activities achieve economic growth in state-related sectors' and maintain some degree of monopoly power in some "national strategic industries."

The incentive structures for state-appointed (or state-influenced) managers are based on a political cadre promotion system with different hierarchical levels. Each level of the cadre is equipped with a different set of benefits, but by nature, all are entitled as government officers to enjoy miscellaneous political and economic types of rewards. For instance, under the career promotion system, a manager who wants to secure his job and ensure promotion has to show loyalty to the party.

The enforcement mechanisms rely on the coercive power of the state to punish the stewards when they violate the state's will or when their behavior and performance are perceived as unsatisfactory. The punishment comprises lowering a SOE manager's rank (seniority) in the civil service hierarchy or removing a manager from his political cadre position. Moreover, the government regularly rotates its officers and state-appointed managers between political and corporate positions to make sure that they are unconditionally loyal to the party.

This state-stewardship concept is not static but has evolved over the past two decades. The massive privatization has reformed the ownership of Chinese enterprises, transiting from entirely state-owned to semi-state owned or privately owned, especially after the split-share structure reform. Correspondingly, the form of control by the Communist-Party-led state has transited from pure state ownership to state-stewardship. We argue that the reforms only privatized the ownership structure and composition but did not really reform the human resources policies at the managerial level. To maintain its control legitimacy, the state *boosts the economy* through privatization (which leads to more efficient allocation of resources and improves production efficiency), and *controls the economy* through maintaining its stewardship system within firms to carry out its political objectives. Table 2 shows a comparison between these two major types of controls exerted by China's state, in terms of their representative periods, control methods, governance models, and managerial incentive structures.

Within this state-stewardship framework, we revisit the executive compensation issues at three levels: the personal level (managerial background), the firm level (ownership, performance, and internal governance mechanisms), and the macroeconomic level, which have been investigated in the literature from the agency perspective. To do so, we develop five testable hypotheses and contrast them with agency predictions in the next section.

HYPOTHESIS

State Control and Gray Income

Our first set of hypotheses explores this question: What drives the managerial compensation in China? (Or why is Chinese compensation so low?) We have seen above that the state puts more emphasis on political and macroeconomic objectives rather than on firm profitability. Consequently, a manager's incentive structure may be geared towards the former objectives.

Table 2.   From State-Ownership to State-Stewardship.

	Pre-2006	Post-2006
State-manager relationship	State ownership and control	State-stewardship (focusing more on managers' political connections)
Governance model (organizing principle)	Unification of ownership and control (large non-tradable government controlled share blocks); more political oriented "command" governance model	Partial separation of ownership and control (dispersed state ownership); more market-oriented "administrative" governance model
Control rights	The state possessed all control rights (in some partially privatized SOEs, voting rights proportional to shareholdings)	Voting rights proportional to shareholdings
Dividend policy	No dividends. Most profit reinvested in focal SOEs	Proposal: at least 10% of profit paid to all shareholders (including state) as dividend
Method of state control	Mainly control through government ownership (large number of non-tradable shares), regulations, and the state's ultimate control (voting rights)	Mainly control through appointment of executive personnel and administrative orders
Incentive structure	Fulfilling political, social, and economic objectives, political and social goals are dominating	Fulfilling political and economic objectives, economic ones growing in importance

As state's stewards, government-appointed managers are government officials who face the threat of punishment for lack of political loyalty (dismissal) but are also offered lower firm-based pecuniary rewards, and lower pay-for-corporate performance. In addition, they are subject to regulatory salary ceilings (e.g., salary grades and brackets based on rank). The prevailing presence of state ownership and state control in Chinese firms is the legacy of China's incomplete privatization, which can be viewed as exogenous from a corporate perspective. Especially for the largest companies and companies in key industries of "national strategic importance," such as oil and telecommunication, the state wants to retain its absolute control (*"retain the large"*). More concentrated state ownership is usually associated with various non-pecuniary benefits for the management such as higher prestige, stronger political cadre promotion incentives, but also with stronger (coercive) state influence, and a stronger concern for public criticism (Kuhnen & Niessen, 2012) — a reason for setting regulatory salary ceilings.

Agency theory predicts a negative relationship between *institutional* ownership concentration and executive compensation, because the major shareholders adopt a monitoring role and are expected to avoid excess managerial compensation (Hartzell & Starks, 2003). However, a positive relation is expected in an environment that lacks effective incentives and monitoring mechanisms due to managerial entrenchment (Bebchuk & Fried, 2003). It is widely believed that even though the ownership is concentrated in Chinese firms, the fact that the controlling shareholder is the state results in little effective monitoring (IIF, 2006). In our state-stewardship view, the institutionalized state-manager relationship ("state-stewardship") makes managers accept lower compensation in companies in which the state retains control. Therefore, we hypothesize that a higher proportion of shares owned by the state results in less cash compensation as there is then a higher probability that the pay schedules for civil servants or political representatives will be applied and higher non-monetary rewards can be enjoyed (subsidized housing, better health insurance). If this hypothesis is true, we will expect a negative association between the state ownership stakes (whereby the state can be a direct or ultimate owner) and managerial pay:

H1a Managerial compensation is lower in firms with stronger state ownership, and in firms whose ultimate controller is the state. The effect of state ownership has become less important since the 2006 reform.

In this state-stewardship framework, besides receiving non-pecuniary benefits, executives in Chinese companies with stronger state ownership may also stealthily compensate their low pay packages by means of gray income through colluding with politicians and state agencies (Wang & Xiao, 2011). Gray income (unlike perquisite consumptions which are legal) resulting from "tunneling" is prevalent among firms in developing countries with strong state influence such as Russia (Johnson, La Porta, Lopez-de-Silanes, & Shleifer, 2000) and China (Jiang et al., 2010). For example, the latter study documents that during the period 1996–2006, the management transferred tens of billions of RMB from listed firms by means of intercorporate loans to blockholders. Information on such intercorporate loans is publically available but the loans do not follow basic business logic. It is fair to expect that managers of the firms where this type of tunneling was rampant, personally benefited by colluding with dominant shareholders (often even state authorities or agencies) and sharing the private benefits the blockholders have extracted from the firm. Jiang et al. (2010) argue that China is an environment highly conducive to tunneling behavior.[9] The lack of clout of the market regulators caused the tunneling practices to persist.

Agency theory which assumes a conflict of interest between shareholders and the managers would predict – in contrast to the state-stewardship framework – a positive relationship between managerial compensation and tunneling by controlling shareholders (Noe, 2009). This is because, in order to benefit from tunneling, controlling shareholders would "bribe" the manager by offering him higher compensation. The split-share reform has been shown in the literature to enhance governance and curb controlling shareholders' expropriation of minority shareholders. In contrast, from our viewpoint, managers are the state's stewards, they collude with shareholders who are usually government authorities stealing from the public. We therefore expect a negative correlation between managers' contractual compensation and the size of the other receivables on the balance sheet because managers with low income may be more prone to resort to tunneling and managers who significantly increase income through tunneling care less about their (low) cash compensation. After the 2006 split-share reform, non-tradable shares became tradable on the stock markets and ownership became more dispersed. Consequently, the use of tunneling by managers and major shareholders to extract private benefits from minority shareholders (public investors) has been reduced so that such gray income opportunities may have become smaller. Therefore, we hypothesize that:

> **H1b** Managerial compensation in China is lower in firms with higher other receivables. The opportunities to complement pay by means of tunneling (through other receivables) have decreased since the 2006 reform.

Value Maximization: Agents versus State's Stewards

Our second hypothesis examines whom Chinese managers are responsible to. State control may decrease managerial pay but may also insulate managers who are inefficient (from a corporate perspective) (Conyon & He, 2011) but still adhere to the political objectives of the state. From an agency perspective, managerial pay should be linked to performance that maximizes shareholder value, whereas from a state-stewardship view, a manager is motivated less by pecuniary rewards but more so by political objectives, which translates into political promotions and prestige. To measure performance, we use the return on assets (ROA) which measures the net income to the assets (still to a large extent) controlled by the state, and Tobin's Q, which is a measure of the market-based return to the shareholder's equity. If there is indeed a discrepancy between being responsible to the state and not to the shareholders, we would observe that managerial compensation is more related to the ROA but less to Tobin's Q (Van Essen, Oosterhout, & Carney, 2012). Since the split-share structure reform of 2006 when most non-tradable shares were sold to the market as tradable equity and corporate governance became more market-oriented, we expect that the increase in market-orientation is reflected in the stronger pay for market-based performance. Therefore,

H2 The managerial compensation in China is significantly positively correlated with the ROA, but not with the market-based return (e.g., Tobin's Q) in the pre-2006 period. Subsequently, we expect that the former relation is attenuated and that pay is significantly positively related to the market-based return.

Political Connections and Managerial Backgrounds

If corporate performance in China is a less important benchmark for managerial pay, what are the main corporate characteristics and managerial traits that are related to higher compensation? Let us first examine whether pay is related to a manager's personality, ability, and political connections. If the state-stewardship concept is valid, we expect managers not to be rewarded for their real abilities to generate financial returns, but to their connectedness to the state and the politicians, and to their degree of compliance to the state order (Fan, Wong, & Zhang, 2007; Peng, Sun, & Markoczy, 2015). Furthermore, a political background increases one's prestige in China substantially. Managers of listed firms who are politically connected are perceived to belong to both the business and political elites which reflects their high status in the social hierarchy of the Chinese society (Li & Zhang, 2007). Therefore, one could hypothesize that managers are paid in line with this hierarchical status. As the direct ownership stakes held by the state have decreased since the (partial) privatization, the importance of state control through political connections has increased, which may be reflected in higher pay for connectedness (especially since 2006) but not necessarily for ability.

In contrast, agency theory implies that politically connected managers are paid more *only if* their connections are beneficial to the firms, for example, in easing financial constraints and securing large contracts, because they increase shareholder value. However, it has been well documented that executives' political connections actually lead to worse financial performance due to politicians' rent extraction from companies they manage, especially in developing countries (Faccio, Masulis, & McConnell, 2006; Shleifer & Vishny, 1994). Therefore, under the agency framework, the board of directors should not allot higher compensation to politically connected managers, while under the state-stewardship framework such managers will be paid more by the state.

H3a Politically connected managers receive higher compensation. This relation is stronger in the post-2006 period.

Under the rule of the communism tenets, the state and its stewards may window-dress their relationship in order to avoid public criticism. They may appease the public by setting relatively higher compensation for some easily observable managerial traits, such as degrees from prestigious universities or academic scholarship. These factors significantly contribute to one's prestige in China which has a long history and tradition (Confucianism) of respecting knowledge and intellectuals. Moreover, in the light of China's lagging intellectual and educational development in modern history (the past 60 years), Chinese hold people who have been educated at foreign top universities or have worked overseas in high esteem. Whereas agency theory states that managerial pay ought to be closely linked to a manager's abilities, under our state-stewardship view managers' actual abilities to efficiently manage their firms are expected to be less important in terms of compensation (Graham, Li, & Qiu, 2012; Rose & Shepard, 1997). Obviously, academic and international experience is not just a factor of prestige, it may also increase Chinese executives' abilities to manage state assets and generate more benefits for the state in their function as responsible stewards. We distinguish between prestige and ability variables by also testing whether experience in specialized fields (technology, finance, and accounting) is priced in the manager's compensation.

We classify the managerial characteristics according to three dimensions: the *prestige*, *ability*, and *personal* dimensions in order to explore which types of characteristics account for higher compensation. Prestige increases for managers with *Political Experience*, with *International Work Experience*, with *Overseas Education*, with *Academic Experience*, and with a higher *Educational Degree*. Ability is captured by *Accounting Experience*, *Financial Experience*, and *Technological Experience*. The personal dimension is determined by *Gender*, *Nationality*, and *Age* (which may also proxy for seniority and entrenchment within the firm). Based on our above discussion, we expect that managerial pay significantly positively correlates with a manager's political and prestige dimensions, but less so to ability and personal characteristics. Therefore, we hypothesize that:

H3b Managerial compensation is significantly positively related to the manager's "prestige," mirrored by international work experience, overseas education, or academic background, but less related to the manager's "ability," reflected by their work experience in specialized industries.

Internal Governance and Symbolic Management

Our fourth set of hypotheses is on the internal corporate governance mechanisms (mainly the structure of the board) that could regulate managerial compensation. An effective board structure could alleviate moral hazard problems and reduce agency costs (Rosenstein & Wyatt, 1990). The effectiveness of the board structure (especially in monitoring managers) should be stronger when firms become more market-oriented, and executive compensation could consequently be driven more towards the Western pay-for-performance model.

Based on our state-stewardship view that managers and the state share the same interests which may conflict with that of the citizens, we question the effectiveness of board structures in relation to regulating managerial compensation in China. The state has little incentive to implement a real corporate governance reform leading to more independence from the state. Some studies suggest that as China's corporate governance gradually converges to the Western market-based model, especially since the issuance of the 2002 CSRC Code which requires the presence of more independent directors and the separation of management and supervision. Since then, board structure should play a stronger role in aligning managerial pay to firm performance (e.g., Cao, Pan, & Tian, 2011; Conyon & He, 2011). Furthermore, as is the case with the nomination of managers, directors are also usually selected by the government and many of them have political connections. In this sense, they are also stewards of the state, and share the same interests as ("collude" with) the managers instead of monitoring them. Therefore, externally visible structures (such as committees, procedures, and formal organizational positions) are mainly used to meet legal requirements or social procedures in China, rather than to reform corporate governance in substance (Markoczy, Sun, Peng, Shi, & Ren, 2013; Sun, Zhu, & Ye, 2015). This practice, often coined as "symbolic management" is used to conform to societal rules, norms, and expectations but not to the essence of the regulation (Westphal & Graebner, 2010; Westphal & Zajac, 1998). For example, Peng (2004) has confirmed that outside directors mostly serve a symbolic purpose without improving firm performance among Chinese firms. IIF (2006) also reports that independent directors have little leeway to influence corporate strategy in China. Also, the setting up of compensation committees is voluntary under the recommendation of CSRC in 1999, and can also service as a symbolic tool in China (Markoczy et al., 2013).

In this light, the symbolic management view can be housed in our state-stewardship perspective that explains executive compensation in Chinese firms. As the state's stewards, the boards do not function to effectively monitor managers and constrain managerial pay, and many of the board structures (such as the ratio of independent directors and the existence of compensation committees) are merely symbolic — they are either not related to or even positively related to pay. In addition, they would not induce stronger pay-for-performance (Van Essen, Heugens, et al., 2012). In contrast, agency theory predicts that well-functioning internal corporate governance mechanisms should be related to lower managerial pay and stronger pay-for-performance (Bebchuk & Fried, 2004). For the Chinese context however, we hypothesize that:

> **H4a** Managerial compensation is not related or even positively related to symbolic features of board structures such as the ratio of independent directors and the setting up of a compensation committee. These board structures do not strengthen pay-for-performance.

Another important internal governance feature is the phenomenon of managerial duality. Managerial duality whereby the manager is also the chairman of the board, and in some cases, even the secretary of the party committee is still prevalent in Chinese corporations.[10] In an agency framework, managerial duality creates conflicts of interests as the manager is put in a position where he has to evaluate and monitor his own performance.[11] The managerial power theory within the agency framework states that duality gives the manager more power over the board, and that top management is likely to abuse their power by rewarding themselves a high compensation (Grabke-Rundell & Gomez-Mejia, 2002). However, given that most managers who hold dual positions in China usually also have significant political stakes and aligned interests with the state as its stewards, it is not likely that they would put their own political fate at risk. Since the 2006 reform, the state has significantly decreased its ownership stakes but has shifted control towards dominating the recruitment/hiring policies of executive employees. The state relies more on appointing (re)liable managers and such liability becomes particularly important when the manager holds a duality position. Therefore, while the agency view predicts a positive relation between managerial pay and managerial duality over our *whole* sample period, the state-stewardship perspective predicts that managerial duality be more positively related to managerial compensation in the post-2006 period. We hypothesize that:

H4b Managerial compensation in China is weakly positively related to managerial duality in the pre-2006 period, but is more significantly positively related to managerial duality in the post-2006 period.

Local and National Political Goals

Whereas the above-mentioned political dimension is based on issues beyond the individual and firm level, our final hypothesis deals with the macroeconomic determinants of managerial compensation. The organizing principles of the state require that firms' business activities should be fundamentally state-driven, and be conformed to the ideological requirements. Macroeconomic performance at the regional level is an important political indicator of how well local politicians are doing in terms of reaching the political goals of the state and the government(s) (Peng et al., 2015; Sun, Peng, Lee, & Tan, 2015). Following this logic, we argue from our state-stewardship view that managerial compensation also reflects those political goals (in Chinese: *Zheng Ji*). We focus on three major political/economic goals that the Chinese government cares about most: gross domestic product (GDP) growth, employment, and inward foreign direct investment (FDI). More precisely, as the executives in the local state-controlled firms are usually selected by the local provincial officers who control huge amounts of resources and enjoy broad autonomies (Xu, 2011), or have closer connections and aligned interests with the local government, their compensation should be positively correlated with the local provincial GDP growth and employment. To test the link between managerial compensation and macroeconomic factors, we use GDP, total employment of the local province where the firm is headquartered, and the number of employees hired by the firm, as measures of how the managers as state's stewards fulfill the local governors' political aims. Prior to 2006, inward FDI (attracting foreign capital and obtaining technological knowhow) was emphasized in the national economic strategy. Subsequently, GDP growth was stressed, also as a consequence of the global economic crisis. It should be noted that the political priorities differ across regions, for instance, the eastern coastal provinces with their high level of economic development versus the inner continental provinces (northern and western regions). The more developed regions have been the engines of China's economic growth, and there the local governors' priorities hinge on GDP growth, whereas in less developed regions, attracting FDI to upgrade the industrial structure is the focus. The agency theory would make no such prediction as there are no mechanical linkage between managerial pay and macroeconomic factors *after controlling for provincial macroeconomic effects* which capture those unobserved macroeconomic factors such as local income, local property prices, labor market prosperity, social safety net, as well as other geographical and demographical factors. Although the values of some macroeconomic variables vary over time, their relative cross-province differences are stable and can be controlled through province fixed effects. Therefore, we hypothesize that:

> **H5** Managerial compensation is positively related to the local macroeconomic (political) achievement indicators such as growth in GDP, inward FDI, and corporate employment.

DATA AND METHODOLOGY

Data

We test our hypotheses on firms listed on the Shanghai and Shenzhen exchanges.[12] We collect our data from the Wind Database, CSMAR, and Peking University's China Center for Economic Research (CCER) database, which comprise all A-share companies[13] listed on the above exchanges since 1990 (Liang, Renneboog, & Sun, 2016; Peng et al., 2015). Financial and operational data, along with information about industry classification, location of headquarters (city and province) are collected from Wind. Information on executive compensation, stock ownership, corporate governance, and board structure are gathered from CSMAR, and information on the ultimate shareholders' names is from CCER. In addition, we manually collected the variables capturing CEOs' characteristics and backgrounds from their curricula published on Wind and CSMAR. To supplement the managerial background data, we collect the profiles from the annual reports, more specifically from the "Profile of Directors and

Senior Managers" sections that comprise the manager's name, gender, education, academic and professional background, and career history. The dataset consists of 17,272 firm-year observations covering more than 92% of all listed firms in mainland China over the period 2001–2011. We excluded the financial and insurance companies, and the firms labeled by the stock exchanges as *Special Treatment* (ST). The latter are firms in financial distress or experiencing financial difficulties (e.g., negative net earnings for two consecutive years) as defined by CSRC. We follow the *Industry Classification Guide of Listed Companies* issued by CSRC in April 2001 to partition our sample firms into 21 industries. Table 3 summarizes the variable definitions, and Table 4 exhibits the summary statistics on the main variables.[14]

Firms could manipulate their financial and compensation information, for example, the gray income accrued to executives. However, the number of falsified financial statements in China appears to be fairly limited; Firth, Rui, and Wu (2011) find that only 271 firms have the restatements during 2000–2005 (3.7% of all observations). In addition, as aforementioned, equity-based pay such as stock options are rare in China, even in recent years. These help justify the reliability of using cash compensation (salaries and bonuses) as the proxy for managerial pay.

Methodology

We estimate the determinants of managerial pay using fixed effects models as the Hausman tests indicates that the covariates are not uncorrelated with the unobserved firm effects. As some of the key independent variables are time-invariant (e.g., managers' personal background), we also estimate random effect models. The dependent variable is top managerial pay, which is defined as the logarithm of the total compensation of the top three highest-paid top managers as there is no transparency requirement at the individual manager or director level. Our independent variables comprise state ownership (shares directly owned by the state, and the dummy variable indicating whether the ultimate controller of the firm is the state), firm performance (ROA, Tobin's Q), macroeconomic factors (the natural logarithm of the local province's annual GDP, of the annual inward FDI, and of corporate employment[15]), board structure (independent director ratio, the existence of a compensation/strategy committee, CEO-chairman duality, top management team size, board size), political connections, managerial backgrounds (education, international experience), and ability

Table 3. Description of Variables.

Variable	Description
Dependent Variable:	
Ln(Compensation)	The natural logarithm of the total compensation in cash of the top three highest-paid top managers. Source: CSMAR (unit: RMB).
State Ownership and Control:	
State direct ownership	The percentage of firm's shares owned by the State. Source: WIND.
State ultimate shareholder	This dummy variable equals one if the ultimate controlling shareholder is the state or a government agency, and zero otherwise. The ultimate controlling shareholder is defined as the largest shareholder (in terms of the number of shares held), or the shareholder whose voting rights exceed those of the largest shareholder (who may be the largest in terms of cash flow rights), or the shareholder who holds more than 30% of cash flow and voting rights, or who can determine the nomination of more than half of the directors through exerting voting rights. The definition of ultimate controller is similar as in the papers by La Porta, Lopez-de-Silanes, Shleifer, and Vishny (1999) and Claessens, Djankov, and Lang (2000). Source: CCER database and CSMAR.
Self-Dealing and Gray Income:	
Other receivables	Other receivables as on the balance sheet
Firm Performance:	
ROA	Annual ROA. Source: WIND.
Tobin's Q	The ratio of the market value of equity to the book value of equity. Source: WIND.
Managerial Expertise, Background, and Education:	
Political experience	This dummy variable equals one if the manager is or was an official in the central government, local government, or the military, and zero otherwise. Source: Manually collected from managers' CVs.
International work experience	This dummy variable equals one if the manager has worked or is working in a foreign multinational firm, a foreign joint venture, an overseas subsidiary of a Chinese company, or has worked abroad (including Hong Kong, Macau, and Taiwan), and zero otherwise. Source: Manually collected from managers' CVs.
Overseas education	This dummy variable equals one if the manager was educated or obtained a degree abroad, and zero otherwise. Source: Manually collected from managers' CVs.
Accounting experience	This dummy variable equals one if the manager has worked in an accounting firm or position before, and zero otherwise. Source: Manually collected from managers' CVs.
Financial experience	This dummy variable equals one if the manager has worked in the financial industry before, and zero otherwise. Source: Manually collected from managers' CVs.

Table 3. *(Continued)*

Variable	Description
Technology experience	This dummy variable equals one if the manager has worked in a technology-related firm or position before, and zero otherwise. Source: Manually collected from managers' CVs.
Academic experience	This dummy variable equals one if the manager has worked in academia as a university professor or researcher before, and zero otherwise. Source: Manually collected from managers' CVs.
Gender	This dummy variable equals one if the manager is female, and zero if he is male. Source: Manually collected from managers' CVs.
Foreign nationality	The dummy variable equals one if the manager is non-Chinese, and zero if Chinese. Source: Manually collected from managers' CVs.
Education level	The score ranges from 0 to 4: zero if his highest education level is below junior college; one in case of junior college; two in case of a bachelor degree; three if the manager has graduated with a master's degree; and four if graduated with a doctoral degree. Source: Manually collected from managers' CVs.
Age	The manager's age in the year reported. Source: Manually collected from managers' CVs.
Internal Corporate Governance:	
Independent director ratio	This ratio is the number the independent directors divided by the total number of directors. Source: CSMAR.
Board size	Total number of the company's board members. Source: CSMAR.
Management team size	Total number of the company's total management team members. Source: CSMAR.
Compensation committee	This dummy variable equals one if the company has a compensation committee, and zero otherwise. Source: CSMAR.
Strategy committee	This dummy variable equals one if the company has a strategy committee, and zero otherwise. Source: CSMAR.
Managerial duality	This dummy variable equals one if the positions of the general manager (president) and chairman are held by the same person, and zero otherwise. Source: CSMAR.
Director interlocks	Number of independent directors who are holding director positions in other listed firms in the year under consideration. Source: Manually collected from independent directors' CVs.
Information centrality	A firm's relative position ("closeness") to the center of its directors' social network (calculated based on the geodesic paths between any pair of firm-nodes − by means of Ucinet 6)
Firm Employment and Provincial Economic Performance:	
Ln(Local GDP)	The natural logarithm of the GDP of the province where the firm is headquartered. Source: NBS (unit: 10,000 million RMB).
Ln(Inward FDI)	The natural logarithm of the flow of inward foreign direct investment (IFDI) of the local province where the firm is headquartered. Source: China Statistical Yearbook (unit: USD10,000).

Table 3.   (*Continued*)

Variable	Description
Ln(Employees)	The natural logarithm of the total number of people employed by the firm. Source: WIND.
Control Variables:	
Leverage	The ratio of the book value of total debts to the book value of total assets. Source: WIND.
Sales growth	Annual sales growth rate. Source: WIND.
Firm size	The natural logarithm of the total book assets value. Source: WIND.
Capital intensity	The ratio of capital expenditure to net sales. Source: WIND.
Ownership concentration	Percentage of total shares owned by the five largest blockholders.

(specialized experience). We control for industry, year, and province fixed effects. We cluster standard errors at the firm level to further adjust for correlation of unobserved characteristics across firms.

Endogeneity is potentially an issue as there may be reverse causality between managerial pay and most firm-level variables. However, under China's unique institutional arrangement, state ownership, managerial backgrounds, board structures are mostly directly determined by the state, and can thus be viewed as exogenous rather than being affected by managerial compensation. Probably, the only potentially endogenous variables are those measuring firm performance: while managerial compensation can be determined by corporate performance, performance results from managerial effort and incentives may hinge on compensation. Such endogeneity problems may be especially severe in a Western context where managers receive a significant amount of their total compensation in the form of stock options or restricted stock, and it is hard to unbundle the short-term and long-term financial incentives (Datta, D'Mello, & Iskandar-Datta, 2009). However, this is much less of a concern in the case of China because equity-based compensation is rare, and executive compensation packages are produced bureaucratically, with weak links to share price (Buck et al., 2008; Liang et al., 2016). There has been no tradition of (marked-oriented) pay-for-performance for individual executives owing to the Chinese national culture with high collectivism and high power-distance tolerance. We still address this endogeneity issue by implementing an instrument variable approach as a robustness check on our results.

Table 4. Descriptive Statistics.

Variable	Observation	Mean	Median	Std. Dev.	Min	Max
Dependent Variable:						
Managerial compensation (000 RMB)	15,314	884	600	1,160	0	43,300
State Ownership:						
State direct ownership	15,544	24.56%	16.98%	25.79%	0%	100%
State ultimate shareholder	14,650	0.64	1	0.48	0	1
Self-Dealing and Gray Income:						
Other receivables/assets	15,356	3.60%	1.60%	4.68%	0.11%	17.63%
Firm Performance:						
ROA	15,618	3.90	3.73	5.44	−9.61	14.24
Tobin's Q	15,519	2.17	1.89	2.25	0.92	9.21
Managerial Expertise, Background, and Education:						
Political experience	16,419	0.20	0	0.40	0	1
Overseas education	16,422	0.04	0	0.20	0	1
International work experience	16,417	0.06	0	0.23	0	1
Education level	16,292	2.36	2	0.90	0	4
Academic experience	16,420	0.11	0	0.31	0	1
Technology experience	16,421	0.43	0	0.49	0	1
Accounting experience	16,421	0.12	0	0.32	0	1
Financial experience	16,421	0.06	0	0.24	0	1
Foreign nationality	16,424	0.01	0	0.10	0	1
Age	16,353	46.43	46	6.89	21	75
Gender	16,423	0.05	0	0.22	0	1
Internal Corporate Governance:						
Independent director ratio	15,499	36.95%	33.33%	18.59%	0%	88.89%
Compensation committee	14,183	0.66	1	0.47	0	1
Strategy committee	14,187	0.51	1	0.50	0	1
Managerial duality	15,508	0.15	0	0.36	0	1
Board size	15,505	8.81	9	2.46	0	24
Management team size	15,464	7.08	6	3.95	1	64

Table 4. (*Continued*)

Variable	Observation	Mean	Median	Std. Dev.	Min	Max
Firm Employment and Provincial Economic Performance:						
Local GDP	15,021	13,568.8	10,552.06	11,209.39	138.73	53,004
Inward FDI	16,132	7.51×10^5	5.85×10^5	7.23×10^5	0	4.01×10^6
Employees	15,545	4,205.03	1,621	16,959.4	1	5.53×10^5
Control Variables:						
Sales growth rate	15,715	18.02%	14.92%	29.61%	−34.51%	87.63%
Capital intensity	15,782	0.21	0.09	0.28	0.00	1.10
Firm size (Ln(Assets))	15,642	21.35	21.21	1.24	10.84	28.66
Leverage	16,666	0.63	0.49	7.12	0	877.26
Ownership concentration	15,329	0.55	0.56	0.14	0.29	0.78

All monetary terms are in **RMB**. Other receivable/assets, ROA, Tobin's Q, sales growth rate, capital intensity, and ownership concentration are winsorized at 5% level. A correlation check suggests there is no multicollinearity between the explanatory and control variables.

RESULTS AND DISCUSSION

Benchmark Results

It is important not just to test the state-stewardship for the whole sample period but also to distinguish between the periods before and after the regulatory structural break of 2006 (the split-share reform) and study the economic transition patterns. To examine the impact of the state on top managerial compensation, we estimate the regression including the degree of state ownership (or whether the state is the ultimate shareholder) (for definitions, see Table 3). A first important observation is that state ownership has a significantly negative impact on managerial pay for the full sample (full sample in Table 5), but this relation only occurs for the pre-2006 period when a 1% increase in state ownership results in an average 0.225% decrease in the managerial pay, *ceteris paribus*. That entails that, for instance, a 30% higher percentage of state ownership drives down the managerial compensation by about 7%. This supports H1a in that managers in more state-oriented companies receive a lower pecuniary compensation, especially when the state control is strong (through direct ownership). This effect disappears from 2006 when the state significantly reduced its (non-tradable) share stakes and direct state control became weaker. Similar results are found when we replace the State direct ownership with State ultimate shareholder dummy as an explanatory variable.

An alternative explanation on the negative association between state ownership control and managerial pay may lie in the tradeoff between incentive and insurance: state ownership and the resulting state appointments insulate top executives from turnover. Therefore, SOE managers may be willing to accept lower compensation in exchange for higher job security. However, we find that managerial turnover is not significantly larger in private firms than in SOEs.[16] Moreover, the job security argument does not explain the statistical significance of the coefficients of Political Experience either: politically connected managers are supposed to have more secure positions and would hence earn less if the above turnover argument were true.

Jiang et al. (2010) suggest that high other receivables represent inter-company loans to firms of blockholders. As the use of this type of loans has been shown to enable tunneling, managers of firms with high other receivables are suspected of collude with blockholders, which are usually state agencies and politicians. In the context of these opportunities for

Table 5. Tests for the State-Stewardship View on Managers.

	Full Sample				Pre-2006 Period				Post-2006 Period			
	Coefficient	Std. Err.	Coefficient	Std. Err.	Coefficient	Std. Err.	Coefficient	Std. Err.	Coefficient	Std. Err.	Coefficient	Std. Err.
State Ownership:												
State direct ownership	-0.091**	(0.029)			-0.225***	(0.057)			0.004	(0.034)		
State ultimate shareholder			-0.013	(0.017)			-0.061**	(0.028)			0.014	(0.021)
Self-Dealing and Gray Income:												
Ln(Other receivables)	-0.011**	(0.005)	-0.010**	(0.005)	-0.020**	(0.008)	-0.019**	(0.008)	-0.000	(0.006)	-0.001	(0.005)
Firm Performance:												
ROA	0.023***	(0.001)	0.023***	(0.001)	0.020***	(0.002)	0.021***	(0.002)	0.020***	(0.001)	0.020***	(0.001)
Tobin's Q	0.015***	(0.003)	0.014***	(0.003)	0.004	(0.009)	0.004	(0.009)	0.012***	(0.001)	0.012***	(0.001)
Managerial Expertise, Background, and Education:												
Political experience	0.041***	(0.015)	0.038**	(0.015)	0.045*	(0.026)	0.046*	(0.026)	0.047**	(0.022)	0.049**	(0.022)
Overseas education	0.057*	(0.031)	0.041	(0.032)	0.091	(0.059)	0.075	(0.059)	0.050	(0.041)	0.074*	(0.041)
International work experience	0.116***	(0.027)	0.112***	(0.027)	0.091**	(0.044)	0.077*	(0.044)	0.147***	(0.042)	0.154***	(0.042)
Education level	0.028***	(0.007)	0.028***	(0.007)	0.024*	(0.013)	0.025*	(0.013)	0.024**	(0.010)	0.023**	(0.010)
Academic experience	0.025	(0.019)	0.021	(0.019)	0.080**	(0.034)	0.073**	(0.034)	0.017	(0.028)	0.016	(0.028)
Technology experience	0.031**	(0.013)	0.030**	(0.013)	0.036	(0.024)	0.036	(0.024)	-0.011	(0.018)	-0.007	(0.019)
Accounting experience	-0.008	(0.017)	-0.009	(0.017)	-0.022	(0.027)	-0.020	(0.027)	0.016	(0.034)	0.029	(0.035)
Financial experience	-0.037	(0.025)	-0.032	(0.025)	-0.034	(0.048)	-0.033	(0.048)	-0.059*	(0.035)	-0.063*	(0.035)
Foreign nationality	0.231***	(0.072)	0.258***	(0.073)	0.139	(0.144)	0.156	(0.144)	0.208**	(0.091)	0.154*	(0.094)
Age	0.005***	(0.001)	0.004***	(0.001)	0.001	(0.002)	0.001	(0.002)	0.006***	(0.001)	0.006***	(0.001)
Gender	-0.031	(0.028)	-0.040	(0.029)	-0.086	(0.055)	-0.091*	(0.055)	-0.037	(0.037)	-0.029	(0.037)
Internal Corporate Governance:												
Independent director ratio	0.020	(0.036)	0.011	(0.037)	0.050	(0.112)	0.048	(0.112)	-0.019	(0.040)	-0.008	(0.039)
Board size	0.012***	(0.003)	0.012***	(0.003)	0.005	(0.005)	0.005	(0.005)	0.019***	(0.005)	0.019***	(0.005)
Management team size	0.013***	(0.002)	0.012***	(0.002)	0.044***	(0.005)	0.043***	(0.005)	0.018***	(0.002)	0.019***	(0.002)
Compensation committee	0.076***	(0.016)	0.078***	(0.017)	0.089***	(0.027)	0.088***	(0.027)	0.055**	(0.024)	0.051**	(0.023)

	(1)	(2)	(3)	(4)	(5)	(6)
Strategy committee	0.005	0.003	0.015	0.024	0.001	−0.003
	(0.014)	(0.014)	(0.029)	(0.029)	(0.016)	(0.016)
Managerial duality	0.041**	0.042**	0.039	0.038	0.040**	0.039*
	(0.017)	(0.017)	(0.032)	(0.032)	(0.020)	(0.021)
Firm Employment and Provincial Economic Performance:						
Ln(Local GDP)	−0.028		0.048		0.121***	
	(0.032)		(0.109)		(0.043)	
Ln(Employees)	0.017**	0.018**	−0.035***	−0.036***	0.039***	0.041***
	(0.008)	(0.008)	(0.013)	(0.013)	(0.009)	(0.009)
Ln(Inward FDI)		0.038***		0.050**		0.020
		(0.013)		(0.026)		(0.020)
Control Variables:						
Leverage	0.002***	0.002***	−0.053*	−0.055*	0.002***	0.002***
	(0.001)	(0.001)	(0.030)	(0.030)	(0.001)	(0.001)
Sales growth rate	−0.009	−0.007	−0.017	−0.019	−0.006	−0.007
	(0.017)	(0.017)	(0.026)	(0.026)	(0.019)	(0.020)
Capital intensity	−0.029	−0.030	−0.105***	−0.105***	−0.001	−0.003
	(0.027)	(0.020)	(0.033)	(0.033)	(0.036)	(0.037)
Firm Size	0.241***	0.238***	0.287***	0.281***	0.194***	0.193***
	(0.010)	(0.010)	(0.021)	(0.021)	(0.012)	(0.012)
Ownership concentration	0.107*	0.077	0.243*	0.072	0.040	0.030
	(0.059)	(0.059)	(0.136)	(0.125)	(0.069)	(0.069)
Constant	6.565***	6.416***	6.232***	6.227***	6.814***	7.755***
	(0.339)	(0.256)	(1.065)	(0.530)	(0.474)	(0.352)
Year fixed effect	Yes	Yes	Yes	Yes	Yes	Yes
Industry fixed effect	Yes	Yes	Yes	Yes	Yes	Yes
Province fixed effect	Yes	Yes	Yes	Yes	Yes	Yes
No. of observations	12,401	12,042	4,916	4,886	7,485	7,156
R-squared adjusted	53%	54%	41%	40%	44%	45%

The dependent variable is the natural logarithm of the top three highest-paid managers' compensation. Independent variables are state ownership (%), a state ultimate shareholder dummy, ROA (winsorized at the 95% level), Tobin's Q (winsorized at the 95% level), independent director ratio, board size, management team size, compensation committee dummy, strategy committee dummy, managerial duality dummy (equals 1 if the manager and chairman is the same person), logarithm of local province's GDP and inward FDI, and of the total number of employees of the firm, a series of managerial background dummies, and control variables (leverage, sales growth rate, capital intensity, firm size (total asset value), and the ownership concentration of the top five blockholders). More information on variable definitions can be found in Table 3. *, **, and *** stand for significance at the 10%, 5%, and 1%, respectively. Standard errors are clustered at the firm level and reported in parentheses. GLS estimations are used.

self-dealing, managers may care less about their regular cash income. Other receivables are always significantly negative in Table 5 (for the full and pre-2006 samples), which supports H1b and indicates that gray income and cash compensation are to some extent substitutes. The fact that the negative relation is not statistically significant in the more recent years implies that this type of tunneling by managers (along with dominant shareholders) is no longer (or less) prevalent and that the government crackdown on this type of self-dealing has been successful (and/or that other channels have been found for tunneling). These results are salient given that we have already controlled for ownership concentration which to some extent captures the agency argument that blockholders can "bribe" managers.

One concern about this result would be that the causality is likely to go in the opposite direction: managers are more likely to engage in gray income-generating behaviors because they have lower monetary compensation. If this were the case, we would expect the negative relation to be stronger in firms with more concentrated state ownership as the manager needs to compensate more for his low pay through gray income. In unreported regressions, we include an interaction term between state ownership and other receivables. However, its coefficients are not statistically significant, neither before nor after 2006, a finding which is also supported by our tests on subsamples of SOEs and private firms.

We document a strong relation between firm performance and managerial compensation (Table 5). For the full sample, the economic significance of the ROA coefficient (12.5% [2.3%×5.44]) is four times bigger than that of Tobin's Q (3.15% [1.4%×2.25]) which implies that the accounting performance is in general more important than the market-based benchmark. A more detailed analysis reveals that ROA is only positively significant in the pre-2006 sample whereas both the accounting and market-based measures are significant for the post-2006 sample. This provides some support for H2 in that the managerial compensation depends on accounting returns, but only since 2006 also on the market-based return. This finding conforms to China's move towards a more market-based economy.

An alternative explanation may be under an optimal contracting framework. For example, Kang and Liu (2008) find that the sensitivity of managerial compensation with respect to stock performance is positively correlated with the measure of stock price informativeness. Before the 2006 split-share reform, most shares were held by the government and its affiliated agencies in China were non-tradable, and the stock market was not efficient which implies that stock prices were at best a coarse measure of underlying firm fundamentals. Therefore, the state linked managerial pay to some other measures such as ROA to capture managerial performance. After the 2006 reform, all the non-tradable shares were gradually floated on the stock market, thus increasing the stock market efficiency (Murillo, Ribas, & Wang, 2011). As a result, executive compensation could now also be tied more closely to firm stock performance such as Tobin's Q. However, this assumes that bonuses are paid out, linked to stock price increases and the compensation contract is revised every year, which is not the case in China (Adithipyangkul et al., 2009). Furthermore, it has been empirically shown that stock price informativeness has actually decreased in China since the split-share reform, due to the risk-sharing induced by the broadened investor base which leads investors to collect less information on the firm's future payoff (Chang, Lin, & Ma, 2012; Li et al., 2011; Peress, 2010), which significantly weakens this explanation.

Managers with political experience receive a higher compensation, and this relation between pay and the political background is stronger in the postreform period. Managers with a political background received 4.5% more compensation prior to 2006, but this increased to 5% post-2006 (a difference which is statistically significantly different but economically small).[17] This echoes — although only weakly — Xu's (2011) claim about the government's control over executive personnel: stronger political ties are reflected in higher executive compensation. These findings fail to reject H3a.

Next, we relate the top managers' "prestige," which is captured by their international work experience, overseas education, educational level, and academic background, to their compensation. We find that international work experience is financially compensated (and even increasingly so), certainly for reasons of prestige in the home country, but possibly also because this type of experience may bring valuable expertise to the company. It should be noted that since Chinese firms turned more market-oriented, international exposure is rewarded more (Table 5) but top management's specialized expertise in finance, accounting, or technology is not priced. We also observe that managers with a higher level of education, overseas education, or an academic (university) background receive higher pay. From a human capital view, specialized expertise, international experience, and education could all contribute to managers' competence, but in China, only those factors with a strong connotation to prestige are priced in terms of higher managerial compensation. This result gives some support to our H3b, and is reinforced by the Chinese culture in which prestige factors play a prominent role. The fact that managerial pay is strongly related to what are considered in China as prestige factors, but less to ability factors, implies that the Chinese compensation policy is somehow a window-dressing corporate governance practice aiming at cherry picking managers who are loyal to the state. We also control for age, which is strongly positively related to compensation, and gender which has a negative (but not statistically significant) impact.

Regarding the internal corporate governance structure, we find that the larger the size of the board and of the management team (which is shown in Fig. 2 not to be part of the board and has a low correlation with board size), the higher the pay of the top management. The proportion of independent directors does not have an impact on compensation implying that independent directors are not effective in regulating managerial pay. In addition, managerial pay is higher in firms with a compensation committee, but not with a strategy committee. The fact that independent director ratio and other board structures are irrelevant while compensation committee is positively related to pay supports H4a that they do not function to *constrain* managerial pay. Our results are also consistent with the findings in Markoczy et al. (2013) that firms set up compensation committees as a symbolic management tool to create the appearance of legitimacy by paying high managerial compensation. In unreported regressions, we create a variable interacting compensation committee dummy with ROA, and find that compensation committees weaken the pay-performance sensitivity. We find similar results for the independent director ratio, and for board structure variables when they are interacted with Tobin's Q (the interaction term does not affect the significance of Tobin's Q in isolation). In general, these findings suggest that the symbolic board structures do not reduce managerial pay and do not induce pay-for-performance. Furthermore, managerial duality does not significantly influence managerial compensation prior to 2006, but subsequently gained significance. The coefficient of the interaction term between managerial duality and political experience (not reported) is significant and positive for SOEs. This is consistent with our prediction in H4b: given the state's reduction of control based on ownership concentration, it wants to appoint more (re)liable or trusted people whom they give more responsibilities and thus compensate better.

One may be concerned that the above findings on board structures may be explained by the managerial power theory. That is, powerful managers can dominate the corporate governance mechanisms (such as the nomination of independent directors and board committees) which enable them to receive higher compensation and contracts with lower pay-for-performance. However, this argument is weakened by the fact that the coefficients of the independent director ratio are never statistically significant. In addition, the positive effect of the interaction between managerial duality and political experience (not reported) indicates that higher pay is based on managers' political reliability rather than managerial power. Another concern about the positive effect of compensation committees may be that one of the roles of the compensation committee is to attract talented managers with higher pay (Markoczy et al., 2013). However, this argument is not supported by its weaker association with pay-for-performance, and the fact that the pay is not linked to managerial expertise in specialized fields.

Interestingly, Table 5 shows that the coefficients of local GDP (*Ln(GDP)*) and inward FDI (*Ln(inward FDI)*), which measure the local provincial governors' political goals and achievements, are significant but in different time periods[18]: the growth of inward FDI is significant pre-2006, whereas GDP growth only plays a role post-2006. This implies that the priority in local governors' political goals has evolved over time: prior to 2006, attracting foreign investment to upgrade the industrial structures and obtain technological knowhow was a major political concern, but since 2006, the stronger market-orientation and widespread financial crisis put more pressure on the state and local governors to boost economic growth so as to maintain legitimacy and political stability. Table 5 also reveals that the number of employees of the firm (*Ln(Employees)*), which proxies for both the level of responsibilities of top management and the firm's contribution to local employment, is positively related to pay. Securing employment has gained importance over time, especially since the economic crisis struck. This supports H5: managerial compensation is tied to macroeconomic political goals and achievement indicators.

We do not find the typical pay-performance relationship documented in some other papers, such as Conyon and He (2011), Chen et al. (2011), and Cao et al. (2011). One key distinction between our model and theirs is that we control for the political dimension such as state ownership, managers' political connections, political achievement variables, etc. We argue that ignoring the strong state involvement could bias the empirical findings and reduce the ability to judge how Chinese managers are actually evaluated. Furthermore, given the large heterogeneity in industrial and regional development within China's economy, what is missing in previous studies is industry and province fixed effects.

SOEs versus Private Firms

In the previous section, we have found that contrary to the predictions of agency theory, managerial compensation is negatively related to state ownership/control and other receivables, positively related to managers' prestige factors and local governors' political goals. Compensation is not related to shareholder value before 2006 (e.g., Tobin's Q), managers' past professional experience, and board structure (with exception of the compensation committee – which can be argued – could be regarded as a "symbolic management" tool). We expect that the impact of the above explanatory variables differ across firm type, and be stronger for SOEs. In this section, we analyze two subsamples: SOEs in which the proportion of state-owned shares amounts to more than 30% and "privately-owned" firms with state ownership below that threshold. We expect that SOEs and private firms generally have different operating objectives. It should be noted that the Chinese definition of a private firm is different from that in western economies: although the average ownership in a Chinese private firm stake can be low, the influence of the party (through the board, party representatives in the company, etc.) is still significant.

Table 6 compares the results for SOEs and private firms for the full sample period and the two subperiods. For SOEs, the previous results supporting our state-stewardship hypotheses still hold for both types of SOE classifications: (1) State ownership is significantly negatively correlated with managerial pay for SOEs, while such effect is not significant in private firms (including the State Ultimate Shareholder variable in our regressions yields similar results; not shown). (2) As before, the tunneling effect through other receivables is significant in the pre-2006 sample but not in the post-2006 sample, and it is particularly strong for private firms. This strengthens our argument that managers collude with the dominant shareholders (see Jiang et al., 2010; Li et al., 2011) to extract private benefits especially in private (less state-owned) firms. (3) ROA still has a positive influence on managerial pay, whereas Tobin's Q only has a significant impact after 2006. The increased focus on market-based performance is visible both for SOEs and for private firms, and the pay-to-market performance tie is stronger in private firms. (4) Prestige (such as international work experience and the level of education) translates into higher compensation, especially for SOEs, while specialized experience does not. (5) Managerial political background is more important for private firms (with less state ownership control) than for SOEs, which indicates a tradeoff between state ownership and managerial political connections between two types of firms. (6) Internal corporate governance mechanisms such as the proportion of independent director are still not statistically significant for SOEs, but are for private firms prior to 2006. The symbolic role of the compensation committee remains strong, and has become stronger for SOEs than for private firms after 2006. Managerial duality is significant and positive in private firms in which

Table 6. SOEs versus Private Firms.

	Full Sample		Pre-2006 Sample		Post-2006 Sample	
	SOE State ownership >30%	Private State ownership <30%	SOE State ownership >30%	Private State ownership <30%	SOE State ownership >30%	Private State ownership <30%
State Ownership:						
State direct ownership	−0.268*** (0.101)	0.054 (0.093)	−0.724*** (0.173)	0.226 (0.221)	−0.323*** (0.128)	0.088* (0.103)
Self-Dealing and Gray Income:						
Ln(Other receivables)	−0.006 (0.007)	−0.015** (0.006)	−0.009 (0.010)	−0.033** (0.014)	0.011 (0.010)	−0.006 (0.007)
Firm Performance:						
ROA	0.026*** (0.002)	0.020*** (0.001)	0.026*** (0.003)	0.013*** (0.004)	0.023*** (0.002)	0.019*** (0.002)
Tobin's Q	0.014*** (0.005)	0.009** (0.004)	−0.001 (0.013)	−0.001 (0.012)	0.010* (0.006)	0.012*** (0.004)
Managerial Expertise, Background, and Education:						
Political experience	0.018 (0.023)	0.039* (0.021)	0.007 (0.034)	0.073* (0.043)	0.042 (0.041)	0.045* (0.026)
Overseas education	0.109** (0.050)	0.039 (0.042)	0.078 (0.076)	0.055 (0.091)	0.151** (0.075)	0.071 (0.049)
International work experience	0.101** (0.043)	0.097*** (0.035)	0.121** (0.058)	0.026 (0.070)	0.250*** (0.088)	0.095** (0.047)
Education level	0.024** (0.011)	0.015 (0.010)	0.015 (0.016)	0.001 (0.021)	0.013 (0.018)	0.034*** (0.011)
Academic experience	0.036 (0.027)	0.040 (0.027)	0.073* (0.042)	0.119** (0.056)	−0.003 (0.051)	0.010 (0.033)
Technology experience	0.005 (0.019)	0.050*** (0.018)	0.019 (0.029)	0.027 (0.040)	−0.065** (0.030)	0.035 (0.022)
Accounting experience	−0.013 (0.024)	−0.006 (0.025)	−0.017 (0.034)	−0.032 (0.043)	0.022 (0.059)	0.029 (0.041)
Financial experience	−0.070* (0.042)	−0.024 (0.032)	0.019 (0.069)	−0.077 (0.067)	−0.030 (0.068)	−0.045 (0.040)
Foreign nationality	0.254 (0.211)	0.237*** (0.081)	−0.128 (0.383)	0.259 (0.168)	0.655** (0.323)	0.133 (0.097)
Age	0.000 (0.001)	0.005*** (0.001)	0.001 (0.002)	−0.003 (0.003)	−0.001 (0.002)	0.008*** (0.002)
Gender	−0.030 (0.048)	−0.033 (0.036)	−0.106 (0.074)	−0.037 (0.079)	0.058 (0.081)	−0.054 (0.042)
Internal Corporate Governance:						
Independent director ratio	−0.129** (0.064)	0.076 (0.047)	−0.146 (0.131)	0.304 (0.200)	−0.031 (0.077)	0.019 (0.048)
Board size	0.003 (0.004)	0.015*** (0.005)	−0.002 (0.006)	0.008 (0.009)	0.013* (0.007)	0.021*** (0.006)
Management team size	0.016*** (0.002)	0.014*** (0.002)	0.039*** (0.006)	0.048*** (0.008)	0.014*** (0.004)	0.018*** (0.003)
Compensation committee	0.079*** (0.023)	0.054** (0.024)	0.059* (0.032)	0.117*** (0.046)	0.071* (0.038)	0.022 (0.029)

Table 6. *(Continued)*

	Full Sample		Pre-2006 Sample		Post-2006 Sample	
	SOE	Private	SOE	Private	SOE	Private
	State ownership >30%	State ownership <30%	State ownership >30%	State ownersh.p <30%	State ownership >30%	State ownership <30%
Strategy committee	0.021 (0.022)	0.000 (0.019)	0.020 (0.035)	0.025 (0.050)	-0.008 (0.029)	-0.002 (0.019)
Managerial duality	0.012 (0.029)	0.064*** (0.022)	0.021 (0.042)	0.057 (0.049)	-0.037 (0.041)	0.067*** (0.024)
Firm Employment and Provincial Economic Performance:						
Ln(Local GDP)					0.156** (0.069)	0.100** (0.049)
Ln(Employee)	-0.007 (0.012)	0.033*** (0.010)	-0.034* (0.017)	-0.018 (0.021)	0.029** (0.015)	0.039*** (0.011)
Ln(Inward FDI)	0.014 (0.019)	0.038* (0.020)	-0.001 (0.029)	0.143*** (0.049)		
Control Variables:						
Leverage	-0.020** (0.008)	0.002*** (0.001)	-0.106** (0.050)	-0.016 (0.039)	-0.012 (0.010)	0.002*** (0.001)
Sales growth rate	-0.015 (0.025)	-0.013 (0.022)	-0.034 (0.033)	-0.026 (0.041)	0.024 (0.034)	-0.007 (0.024)
Capital intensity	-0.109*** (0.030)	0.029 (0.029)	-0.149*** (0.043)	-0.068 (0.051)	-0.073 (0.064)	0.011 (0.046)
Firm size	0.235*** (0.016)	0.244*** (0.013)	0.251*** (0.026)	0.329*** (0.035)	0.183*** (0.019)	0.210*** (0.014)
Ownership concentration	0.379*** (0.126)	0.005 (0.072)	0.878*** (0.221)	0.083 (0.196)	0.224** (0.151)	-0.028 (0.081)
Constant	7.335*** (0.387)	6.350*** (0.365)	7.382*** (0.637)	4.076*** (0.951)	7.298*** (0.752)	6.700*** (0.543)
Year FE	Yes	Yes	Yes	Yes	Yes	Yes
Industry FE	Yes	Yes	Yes	Yes	Yes	Yes
Province FE	Yes	Yes	Yes	Yes	Yes	Yes
No. of observations	5,207	6,825	2,993	1,895	2,294	5,191
R-squared adjusted	59%	50%	46%	38%	51%	44%

The dependent variable is the natural logarithm of the top three highest-paid managers' compensation. Independent variables are state ownership (%), ROA (winsorized at the 95% level), Tobin's Q (winsorized at the 95% level), independent director ratio, board size, management team size, compensation committee dummy, strategy committee dummy, managerial duality dummy (equals 1 if the manager and chairman is the same person), logarithm of local province's GDP and inward FDI, and of total number of employees of the firm, a series of managerial background dummies, and control variables (leverage, sales growth rate, capital intensity, firm size (total asset value), and the ownership concentration of the top five blockholders). More information on variable definitions can be found in Table 3. *, **, and *** stand for significance at the 10%, 5%, and 1%, respectively. Standard errors are clustered at the firm level and reported in parentheses. GLS estimations are used.

ownership control by the state is weaker, especially after 2006. The coefficient on the interaction term between managerial duality and political experience (unreported) is only significant in the private firm post-2006 subsample but neither for SOEs nor for pre-2006 samples. (7) Political goals (firm employment and provincial economic performance) variables still matter for managerial pay. In general, our perspective is still robust within SOE and private subsamples.

The Regional Analysis

One important characteristic of China is its geographic heterogeneity. Even though we have controlled for province fixed effects, an analysis by region is warranted. There are 31 provinces/regions in mainland China that they are grouped based on geographic and demographic characteristics (excluded are Hong Kong and Macau, and included are five ethnic minority autonomous regions: Inner Tibet, Ningxia, Mongolia, Xinjiang, Guangxi, and four municipalities: Beijing, Shanghai, Tianjin, and Chongqing). We group the provinces into North China, South China, East China, and West China,[19] and also analyze the regional North, Northwest, and Southwest[20] separately given their lower level of industrialization and development.[21]

Table 7 displays that the effects of state influence vary substantially across regions.[22] For example, in East China which is the most economically developed and market-oriented region, the influence of state ownership is insignificant (model (1) in Table 7). The East China region consists of mostly coastal provinces which opened their ports to foreign trade already more than one century ago. In the West, North, or Northwest regions (models (3), (4), and (6)), state influence is much stronger than in the South (model (2)) or Southwest (model (7)), which can be explained by the fact that these regions were historically considered as strategically located. Most of the ancient imperial capitals were established in these regions (e.g., Xi'an, the capital city of Shaanxi Province, was the capital for six imperial dynasties) and they are now the key places in which the state is implementing the pervasive *"Western Development Strategy"* (in Chinese, *Xibu Dakaifa Zhanlve*). It is therefore not surprising that the tradition of state-influence remains most significant in these regions. Furthermore, a comparison between the minority autonomous region sample and the municipality sample shows that political connections, symbolic management (compensation committees), and political goals are more important in municipalities which are directly controlled by the state. These state-stewardship factors

Table 7. Regional Subsamples (2001–2011).

	(1) East		(2) South		(3) West		(4) North		(5) Regional North		(6) Northwest		(7) Southwest		(8) Auto-region		(9) Municipality	
State Ownership:																		
State direct ownership	-0.078	(0.049)	0.281***	(0.091)	-0.124*	(0.069)	-0.110*	(0.059)	-0.090	(0.070)	-0.311***	(0.121)	0.002	(0.091)	-0.093	(0.137)	-0.040	(0.053)
Self-Dealing and Gray Income:																		
Ln(Other receivables)	-0.008	(0.049)	0.014	(0.014)	-0.015	(0.011)	-0.022**	(0.010)	-0.022*	(0.012)	-0.037*	(0.019)	-0.006	(0.015)	-0.016	(0.023)	-0.007	(0.009)
Firm Performance:																		
ROA (winsorized)	0.024***	(0.002)	0.020***	(0.003)	0.026***	(0.002)	0.017***	(0.003)	0.020***	(0.003)	0.028***	(0.004)	0.020***	(0.003)	0.027***	(0.005)	0.017***	(0.002)
Tobin's Q (winsorized)	0.019***	(0.005)	0.022**	(0.009)	0.019***	(0.006)	0.002	(0.007)	0.011	(0.008)	-0.004	(0.040)	0.030***	(0.008)	0.036***	(0.013)	0.005	(0.006)
Managerial Expertise, Background, and Education:																		
Political experience	0.051**	(0.025)	-0.012	(0.041)	0.069*	(0.036)	0.035	(0.036)	0.093**	(0.044)	0.075	(0.067)	0.078*	(0.047)	-0.008	(0.067)	0.099***	(0.033)
Overseas education	0.009	(0.051)	0.104	(0.092)	0.149*	(0.088)	0.071	(0.066)	0.092	(0.082)	0.264	(0.175)	0.120	(0.106)	-0.171	(0.321)	0.083	(0.053)
International work experience	0.083**	(0.042)	0.194***	(0.066)	0.031	(0.074)	0.050	(0.060)	0.002	(0.066)	0.171	(0.196)	0.016	(0.086)	0.043	(0.166)	0.060	(0.043)
Education level	0.032**	(0.012)	-0.018	(0.023)	0.017	(0.016)	0.049***	(0.017)	0.045**	(0.021)	0.066**	(0.030)	-0.006	(0.021)	0.070**	(0.032)	0.001	(0.015)
Academic experience	0.021	(0.032)	0.032	(0.050)	-0.016	(0.047)	0.025	(0.040)	0.019	(0.046)	-0.101	(0.096)	0.047	(0.057)	-0.105	(0.103)	0.078**	(0.034)
Technology experience	0.043**	(0.021)	-0.036	(0.038)	0.110***	(0.030)	0.056*	(0.029)	0.051	(0.035)	0.065	(0.054)	0.082**	(0.040)	0.156***	(0.058)	0.076***	(0.027)
Accounting experience	-0.032	(0.027)	0.072	(0.051)	0.006	(0.041)	0.036	(0.037)	0.045	(0.044)	0.032	(0.072)	-0.063	(0.054)	0.138*	(0.084)	0.049	(0.030)
Financial experience	-0.090**	(0.044)	0.081	(0.064)	-0.194***	(0.059)	0.071	(0.054)	0.004	(0.067)	-0.301***	(0.105)	-0.171**	(0.081)	-0.203*	(0.109)	0.066	(0.045)
Foreign nationality	0.360***	(0.091)	-0.267	(0.241)	0.347	(0.303)	0.503***	(0.170)	0.721***	(0.365)	-0.157	(0.371)	1.036**	(0.499)	0.116	(0.418)	0.619***	(0.130)
Age	0.006***	(0.001)	0.003	(0.003)	0.006***	(0.002)	0.006***	(0.002)	0.012***	(0.003)	-0.002	(0.004)	0.006**	(0.003)	0.010***	(0.005)	0.005***	(0.002)
Gender	-0.035	(0.041)	-0.127*	(0.076)	0.060	(0.069)	-0.019	(0.074)	-0.143	(0.099)	-0.059	(0.138)	0.144	(0.104)	0.087	(0.115)	-0.065	(0.056)
Internal Corporate Governance:																		
Independent director ratio	0.058	(0.082)	0.065	(0.079)	0.059	(0.075)	-0.105	(0.085)	-0.073	(0.113)	-0.130	(0.133)	0.139	(0.085)	0.109	(0.216)	-0.150	(0.096)
Board size	0.012**	(0.005)	0.042***	(0.009)	0.011	(0.007)	-0.003	(0.007)	-0.009	(0.008)	-0.001	(0.012)	0.021**	(0.009)	0.010	(0.015)	0.000	(0.006)
Management team size	0.013***	(0.003)	0.017***	(0.004)	0.017***	(0.004)	0.008**	(0.004)	0.004	(0.005)	0.017**	(0.007)	0.013***	(0.005)	0.027***	(0.007)	0.004	(0.004)
Compensation committee	0.068***	(0.026)	0.032	(0.051)	0.136***	(0.040)	0.039	(0.037)	0.007	(0.045)	0.171***	(0.069)	0.144***	(0.054)	0.065	(0.072)	0.124***	(0.032)
Strategy committee	0.032	(0.022)	-0.020	(0.042)	-0.119***	(0.035)	0.082***	(0.031)	0.087***	(0.038)	-0.103*	(0.058)	-0.129***	(0.049)	-0.084	(0.062)	0.008	(0.027)
Managerial duality	0.054**	(0.027)	0.044	(0.047)	0.037	(0.041)	-0.008	(0.038)	-0.020	(0.052)	0.035	(0.082)	0.078	(0.053)	0.007	(0.078)	0.091**	(0.036)

Firm Employment and Provincial Economic Performance:

Ln(Local GDP)	0.020	0.131***	0.020				−0.049		0.191***
	(0.013)	(0.131)	(0.030)				(0.043)		(0.054)
Ln(Employee)		0.073***	−0.016	−0.008	−0.001	−0.080***	−0.020	0.004	0.001
		(0.020)	(0.017)	(0.017)	(0.017)	(0.031)	(0.023)	(0.036)	(0.013)
Ln(Inward FDI)	0.035			0.158***	0.138***	−0.059		0.022	
	(0.021)			(0.026)	(0.026)	(0.036)		(0.032)	
Control Variables:									
Leverage	0.004	−0.004	0.002***	−0.147***	−0.059	−0.063	0.002***	−0.112	0.009
	(0.008)	(0.009)	(0.001)	(0.042)	(0.046)	(0.095)	(0.001)	(0.116)	(0.008)
Sales growth rate	−0.056**	−0.057	0.003	0.073**	0.026	−0.002	−0.000	−0.013	0.019
	(0.027)	(0.047)	(0.037)	(0.036)	(0.044)	(0.062)	(0.050)	(0.066)	(0.031)
Capital intensity	−0.032	0.044	−0.122***	−0.066	−0.083	−0.072	−0.170***	−0.127	−0.090**
	(0.036)	(0.058)	(0.043)	(0.042)	(0.054)	(0.074)	(0.058)	(0.081)	(0.040)
Firm size	0.211***	0.211***	0.275***	0.251***	0.250***	0.323***	0.294***	0.206***	0.227***
	(0.018)	(0.029)	(0.024)	(0.021)	(0.025)	(0.042)	(0.032)	(0.047)	(0.019)
Ownership concentration	0.088	0.090	0.044	0.308**	0.266	0.641***	−0.125	−0.119	0.216*
	(0.098)	(0.157)	(0.148)	(0.140)	(0.176)	(0.265)	(0.199)	(0.279)	(0.129)
Constant	6.453***	5.584***	5.602***	4.855***	4.892***	6.201***	5.996***	6.688***	5.626***
	(0.430)	(0.634)	(0.475)	(0.495)	(0.582)	(0.821)	(0.659)	(0.873)	(0.537)
Year fixed effect	Yes	Yes	Yes	Yes	Yes	Yes	Yes	Yes	Yes
Industry fixed effect	Yes	Yes	Yes	Yes	Yes	Yes	Yes	Yes	Yes
Province fixed effect	Yes	Yes	Yes	Yes	Yes	Yes	Yes	Yes	Yes
No. of observations	4,289	1,810	2,384	2,340	1,591	800	1,220	770	2,376
R-squared adjusted	48%	50%	48%	57%	59%	58%	53%	49%	58%

The dependent variable is the natural logarithm of the top three highest-paid managers' compensation. Independent variables are state ownership (%), ROA (winsorized at the 95% level), Tobin's Q (winsorized at the 95% level), managerial duality dummy (equals 1 if the manager and chairman is the same person), logarithm of local province's GDP and inward FDI, and of total number of employees of the firm, a series of managerial background dummies, and control variables (leverage, sales growth rate, capital intensity, firm size (total asset value), and the ownership concentration of the top five blockholders). More information on variable definitions can be found in Table 3. *, **, and *** stand for significance at the 10%, 5%, and 1%, respectively. Standard errors are clustered at the firm level but not reported so as to save space. GLS estimations are used.

are less emphasized in autonomous regions. In addition, managerial pay is tied to market-based returns (Tobin's Q) in autonomous regions but not in municipalities. It is also interesting to note that wherever the state owner-ship does not have a significant impact on managerial pay, the manager's political background variable has a significant effect, which implies a potential tradeoff between state ownership and political connections. This confirms our argument that state ownership and state-stewardship are sub-stitutes for the state to maintain control over the firms.

Robustness Checks

Results from Alternative Panel Data Models

To test the robustness of our results, we conduct some more empirical tests with different specifications. Our aforementioned results are based on a random effect model controlling for year, industry, and province fixed effects. As alternative estimation methods, we use pooled OLS models (while controlling for year, industry, and province), pure random effect models (without controlling for year, industry, and province effects), and firm-fixed effect models. Obviously, the non-time-variant variables yield no results in a firm-fixed effects model. The first three models of Table 8 report that the coefficients on the state ownership variable are significantly nega-tive and the coefficients on the politically connected managers are signifi-cantly positive. Other receivables have a significant negative relationship with managerial pay. The pay for performance (ROA and Tobin's Q) is positively significant. The coefficients on independent directors are again not significant when we control for year, industry, and province fixed effects, but are significant when we use a pure random effects model. We argue that the insignificance of the results with fixed effects models make more sense: given the large heterogeneity among different industries and regions, we need to control for provincial and industrial variation by including their fixed effects. The same arguments apply to the sign and sig-nificance of internal governance variables − again, we find that only the coefficient on the compensation committee (a symbolic feature) is signifi-cant, while that on independent director ratio is not. The results of the managerial characteristics remain as before; prestige factors are positively and significantly influencing managerial pay whereas the variables captur-ing ability are not.

Table 8. Other Robustness Checks.

| | Pooled OLS (2001–2011) | | Random Effects (2001–2011) | | Firm Fixed Effects (2001–2011) | | IV Result (2SLS) 2001–2005 | |
| | | | | | | | 1st stage (ROA) | 2nd stage (Compensation) |
	Coefficient	Std. Err.	Coefficient	Std. Err.	Coefficient	Std. Err.		
State Ownership:								
State direct ownership	-0.129***	(0.030)	-0.204***	(0.029)	-0.083*	(0.047)	-1.102	(0.741)	-0.170***	(0.059)
Self-Dealing and Gray Income:								
Ln(Other receivables)	0.007	(0.005)	-0.019***	(0.005)	-0.015**	(0.007)		
Firm Performance:								
ROA (winsorized)	0.036***	(0.001)	0.024***	(0.001)	0.019***	(0.002)	0.002***	(0.000)	
Tobin's Q (winsorized)	0.016***	(0.004)	0.022***	(0.003)	0.013***	(0.004)	(Information centrality)		0.088***	(0.017)
Managerial Expertise, Background, and Education:								
Political experience	0.029*	(0.016)	0.033**	(0.016)	0.047**	(0.024)	-0.017	(0.376)	0.049*	(0.026)
Overseas education	0.087**	(0.034)	0.070**	(0.033)	0.030	(0.054)	0.834	(0.877)	-0.048	(0.060)
International work experience	0.122***	(0.025)	0.148***	(0.028)	0.109***	(0.038)	-0.760	(0.670)	0.180***	(0.046)
Education level	0.048***	(0.007)	0.057***	(0.008)	0.018	(0.012)	-0.112	(0.183)	0.024*	(0.013)
Academic experience	0.045**	(0.020)	0.015	(0.020)	0.018	(0.028)	1.110**	(0.478)	0.002	(0.039)
Technology experience	0.020	(0.013)	0.017	(0.014)	0.023	(0.021)	0.717***	(0.336)	-0.020	(0.027)
Accounting experience	0.012	(0.019)	-0.046***	(0.018)	-0.014	(0.027)	-0.023	(0.388)	0.008	(0.027)
Financial experience	-0.036	(0.029)	0.003	(0.026)	-0.033	(0.039)	0.649	(0.749)	-0.048	(0.049)
Foreign nationality	0.273***	(0.067)	0.206***	(0.076)	0.253***	(0.104)	2.306	(2.152)	0.083	(0.154)
Age	0.006***	(0.001)	0.008***	(0.001)	0.004***	(0.001)	0.014	(0.024)	-0.002	(0.002)
Gender	-0.081***	(0.027)	-0.029	(0.030)	-0.023	(0.043)	1.234	(0.759)	-0.169***	(0.056)
Internal Corporate Governance:								
Independent director ratio	-0.019	(0.045)	0.284***	(0.034)	0.021	(0.058)	3.451*	(1.932)	-0.133	(0.124)
Board size	0.023***	(0.003)	0.012***	(0.003)	0.006	(0.005)	0.024	(0.066)	0.036***	(0.004)
Management team size	0.019***	(0.002)	0.013***	(0.002)	0.009***	(0.003)	-0.178*	(0.099)	0.006	(0.005)
Compensation committee	0.095***	(0.020)	0.196***	(0.016)	0.069***	(0.023)	-0.242	(0.385)	0.111***	(0.027)
Strategy committee	0.024	(0.016)	0.056***	(0.014)	0.000	(0.019)	0.045	(0.420)	0.022	(0.029)
Managerial duality	0.028	(0.019)	0.053***	(0.018)	0.045*	(0.027)	-0.043	(0.487)	0.032	(0.031)

Table 8. (Continued)

	Pooled OLS (2001–2011)		Random Effects (2001–2011)		Firm Fixed Effects (2001–2011)		IV Result (2SLS) 2001–2005	
	Coefficient	Std. Err.	Coefficient	Std. Err.	Coefficient	Std. Err.	1st stage (ROA)	2nd stage (Compensation)
Firm Employment and Provincial Economic Performance:								
Ln(Local GDP)	−0.008	(0.007)	0.305***	(0.012)				
Ln(Employee)	0.042**	(0.018)	−0.015**	(0.008)	0.028*	(0.015)	0.741*** (0.142)	−0.013 (0.018)
Ln(Inward FDI)					0.033*	(0.020)	−0.655 (0.495)	0.113*** (0.027)
Control Variables:								
Leverage	0.002***	(0.000)	0.002***	(0.001)	0.002***	(0.000)	−5.090*** (0.192)	0.333*** (0.091)
Sales growth rate	0.002	(0.023)	−0.002	(0.017)	−0.007	(0.019)		
Capital intensity	−0.100***	(0.023)	−0.096***	(0.020)	−0.004	(0.029)		
Firm size	0.252***	(0.009)	0.306***	(0.010)	0.211***	(0.021)		
Ownership concentration	−0.116***	(0.050)	−0.149**	(0.060)	0.339***	(0.118)	8.433*** (1.499)	−0.189 (0.199)
Constant	5.888***	(0.281)	3.326***	(0.185)	6.958***	(0.438)	2.305 (7.132)	10.733*** (0.381)
Year fixed effect	Yes		No		Yes		Yes	Yes
Industry fixed effect	Yes		No		No		Yes	Yes
Province fixed effect	Yes		No		No		Yes	Yes
Firm-fixed effect	No		No		Yes		No	No
No. of observations	12,032		12,401		12,032		5,776	5,564
R-squared adjusted	55%		43%		43%		20%	33%

The dependent variable is the natural logarithm of the top three highest-paid managers' compensation. Independent variables are state ownership (%), a state ultimate shareholder dummy, ROA (winsorized at the 95% level), Tobin's Q (winsorized at the 95% level), Independent director ratio, board size, management team size, compensation committee dummy, strategy committee dummy, managerial duality dummy (equals 1 if the manager and chairman is the same person), logarithm of local province's GDP and inward FDI, and of total number of employees of the firm, a series of managerial background dummies, and control variables (leverage, sales growth rate, capital intensity, firm size (total asset value), and the ownership concentration of the top five blockholders). More information on variable definitions can be found in Table 3. *, **, and *** stand for significance at the 10%, 5%, and 1%, respectively. Standard errors are robust or clustered at the firm level (for panel data estimations) and reported in parentheses. The standard errors for the second stage of 2SLS estimation are after adjustment. GLS estimations are used for all specifications.

Pay and Performance Revisited: Instrumental Variable Strategy

Most studies deal with the pay-performance causation issue by including the one-year lagged value of profitability measures as independent variables. An alternative (and maybe more robust) approach is an instrumental variable (IV) strategy with a good instrument at the firm-, industry- or regional-level financial and economic factors (as they are most relevant to corporate performance) provided that this instrument does not directly influence managerial pay.[23] The Chinese unique social and cultural background gives us a plausible IV: the interlocking network of directors among Chinese firms. A key issue of Chinese business is the extensive use of personal connections (in Chinese, *Guanxi*) and network strategies (Ren, Au, & Birtch, 2009). Such connections and networks are part of the informal institutions that also influence business activities and economic development (North, 1990). Director interlocks are an important form of such network ties that can shape firm behavior and hence performance (Renneboog & Zhao, 2011). Such a professional network may give access to information within the network (Davis, 1991) and enables network members to handle uncertainties better (Shipilov, Greve, & Rowley, 2010; Shropshire, 2010). However, in the Chinese context, we expect *interlocked director* networks to have little direct impact on managerial compensation, because managers are not directors, usually do not own an equity stake (in contrast to the directors), and are usually appointed by the state (even in "private" firms, the state has a large impact on top managerial appointments). Director networks in China are highly developed because of (past) informal and political connections (Ren et al., 2009) but are not the result of current and past firm performance.

A network based on director interlocks can be represented by the *information centrality* which measures the position of the firm within the network and is based on the "information" contained in all possible geodesic paths between pairs of nodes (firms).[24] We use this information centrality variable to run a 2SLS regression, controlling for the same variables and fixed effects as in the regressions explained in sections from "Benchmark Results" to "The Regional Analysis."[25,26] The last two columns of Table 8 report the IV results from a 2SLS estimation, with information centrality of the director networks as an instrument variable for ROA.[27] The one but last column is the first-stage estimation with ROA as dependent variable, and information centrality along with all other key and control variables as independent variables. We find that information centrality is loading significantly on ROA. Academic experience and specialized expertise in technology lead to higher reported accounting returns whereas international work experience, overseas education, educational level do not. Expectedly, stronger state ownership and political experience do not yield a higher ROA. The last column is the second-stage estimation with managerial pay as dependent variable and the predicted ROA along with all other variables as independent variables. One can easily verify that the results remain similar as in previous estimations, and most key variables (state ownership, political experience, ROA, Ln(inward FDI), international prestige, education degree, compensation committee, etc.) are highly significant. Compensation is lower in state-controlled firms and higher when top managers have built up political experience. Only "prestige" is significantly and positively associated with managerial pay, and the existence of the compensation committee is positively related to higher compensation while the ratio of independent director is not. Political goals still play a role, as manifested by the significant coefficient on corporate employment. All of our five hypotheses are still receiving support in the IV estimations. In addition, the fact that the IV results are not significantly different from our basic results (of sections from "Benchmark Results" to "The Regional Analysis") implies that the endogeneity problem may not be that severe in our basic specifications.[28]

In sum, the empirical evidence so far largely confirms our five sets of hypotheses developed under the state-stewardship framework.

Generalizability and Alternative Explanations

Is our state-stewardship view context-specific or can it be generalized to other emerging markets with strong political involvement in business? Essentially, to answer this question is to ask: whether political institutions (e.g., autocratic regime, state ownership and control, political connections under administrative rules, etc.) are the key determinants of corporate governance outcomes, including executive compensation. One potential alternative explanation on the China's executive compensation is related to the unique Chinese cultural and social norms. One can argue that the prevailing social norms in China prevent executives from being paid excessively more than other employees and paid for performance. However, it is empirically found that firms in Hong Kong, Taiwan, and Singapore which are also Chinese communities with similar cultural origin but different political regimes, have corporate governance structure and executive compensation schemes that conform to the agency theory (Sun, Zhao, & Yang, 2010), rather than the institutional-based state-stewardship view.

Meanwhile, in many transitional economies (under the Socialist legal origin), executive compensation is found to be not tied to profitability but rather to political connection and political goals (e.g., Eriksson, 2005; Jones & Kato, 1996). These conform that the executive compensation patterns in China and other emerging economies under strong state involvement are a direct result of political institutions and institutional change, rather than cultures and social norms. Such effects remain even after massive privatization in these economies.

CONCLUSION

This paper proposes a state-stewardship view (which competes with the agency perspective) to explain China's state-manager relationship, as well as the corporate governance model and executive compensation schemes which are under the political influence of the state. As the world's largest country transiting from a fully state-controlled economy to a more market-oriented one through partial privatizations of firms, China offers the right context to test this theory. We hypothesize that Chinese executives act as responsible stewards of the state and run their companies in such a way that the firm's objectives are aligned with those of the state. Consequently, managers' compensation schemes are set to reflect their loyalty to the state and abilities to fulfill both the political objectives and the economic targets (with the political aims dominating). Since the 2006 reforms, the state influence has transited from state control through ownership to state-stewardship. Our state-stewardship framework hinges on five testable hypotheses. We use firm-level microdata for almost all public non-financial listed firms for the period 2001−2011 as well as regional-level macrodata to test our hypotheses at three levels: the personal-level, the corporate level, and the macroeconomic level. Chinese managers are paid much less than their international counterparts. The lower is the compensation in China, the larger is the ownership stake held by the state (or the stronger is the ultimate control of the state). Such lower pay seems to be compensated by higher gray income through colluding on tunneling activities. Also, the management seems to be remunerated not for maximizing shareholder shareholders (proxied by Tobin's Q) but that of the state-owned assets (proxied by ROA). In addition, compensation is not linked to ability or personality, but to political connections and prestige. Furthermore, internal governance mechanisms such as the percentage of independent directors and the compensation committee on the board are symbolic and do neither constrain managerial pay nor strengthen pay-for-performance. Moreover, CEO-chairman duality is used by the state to give more responsibilities to reliable state-stewards. Finally, managerial pay is closely tied to local officials' political goals and achievements, even after controlling for provincial fixed effects. These effects are stronger in the pre-2006 period because subsequent to the split-share reform, companies became more market-oriented.

Our empirical results lead to a critical evaluation of the relationships among the state, the firm, and the managers. Whereas most academic studies apply the western agency theory on China's corporate governance model and executive compensation, we take a state-stewardship perspective and argue that the state is actually seized by and represents the interest of the ruling government and its politicians rather than its citizens, as argued by North's (1990) predatory theory of the state and the seminal work by Acemoglu and Johnson (2005). Note that our basic argument is that Chinese managers are the stewards of the *state*, but not necessarily of the *nation* – the private citizens. In this context, the motivation of the manager would be substantially different. As China has been a communist country with a single ruling party for decades, the ideas of socialism still have a strong impact on how companies are run. As a powerful social elite, the state-steward managers in China have the same interests as the state (the government), namely extracting rents that should adhere to the nation (which stands for the society at large or the collective private citizens). The state and its steward managers form the same interest group and expropriate the private sector (and the citizens). The legitimacy of the elite's privileged rights over private sectors is central to our question.

NOTES

1. In 2010, *Jiangling Motors*, one of China's biggest commercial vehicle companies and Ford's joint venture partner, achieved sales revenues of over $2.5 billion following strong growth. Its CEO, York Chen, received an annual total compensation of $375,000, at par with his 2009 pay (but higher than that of any other CEO in this sector). In marked contrast, Dieters Zetsche, the CEO of the European automobile giant *Daimler AG*, earned €8.7 million euro ($12 million), twice his pay in 2009 and more than 30 times Chen's salary. This discrepancy in pay is even larger when one considers *Ford*'s CEO Allan Mulally, who received $26.5 million in 2010, 48% more than in 2009 (*Bloomberg*, April 1, 2011).

2. Stock options were rarely used before 2008, and even subsequently, merely 5% of listed companies report the use of stock options to remunerate their managers.

3. These are usually the state (including the central or local governments) and their affiliated SOEs and legal shareholders (the business agencies controlled by local government) (Sun & Tong, 2003). The owners of these non-tradable shares have the privileges of the same voting and cash flow rights as the owners of tradable shares (Li, Wang, Cheung, & Jiang, 2011).

4. The de facto privatization has been underway as so-called "shareholding system reform" since mid-1980s (in Chinese, *gufenzhi gaige*).

5. In general, executive directors and non-executive directors of US and UK firms man one organizational body which is chaired by the CEO (as is frequently the case in the United States) or not (in the United Kingdom). Such one-tier boards also comprise audit, remuneration, and nomination committees. In contrast, firms from German legal origin countries such as Austria, Germany, and Japan, separate the executive and supervisory boards (the latter then only consists of non-executive directors with advisory and monitoring roles who represent shareholders and employees).

6. Henceforth, when we mention the "board," we refer to the board of directors consisting of both executive and non-executive directors, but not the supervisory board.

7. There are two types of SOEs. Most SOEs are directly (or ultimately) controlled by the central government under China's State-owned Assets Supervision and Administration Commission (SASAC) of the State Council, and enjoy monopoly power in certain industries such as energy and telecommunication. Other SOEs are controlled by local government under the local SASAC.

8. Under government regulations, the executive compensation can only be up to 10−12 times that of an average worker.

9. Jiang et al. (2010) give the following reasons: (i) all Chinese listed firms have a dominant/controlling shareholder; (ii) prior to 2006, the trading of controlling shares was restricted, thus limiting the ownership benefits of price appreciation to the controlling shareholder.

10. A good example of this managerial duality is the General Manager of PetroChina Jiang Jiemin, who served as the Deputy Provincial Governor of the Qinghai Province and the deputy secretary of the province during 2000−2003. He has been the General Manager of CNPC, the chairman, the president, and the party secretary of PetroChina all at the same time, and he is also an alternate member of the 17th CPC Central Committee. However, Jiang's compensation was not high: according to *Reuters*, Jiang's 2010 compensation was only RMB 916,000 (approximately $140,000).

11. For example, Core et al. (1999) found that CEO with duality role has significantly higher managerial compensation.

12. We exclude Chinese firms listed in Hong Kong or abroad as they operate in a different institutional environment and are subject to different regulations.

13. A-shares are stocks valued in RMB and available only to Chinese citizens; B-shares are also denominated in RMB but traded in such foreign currencies (USD or Hong Kong dollar).

14. A correlation check indicates there is no multicollinearity problem between these variables.

15. As both the macro(-economic) variables and the dependent variables are in natural logarithms, the beta coefficient also measures the effects of change of these variables, since the first-order approximation of its Taylor serial is its growth rate.

16. To check this, we collected information on managerial turnover in the pre-2006 subsample, and generated a dummy variable that equals 1 if there was a change in managers in the year under consideration, and 0 otherwise. The average managerial change for SOEs is 24% while the average managerial change for private firms is 20%.

17. We use a dummy variable to show whether the observation belongs to the post-2006 sample (or not), and an interaction term between this dummy variable and the manager's "political experience" variable (Liang et al., 2015). The F-test rejects the null hypothesis that the coefficients of these variables are jointly zero, implying the coefficients of "political experience" in the pre-2006 and post-2006 samples are statistically significantly different (the effect of including the post-2006 dummy in the regression is significant).

18. As Ln(GDP) and Ln(Inward FDI) are highly correlated (over 80%), we do not include these variables in the same regression.

19. Our regional partition of China's provinces is slightly different from the conventional administrative division that classifies China into six regions. We distinguish between: (i) North China (including the North East and North but excluding Inner Mongolia): Heilongjiang, Jilin, Liaoning, Beijing, Tianjin, Hebei, and Shanxi. (ii) South China: Guangdong, Guangxi, and Hainan. (iii) West China (including Southwest, Northwest, Inner Mongolia, and Guangxi): Sichuan, Chongqing, Yunnan, Guizhou, Tibet, Shaanxi, Gansu, Qinghai, Ningxia, Xinjiang, Inner Mongolia, and Guangxi. (iv) East China: Shandong, Jiangsu, Zhengjiang, Anhui, Fujian, and Shanghai.

20. Regional North includes the following municipalities and provinces: Beijing, Tianjin, Hebei, Shanxi, and Inner Mongolia; Northwest includes Liaoning, Jilin, and Heilongjiang; Southwest includes Sichuan, Yunnan, Guizhou, Tibet, and Chongqing.

21. For reasons of conciseness, we only report the results for the full sample by region.

22. In unreported regressions, we replace state ownership by state control and reach similar conclusions.

23. A valid IV should be correlated with the endogenous regressor (performance measure) but orthogonal to any other omitted characteristics. However, one major difficulty is that likely candidates at the level of formal economic factors may be significantly affected by the state's political influence, and may thus be correlated with managerial pay through those channels. Therefore, we turn to individual-level factors.

24. The centrality measurement method assumes that each link in a network path is independent, with the variance of a single link between nodes being unity. Therefore, the variance of a path is simply its length. This measure captures the communication in corporate interlocks that occurs along reachable, non-geodesic pathways (Stephenson & Zelen, 1989, p. 3). We calculate this information centrality

measure using software Ucinet 6 as in Borgatti, Everett, and Freeman (2002). We then calculate it as $I_i = n/(\sum_{j=1}^{n} 1/I_{ij})$, where I refers to the centrality or information of (i), the harmonic average of the information associated with the path from (i) to the other nodes.

25. We do exclude a few variables which could serve as alternative channels for networks. We exclude the tunneling variable (because director network may affect managerial pay through the tunneling network), as well as size, capital intensity, and sales growth rate (which may all be influenced by information centrality and serve as alternative channels for information centrality to affect firm performance). Political experience is included in the model as it is not related to our networks measure (the correlation is only −0.02).

26. Due to the data availability issue, we perform this IV exercise on the pre-2006 sample only.

27. We only use an instrument for ROA since we found that Tobin's Q was not a key determinant for managerial pay before 2006.

28. The F-statistics against the null that the excluded instrument (information centrality) is irrelevant in the first-stage regression is larger than 10, which indicates that information centrality qualifies as a strong instrument variable.

ACKNOWLEDGMENTS

We thank Lucian Bebchuk, Fabio Braggion, Jerry Cao, Joost Driessen, Olivier de Jonghe, Michael Firth, Wayne Guay, Xu Lang, Chris Marquis, Dwight Perkins, Bing Ren, Oliver Spalt, Dylan Sutherland, Yuhai Xuan, and the seminar and conference participants at Harvard Kennedy School, Harvard Law School, London School of Economics, Copenhagen Business School, CESifo Venice Summer Institute, Asian Finance Association conference, Peking University, Tsinghua University, Nankai University, and Tilburg University for their valuable comments. Special thanks to Bing Ren at Nankai University for providing data on Chinese directors' interlocking network to us. We are also grateful to Yan Wang, Ying Zheng, Haoyu Wu, and Haikun Zhu for the excellent research assistant work.

REFERENCES

Acemoglu, D., & Johnson, S. (2005). Unbundling institutions. *Journal of Political Economy*, *113*, 949–995.

Adithipyangkul, P., Alon, I., & Zhang, T. (2009). Executive perks: Compensation and corporate performance in China. *Asia Pacific Journal of Management*, *28*, 401–425.

Bebchuk, L. A., & Fried, J. M. (2003). Executive compensation as an agency problem. *Journal of Economic Perspectives, 17*, 71–92.

Bebchuk, L. A., & Fried, J. M. (2004). *Pay without performance: The unfulfilled promise of executive compensation.* Cambridge, MA: Harvard University Press.

Bebchuk, L. A., Fried, J. M., & Walker, D. I. (2002). Managerial power and rent extraction in the design of executive compensation. *University of Chicago Law Review, 69*, 751–846.

Borgatti, S. P., Everett, M. G., & Freeman, L. C. (2002). *Ucinet for windows: Software for social network analysis.* Harvard, MA: Analytic Technologies.

Buck, T., Liu, X., & Skovoroda, R. (2008). Top executive pay and firm performance in China. *Journal of International Business Studies, 39*, 833–850.

Cao, J., Lemmon, M., Pan, X., Qian, M., & Tian, G. (2011). *Political promotion, CEO incentives, and the relationship between pay and performance.* Wharton Financial Institutions Center Working Paper #11-53. Retrieved from http://fic.wharton.upenn.edu/fic/papers/11/p1153.htm

Cao, J., Pan, X., & Tian, G. (2011). Disproportional ownership structure and pay-performance relationship: Evidence from China's listed firms. *Journal of Corporate Finance, 17*, 541–554.

Chang, E. C., Lin, T.-C., & Ma, X. (2012). Risk sharing and stock price informativeness: Evidence from stock-split natural experiment. *Proceedings of the 10th China International Conference in Finance*, Chongqing, China, 9–12 July 2012.

Chen, J., Ezzamel, M., & Cai, Z. (2011). Managerial power theory, tournament theory, and executive pay in China. *Journal of Corporate Finance, 17*, 1176–1199.

Chen, J. J., Liu, X., & Li, W. (2010). The effect of insider control and global benchmarks on Chinese executive compensation. *Corporate Governance: An International Review, 18*, 107–123.

Claessens, S., Djankov, S., & Lang, L. (2000). The separation of ownership and control in East Asian corporations. *Journal of Financial Economics, 58*, 81–112.

Clarke, D. C. (2003). Corporate governance in China: An overview. *China Economic Reviews, 14*, 494–507.

Conyon, M. J., & He, L. (2011). Executive compensation and corporate governance in China. *Journal of Corporate Finance, 17*, 1158–1175.

Core, J. E., Holthausen, R., & Larcker, D. (1999). Corporate governance, chief executive officer compensation, and firm performance. *Journal of Financial Economics, 51*, 371–406.

Datta, S., D'Mello, R., & Iskandar-Datta, M. (2009). Executive compensation and internal capital market efficiency. *Journal of Financial Intermediation, 18*, 242–258.

Davis, G. F. (1991). Directors without principles? The spread of the poison pill through the intercorporate network. *Administrative Science Quarterly, 36*, 583–613.

Davis, J. H., Schoorman, F. D., & Donaldson, L. (1997). Toward a stewardship theory of management. *Academy of Management Review, 22*, 20–47.

Donaldson, L., & Davis, J. H. (1991). Stewardship theory or agency theory: CEO governance and shareholder returns. *Australian Journal of Management, 16*, 49–65.

Eriksson, T. (2005). Managerial pay and executive turnover in the Czech and Slovak republics. *Economics of Transition, 13*, 659–677.

Faccio, M. (2006). Politically connected firms. *American Economic Review, 96*, 369–386.

Faccio, M., Masulis, R. W., & McConnell, J. J. (2006). Political connections and corporate bailouts. *Journal of Finance, 61*, 2597–2635.

Fan, J. P. H., Wong, T. J., & Zhang, T. (2007). Politically connected CEOs, corporate govern-ance, and post-IPO performance of China's newly partially privatized firms. *Journal of Financial Economics, 84*, 330−357.

Firth, M., Fung, P. M. Y., & Rui, O. M. (2006). Corporate performance and CEO compensa-tion in China. *Journal of Corporate Finance, 12*, 693−714.

Firth, M., Fung, P. M. Y., & Rui, O. M. (2007). How ownership and corporate governance influence chief executive pay in China's listed firms. *Journal of Business Research, 60*, 776−785.

Firth, M., Rui, O. M., & Wu, W. (2011). Cooking the books: Recipes and costs of falsified financial statements in China. *Journal of Corporate Finance, 17*, 371−390.

Garen, J. E. (1994). Executive compensation and principal-agent theory. *Journal of Political Economy, 102*, 1175−1199.

Gimeno, J. F., Folta, T. B., Cooper, A. C., & Woo, C. Y. (1997). Survival of the fittest? Entrepreneurial human capital and the persistence of underperforming firms. *Administrative Science Quarterly, 42*, 750−783.

Grabke-Rundell, A., & Gomez-Mejia, L. R. (2002). Power as a determinant of executive com-pensation. *Human Resource Management Review, 12*, 3−23.

Graham, J. R., Li, S., & Qiu, J. (2012). Managerial attributes and executive compensation. *Review of Financial Studies, 25*, 144−186.

Groves, T., Hong, Y., McMillan, J., & Naughton, B. (1994). Autonomy and incentives in Chinese state enterprises. *Quarterly Journal of Economics, 109*, 183−209.

Groves, T., Hong, Y., McMillan, J., & Naughton, B. (1995). China's evolving managerial labor market. *Journal of Political Economy, 4*, 873−892.

Hartzell, J. C., & Starks, L. T. (2003). Institutional investors and executive compensation. *Journal of Finance, 58*, 2351−2374.

IFF Task Force Report. (2006). *Corporate governance in China: An investor perspective.* Washington, DC: Institute of International Finance.

Jensen, M. C., & Murphy, K. J. (1990). Performance pay and top-management incentives. *Journal of Political Economy, 98*, 225−264.

Jensen, M. C., Murphy, K. J., & Wruck, E. (2004). *Remuneration: Where we've been, how we got to here, what are the problems, and how to fix them.* ECGI Working Paper Series, No. 44−2004, July 2004 (Also in the Negotiation, Organizations and Markets Research Paper Series No. 04-28).

Jiang, G., Lee, C. M. C., & Yeung, H. (2010). Tunneling through intercorporate loans: The Chinese experience. *Journal of Financial Economics, 98*, 1−20.

Johnson, S., La Porta, R., Lopez-de-Silanes, F., & Shleifer, A. (2000). Tunneling. *American Economic Review, 90*, 22−27.

Jones, D. C., & Kato, T. (1996). The determinants of chief executive compensation in transi-tional economies: evidence from Bulgaria. *Labour Economics, 3*(3), 319−336.

Kang, Q., & Liu, Q. (2008). Stock trading, information production, and executive incentives. *Journal of Corporate Finance, 14*, 484−498.

Kuhnen, C. M., & Niessen, A. (2012). Public opinion and executive compensation. *Management Science, 58*, 1249−1272.

La Porta, R., Lopez-de-Silanes, F., Shleifer, A., & Vishny, R. (1999). The quality of govern-ment. *Journal of Law, Economics and Organization, 15*, 222−279.

Li, H., & Zhang, Y. (2007). The role of managers' political networking and functional experience in new venture performance: Evidence from China's transition economy. *Strategic Management Journal, 28,* 791–804.

Li, K., Wang, T., Cheung, Y. L., & Jiang, P. (2011). Privatization and risk sharing: Evidence from the split share structure reform in China. *Review of Financial Studies, 24,* 2499–2525.

Liang, H., Ren, B., & Sun, S. L. (2015). An anatomy of state control in the globalization of state-owned enterprises. *Journal of International Business Studies, 46*(2), 223–240.

Liang, H., Renneboog, L., & Sun, S. L. (2016). The political determinants of executive compensation: Evidence from an emerging economy. *Emerging Markets Review, 25,* 69–91. doi:10.1016/j.ememar.2015.04.008

Markoczy, L., Sun, S. L., Peng, M. W., Shi, W., & Ren, B. (2013). Social network contingency, symbolic management, and boundary stretching. *Strategic Management Journal, 34,* 1367–1387.

Murillo, C., Ribas, R. P., & Wang, Y. A. (2011). *Is the stock market just a side show? Evidence from a structural reform.* Retrieved from http://ssrn.com/abstract=1954234

Noe, T. H. (2009). Tunnel-proofing executive suite: Transparency, temptation, and the design of executive compensation. *Review of Financial Studies, 22,* 4849–4880.

North, D. C. (1990). *Institutions, institutional change and economic performance.* Cambridge: Cambridge University Press.

Peng, M. W. (2004). Outside directors and firm performance during institutional transitions. *Strategic Management Journal, 25,* 453–471.

Peng, M. W., Sun, S. L., & Markoczy, L. (2015). Human capital and CEO compensation during institutional transitions. *Journal of Management Studies, 52*(1), 117–147.

Peress, J. (2010). The tradeoff between risk sharing and information production in financial markets. *Journal of Economic Theory, 145,* 124–155.

Ren, B., Au, K., & Birch, T. (2009). China's business network structure during institutional transitions. *Asia Pacific Journal of Management, 26,* 219–240.

Renneboog, L., & Zhao, Y. (2011). Us knows us in UK: On director networks and managerial compensation. *Journal of Corporate Finance, 17,* 1132–1157.

Rose, N. L., & Shepard, A. (1997). Firm diversification and CEO compensation: Managerial ability or executive entrenchment? *Rand Journal Economics, 28,* 489–514.

Rosenstein, R., & Wyatt, J. G. (1990). Outside directors, board independence, and shareholder wealth. *Journal of Financial Economics, 26,* 175–191.

Shipilov, A. V., Greve, H. R., & Rowley, T. J. (2010). When do interlocks matter? Institutional logics and the diffusion of multiple corporate governance practices. *Academy of Management Journal, 53,* 846–864.

Shleifer, A. (1998). State versus private ownership. *Journal of Economic Perspectives, 12,* 133–150.

Shleifer, A., & Vishny, R. (1994). Politicians and firms. *Quarterly Journal of Economics, 109,* 995–1025.

Shropshire, C. (2010). The role of the interlocking director and board receptivity in the diffusion of practices. *Academy of Management Review, 35,* 246–263.

Stephenson, K., & Zelen, M. (1989). Rethinking centrality: Methods and examples. *Social Network, 11,* 1–37.

Sun, L., Zhao, X., & Yang, H. (2010). Executive compensation in Asia: A critical review and outlook. *Asia Pacific Journal of Management, 27,* 775–802.

Sun, Q., & Tong, W. H. S. (2003). China share issue privatization: The extent of its success. *Journal of Financial Economics, 70*, 183–222.

Sun, S. L., Peng, M. W., Lee, R. P., & Tan, W. (2015). Institutional open access in the home country and outward internationalization. *Journal of World Business, 50*(1), 234–246.

Sun, S. L., Zhu, J., & Ye, K. (2015). Board openness during an economic crisis. *Journal of Business Ethics, 129*(2), 363–377.

Tam, O. K. (2002). Ethical issues in evolution of corporate governance in China. *Journal of Business Ethics, 37*, 303–320.

Tenev, D., & Zhang, C. (2002). *Corporate governance and enterprise reform in China.* Washington, DC: World Bank and the International Finance Corporation.

Van Essen, M., Heugens, P. P., Otten, J., & Van Oosterhout, J. H. (2012). An institution-based view of executive compensation: A multilevel meta-analytic test. *Journal of International Business Studies, 43*, 396–423.

Van Essen, M., Oosterhout, J., & Carney, M. (2012). Corporate boards and the performance of Asian firms: A meta-analysis. *Asia Pacific Journal of Management, 29*, 873–905.

Wang, K., & Xiao, X. (2011). Controlling shareholders' tunneling and executive compensation: Evidence from China. *Journal of Accounting and Public Policy, 30*, 89–100.

Westphal, J. D., & Graebner, M. (2010). A matter of appearances: How corporate leaders manage the impressions of financial analysts about the conduct of their boards. *Academy of Management Journal, 53*, 15–44.

Westphal, J. D., & Zajac, E. J. (1998). The symbolic management of stockholders: corporate governance reforms and external constituent reactions. *Administrative Science Quarterly, 43*, 127–153.

Xu, C. (2011). The fundamental institutions of China's reforms and development. *Journal of Economic Literature, 49*, 1076–1151.

NETIZENS AND PRIVATE MONITORING IN CHINESE BANKING

W. Travis Selmier, II

ABSTRACT

Purpose — *Much of the criticism directed toward banking in China revolves around self-dealing in relationships between bankers and their clients. Corruption, nepotism, high levels of non-performing loans, and the inefficiency of government-directed lending have all been laid at the door of embedded* guanxi *networks. While valid to an extent, this criticism ignores two important, related points:* guanxi *networks bring disciplining mechanisms as well as the potential for corruption, and those mechanisms may improve banking governance.*

Methodology/approach — *Employing theory from relationship banking, information economics, and the business ethics of* guanxi, *I examine how monitoring by netizens will lead to greater disclosure.*

Findings — *Relationship banking in a Chinese context — with the influence of* guanxi *in banking — further increases reputational costs when self-dealing is uncovered. Costs of bad banking behavior are increasing just as benefits from staying rich increase. Increased disclosure affects*

The Political Economy of Chinese Finance
International Finance Review, Volume 17, 93–113
ISSN: 1569-3767/doi:10.1108/S1569-376720160000017010

chances of staying rich as disclosure increases the chance that a corrupt relationship will lead to loss of wealth and reputation.

Research limitations/implications – *This paper presents a theoretical construct informed by selected examples. An empirical analysis of netizen monitoring leading to improved banking governance would provide additional support for the theoretical construct.*

Practical implications – *Bankers, financiers, and government officials must be aware of monitoring by netizens, which forces more ethical financial contracting.*

Social implications – *Rather than weakening financial system governance,* guanxi *may begin to strengthen the disciplinary measures inherent in relationship banking as information disclosure increases and private sector monitoring grows.*

Originality/value – *This paper provides an extension to private monitoring theory in financial contracting which may be applied to netizen monitoring in other regions and countries.*

Keywords: Chinese banking; relationship banking; information economics; *guanxi*; private monitoring; netizens

JEL classifications: G2; P3; Z1

INFORMATION AND PRIVATE MONITORING IN CHINESE BANKING

A significant amount of the criticism directed toward banking revolves around claims of self-dealing by bankers. Close ties between bankers and their clients have been cited as evidence of corruption and nepotism, and as leading to high levels of non-performing loans around the world (Kane, 2003; Kang, 2002; Rose-Ackerman, 1999). These problems have been laid at the door of Chinese banks and partly blamed on the embedded nature of *guanxi* networks (Cousin, 2007, p. 85; Shih, 2008; Tan, 2013). While partially valid, this criticism ignores the positive side of *guanxi* in instilling discipline and providing private governance (Li, 2009; Park & Luo, 2001; Selmier, 2013). I argue *guanxi* may begin to strengthen the disciplinary measures inherent in banking governance through private monitoring by an emerging group of new private monitors, netizens. Netizens are defined as citizens who engage in social activities and social activism through employing internet resources.

This paper asks whether a confluence of factors — the social obligations embedded in the Chinese relational system of *guanxi* (Han & Altman, 2009; Huang, 1998; Yeung & Tung, 1996), information dynamics released through internet and other media channels which wash away informational opacity (Qiu, Lin, Chiu, & Liu, 2015; Yang, 2009, 2014), and unique aspects of Chinese banking and finance (Bailey, Huang, & Yang, 2011; Fu & Bao, 2011; Li, Makaew, & Winton, 2014) — may lead to a better-functioning, better-governed banking system. Ours is a simple transactional cost argument: costs to bad banking behavior in China are increasing just as benefits from staying rich are concurrently growing. As information becomes more available to private monitors the power of private monitoring grows, leading to increased likelihood that bad behavior would be disclosed. Government's difficulty in controlling information flow also increases probability of disclosure of bank-related transactions. In short, the benefits to staying rich are growing in China, while disclosure of self-dealing lessens the chances of staying rich as public knowledge of a corrupt relationship and the resulting shame will lead to loss of wealth and reputation.

The Xi Jinping Administration's focus on corruption enhances these effects, and China has entered a period of rapid and extensive disclosure of self-dealing. Disclosure has occurred not only through government policy, but also as the internet leads to a burgeoning civil society (Shi, 2013; Yang, 2009, 2014) which empowers monitoring and criticism (Meng, 2011; Yang, 2012). While the Chinese government may attempt to channel and even contain these releases, governmental capacity is compromised as web users progressively circumvent such attempts (Clayton, Murdoch, & Watson, 2006; MacKinnon, 2009; Yang, 2012).

This general concept may be extended to other countries' banking systems as netizen monitoring grows and disclosure increases reputational risk for bankers and financiers, but several factors make China a particularly interesting economy to look for emergence of netizen private monitoring. First, *guanxi* involves significant personal commitment in that a debt is created when one party does something to the other (Huang, 1998; Yeung & Tung, 1996). The "tail" created in this relational binding links both parties; subsequent discovery of ill deeds harms each party by engendering shame, or worse for each (Li, 2009; Yeung & Tung, 1996). Second, there is also an intense interest in tapping into electronic media coupled with increasingly open information flows (MacKinnon, 2009; Qiu et al., 2015; Yang, 2009).

Lastly, a willingness of Chinese people to stand up and criticize when they see bankers and government officials engaged in self-dealing, heightening risks associated with discovery of self-dealing to both bankers and government which wishes to have a happy (and not revolting) citizen base.

This paper proceeds in four sections. The first examines certain fundamental tenets of banking theory, differentiating between relationship and transactional banking and looking at Chinese banking through the theoretical lens they provide. The second examines how pathologies in Chinese banking create governance issues which may be alleviated through private monitoring. The third applies ideas of Chinese internet dynamics to sketch a model of how netizens' monitoring could expose self-dealing Chinese banking. The fourth notes extensions and limitations in this model's approach.

RELATIONSHIP AND TRANSACTIONAL BANKING MODELS IN CHINESE BANKING

The Chinese economy suffers from several inefficiencies in Chinese banking: first, credit may be mispriced due to interference in allocation decisions. This interference distorts the true value of money; not only are projects funded which may not be economically viable, but self-dealing may be encouraged. When market-set prices of money and capital are distorted, actors may think money has less "value." Second, state-owned enterprises (SOEs) are able to obtain loans beyond what an arms-length banker would normally extend in a credit analysis-based transaction while third, small and medium-sized enterprises (SMEs) and other less-connected firms experience greater difficulty sourcing credit. Reconsidering classic banking theory helps to understand why these inefficiencies may be more manifest in China in comparison with other countries.

Banking theory posits that banks possess three forms of capital: financial capital, informational capital, and reputational capital (Boot, Greenbaum, & Thakor, 1993; Hidy, 1941, p. 58; Morrison & Wilhelm, 2004). Financial capital provides a bank's *raison d'être* – to store excess capital from suppliers and then allocate it to those in need of that capital. Possessing reputational capital enables a well-regarded financial firm to leverage and increase its financial capital in structuring deals, to engage in financial contracting while running higher assets-to-deposits ratios, and to capture a stronger capacity to garner deposits. Informational capital – embedded in bank management experience, contacts, and expertise — lowers risks and enables engineering of financially complex deals. These three forms of capital exist in both relationship and transaction-oriented banking forms, but may be utilized in different proportions.

Relationship and transactional banking have been reified in the banking finance literature as archetypal models of banking strategy and organization. Relationship banking does not exclude hard data per se, but rather must include data analysis often ascribed to the realm of transaction-oriented banking (see Boot on securitization, 2000, pp. 11–12; Hayes, 1979). While the practice of relationship banking still necessitates utilizing "numbers," practicing transaction-oriented banking may require little beyond point-of-transaction relationships in that the point of banking activity focuses on that transaction core rather than peripheral, softer data which require relational intensity developed through temporal length.

Information availability is essential for banks to properly function. A fundamental paradigm of banking theory is that banks overcome financial market inefficiencies by acting as information conduits. This theory is posited to exist in developed as well as in less-developed markets (Rajan, 1992; Rajan & Winton, 1995; Stallings & Studart, 2006). Financial institutions are necessary to move financial contracting away from face-to-face, immediate transactions toward transactions which span broader geographic and temporal horizons. Financial intermediation enables capital deployment across both time and space; such deployment requires aggregation and use of proprietary information by those intermediaries, which results in informational asymmetries in money and capital markets. In both relationship and transactional banking there are substantial information search costs, as well as costs associated with information capture, storage, usage, and transmission. The resulting investment requirement in relationship banking operations is considered both large and asset-specific to the relationship, and it is assumed that smaller banks have an advantage in controlling such costs while maximizing the benefits when engaged in SME lending. This leads to the eponymous "small bank advantage" (Berger & Udell, 1992; Boot & Marinč, 2008, pp. 1190–1191; Zhang, 2002) which is a foundation of relationship banking.

However the idea that these information costs dynamics lead to a small bank advantage in SME relationship lending which, when reversed, lead large financial institutions to engage solely in transactions-oriented banking is not an entirely accurate way to look at the issue. Even in highly transactions-oriented environments, a strong relationship still exists (Boot, 2000; Hayes, 1979). As I argue below, large Chinese state-owned banks hew more closely to a relationship banking model in part because longer-term relationships, which I describe using the broader term *guanxi*, are embedded in Chinese financial contracting. Relational networks are embedded within financial contracting generally (Boot, 2000; Boot et al., 1993; Carruthers & Kim, 2011) and Chinese banking relationships specifically (Keister, 2004; Shih, 2008; Tanaka & Molnar, 2008).

In effect, *guanxi* is a kind of bridging function which enables market actors to overcome inefficiencies due to imperfect or incomplete information. But a debt is incurred when one party does something for the other (Huang, 1998; Yeung & Tung, 1996). *Guanxi* entails significant personal risk, in that the relationship between two parties is supportive and long-lasting, the influence of *guanxi* in Chinese banking and financial contracting means that when losses occur through bad behavior there is a heightened reputational cost should that bad behavior be uncovered. In a sense, the *guanxi* relationship may lead to a quasi-contractual debt obligation, and that debt must be repaid. The "tail" created in this relational binding links both parties; subsequent discovery of ill deeds harms each party by engendering shame, or worse, for each (Li, 2009; Selmier, 2013; Yeung & Tung, 1996).

PATHOLOGIES IN CHINESE RELATIONSHIP AND TRANSACTIONAL BANKING

Chinese banks are subject to the same advantages and disadvantages inherent in relationship banking and transactional banking models which affect other countries' banks. Table 1 summarizes the advantages of each model. Generally, relationship banking enables a banker to obtain deeper information (so-called "soft information"), carries substantial ex post advantages as financial contracts may be easier to negotiate, and allows more flexible covenants in a financial contract. Advantages of transactions-oriented banking may minimize human error and bias toward or against a particular borrower, and privilege a portfolio approach with statistically robust analytics and risk-sharing.

Both relationship and transactional archetypal banking models lower transaction costs (Berger & Udell, 2006; Boot et al., 1993; Boot & Marinč, 2008), but each banking model brings certain pathologies as well, as shown in Table 2. One might argue that the advantages which each offer have a dark side; how these pathologies manifest in Chinese banking leads to possible solutions which are strengthened through private monitoring. Chinese

Table 1. Advantages in Relational and Transactional Banking.

Banking Type	
Relational	Deeper information held by the bank may lead to better capital allocation decisions, as the client is willing to selectively disclose to his or her primary bank(s) so as not to leak information to competitors to see.
	Capacity for financial contracting is not just simply an ex ante proposition, but carries ex post advantages as well.	<ul><li>Financial contracting occurs under bounded knowledge, so it is not possible to include all the contingent clauses ex post.</li><li>Known risks are included when pricing credit, but uncertainty is present at the time of contracting. Although forecasting of future events may be probabilistically estimated, the distribution probabilities are based on known risks.</li><li>Relationship banking allows for significant negotiating latitude ex ante and ex post due to the inherent trust in the relationship.</li></ul>
	Covenants are easier to negotiate and collateral monitoring more effective under relationship banking.
Transactional	Reliance on hard information ameliorates mistakes which may arise through human error or, more critically, human bias toward or against a particular borrower.
	Uniform analytical approach is possible, as transactions-oriented banking.	<ul><li>Brings a statistically stable approach to the credit allocation/capital commitment decision.</li><li>Creates capacity to do a large number of deals, thereby lowering transactions costs while enabling a portfolio approach which is more difficult to achieve under a relationship banking model.</li></ul>

Sources: Berger and Udell (1992, 2006), Bhattacharya and Thakor (1993), Boot (2000), Rajan and Winton (1995), and Zhang (2002).

Table 2. Pathologies in Relational and Transactional Banking.

Banking Type	Nature of Relationship		Informational Axis	
	Problem	Issue	Problem	Issue
Relational	Too close	Self-dealing; commitment to borrower	Information too tightly held	Non-disclosure
Transactional	Too distant	Little commitment to borrower, so incentive to monitor now weakened	Little informational advantage	Information feed is now weaker, more dispersed. Asymmetric information access is not as much value

netizens provide a new type of private monitoring which would help to alleviate these pathologies through providing additional information.

Through intermediation processes, banks disclose information to those who observe banks' actions and glean information from those actions. But this information may sometimes be screened out, withheld, or signal-jammed by banks for their own benefit rather than permit information to flow beyond banks information firewalls (Stallings & Studart, 2006; Yosha, 1995). Bank managers may also privately benefit from an informational advantage in their banks, using this advantage for their own financial investments, or seeking to capture revenues through skimming. In addition, banks may send mixed or incorrect signals. Sometimes the observer assumes the bank is in possession of more information than it actually is, or sometimes the banker protects or fails to financially discipline a client.

As summarized in Table 3 below, the Chinese banker's relationship with his or her client may literally be too close, leading to over-commitment to a borrower and inefficient budget constraints. Leaving aside this soft-budget constraint for a moment, let us first consider the opposite issue, where being too close to the client enables the banker to extract additional fees. Known as the hold-up problem, in this pathology a bank is able to hold hostage a client who has committed in a main banking relationship with that bank and has nowhere else to turn. This is particularly pernicious for Chinese SMEs, which face great difficulty obtaining finance as larger banks ignore them and capital markets focus on larger firms (Bailey et al., 2011; Lin & Chen. 2012; Tanaka & Molnar, 2008).

Table 3. Relationship Banking Challenges with Chinese Socialist Characteristics.

Challenge	Description	Chinese Enterprise Level			
		SOE/VLE		SME	
		Problem	Solution	Problem	Solution
Hold-up problem	Bank obtains informational monopoly in client relationship	Not really a problem; firm has options to go to other banks		Huge problem – SMEs are held hostage by banks extracting fees, higher rates	Encourage Big Four participation in SME lending; transparent reporting
Soft-budget constraint	Bank is reluctant to enforce client's contractual obligations	Huge problem – SOEs, especially, have political clout to obtain additional loans	Stricter lending practices; more transparency in reporting internally and externally; enhance private monitoring function of individuals and investors	Problem exists when banking relationship enables nontransparent dealing	Stricter lending practices; more transparency in reporting to regulators; encourage private monitoring by individuals

Fu and Bao (2011) argue that relationship banking not only overcomes critical financing limitations faced by Chinese SMEs shut out of the equity and bond markets, but serves to lower financing charges directly through lower interest rates and indirectly through reduced collateral requirements. But one doubts whether Chinese SMEs will migrate toward a more transactional banking model. First, Chinese SMEs typically do not enter into multiple formal banking relationships but rather may rely in part on kerb market transactions to raise capital, an outcome Kellee Tsai has charmingly named "back-alley banking" (Tsai, 2002; also see Ding, 2012; Zhang, Xu, & Qin, 2013). Second, there is a large body of empirical evidence supporting the opacity of Chinese SMEs as a main reason they encounter severe credit rationing (Lin & Chen, 2012; Tanaka & Molnar, 2008, and Zhang, 2002; are representative).

Zhang (2002) employs Berger and Udell's (2002) discussion of different types of lending, noting that archetypal relationship lending not only includes financial information but can encompass the vast array of information held by the company's circle of stakeholders, including "information about corporate behavior, [firm and management] credibility, and the owner's personal conduct."[1] In fact, Cousin (2007, pp. 106–109), and others who have found bankers sometimes turn this information to extract fees from Chinese SMEs; the China Banking Regulatory Commission (CBRC) has investigated cases were SMEs were paying an "application fee" of ~3.8% of loan amount. We might then describe the soft information arising in Chinese SME relationship banking as too tightly held; non-disclosure of this information is part of the reason for the hold-up problem.

Except for the very largest privately held companies, the "Big Four" Chinese banks – the Bank of China, the China Construction Bank, the Industrial and Commercial Bank of China, and the Agricultural Bank of China – ignore SMEs and leave their banking business to joint-stock banks and city commercial banks (Bailey et al., 2011; Cousin, 2007; Tan, 2013). (A rough structure of the Chinese banking industry is provided in the Appendix.) The Big Four Chinese banks – all state-owned – focus on other SOEs and the largest private firms.

The nature of lending to SOEs leads to another pathology, the "soft-budget constraint." Kornai's (1986) early examinations of the soft-budget constraint focused on the lack of a market solution to centrally planned economies' unwillingness to discipline underperforming firms through credit restriction. The problem had clear resonance in relationship banking, and so financial economists expanded Kornai's concept into both state-owned and private banking (Qian, 1994; sees extension of state bank lending leading to suboptimal social welfare). Chinese banking analysts loosely term this issue of the soft-budget constraint as one of "lending new to repay old"[2] (Cousin, 2007, p. 88).

Governance issues with the soft-budget constraint manifest in Chinese banking in two ways. The first is through loose credit to SOEs. "Lending new to repay old" does merely occur through rolling over loans. Different lending channels lead to different requirements for credit allocation sign-offs; as is common in banking management practice anywhere, the larger the commitment, the further up the ladder the loan must climb to be approved. For the larger SOEs (and a few very large private firms), large banks' lending policies mandate a national credit check and sign off by a senior, national-level credit committee before disbursement (Cousin, 2007, pp. 101–104). A local bank manager may disburse smaller amounts of credit to SOEs or to private firms. Yeung (2009) find some bankers escape "climbing the ladder" by splitting a loan into smaller pieces.

Personal Relationships between Senior Bankers and SOE Senior Managers

Given the relative size of the Big Four (see Appendix), one might expect little chance for a personal relationship to exist between a senior banker and a senior SOE manager. But this expectation ignores four important aspects of managerial appointments for SOEs generally (Bian, 1997; Huang, 1998; Keister, 1998) and for state-owned banks specifically[3] (Cousin, 2007; Nee & Opper, 2010, p. 2122; Shih, 2008):

1. Senior managers are appointed by the central government for both banks and for SOEs from a small candidate pool in which strong competition exists for the top positions in banks and SOEs;
2. Each appointee's record is heavily scrutinized for a history of success by the government organizations responsible for the appointment and the new posting's firm. While political interference may color an appointment and increase or decrease the probability of an appointment, it is certainly true that incompetent managers face increasing resistance to higher-level appointments;
3. Local governments exert influence on appointments even at a senior level, and weigh in based on their pleasure or displeasure with the prospective appointee. This additional veto players increase potential

interference in an appointment by injecting political influence as well as increasing the level of scrutiny on past scandals;

4. The rotating nature of the appointments may militate against forming relationships earlier in a manager's career but, as decades of service increase, the chances of two appointees either having a relationship (bad as well as good) or knowing someone in the counterparty's *guanxi* network increase commensurately.

When a personal relationship exists between a senior banker on a credit committee and a senior member of the borrower's management, then we would expect relationship-embedded financial contracting should occur. This expectation arises not only through the nature of a relationship, but also because important information embedded in the relationship will naturally influence the banker in his or her decision. Such information may enable the banker to structure a better financial contract (or influence his or her to choose a worse outcome). Bankers involved in such credit decisions have access to additional data from the narrowly defined banking relationship as well as from the wider web of *guanxi* relationships (Yeung, 2009; a broader contextual analysis is provided in Park & Luo, 2001; Yeung & Tung, 1996).

SOEs continue to draw support beyond what would be given in an arms-length financial contracting arrangement, hence Hsieh and Wu (2012) find a negative correlation between loan size and profitability of firm, indicating those better-connected firms — nearly always SOEs — receive excess lending. And the converse — that banks do not withhold lending — is borne out by their research as well as that of Bailey et al. (2011), Yeung (2009), and others.

A SIMPLE ARGUMENT FOR BETTER CHINESE BANKING GOVERNANCE

The capacity to hide self-dealing in banking has become more difficult as information is more difficult to keep hidden. China has become one of the world's more wired nations, with the most internet users; most texters; most tweeters; incredible growth in chat rooms and in servers (Yang, 2009, 2012; also see Meng, 2011; Minter, 2013; Zhou, 2011). The chances of disclosure have increased due to an emergent internet-based civil society (Qiu et al., 2015; Shi, 2013; Yang, 2009) whose members are increasingly monitoring, criticizing, and actively protesting bad behavior (Meng, 2011; Yang, 2012). Costs of discovery have increased just as the chances of discovery have also increased.

Over the history of the internet, the Chinese government has attempted to contain the availability of online and other new media information through numerous means (Yang, 2014). But in each case that capacity has been compromised as web users effectively circumvent such attempts. Clayton et al. (2006) showed that attempts to create a "Great Firewall of China" were easily evaded through creative addressing of information packets, and outlined how to set up a system to evade the firewall; MacKinnon (2009) examined how bloggers were censored and found that much political information still made it into the blogosphere. Maintaining blogger anonymity was a key to create some space from government eyes. Beginning of 2013 brought another government attempt to curb anonymity by requiring that a new internet user must register in his or her own name (Minter, 2013). While not affecting directly the 540 million internet users (Minter, 2013 estimate), extensive discussions on China's blogs illustrate this casts a near-term pall on dissent.

However, this effort appears to have had a temporary effect just as other attempts to control have failed (Yang, 2009, 2014).[4] The Chinese government can neither control the use of the internet nor close off access as the Chinese economy is now so wired into the web. Nor can the government manage the creative range of criticism which its netizens put forth, including use of code words, pictures, videos, and veiled references (Meng, 2011; Yang, 2009).

These increasingly open information flows are paired with a willingness of Chinese people to stand up and criticize when they see bankers and government officials engaged in self-dealing. This criticism imparts a tremendous social and, sometimes, reputational toll as officials are fired or demoted. Internet outings of apparently illicit gain include pictures of officials with multiple expensive watches or in sports cars; maps of multiple apartment ownership; online analysis of financials behind large construction projects, and consumption of expensive wine to name just a few (Economist, 2012). Traditional media, both domestic and foreign, are joining in the fray, as Barboza's analysis of the Wen family riches exemplifies (Barboza, 2012). The interaction between *guanxi* and increasing information access exacerbates that powerful social fear of being found doing wrong. And the Chinese government pays attention to citizens' complaints – the predominant view of officials and Communist Party members is that government exists to create a strong, powerful state and

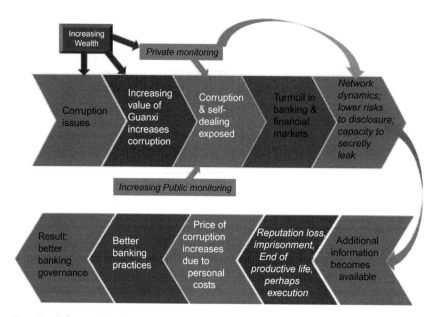

Fig. 1. Private Monitoring through Chinese Netizens Provides Better Banking Governance.

this goal is helped by having a happy citizenship. Xi Jinping's administration has recognized this, showing a strong commitment to curtailing corruption.[5]

Chinese people may be a tough lot capable of enduring great hardships, but this is not a passive society as shown through China's long history. Speaking truth to power is not only part of Chinese social custom, it is revered in Chinese history (Alford, 1993) and celebrated today in national holidays (as an example, I direct the reader to May 5 celebrations which continue to honor the suicide of a Chinese patriot who protested corrupt government nearly 2,300 years ago).

The model shown in Fig. 1 details the flow of my argument as outlined in this paper.

FINAL THOUGHTS

This paper has proposed a model of Chinese banking in which relationship banking combined with *guanxi* networks increased information access and a critical, empowered citizenry improve banking governance through private monitoring. Growing private monitoring through financial institutional channels will further enhance this governance. One might ask about the strength of this private monitoring mechanism I have outlined above, whether the mechanism actually will come to pass, and whether it can be reversed. Again, the basic idea of the argument is that Chinese banking tends to hew to the relationship banking model; this, and the nature of the Chinese economy, makes the soft-budget constraint a particularly knotty problem. The soft-budget constraint, the underlying structure of state involvement in Chinese banks, the "weak side" of *guanxi* relationships, and a desire to get rich all add to the probability of self-dealing occurring in Chinese banking transactions.

Yet reinforcement of private monitoring may be at hand in Chinese banking and financial contracting, delivered through new information sources empowering netizens to bring self-dealing to light, by a Chinese government concerned about a populace angry about corruption, and with the "good side" of *guanxi* bringing a powerful set of disciplinary cudgels wielded through netizen monitoring (see Qiu et al., 2015; Yang, 2014). The preponderance of recent high-profile financial dealings which indicate self-dealing in China shows that, once uncovered, the stories not only have an impact on public opinion but also disciplining mechanisms lock into place.

At first, this may appear a naïve argument. After all, information availability and social disciplinary measures in *guanxi* seem like weak necessary conditions for more banking transparency. In fact, a frequent criticism of *guanxi* is the claim that it is a kind of a gateway drug to corruption. But is it? *Guanxi* has also acted as a disciplining device throughout Chinese history, as shame accruing to a transgressor not only injures himself or herself but also his or her relationship, leading in more extreme cases to ostracism from the network and, sometimes, the country or kingdom (Alford, 1993; Li, 2009; Yeung & Tung, 1996). The social value of *guanxi* is not to be lightly considered by anyone in a *guanxi* network.

And the Chinese government has begun responding to the internet in ways other than attempting to control content and access. Local governments have begun microblogging efforts to better engage citizenry and gather complaints and information before anger spirals out of hand (Schlæger & Jiang, 2014; Yang, 2014). Government officials are learning that, "In the past we could avoid the press ... we could remain silent, but now we can no longer avoid it," and training to deal with an inquisitive press and online public is now given to senior government employees (quoted and noted in the Economist, 2014). I am not arguing that this mechanism is free from political vendettas or cyber-bullying (Qiu et al., 2015), but suggest that Chinese netizens and government officials and organizations will continue to adapt to a changing environment which would improve private monitoring.

Chinese banking provides a powerful case to examine these issues, but it is not the only country where this argument may work. The difficulties encountered by the Chinese government and banks in controlling information flow will empower private monitoring and lead to greater disclosure in many countries. When information networks make hiding corruption more difficult by forcing economic transactions into the open, bank governance gains an additional mechanism through a stronger private monitoring function. This mechanism should be further strengthened where relationship banking imposes additional reputational risks through the banker-creditor personal relationship combined with the institutional relationship inherent in any banking model.

NOTES

1. "有关企业行为、信誉和业主个人品行的信息."
2. "借新還舊."
3. Also see Shen and Lin (2012) for an interesting "political interference hypothesis" which suggests political appointment is endemic in developing economies' state-owned banks.
4. Because efforts to quash use of virtual private networks (VPNs) within China began in early 2015, so it is too early to forecast the effects. As elsewhere, VPNs are used by Chinese netizens to mask internet usage by creating a more secure point-to-point data channel.
5. It is beyond the scope of this paper to comment if these efforts are completely apolitical or partially apolitical.

REFERENCES

Alford, W. P. (1993). Double-edged swords cut both ways: Law and legitimacy in the people's republic of China. *Daedalus, 122*(2), 45−69.
Bailey, W., Huang, W., & Yang, Z. S. (2011). Bank loans with Chinese characteristics: Some evidence on inside debt in a state-controlled banking system. *The Journal of Financial and Quantitative Analysis, 46*(6), 1795−1830.
Barboza, D. (2012). Lobbying, a windfall and a leader's family. *New York Times*, November 24.
Berger, A. N., & Udell, G. F. (1992). Some empirical evidence on the empirical significance of credit rationing. *Journal of Political Economy, 100*, 1047−1077.

Berger, A. N., & Udell, G. F. (2002). Small business credit availability and relationship lending: The importance of bank organizational structure. *Economic Journal, 112*(477), F32—F53.

Berger, A. N., & Udell, G. F. (2006). A more complete conceptual framework for SME finance. *Journal of Banking & Finance, 30*(11), 2945—2966.

Bhattacharya, S., & Thakor, A. V. (1993). Contemporary banking theory. *Journal of Financial Intermediation, 3*, 2—50.

Bian, Y. (1997). Bringing strong ties back in: Indirect ties, network bridges, and job searches in China. *American Sociological Review, 62*(3), 366—385.

Boot, A. W. A. (2000). Relationship banking: What do we know? *Journal of Financial Intermediation, 9*, 7—25.

Boot, A. W. A., Greenbaum, S. I., & Thakor, A. V. (1993). Reputation and discretion in financial contracting. *American Economic Review, 83*(5), 1165—1183.

Boot, A. W. A., & Marinč, M. (2008). The evolving landscape of banking. *Industrial and Corporate Change, 17*(6), 1173—1203.

Carruthers, B. G., & Kim, J. C. (2011). The sociology of finance. *Annual Review of Sociology, 37*, 239—259.

Clayton, R., Murdoch, S. J., & Watson, R. N. (2006). *Ignoring the great firewall of China.* Cambridge: University of Cambridge. Computer Laboratory paper. Retrieved from http://www.cl.cam.ac.uk/~rnc1/ignoring.pdf. Accessed on January 6, 2013.

Cousin, V. (2007). *Banking in China.* Basingstoke: Palgrave Macmillan.

Ding, Q. [丁琪] (2012). Resolution on folk lending in Wenzhou [解析温州民间借贷]. *Technological Development of Enterprise, 31*(4,7) [企业技术开发], 165—166.

Economist. (2012). Life and death struggle. December 8.

Economist. (2014). Learning to spin. February 8.

Fu, X. L., & Bao, Q. H. [付晓亮 & 包清华] (2011). Theoretical research on application of relationship banking loans in China. [关系型银行贷款理论及其在我国的应用研究]. *Operations and Management, 16.* 《经营管理者: 16期》.

Han, Y., & Altman, Y. (2009). Supervisor and subordinate Guanxi: A grounded investigation in the People's Republic of China. *Journal of Business Ethics, 88*(Suppl. 1), 91—104.

Hayes III, S. L. (1979). The transformation of investment banking. *Harvard Business Review, 57*(1), 153—170.

Hidy, R. W. (1941). The organization and functions of Anglo-American merchant bankers, 1815–1860. *Journal of Economic History, 1*, 53—66.

Hsieh, C.-C., & Wu, S.-J. (2012). Monitoring the monitors: The effect of banking industry reform on earnings management behavior in an emerging market. *Corporate Governance: An International Review, 20*(5), 451–473.

Huang, X. B. (1998). Guanxi networks and job searches in China's emerging labour market: A qualitative investigation. *Work, Employment and Society, 22*(3), 467—484.

Kane, E. J. (2003). What lessons might crisis countries in Asia and Latin America have learned from the S&L Mess? *Business Economics, 38*(1), 21—30.

Kang, D. C. (2002). Bad loans to good friends: Money politics and the developmental state in South Korea. *International Organization, 56*(1), 177—207.

Keister, L. A. (1998). Engineering growth: Business group structure and firm performance in China's transition economy. *American Journal of Sociology, 104*(2), 404—440.

Keister, L. A. (2004). Capital structure in transition: The transformation of financial strategies in China's emerging economy. *Organization Science, 15*(2), 145—158.

Kornai, J. (1986). The soft budget constraint. *Kyklos, 39,* 3–30.

Li, M.-W., Makaew, T., & Winton, A. (2014). *Cheating in China: Corporate fraud and the roles of financial markets.* Retrieved from http://ssrn.com/abstract=2521151 or http://dx.doi.org/10.2139/ssrn.2521151. Accessed on August 1, 2015.

Li, P. P. (2009). The duality of crony corruption in economic transition: Toward an integrated framework. *Journal of Business Ethics, 85*(1), 41–55.

Lin, G., & Chen, T. [林贵 & 陈婷] (2012). Risk and prevention of establishing private banks in Wenzhou [温州建立与发展民营银行的风险与防范]. *Journal of Wenzhou Vocational & Technical College, 12*(1), [温州职业技术学院学报], 8–23.

MacKinnon, R. (2009). China's censorship 2.0: How companies censor bloggers. *First Monday,* 14(2).

Meng, B. (2011). From steamed bun to grass mud horse: E Gao as alternative political discourse on the Chinese internet. *Global Media and Communication, 7*(1), 33–51.

Minter, A. (2013). Chinese censors lift the veil on bloggers. *Bloomberg View.* Retrieved from http://www.bloomberg.com/news/2013-01-04/chinese-censors-lift-the-veil-on-bloggers.html

Morrison, A. D., & Wilhelm, W. J. (2004). Partnership firms, reputation, and human capital. *American Economic Review, 94*(5), 1682–1692.

Nee, V., & Opper, S. (2010). Political capital in a market economy. *Social Forces, 88*(5), 2105–2132.

Park, S. H., & Luo, Y. (2001). Guanxi and organizational dynamics: Organizational networking in Chinese firms. *Strategic Management Journal, 22*(5), 455–477.

Qian, Y. (1994). A theory of shortage in socialist economies based on the 'Soft Budget Constraint'. *American Economic Review, 84*(1), 145–156.

Qiu, L., Lin, H., Chiu, C.-y., & Liu, P. (2015). Online collective behaviors in China: Dimensions and motivations. *Analyses of Social Issues and Public Policy, 15*(1), 44–68. Retrieved from http://onlinelibrary.wiley.com.proxyiub.uits.iu.edu/doi/10.1111/asap.12049/full

Rajan, R. G. (1992). Insiders and outsiders: The choice between informed and arm's-length debt. *Journal of Finance, 47*(4), 1367–1400.

Rajan, R., & Winton, A. (1995). Covenants and collateral as incentives to monitor. *Journal of Finance, 50*(4), 1113–1146.

Rose-Ackerman, S. (1999). *Corruption and government: Causes, consequences, and reform.* Cambridge: Cambridge University Press.

Schlæger, J., & Jiang, M. (2014). Official microblogging and social management by local governments in China. *China Information, 28*(2), 189–213.

Selmier II, W. T. (2013). Stand by me: Friends, relationship banking and banking governance in Asia. *Business Horizons, 56*(6), 733–741.

Shen, C. H., & Lin, C. Y. (2012). Why government banks underperform: A political interference view. *Journal of Financial Intermediation, 21,* 181–202.

Shi, S. (2013). The use of Web2.0 style technologies among Chinese civil society organizations. *Telematics and Informatics, 30*(4), 346–358.

Shih, V. C. (2008). *Factions and finance in China: Elite conflict and inflation.* New York, NY: Cambridge University Press.

Stallings, B., & Studart, R. (2006). *Finance for development: Latin America in comparative perspective.* Washington, DC: Brookings Institution Press.

Tan, M. N. T. (2013). *Corporate governance and Banking in China.* New York, NY: Routledge.

Tanaka, K., & Molnar, M. (2008). What is different about informal finance? Financing of private firms in China. *Revue Économique, 59*(6), 1131–1143.

Tsai, K. S. (2002). *Back-Alley banking: Private entrepreneurs in China.* Ithaca, NY: Cornell University Press.

Yang, G. B. [楊國斌] (2009). The internet and China's civil society. 互聯網與中國公民社會. *Twenty-first Century Review [二十一世纪评论], 114,* 14–25.

Yang, G. B. (2012). A Chinese internet? History, practice, and globalization. *Chinese Journal of Communication, 5*(1), 49–54.

Yang, G. B. (2014). Internet activism & the party-state in China. *Daedalus, 143*(2), 110–123.

Yeung, G. (2009). How banks in China make lending decisions. *Journal of Contemporary China, 18*(59), 285–302.

Yeung, I. Y. M., & Tung, R. L. (1996). Achieving business success in Confucian societies: The importance of guanxi (connections). *Organizational Dynamics, 25*(2), 54–65.

Yosha, O. (1995). Information disclosure costs and the choice of financing source. *Journal of Financial Intermediation, 4*(1), 3–20.

Zhang, J. [张捷] (2002). 中小企业的关系型借贷与银行组织结构. [Relationship lending to small and medium enterprises and the organizational structure of banks]. 经济研究 *[Economic Research]*, 2002, (6).

Zhang, X.-C., Xu, Z., & Qin, D. [张雪春, 徐忠 & 秦朵] (2013). The outlet of folk lending interest rates and folk capital: The case of Wenzhou [民间借贷利率与民间资本的出路：温州案例]. *Journal of Financial Research, 3*(393), [金融研究], 1–14.

Zhou, H. Z. (2011). Most avid internet users are found in the BRICS. *China Daily.* Retrieved from http://www.chinadaily.com.cn/china/2011-12/16/content_14277697.htm. Accessed on December 16, 2011.

APPENDIX

Table A1. Structure of the Chinese Banking Industry (Figures Year End 2005).

Banking Type	Nick-Name	Number	Assets in System[a] Profitability// NPLs	Notes
State-owned Commercial Banks	SOCBs	4	52% of BS assets ROE: 1.3–16.4% ROA: 0.02–1.03% NPLs: 3.8–26.2%	SOCBs are legally enjoined "to provide loans for special projects approved by the State Council. Losses resulting from such loans shall be compensated with appropriate measures taken by the State Council." Article 41, Common Bank Law (Cousin, 29)
Joint-stock Commercial Banks	JSCBs	13	15% of BS assets[b] ROE: 7.0–20.3% ROA: 0.15–0.65% NPLs: 1.3–10.6%	Set up in 1994, these are more entrepreneurial, the most competitive, and a prime target of foreign investment. SDB (case analyzed below) had the highest NPL level and lowest ROE and ROA figures among the 8 banks' numbers at left
City Commercial Banks	CCBs	115	5.4% of BS assets ROE: 4.4–20.0% ROA: 0.16–0.67% NPLs: 4.0–20.0% *Top 12 CCBs:* *ROE,* *13.6%;*	Vary tremendously in size, management capacity, degree of political interference, and loan policy. Largest two (Bank of Shanghai and Bank of Beijing) account for 13% and 12% of CCB total assets, respectively. Local

Table A1. (*Continued*)

Banking Type	Nick-Name	Number	Assets in System[a] Profitability// NPLs	Notes
			ROA, 0.55%; NPLs, 6.0%	governments own ˜75% of CCB shares. All CCB NPL ratio was 11.7% YE 2004
Foreign Banks	FBs	244 (from 60 countries)	2% of BS assets ROE, ROA, NPLs: not available	FBs geographic location breakdown: Shanghai (28%); Beijing (13%); Shenzhen (13%). FBs have 12.4% of total banking assets in Shanghai
Non-bank Financial Institutions	NBFIs			The most important NBFIs are the Trust and Investment Companies (TICs), whose fortunes have been in decline since the 1998 collapse of Guangdong Intl TIC
Rural Credit Cooperatives	RCCs	30,438	4.4% of BS assets NPLs: 14.8%	High degree of political interference, often managed by local cadres
Policy Banks	Policy Banks	3		Established in 1994 to assume SOCBs' policy lending role, with weak branch network and inadequate capital structure

Source: Cousin, Banking in China (2007).
[a]Assets as a percent of total domestic banking system.
[b]As of YE 2004. ROA, ROE, NPLs for selected JSC banks: BoComm, Minsheng, Merchants, Huaxia, CITIC, SPDB, Industrial, SDB.

CEO PROMOTION, RELATIVE PERFORMANCE MEASURES, AND INSTITUTIONS IN AN EMERGING MARKET: EVIDENCE FROM CHINA'S LISTED STATE-OWNED ENTERPRISE

Fang Hu and Yahua Zhang

ABSTRACT

Purpose — *This paper investigates CEO turnover and the usefulness of relative performance evaluation (RPE) as a management incentive in an emerging economy lacking market-based competition.*

Methodology/approach — *In a sample of China's listed state-owned enterprises (SOEs) from the period 2001 to 2005, we manually collect the data where a CEO has gone after being removed by reading the annual reports of the firms and searching the major news and business publications, and run OLS regressions to examine how various incentives provided by different CEO turnovers such as promotion, demotion, and rotation affect the firm performance.*

The Political Economy of Chinese Finance
International Finance Review, Volume 17, 115–148
Copyright © 2016 by Emerald Group Publishing Limited
ISSN: 1569-3767/doi:10.1108/S1569-376720160000017011

Findings — *We find that 41% of departing CEOs in SOEs is being promoted. The promotion is positively associated with preceding firm performance relative to peers in the same region and this association is more significant than that between the promotion and firm's specific performance. Furthermore, the promotion outperforms other incentive schemes such as CEO demotions by 5–8% in terms of subsequent Tobin's* q *in three years. These consequences persist in undeveloped regions where there are fewer firms listed on the stock market, a lower stock market capitalization, or a higher regional Herfindahl–Hirschman Index (*HHI*).*

Research implications — *The findings imply that promotion based on RPE provides an important incentive by creating competitions.*

Keywords: Incentive scheme; promotion; relative performance evaluation (RPE); market competition; China's SOEs

INTRODUCTION

Previous studies have implied that the tournament based on relative performance evaluation (RPE) plays a crucial role in contracting because RPE gives accurate information on an agent's actions in a competitive market by filtering out the common factors faced by the agent's peers (Aggarwal & Samwick, 1999; Antle & Smith, 1986; Barro & Robert, 1990; DeFond & Park, 1999; Dye, 1992; Garvey & Milbourn, 2003; Gibbons & Murphy, 1990; Janakiraman, Lambert, & Larcker, 1992). However, there is little empirical evidence on this issue. This study attempts to fill this void by investigating the incentive role of RPE in a unique institutional setting in China.

In the market competition, RPE provides a more precise measure of the idiosyncratic efforts of agents by eliminating common factors such as market or industry conditions (Diamond & Verrechia, 1982; Holmstrom, 1979, 1982). This gives a principal more accurate information on an agent's effort and thus reduces agency costs. The information role of RPE is enhanced in a competitive environment because agents are more likely to be subject to similar uncertainties and to have more peers, and because any given agent's actions are unlikely to affect the output of other agents (DeFond & Park, 1999; Holmstrom, 1982). However, there is a little evidence that RPE is effective in environments lack of market competition as an incentive to motivate agents' actions. Shleifer (1985) suggests that in theory RPE is the first-best incentive in a highly regulated environment in which regulators determine the price rating and tends to motivate agents' effort by artificially creating competition. A few studies provide evidence that RPE is a useful incentive in the public sector. For example, Besley and Case (1996) show that the economic performance of a state relative to neighboring states has a positive impact on the re-election prospects of US governors as a consequence of the states' relative taxation behavior.[1] Matsumura and Shin (2006) find evidence that financial performance improves following the implementation of an incentive scheme that includes relative performance measures in a sample of 214 postal stores in South Korea, because RPE motivates reduced effort when workers perceive unfairness in competition. Those studies only describe the incentive role of RPE in behavioral theories given the regulated environment or public sectors.

A sample of China's state-owned enterprises (SOEs) is a natural laboratory to empirically test the theory of the incentive role of RPE in a weak market competition for several reasons. First, China's SOEs are affiliated with the Chinese bureaucratic hierarchy, and are thus scarcely subject to market-based competition. Although SOEs are listed and traded on the stock, a significant portion of state shares remain non-tradable (Alchian, 1965; Fan, Wong, & Zhang, 2007; Jensen & Meckling, 1979; Karpoff & Rice, 1989). As the `management of SOEs remains under the authority of the Central Committee of the Communist Party of China (CPC), it also lacks a competitive managerial labor market (Groves, Hong, McMillan, & Naughton, 1995; Li & Zhou, 2005). Second, China's government has explicitly incorporated relative economic performance criteria into the procedure of evaluating officials since economic reforms were launched in 1980s (Li & Zhou, 2005; Oi, 1992; Qian, 2000; Qian & Weingast, 1997). Government reports or yearbooks and the mass media regularly publish detailed information on relative provincial performance rankings in such varied areas as GDP growth, sales revenue, profit, steel production, and miles of road constructed. Third, there is considerable variation across jurisdictional regions in China in terms of both market development and the extent of government control. A large sample of listed SOEs affiliated with different regional governments thus allows us to examine the incentive role of RPE tangled with institutions in regions.

As Chinese governments usually rely on administrative approaches such as appointment and removal of senior officials to administer SOEs and design the incentive schemes for managers in SOEs, this study investigates the research questions as follows. First, how have the incentive schemes been designed in SOEs and what are the determinants of incentive schemes? Second, is the incentive scheme linked to firm performance, especially, is it linked to relative performance measure? Third, what consequences have those incentive schemes caused? Forth, how do those incentive schemes work with institutions in Chinese emerging market?

The results reveal several key findings. First, promotion is most frequently adopted in Chinese SOEs as an incentive for CEOs. Among the CEOs leaving office in the study period, 41% were promoted within the firm, or to the parent firm, or to another firm in higher layer of Chinese bureaucratic hierarchy; 15% were demoted (most often internally); 15% were rotated or reassigned to an equivalent-ranking position; 13% entered a government entity; 8% were imprisoned, and 8% were assigned another usually honorary position, such as honorary chairman or supervising board director. Further, the promotion occurs more frequently in SOEs affiliated with the central government, in SOEs located in undeveloped or poorer regions, and in SOEs in regulated industries. Second, the promotion is significantly associated with the firm's individual performance (ROA) but more significantly associated with the firm's performance relative to peers in the region. Third, the promotion is positively associated with the subsequent three-year Tobin's q and outperforms other incentive schemes by $5-8\%$. These effects are significant in the subsample where there are fewer firms listed on the stock market, a lower stock market capitalization, or a higher regional Herfindahl–Hirschman Index (*HHI*) value.

Our findings make several contributions as follows. First, it extends the literature on executive compensation and incentive. DeFond and Park (1999) find that RPE is useful in highly competitive environments and that competitive environments are more conducive to RPE. By examining the use of RPE in an emerging market lack of market competition, this study complement prior studies by demonstrating that RPE might lead to tournament and play an important role for incentive in a market lack of competition. Second, our student extends the accounting literature on performance measures. Previous studies have cast doubt on the usefulness of accounting information in a developing economies such as China in which the market is less functional, government intervention is strong, and state-owned firms dominate (Ball, Kothari, & Robin, 2000; Ball, Robin, & Wu, 2003; Bushman and Piotroski, 2006; Fan and Wong, 2002; Li, Park, & Li, 2004; Opper & Brehm, 2007). This study implies that accounting measures are useful for contracting in such an environment if they are properly designed. Third, our study sheds insights on the corporate governance of China's SOEs. We look into the executive incentives in SOEs and shed lights on the performance measures used in executive compensation in an emerging market.

The remainder of this paper is organized as follows. The section "Background and Hypothesis" discusses the background and develops the hypotheses. The section "Variables and Models" presents the variables measures and research model. The section "Data and Sample" describes the data and sample. The section "Results" reports the results. The final section concludes the paper.

BACKGROUND AND HYPOTHESIS

Incentive Schemes in China's SOEs

China's SOEs are affiliated with a huge Chinese bureaucratic hierarchy that is lack of market competition. The Chinese governments have ultimate ownership of SOEs that cannot be freely traded in the market (Alchian, 1965; Fan et al., 2007; Jensen & Meckling, 1979; Karpoff & Rice, 1989).[2] The lack of market competition is exacerbated by the absence of a large secondary owner who serves as a powerful monitor and benefits from additional firm productivity (Shleifer & Vishny, 1986). In such a bureaucratic hierarchy, the Central Committee of the Communist Party of China (CPC), which functions more or less as the personnel department of this enormous organization, ultimately controls the mobility of officials within the system, maintaining dossiers and tracking managerial careers.[3] If an official is separated from the government hierarchy, then his or her career in the political system is disrupted (Li & Zhou, 2005). Hence, Chinese government officials have few options outside the internal labor market.[4] This highly centralized personnel machine relies heavily on administrative means of control such as personnel appointments and removes. Monetary rewards play a much less prominent role either in implicit contracts or remuneration in a bureau. In part, this is because the relationship between a bureaucratic superior and his or her subordinates is authoritative, and administrative compulsion is more likely to elicit compliance than would be the case under market pressure. In addition, the lock-in effect, coupled with the huge difference in the personal benefits of staying in power and relinquishing power, greatly reinforces the incentive for Chinese officials to remain in office.[5]

The Relative Performance Measure as Explicit Incentive in China's SOEs

The Chinese government has explicitly incorporated RPE into the control mechanism of the bureaucratic hierarchy. The use of RPE encourages better economic performance by artificially creating competition among regions or local governments. In the economic reforms implemented since the 1980s, the Chinese central government has pursued an explicit policy of stimulating regional competition, such as encouraging regions to "get rich first." Indeed, both the lobbying position of a local government and the careers of local governor in a higher government entity or the central government are determined by local economic performance relative to similar jurisdictions or areas (Montinola, Qian, & Weingast, 1995; Oi, 1992; Qian & Weingast, 1997; Qian & Xu, 1993). In the contest, Chinese government would like to select "elites" to lead the bureaucratic hierarchy and one of the major channels of elite recruitment appears to promote persons based on the rankings of performance in related fields (Li & Bachman, 1989).[6] In addition, government reports or yearbooks and the mass media regularly publish detailed information on relative provincial performance rankings in varied areas such as GDP growth, sales revenue, profit, steel production, and miles of road constructed. In an analysis of 520 Chinese SOEs, Maskin, Qian, and Xu (2000) find that firm performance across regions is more useful than inter-industry performance, and document a positive relationship between the lobbying status of a Chinese province (as measured by the ranking of the provincial per capita number of Central Committee members in the Party Congress) and its economic performance ranking in terms of growth rate one year before the Party Congress.[7] Second, the use of RPE may be especially helpful in less competitive markets to mitigate the information costs and efficiency problems arising from political competition encouraged by the central government. In the appraisals of SOE managers, the government or regulator may evaluate economic outcomes by firm-specific earnings, thus requiring firms to reveal private information (Laffont, 1994; Stigler, 1971).[8,9] When RPE is used, an SOE's performance is related to other similar firms in the same region. In this case, managers may make greater effort to adjust to changes in circumstances to improve firm performance, much as they would in a competitive market.

This setting with weak market competition and the explicit policy of RPE make it ideal to test the incentive and the role RPE for incentive.

VARIABLES AND MODELS

Incentive Schemes in China's SOEs

Based on administrative means of personnel control in China's SOEs (Huang, 1998), we classify the incentives as follows.

Promotion

Promotion has substantial motivation effects when employees know in advance that there is a likelihood of promotion and are aware of the personal benefits afforded by the higher position. According to Gibbs (1996), promotion is usually based on one of two extreme models: the first is to run a contest or tournament and the second is to set a quota or absolute performance standard. Although these seemingly disparate means are almost identical in terms of their incentive properties, the tournament model based on relative performance measures is generally more applicable in empirical work. Lazear and Rosen (1981) suggest that it might be less costly to observe relative performance than to measure the level of a worker's individual output when monitoring is so difficult that moral hazard is a serious problem. While promotion on the basis of RPE might be preferable in an undeveloped market with a serious monitoring problem such as the information cost and efficiency problems mentioned above, it is an open issue to be tested. Here, promotion is identified as: (i) a CEO being appointed as chairman of the board or vice-chairman within a firm; (ii) a chairman of the board or CEO being appointed as a senior executive in the parent firm; (iii) a chairman of the board or a CEO being appointed as a senior executive in another SOE in an equivalent bureaucratic layer or to an equal-ranking position in another SOE in a higher bureaucratic layer.

Entering Government

Future opportunities for SOE managers include entering a government entity to take up a position in an industrial bureau or administrative division of the government or even as a governor, such as a mayor, provincial governor, or party secretary. The incentive effect derives from SOE managers observing that government positions will not be snatched up by outsiders every time they become available, and that incumbents in these positions are afforded certain privileges, such as a secretary, company car, and access to political resources.

Rotation

Rotation is a practice whereby officials are regularly rotated in bureaucratically equivalent positions. For example, the CEO of ChinaTelecom Co., a company held by the central government, may be reassigned to manage ChinaUnicom Co., which is also held by the central government. A chairman of the board or CEO taking up an equivalent position in an SOE affiliated with the equivalent layer of government is classed as a rotation.

Demotion

Demotion is defined as: (i) a chairman of the board being appointed as the director, CEO, or executive of the firm or other SOE affiliated with the equivalent bureaucratic layer; and (ii) a CEO being appointed as a non-chief executive in the firm or other SOE affiliated with the equivalent bureaucratic layer. Relinquishing power greatly reinforces the incentive for SOE managers, because terminated managers lose the major source of benefits associated with such power. Existing studies, which focus on privately held firms in developed market economies, have tested the relation between the forced management turnover (presumably demotion) and firm performance. For example, some demonstrate that forced management turnover is significantly negatively associated with firm-specific accounting performance (Brickley, 2003; Engel, Hayes, & Wang, 2003; Kaplan & Minton, 1994; Weisbach, 1988); others find that the disciplinary turnover is negatively related to the RPE (Cannella, Fraser, & Lee, 1995; DeFond & Park, 1999; Huson, Malatesta, & Parrino, 2004).

Imprisonment

If SOE managers engage in gross misconduct, then they may suffer consequences beyond losing their jobs or being demoted or fined, such as serving a prison sentence. The risk of litigation acts as an incentive in undeveloped markets while legal enforcement is weak (Sun & Zhang, 2006).

Other Honorary Positions

The managers of SOEs may be assigned to an honorary yet virtually powerless position, such as honorary chairman of the board, non-executive director of the board, grass-roots party secretary, or chairman of a supervisory committee. Whatever gloss may be put on this, they lose the decision rights that they had as chairman of the board or CEO. Because the difference in these positions is subtle, they are grouped under the heading "other honorary positions."

Relative Performance Evaluation (RPE)

In an attempt to encourage regions to "get rich first," the Chinese government evaluates economic performance by comparing performance between regions. For the administration of the nation, China is partitioned into jurisdictions based on provincial units. There are 31 provincial units, including four directly ruled municipalities, 22 provinces, and five autonomous regions.[10] Based on this jurisdictional partitioning, the Chinese bureaucratic hierarchy broadly consists of four layers for administration of SOEs: central, provincial, municipal, and county (see Appendix for more details). Hence, SOEs in the same bureaucratic layer and located in the same provincial unit are defined as a reference group. There are 124 (31 provincial units × 4 layers) reference groups in total. The RPE is then defined as a firm i's return on assets (ROA) less the average ROA in the reference group.

Other Factors

$SIZE_{it}$, which is measured as the log of the total assets of a firm, is a proxy for firm size. Berry, Bizjak, Lemmon, and Naveen (2006) suggest that an increase in size increases management entrenchment, and thus top executives are less likely to be found "incompetent."

DA_{it}, which is the debt-to-assets ratio of a firm, is a proxy for leverage risk or financial distress. This is included because Gilson (1990) provides evidence that management turnover is greater in financially distressed firms.

$OWNERSHIP_{it}$, which is the percentage of state ownership ultimately held by the government, is a proxy for the level of government ownership. Highly concentrated ownership will presumably give the controlling shareholder more incentive to monitor management (La Porta, Lopez-de-Silanes, Shleifer, & Vishny, 2000). When the incumbent manager is doing a poor job, the controlling owner has a strong incentive to select the "right" person to ensure that management acts in his or her interests (Fama & Jensen, 1983; Jensen & Meckling, 1976). This factor often determines the adoption by state owners of administrative means as an incentive.

$Indusmb_{it}$, which is the industry (two-digit SIC code) median market-to-book ratio, is a surrogate for the investment opportunity set (IOS). Previous research indicates that the IOS may be associated with management change because firms with a good IOS demand high-quality managers and thus engage in more frequent management changes (Smith & Watts, 1992).

AGE is included because it affects the retirement or termination incentives. When an incumbent chairmen or CEO is close to retirement, the incentive effect of promotion should be stronger (Kale, Reis, & Venkateswaran, 2009).

Employee$_{it}$, which is the log of the number of employees in a firm, is included to control for the effect of political factors on the selection of managers by the Chinese political hierarchy, because both SOEs and politicians have a social obligation to maintain the rate of employment (Fan et al., 2007).

GDP$_{it}$, which is the log of the local (provincial) gross domestic product (GDP), is included to control for variety in economic conditions across regions (Fan et al., 2007).

HHI$_{it}$, which is the industrial HHI by two-digit SIC code,[11] is included to control for industrial competition. Strong industrial competition reinforces the usefulness of RPE in contracts (DeFond & Park, 1999).

DATA AND SAMPLE

Data

Regarding CEO's turnover, we track where a CEO has gone after being removed by reading the annual reports of the firms and searching the major news and business publications, including the top 50 newspapers and news wire services. Firms are excluded from the sample if a CEO was removed due to "natural" reasons, which include (i) natural retirement or the expiration of an acting position; (ii) death; (iii) change of ownership, such as privatization; and (iv) resignation, or if there are missing values. The final sample includes 462 listed SOEs in China for the period 2001−2005.

All of the financial data, including return on assets (ROA), total assets, debt, sales, percentage shareholding, market-to-book ratio, managers' ages, number of employees, and Tobin's q, are obtained from the China Securities Markets and Accounting Research (CSMAR) database. The institutional data, such as local (provincial) GDP, are collected from government yearbooks.

Sample Description

Table 1 shows the number and frequency of incentive schemes used in SOEs from the raw data without processing the other variables. The sample

Table 1.   Incentive Plans for the Administration of CEOs in China's SOEs during 2001—2005.

Classification of CEO Turnover	Observation No.	Freq.
Demotion	183	0.15
Promotion		
Within firm	238	0.21
To parent firm	220	0.19
To the other firm within bureaucratic hierarchy	16	0.01
Subtotal	474	0.41
Rotation	169	0.15
Entering government		
Industry bureau	54	0.05
Administration division	57	0.05
Governor of government	38	0.03
Subtotal	149	0.13
Imprisonment	96	0.08
Others		
As board director	40	0.03
As party sectary/supervisory committee/honorary position	48	0.04
Subtotal	88	0.08
Total	1,159	1.00

This table summarizes the number and frequency of SOEs adopting the administrative means for incentive mechanism such as promotion, demotion, rotation, entering government entities, imprisonment and others in a sample of raw data. The total sample consists of 1,650 firm-year observations where CEO has been forced to leave the office in the SOEs. The observation number shows the number of sample. Freq. shows the percentage of the total sample.

consists of 1,159 firm years in the period 2001—2005 in which a CEO left his or her position. After leaving office, 41% of CEOs were promoted, among which half were promoted to the position of chairman or vice-chairman within the firm and the other half were promoted to top management in the parent firm. In addition, 15% of removed CEOs get demoted, 15% being rotated, 13% entering government, 8% being imprisoned, and 8% taking an honorary position.

Table 2 shows the distribution of the incentive schemes by partitions based on institutions. Panel A of Table 2 presents the distribution by bureaucratic layers with which SOEs are affiliated. The promotion is more commonly used for incentives in all bureaucratic layers, compared with other incentives. At the central level of administration,[12] especially, promotion occurs more frequently than that at other local levels of administration, 43% of removed CEOs being promoted (10% more than that at the county level). CEOs at the county level are more frequently demoted.

Table 2. Incentive Plans for CEOs in China's SOEs by Partitions.

	County		City		Province		Central	
	No.	Freq.	No.	Freq.	No.	Freq.	No.	Freq.
Panel A								
Demotion	10	0.23	51	0.16	69	0.16	47	0.14
Rotation	10	0.23	35	0.11	46	0.1	78	0.22
Promotion								
Within firm	9	0.21	80	0.25	92	0.21	61	0.18
To parent firm	3	0.07	47	0.15	88	0.2	82	0.24
To the other firm within bureaucratic hierarchy	2	0.05	6	0.02	4	0.01	4	0.01
Subtotal	14	0.33	133	0.42	184	0.42	147	0.43
Entering government								
Industry bureau	–	–	20	0.06	20	0.05	14	0.04
Administration division	2	0.05	10	0.03	35	0.08	10	0.03
Governor of government	2	0.05	8	0.02	15	0.03	13	0.04
Subtotal	4	0.1	38	0.11	70	0.16	37	0.11
Imprisonment	1	0.02	43	0.13	31	0.07	21	0.06
Others								
As board director	3	0.07	13	0.04	20	0.05	10	0.03
As party sectary/supervisory committee/honorary position	1	0.02	11	0.03	23	0.05	8	0.02
Subtotal	4	0.09	24	0.07	43	0.1	18	0.05
Total	43	1	324	1	443	1	348	1

This table summarizes the number and frequency of SOEs adopting the administrative means for incentive mechanism such as promotion, demotion, rotation, entering government entities, imprisonment, and others by four bureaucratic layers – the county, city, province, and central level. The total sample consists of 1,650 firm-year observations where CEO has been forced to leave the office in the SOEs. No. shows the number of sample. Freq. shows the percentage of the total sample in the bureaucratic layer.

	North (Mean GDP 36.32[a])		Southwest (Mean GDP 41.31[a])		Northwest (Mean GDP 45.55[a])		Northeast (Mean GDP 46.58[a])		East (Mean GDP 87.18[a])		Central (Mean GDP 99.79[a])	
	No.	Freq.	No.	Freq.	No.	Freq.	No.	Freq.	No.	Freq.	No.	Freq.
Panel B												
Demotion	18	0.12	19	0.18	32	0.12	19	0.21	49	0.19	40	0.14
Rotation	34	0.23	12	0.12	41	0.16	10	0.11	22	0.08	50	0.17
Promotion												
Within firm	34	0.23	27	0.26	59	0.22	14	0.16	46	0.18	62	0.21
To parent firm	38	0.26	11	0.11	48	0.18	19	0.21	55	0.21	49	0.17
To the other firm within bureaucratic hierarchy	1	0.01	1	0.01	0	0	0	0	7	0.03	7	0.02
Subtotal	73	0.5	39	0.38	107	0.4	33	0.37	108	0.42	118	0.4
To government entities												
Industry bureau	5	0.03	8	0.08	8	0.03	6	0.07	12	0.05	15	0.05
Administration division	1	0.01	5	0.05	18	0.07	4	0.04	10	0.04	19	0.07
Governor of government	2	0.01	8	0.08	3	0.01	8	0.09	7	0.03	10	0.03
Subtotal	8	0.05	21	0.21	29	0.11	18	0.2	29	0.12	44	0.15
Imprisonment	5	0.03	9	0.09	26	0.1	3	0.03	25	0.1	28	0.09
Others												
As board director	5	0.03	2	0.02	11	0.04	5	0.06	12	0.05	11	0.04
As party sectary/supervisory committee/honorary position	3	0.02	2	0.02	17	0.06	2	0.02	15	0.06	4	0.01
Subtotal	8	0.05	4	0.04	28	0.1	7	0.08	27	0.11	15	0.05
Total	146	1	104	1	263	1	90	1	260	1	295	1

This table summarizes the number and frequency of SOEs adopting the administrative means for incentive mechanism such as promotion, demotion, rotation, entering government entities, imprisonment, and others by six administrative areas – North, Northeast, East, Central, Southwest, and Northwest. The total sample consists of 1,650 firm-year observations where the chairman or CEO has been forced to leave the office in the SOEs. No. shows the number of sample. Freq. shows the percentage of the total sample in the area.

Table 2. (Continued)

| | A | | B[b] | | C | | D[b] | | E | | F[b] | | G | |
| | Agriculture production | | Mining | | Manufacturing & Petro-chemicals | | Power, oil & water | | Heavy construction | | Transportation | | Telecom | |
	No.	Freq.	No.	Freq.	No.	Freq.	No.	Freq.	No.	Freq.	No.	Freq.	No.	Freq.
Panel C														
Demotion	6	0.2	5	0.19	120	0.17	11	0.18	1	0.08	7	0.15	4	0.08
Rotation	3	0.1	5	0.19	94	0.13	7	0.11	0	0	3	0.06	11	0.22
Promotion														
Within firm	8	0.27	3	0.11	151	0.21	12	0.19	1	0.08	10	0.21	12	0.24
To parent firm	0	0	8	0.3	123	0.17	25	0.4	5	0.38	11	0.23	8	0.16
To the other firm within bureaucratic hierarchy	0	0	0	0	14	0.02	0	0	0	0	0	0	0	0
Subtotal	8	0.27	11	0.41	288	0.4	37	0.59	6	0.46	21	0.44	20	0.4
To government entities														
Industry bureau	0	0	4	0.15	19	0.03	1	0.02	2	0.15	5	0.1	4	0.08
Administration division	4	0.1	0	0	30	0.04	4	0.07	1	0.08	6	0.12	2	0.04
Governor of government	3	0.1	0	0	31	0.04	0	0	0	0	0	0	2	0.04
Subtotal	7	0.2	4	0.15	80	0.11	5	0.09	3	0.23	11	0.22	8	0.16
Imprisonment	1	0.03	2	0.07	59	0.08	2	0.03	1	0.08	4	0.08	4	0.08
Others														
as board director	1	0.03	0	0	29	0.04	0	0	2	0.15	2	0.04	2	0.04
as party sectary/ supervisory committee/ honorary position	4	0.13	0	0	34	0.05	0	0	0	0	0	0	1	0.02
Subtotal	5	0.16	0	0	63	0.09	0	0	2	0.15	2	0.04	3	0.06
Total	30	1	27	1	704	1	62	1	13	1	48	1	50	1

This table summarizes the number and frequency of SOEs adopting the administrative means for incentive mechanism such as promotion, demotion, rotation, entering government entities, imprisonment, and others by 1-digit industry. The total sample consists of 1,650 firm-year observations where the chairman or CEO has been forced to leave the office in the SOEs. No. shows the number of sample. Freq. shows the percentage of the total sample in the industry.

	H		I[b]		J		K		L		M	
	Wholesale trade and Retails		Banking and Financial institutes		Real Estate		Social service and Infrastructure		Media and Communication		Others	
	No.	Freq.	No.	Freq.	No.	Freq.	No.	Freq.	No.	Freq.	No.	Freq.
Demotion	7	0.1	0	0	3	0.08	4	0.11	2	0.4	7	0.1
Rotation	12	0.18	2	0.5	5	0.14	7	0.2	2	0.4	18	0.25
Promotion												
Within firm	14	0.21	2	0.5	5	0.14	7	0.2	0	0	15	0.21
To parent firm	11	0.16	0	0	9	0.24	3	0.09	0	0	17	0.23
To the other firm within bureaucratic hierarchy	2	0.03	0	0	0	0	0	0	0	0	0	0
Subtotal	27	0.4	2	0.5	14	0.38	10	0.29	0	0	32	0.44
To government entities												
Industry bureau	3	0.04	0	0	5	0.14	5	0.14	0	0	6	0.08
Administration division	5	0.07	0	0	1	0.03	1	0.03	0	0	3	0.04
Governor of government	0	0	0	0	0	0	2	0.06	0	0	0	0
Subtotal	8	0.11	0	0	6	0.17	8	0.23	0	0	9	0.12
Imprisonment	6	0.09	0	0	6	0.16	6	0.17	1	0.2	4	0.05
Others												
As board director	6	0.09	0	0	1	0.03	0	0	0	0	3	0.04
As party sectary/supervisory committee/honorary position	2	0.03	0	0	2	0.05	0	0	0	0	0	0
Subtotal	8	0.12	0	0	3	0.08	0	0	0	0	3	0.04
Total	68	1	4	1	37	1	35	1	5	1	73	1

[a]Money unit = 1 million RMB.
[b]Regulated industry.

CEOs at the middle level — the city level or provincial level — are more likely to enter governments or be imprisoned.

Panel B of Table 2 presents the distribution of the sample by regions ranked by local GDPs.[13] The frequency of promotion (50%) is the highest in the poorest area, the North, where the market is undeveloped and market forces are weakest. The frequency of demotion or imprisonment is higher in the richer areas of the Northeast and East. The potential reasons are that the regulations and legal enforcement are more effective in more developed areas. The frequency of entering government is 21% in the less developed area — the Southwest.

Panel C of Table 2 describes the distribution of the sample by industries according to the one-digit Chinese SEC code. The table shows that promotion is more common in the regulated industries. For example, there are 41% of CEOs being promoted in the mining (B) industry, 59% in the power, oil, and water (D) industries, 44% in the transportation (F) industry, and 50% in the banking and finance (I) industries. In strategic industries such as telecoms (G) and banking and finance (I), the rotation of key personnel is more frequent. The agricultural production (A) and media and communications (L) industries have a lower frequency of promotion and a higher frequency of demotion. In the heavy construction (E) and transportation (F) industries, which are critical to the national economy, and in the social service and infrastructure (K) industries, chairmen and CEOs are more frequently appointed as government officials, and are also most frequently appointed as top-ranking government leaders. Criminal conduct most frequently occurs in the real estate (J), social service and infrastructure (K), and media and communications (L) industries. This implies that managerial misconduct in these industries carries a greater litigation risk. In summary, the results imply that promotion is the most frequently used incentive scheme in the higher bureaucratic layers of government control and in the poorer or undeveloped regions and regulated industries where the market is less free.

Panel A of Table 3 reports the descriptive statistics for the sample firms and shows the tests of differences. A control group consists of firms without CEO turnover. The comparison is between firms with different incentive schemes and the control group. The first two variables are firm-specific accounting measures of firm performance used in previous studies (Chang & Wong, 2004; Engel et al., 2003; Kato & Long, 2006; Weisbach, 1988). Firms in which the departing manager was promoted on average demonstrate both positive current performance (ROA_{it}) and positive lagged performance (ROA_{it-1}). The average lagged performance (ROA_{it-1}) is

Table 3. Summary Statistics for Incentive Plans, Firm Performance Measures, and Other Variables.

	Control group Mean	Demotion Mean	Demotion Diff. (t-test)	Rotation Mean	Rotation Diff. (t-test)	Promotion Mean	Promotion Diff. (t-test)	Government Mean	Government Diff. (t-test)	Imprisonment Mean	Imprisonment Diff. (t-test)	Other Mean	Other Diff. (t-test)
Panel A: Preceding firm performance and characteristics													
ROA_{it}	0.029	0.017	−0.012(2.09**)	0.017	−0.012(1.92*)	0.029	0(−0.06)	0.027	−0.002(0.23)	0.014	−0.015(1.12)	0.015	−0.014(2.43**)
ROA_{it-1}	0.03	0.018	−0.012(1.78*)	0.03	0(−0.01)	0.037	0.007(−2.39**)	0.031	0.001(−0.15)	0.026	−0.004(0.24)	0.01	−0.02(2.55**)
RPE_{it-1}	0.0001	−0.008	−0.008(1.28)	0	−0.0001(0.12)	0.006	0.006(−2.01**)	−0.003	−0.0031(0.45)	−0.002	−0.002(0.12)	−0.019	−0.02(2.28**)
$Size_{it}$	21.44	21.22	−0.22(2.33**)	21.3	−0.14(1.66*)	21.45	0.01(−0.07)	21.38	−0.06(0.56)	21.48	0.04(−0.22)	21.21	−0.23(1.41)
DA_{it}	0.061	0.049	−0.012(0.95)	0.036	−0.025(2.87***)	0.056	−0.005(0.87)	0.047	−0.014(1.25)	0.067	0.006(−0.50)	0.081	0.02(−0.92)
$Ownership_{it}$	0.338	0.347	0.009(−0.30)	0.374	0.036(−1.96**)	0.338	0(0.06)	0.318	−0.02(1.18)	0.322	−0.016(0.57)	0.289	−0.05(1.65)
$Indusmb_{it}$	2.333	2.533	0.2(−1.59)	2.626	0.293(−2.06**)	2.434	0.101(−1.67*)	2.458	0.125(−1.07)	2.482	0.149(−0.89)	2.241	−0.092(0.70)
Age	48.82	44.92	−3.9(4.63***)	45.73	−3.09(3.91***)	47.1	−1.72(3.17***)	46.1	−2.72(3.62***)	44.97	−3.85(2.84***)	45.71	−3.11(2.22**)
$Employee_{it}$	7.588	7.088	−0.5(2.34**)	7.135	−0.453(2.50**)	7.453	−0.135(1.32)	7.27	−0.318(1.92*)	7.398	−0.19(0.70)	7.635	0.047(−0.17)
GDP_{it}	7433.2	7629.6	196.4(−.27)	7651.6	218.4(−.31)	6359.7	−1074(3.66***)	7493.7	60.5(−.05)	9488.7	2055.5(−2.49**)	8060.6	627.4(−.64)
HHI_{it}	0.075	0.07	−0.005(0.85)	0.077	0.002(−0.15)	0.079	0.004(−0.74)	0.095	0.02(−1.75*)	0.09	0.015(−0.94)	0.056	−0.019(4.03***)
Panel B: Post-firm value													
Tobin q 0 yr after turnover	1.692	1.591	−0.101(1.18)	1.655	−0.037(0.43)	1.834	0.142(−1.79*)	1.825	0.133(−1.23)	1.622	−0.07(0.62)	1.608	−0.084(0.50)
Tobin q 1 yr after turnover	1.628	1.445	−0.183(2.75***)	1.616	−0.012(0.14)	1.692	0.064(−0.82)	1.777	0.149(−1.40)	1.639	0.011(−0.10)	1.483	−0.145(0.99)
Tobin q 2 yr after turnover	1.823	1.59	−0.233(2.71***)	1.768	−0.055(0.63)	1.805	−0.018(0.22)	2.048	0.225(−1.62)	1.706	−0.117(1.13)	1.568	−0.255(2.04**)
Tobin q 3 yr after turnover	1.998	1.792	−0.206(1.85*)	1.943	−0.055(0.61)	1.95	−0.048(0.64)	2.133	0.135(−1.08)	1.892	−0.106(0.77)	1.59	−0.408(4.31***)
Obs. #	1,621	49		63		193		71		35		24	

This table presents the mean values of firm performance measures and other variables for the subsample of incentive plans. consisting of firms in which there was no turnover in those top managers, chairman or CEO, are also provided. Then the difference between the incentive group and control group is computed in the next column with *t*-test in the parenthesis. ***, **, and * indicate statistical significance at 1%, 5%, and 10% levels.

significantly higher in this sample than in the non-turnover sample (t-value $= -2.39$, significant at the 5% level). Firms in which the departing manager was demoted on average underperform those in the non-turnover sample in terms of both current and lagged performance (ROA$_{it}$: t-value $= 2.09$, significant at the 5% level; ROA$_{it-1}$: t-value $= 1.78$, significant at the 10% level). Firms in which the departing manager was assigned to another honorary position also on average underperform those in the non-turnover sample in terms of both measures of firm-specific performance (ROA$_{it}$: t-value $= 2.43$, significant at the 5% level; ROA$_{it-1}$: t-value $= 2.55$, significant at the 5% level). Although the firms in which the departing manager was imprisoned underperform the control group, the difference is not significant.

The next variable of interest is the RPE measure. The lagged performance (RPE$_{it-1}$) is significantly higher in the turnover sample than in the non-turnover sample (t-value $= -2.01$, significant at the 5% level). Firms in which the departing manager was assigned to another honorary position on average underperform the non-turnover group in terms of relative performance (t-value $= 2.28$, significant at the 5% level for RPE$_{it-1}$).

Several of the firm characteristics variables are also associated with management change. Firm size, as proxied by SIZE$_{it}$, has a significant effect on certain incentive schemes, with demotion and rotation occurring significantly more often in smaller firms compared with the control group. However, firm size does not significantly affect the frequency of promotion, entering government, imprisonment, or assignment to another honorary position. DA$_{it}$, which is the debt-to-assets ratio of a firm, is a proxy for leverage risk or financial distress. Firms in which the departing manager was rotated have a significantly lower leverage risk (t-value $= 2.87$, significant at the 1% level). Firms in which the departing manager was promoted also have a lower leverage risk, but the difference is not significant. Firms in which the departing manager was imprisoned have a higher leverage risk, but again the difference is not significant. OWNERSHIP$_{it}$, or the percentage of state ownership ultimately held by the government as a proxy for government ownership, has a limited impact, in that firms in which the departing manager was rotated have a significantly higher level of government ownership (t-value $= -1.96$, significant at the 5% level for OWNERSHIP$_{it}$). There is almost no difference in the level of government ownership between the promotion group and the control sample. None of the other between-group differences are significant.

Indusmb$_{it}$ (industry median market-to-book ratio by two-digit SIC code), which is a surrogate for the investment opportunity set (IOS), has some effect in firms in which the departing manager was promoted or rotated, as their IOS (Indusmb$_{it}$) is significantly higher. There is no significant difference in the values for this variable among the other groups. Excluding natural retirement or termination, Table 3 shows AGE to have some effect, with managers forced to leave office being on average significantly younger than the managers in the control sample. Among those forced to leave or reappointed, however, the promotion group has the highest average age of 47.1 years. This is consistent with the argument of Kale et al. (2009) that when an incumbent chairmen or CEO is close to retirement, the incentive effect of promotion should be stronger. Finally, the remaining variables affecting management change are institutional factors. Employee$_{it}$, which is the log of the number of employees and controls for the effect of non-economic factors on the selection of managers, is significantly lower in the demotion, rotation, and entering government incentive groups. However, there is no significant difference between the promotion group and the control sample. GDP$_{it}$ is the log of local (provincial) GDP and controls for variation in economic conditions across regions (Fan et al., 2007). In the sample of firms in regions with a significantly lower local GDP, which indicates a poorer or undeveloped economic environment, only the promotion incentive is adopted. HHI$_{it}$, which is the industrial HHI by two-digit SIC code and controls for industrial competition, is higher among firms in which the departing manager entered government, indicating that these firms operate in near-monopoly industries. The group of firms in which the departing manager was reassigned to another honorary position are mainly in the more competitive industries with a lower industrial HHI.

RESULTS

Association between Incentive Schemes and Prior Firm Performance

This section presents empirical evidence on the relation between incentive schemes and preceding RPE. Logistic regression model is employed for the data analysis. The dependent variable is the likelihood of an incentive scheme, whether demotion, rotation, promotion, entering government, imprisonment, or being assigned another honorary position, being used. The independent variable is the preceding performance of the firm (preceding RPE), and personal features, institutional factors, and the preceding firm characteristics are included as control variables. Industry dummy and year dummy variables are also included, but for the sake of brevity the results are not reported in the table. Table 4 reports the summary results of the logistic regressions.

There is evidence to support the usefulness of RPE in promotion incentive schemes. After deleting the top and bottom 1% of the distribution for the financial variables used in the regression, the final sample consists of 462 unique SOEs and 2,056 firm-year observations, including all listed SOEs that underwent and did not undergo management change. As reported in the table, the likelihood of promotion is significantly positively associated with the firm's preceding firm-specific accounting performance (coefficient of $ROA_{it-1}= 3.91$; p-value $= 0.093$) and also significantly positively associated with the firm's preceding relative accounting performance (coefficient of $RPE_{it-1}= 3.82$; p-value $= 0.060$). However, its sensitivity to RPE (RPE_{it-1}) is more significant. Among the control variables, GDP_{it-1} is significantly negatively associated with the likelihood of promotion, supporting the usefulness of RPE as an incentive in less developed markets. HHI_{it-1} is significantly positively associated with the likelihood of promotion. This result can be explained by the argument of DeFond and Park (1999) that the usefulness of RPE is greater in highly competitive industries. Previous studies also demonstrate that when firm performance deteriorates, shareholders are likely to discipline managers by demoting them or terminating their positions (Banker & Datar, 1989; Bushman, Chen, Engel, & Smith, 2004; Chang & Wong, 2004; Engel et al., 2003; Holmstrom & Milgrom, 1991; Kato & Long, 2006; Murphy & Zimmerman, 1993; Weisbach, 1988). As suggested by these studies, the likelihood of demotion is negatively associated with the firm's preceding firm-specific accounting performance (coefficient of $ROA_{it-1}= -0.39$), but not significantly so (p-value $= 0.895$), and significantly positively associated with the departing manager's age (coefficient of AGE$= -1.95$; p-value $= 0.075$). In addition, the likelihood of imprisonment is significantly negatively associated with the firm's preceding firm-specific accounting performance (coefficient of $ROA_{it-1}= -3.81$; p-value $= 0.090$). This is consistent with evidence in previous studies that when firms violate regulations or laws, they suffer severe financial distress (Agrawal, Jaffe, & Karpoff, 1999; Sun & Zhang, 2006). Imprisonment is more likely to occur in more developed regions with a higher GDP. This may be because legal enforcement in these regions is stronger. Interestingly, managers demoted or imprisoned are generally younger in age.

Table 4. Regression Results of the Relation between the Incentive Plans and Preceding Firm Performance Measures.

	Demotion		Rotation		Promotion		Government		Imprisonment		Other	
Intercept	7 (0.975)	7.31 (0.974)	-2.82 (0.987)	-2.74 (0.988)	-12.12 (0.948)	-11.83 (0.950)	-13.21 (0.943)	-13.48 (0.941)	-13.94 (0.950)	-14.09 (0.948)	-7.5 (0.969)	-7.69 (0.968)
ROA_{it-1}	-0.39 (0.895)		-0.95 (0.739)		3.19 (0.093*)		-3 (0.147)		-3.81 (0.090*)		-1.46 (0.708)	
RPE_{it-1}		1.13 (0.747)		-0.44 (0.891)		3.82 (0.060**)		-3.62 (0.126)		-4.09 (0.123)		-2.53 (0.552)
$Size_{it-1}$	-0.49 (0.058*)	-0.50 (0.050**)	-0.01 (0.975)	-0.01 (0.954)	0.03 (0.782)	0.03 (0.819)	0.26 (0.174)	0.27 (0.173)	0.39 (0.112)	0.39 (0.116)	-0.36 (0.347)	-0.36 (0.356)
DA_{it-1}	-0.47 (0.840)	-0.45 (0.848)	-3.44 (0.237)	-3.42 (0.239)	-1.63 (0.166)	-1.66 (0.159)	-1.44 (0.463)	-1.44 (0.463)	-0.66 (0.792)	-0.60 (0.810)	3.41 (0.200)	3.45 (0.194)
$Ownership_{it-1}$	0.35 (0.765)	0.34 (0.771)	2.62 (0.004***)	2.61 (0.004***)	-0.52 (0.365)	-0.48 (0.400)	0.15 (0.873)	0.13 (0.888)	-0.95 (0.463)	-1.00 (0.440)	-0.63 (0.724)	-0.67 (0.707)
$Indusmb_{it-1}$	-0.35 (0.266)	-0.35 (0.259)	0.002 (0.991)	0.001 (0.996)	-0.11 (0.516)	-0.12 (0.493)	-0.04 (0.866)	-0.04 (0.882)	-0.07 (0.831)	-0.06 (0.845)	0.18 (0.757)	0.18 (0.751)
Age	-1.95 (0.075*)	-1.97 (0.072*)	-2.45 (0.017**)	-2.45 (0.017**)	-0.01 (0.983)	-0.04 (0.947)	-1.16 (0.201)	-1.12 (0.220)	-2.47 (0.038**)	-2.43 (0.041**)	-0.92 (0.553)	-0.89 (0.569)
$Employee_{it-1}$	-0.09 (0.562)	-0.08 (0.601)	-0.08 (0.567)	-0.07 (0.577)	0.01 (0.874)	0.01 (0.857)	-0.14 (0.221)	-0.14 (0.227)	-0.32 (0.040**)	-0.32 (0.041**)	-0.06 (0.838)	-0.07 (0.827)
GDP_{it-1}	-0.04 (0.889)	-0.04 (0.889)	0.097 (0.718)	0.10 (0.714)	-0.33 (0.008***)	-0.34 (0.007***)	-0.05 (0.807)	-0.05 (0.820)	0.68 (0.038***)	0.68 (0.037***)	-0.27 (0.385)	-0.28 (0.376)
HHI_{it-1}	0.34 (0.915)	0.36 (0.909)	-5.21 (0.120)	-5.19 (0.120)	2.83 (0.058*)	2.86 (0.056*)	3.05 (0.096*)	2.98 (0.105)	-1.5 (0.631)	-1.53 (0.622)	-4.68 (0.596)	-4.78 (0.589)
Year_Dummy	Yes	Yes	Yes	Yes	Yes	Yes	Yes	Yes	Yes	Yes	Yes	Yes
Indus_Dummy	Yes	Yes	Yes	Yes	Yes	Yes	Yes	Yes	Yes	Yes	Yes	Yes
Quasi R-square	0.01	0.01	0.03	0.03	0.02	0.02	0.01	0.01	0.01	0.01	0.01	0.01
Obs. #	2,056		2,056		2,056		2,056		2,056		2,056	

This table reports the results of a logistic regression. The dependent variable is the likelihood of one of incentive plans – demotion, rotation, promotion, entering government, imprisonment, or others. The independent variables include the preceding firm performance (preceding RPE) and the preceding firm characteristics, personal feature, and institutional factors as control variables. The industry dummy and year dummy variables are also included, but for the sake of brevity, their results are not reported in the table. ***, **, and * indicate statistical significance at 1%, 5%, and 10% levels.

Incentive Schemes and Subsequent Firm Performance

Univariate Tests

Panel B of Table 3 shows that the average Tobin's q for the promotion group of firms is higher, and the difference is positively significant. Table 3 reports the descriptive statistics for the sample firms using between-group mean tests. As in Panel A, where the sample consisting of firms in which there was no management change is taken as the control group, the average firm performance after the adoption of an incentive scheme is reported and its difference from the average for the control sample is tested. The average Tobin's q is highest in the year of promotion among all firms in the management change sample and significantly higher than the control group. The average Tobin's q 1 year, 2 years, and 3 years after promotion remains high, and is second only to that of the entering government incentive, although the difference is not significant. Although the entering government group has the highest Tobin's q over the long term, the difference is not significant. In contrast, the demotion group has the lowest post Tobin's q. The average Tobin's q 1 or 2 years after demotion is significantly lower than that of the control group (significant at the 1% level). The average Tobin's q 3 years after demotion is also significantly lower than that of the control group, although at the 10% significance level. The reassignment to another honorary position group also has a lower post Tobin's q that is significantly lower than that of the control group 2 or 3 years after incentive implementation (both significant at the 1% level). In summary, disciplinary mechanisms such as demotion provide a weaker management incentive, whereas promotion and entering government may provide a stronger incentive under the Chinese political hierarchy, which is characterized by a lack of free-market conditions or competitive managerial labor market.

Regression Results

Regression analyses are performed to examine the effects of incentive schemes with RPE on firm performance (post-performance). The dependent variable is post-performance, which is the average Tobin's q 1 year, 2 years, or 3 years after the incentive scheme was implemented. The independent variables include dummy variables for the incentive schemes, RPE, and the interaction between an incentive scheme and RPE. When an incentive scheme is chosen as the test variable, the remaining schemes are included as control variables. For example, when "promotion" is the test variable, the dummy variables of demotion, rotation, entering government, imprisonment, and assignment to another position are included as control variables. The industry dummy and year dummy variables are also included, but for the sake of brevity are not reported in the table.

Using the sample of all listed SOEs that underwent and did not undergo management changes, the multivariate regression results show no significant evidence that promotion with RPE is positively associated with the post Tobin's q. The dummy variable for promotion is positively associated with the Tobin's q 1, 2, and 3 years after the implementation of the incentive scheme (coefficients are 0.08, 0.06, 0.05, respectively), but not significantly so. The association between the interaction of promotion and RPE is mixed and insignificant. As with "promotion," the dummy variable for entering government is also positively and insignificantly associated with the post Tobin's q. Interestingly, the interaction of entering government and RPE is significantly and negatively associated with the Tobin's q 2 years after implementation. Although it improves firm performance significantly, the entering government incentive relies less on the use of RPE. In the regression, the dummy variable for demotion is negatively associated with the post Tobin's q, but not significantly so. The dummy variable for rotation is significantly and negatively associated with the Tobin's q 1, 2, and 3 years after implementation. The interaction of rotation and RPE is significantly and negatively associated with the Tobin's q 1 year after implementation. These findings imply that rotation, which also relies less on RPE, decreases a firm's post-change performance. Overall, rotation provides a significantly weaker management incentive. Consistent with the statistics in Panel B of Table 3, demotion provides a weaker incentive, but not significantly so. Promotion and entering government provide a stronger incentive, but again not significantly so (Table 5).

To provide more evidence on the effect of incentive schemes with RPE, the whole sample is partitioned into two subsamples according to the level of market competition in the region or provincial unit. The regression model testing the effect of promotion in the section "Incentive schemes and subsequent firm performance" runs again. Again, the independent variables include a dummy variable for promotion, RPE, the interaction of promotion and RPE, dummy variables for the other incentive schemes, an industry dummy, and year dummies.

Table 6 shows that promotion and the interaction of promotion with RPE are significantly positively associated with the post Tobin's q in regions with weak market-based competition. Panel A partitions the sample into high- and low-competition subsamples by the yearly median value of the number of firms listed in a given region (province) (La Porta, Lopez-de-Silanes, Shleifer, & Vishny, 1997). The results show that the dummy

Table 5. Regression Analyses of the Effect of the Incentive Plans with RPE on the Post-firm Performance in a Full Sample.

Independent Variables	Intercept	X						RPE_{it-1}	$X \times RPE_{it-1}$	Incentive_ Dummy	Year_ Dummy	Indus_ Dummy	Adj. R-square	Obs. #
		Demotion	Rotation	Promotion	Government	Imprisonment	Other							
Panel A: Dependent variable is Tobin q 1 year after the turnover														
	1.69	-0.15						1.44	0.27	Yes	Yes	Yes	0.14	2,056
	(<.001***)	(-1.00)						(0.001***)	(0.950)					
	1.7		-0.33					1.56	-10.91	Yes	Yes	Yes	0.14	2,056
	(<.001***)		(0.014***)					(<.001***)	(0.012***)					
	1.69			0.08				1.54	-1.72	Yes	Yes	Yes	0.14	2,056
	(<.001***)			(0.293)				(<.001***)	(0.343)					
	1.69				0.09			1.55	-2.78	Yes	Yes	Yes	0.14	2,056
	(<.001***)				(0.44)			(<.001***)	(0.209)					
	1.69					-0.11		1.46	-0.27	Yes	Yes	Yes	0.14	2,056
	(<.001***)					(0.507)		(<.001***)	(0.889)					
	1.69						0.05	1.42	6.01	Yes	Yes	Yes	0.14	2,056
	(<.001***)						(0.813)	(<.001***)	(0.419)					
Panel B: Dependent variable is Tobin q 2 year after the turnover														
	-0.14							1.14	0.41	Yes	Yes	Yes	0.23	2,056
	1.47	(0.356)						(0.013***)	(0.929)					
	(<.001***)													
	1.47		-0.39					1.21	-5.61	Yes	Yes	Yes	0.23	2,056
	(<.001***)		(0.006***)					(0.009***)	(0.227)					
	1.47			0.06				1.18	-0.64	Yes	Yes	Yes	0.23	2,056
	(<.001***)			(0.484)				(0.012***)	(0.739)					
	1.47				0.21			1.36	-5.61	Yes	Yes	Yes	0.23	2,056
	(<.001***)				(0.100*)			(0.004***)	(0.017**)					
	1.47					-0.25		1.15	0.01	Yes	Yes	Yes	0.23	2,056
	(<.001***)					(0.138)		(0.015**)	(0.955)					
	1.47						-0.15	1.12	7.06	Yes	Yes	Yes	0.23	2,056
	(<.001***)						(0.525)	(0.014***)	(0.374)					

Panel C: Dependent variable is Tobin q 3 year after the turnover

1.27	−0.15	1.03	−0.59	Yes	Yes	Yes	0.25	2,056
(<.001***)	(0.279)	(0.015**)	(0.889)					
1.27	−0.29	1.06	−3.65	Yes	Yes	Yes	0.25	2,056
(<.001***)	(0.029**)	(0.012***)	(0.392)					
1.27	0.05	1.01	0.26	Yes	Yes	Yes	0.25	2,056
(<.001***)	(0.487)	(0.020**)	(0.885)					
1.27	0.15	1.08	−1.49	Yes	Yes	Yes	0.25	2,056
(<.001***)	(0.195)	(0.012***)	(0.493)					
1.27	−0.22	1.14	−2.29	Yes	Yes	Yes	0.25	2,056
(<.001***)	(0.153)	(0.008***)	(0.221)					
1.27	−0.27	1	8.76	Yes	Yes	Yes	0.25	2,056
(<.001***)	(0.218)	(0.018**)	(0.230)					

This table reports the results of a multivariate regression. The dependent variable is post-performance – the average Tobin's q of 1 year, 2 years, or 3 years after the incentive plan being implemented. The independent variables include the dummy variable of one incentive scheme (X), relative performance evaluation (RPE), and interaction of the incentive scheme (X) and RPE. If one incentive scheme is chosen as test variable, then the remainders are included as control variables. For example, when the "promotion" is the test variable, the remainders – the dummy variable of demotion, rotation, entering government, imprisonment, or others are the control variables. The industry dummy and year dummy variables are also included, but for the sake of brevity, their results are not reported in the table. ***, **, and * indicate statistical significance at 1%, 5%, and 10% levels.

Table 6.   Regression Analyses of the Effect of the Promotion Incentive with RPE on the Post-Firm Performance in a Subsample Partitioned by the Extent of Market Competition of the Region.

	Tobin q 1 yr after Turnover		Tobin q 2 yr after Turnover		Tobin q 3yr after Turnover	
	High	Low	High	Low	High	Low

Panel A: Partition the sample into high- and low-competitive region according to the number of listed firms in the region of year (La Porta et al., 1997)

Intercept	1.64	2.08	1.38	1.91	1.12	1.71
	(< .001***)	(< .001***)	(< .001***)	(< .001***)	(< .001***)	(< .001***)
Promotion	−0.01	0.35	0.02	0.29	0.04	0.09
	(0.890)	(0.040**)	(0.852)	(0.089*)	(0.631)	(0.574)
RPE_{it-1}	1.41	1.67	1.23	0.48	1.09	0.34
	(0.003***)	(0.226)	(0.014***)	(0.736)	(0.017**)	(0.803)
Promotion*RPE_{it-1}	−2.61	17.57	−1.51	13.55	−0.46	6.93
	(0.154)	(0.026**)	(0.445)	(0.096*)	(0.798)	(0.372)
Incentive_Dummy	Yes	Yes	Yes	Yes	Yes	Yes
Year_Dummy	Yes	Yes	Yes	Yes	Yes	Yes
Indus_Dummy	Yes	Yes	Yes	Yes	Yes	Yes
Adj. R-square	0.15	0.15	0.23	0.24	0.25	0.24
Obs. #	1,646	410	1,646	410	1,646	410

Panel B: Partition the sample into high- and low-competitive region according to the stock market capitalization in the region of year (La Porta et al., 1997)

Intercept	1.7	2.05	1.32	1.97	1.06	1.74
	(< .001***)	(< .001***)	(0.001***)	(0.001***)	(0.004***)	(< .001***)
Promotion	−0.01	0.31	−0.01	0.31	0.04	0.16
	(0.930)	(0.072*)	(0.898)	(0.070*)	(0.670)	(0.318)
RPE_{it-1}	1.19	2.75	1.21	0.35	1.06	0.25
	(0.011***)	(0.033**)	(0.019**)	(0.779)	(0.024**)	(0.833)
Promotion*RPE_{it-1}	−2.44	18.86	−1.56	16.79	−0.46	9.74
	(0.178)	(0.026**)	(0.436)	(0.040**)	(0.800)	(0.204)
Incentive_Dummy	Yes	Yes	Yes	Yes	Yes	Yes
Year_Dummy	Yes	Yes	Yes	Yes	Yes	Yes
Indus_Dummy	Yes	Yes	Yes	Yes	Yes	Yes
Adj. R-square	0.15	0.13	0.23	0.23	0.26	0.23
Obs. #	1,628	428	1,628	428	1,628	428

Panel C: Partition the sample into high- and low-competitive region according to the number of initial public offerings of equity in a region of year (La Porta et al., 1997)

Intercept	1.70	1.96	1.42	1.53	1.15	1.34
	(< .001***)	(< .001***)	(< .001***)	(< .001***)	(< .001***)	(0.001***)
Promotion	−0.005	0.02	−0.05	0.14	0.03	0.03
	(0.958)	(0.893)	(0.540)	(0.424)	(0.777)	(0.879)
RPE_{it-1}	1.00	1.98	0.19	2.82	−0.03	3.91
	(0.03**)	(0.025**)	(0.675)	(0.010***)	(0.943)	(0.002***)
Promotion*RPE_{it-1}	−1.89	1.69	−0.19	2.69	0.67	3.54
	(0.278)	(0.686)	(0.911)	(0.601)	(0.710)	(0.553)
Incentive_Dummy	Yes	Yes	Yes	Yes	Yes	Yes
Year_Dummy	Yes	Yes	Yes	Yes	Yes	Yes
Indus_Dummy	Yes	Yes	Yes	Yes	Yes	Yes
Adj. R-square	0.16	0.20	0.20	0.16	0.21	0.19
Obs. #	1,767	289	1,767	289	1,767	289

Table 6. (*Continued*)

Panel D: Partition the sample into high- and low-competitive region according to the regional HHI of year (DeFond &
Park, 1999)

Intercept	1.46	1.70	0.99	1.60	0.77	1.37
	(< .001***)	(< .001***)	(0.012***)	(< .001***)	(0.033**)	(< .001***)
Promotion	−0.05	0.46	−0.03	0.32	0.03	0.13
	(0.557)	(0.001***)	(0.739)	(0.05**)	(0.709)	(0.403)
RPE_{it-1}	1.67	0.59	1.47	−0.28	1.24	0.48
	(0.001***)	(0.543)	(0.005***)	(0.801)	(0.011***)	(0.639)
Promotion*RPE_{it-1}	−3.08	8.64	−1.81	7.63	−0.80	6.50
	(0.117)	(0.085*)	(0.376)	(0.188)	(0.672)	(0.215)
Incentive_Dummy	Yes	Yes	Yes	Yes	Yes	Yes
Year_Dummy	Yes	Yes	Yes	Yes	Yes	Yes
Indus_Dummy	Yes	Yes	Yes	Yes	Yes	Yes
Adj. R-square	0.15	0.11	0.23	0.24	0.25	0.28
Obs. #	1,524	532	1,524	532	1,524	532

The dependent variable is post-performance − the average Tobin's q of 1 year, 2 years, or 3 years after the adoption of incentive plan. The independent variables include the dummy variable of promotion incentive, relative performance evaluation (RPE), and interaction of the promotion incentive and RPE. Then the remainders − the dummy variable of demotion, rotation, entering government, imprisonment, or others are included as control variables. The industry dummy and year dummy variables are also included. Panel A partitions the sample into high- and low-competition subsamples by the yearly median value of the number of firms listed in a given region (province) (La Porta et al., 1997). Panel B partitions the sample by the yearly median value of stock market capitalization in a region (province) (La Porta et al., 1997). Panel C divides the sample by the yearly median value of the number of initial public offerings of equity in a region (province) (La Porta et al., 1997). Panel D partitions the sample by the yearly median value of the regional Herfindahl-Hirschman Index (HHI) in a region (province) (DeFond & Park, 1999). ***, **, and * indicate statistical significance at 1%, 5%, and 10% levels.

variable for promotion is significantly and positively associated with the Tobin's q 1 and 2 years after management change if there are fewer listed firms in a region, which indicates that the market is undeveloped and less competitive. The interaction of promotion and RPE is also significantly positive for the Tobin's q 1 and 2 years after implementation in undeveloped and less competitive regions (the effect of Promotion*RPE_{it-1} on the Tobin's q 1 year after implementation is 17.57 with a p-value of 0.026, and that of the Tobin's q 2 years after implementation is 13.55 with a p-value of 0.096). However, the positive effect of promotion with RPE does not persist nor is it significant for firms in regions with a greater number of listed firms. Panel B partitions the sample by the yearly median value of stock market capitalization in a region (province) (La Porta et al., 1997).[14] The results show that the dummy variable for promotion and the interaction of promotion and RPE are significantly positively associated with the Tobin's q 1 and 2 years after implementation for firms in regions with a lower stock market capitalization in which the market is undeveloped and less competitive. Consistent with Panel A, the positive effect of promotion with RPE does not persist nor is it significant for firms in regions with a higher stock market capitalization. Panel C divides the sample by the yearly median value of the number of initial public offerings of equity in a region (province) (La Porta et al., 1997). The results show that the dummy variable for promotion and the interaction of promotion and RPE are positive, but not significantly so, if fewer firms issue IPOs in a given region (province), thus implying a less developed market. However, the dummy variable for promotion and the interaction of promotion and RPE are negative and not significant when more firms issue IPOs in a region (province). Panel D partitions the sample by the yearly median value of the regional HHI in a region (province) (DeFond & Park, 1999).[15] Differing from the aforementioned partitioning scenarios, a higher HHI index indicates a monopoly or a less competitive market, whereas a value close to zero indicates near perfect competition. The results show that the dummy variable for promotion and the interaction of promotion and RPE are significantly positively associated with the Tobin's q 1 year after the implementation of an incentive scheme or management change for firms in regions with a higher HHI and thus an undeveloped and less competitive market. The positive effect of promotion with RPE on the Tobin's q 2 and 3 years after implementation remains, but is not significant. Consistently, the effect of promotion with RPE on post-performance is negative and insignificant for firms in regions with a lower HHI. Partitioning the sample provides evidence that promotion with RPE is a stronger management incentive in regions lacking market-based competition.

CONCLUSION

The primary motivation for this study is to empirically examine the incentives and usefulness of RPE for incentives in an emerging market lack of market competition. A sample of Chinese SOEs is used for testing this argument for two reasons. First, China's SOEs are affiliated with governments without free-market conditions and competitive managerial labor market. Second, the Chinese government formally incorporates RPE in the control mechanisms for administration.

The findings of this study show that promotion is the most frequently used for incentives in SOEs. Regression analysis shows that promotion is more significantly associated with a firm's preceding RPE. Then the effects of promotion on firm performance after a CEO turnover is examined, and the results show that promotion results in a higher Tobin's q than other incentive schemes. Further, we conduct the tests based on subsamples partitioned by the level of market competition and find that the promotion is significantly and positively associated with Tobin's q 1 and 2 years in subsequent periods in regions with fewer listed firms, a lower stock market capitalization, or a higher regional HHI, implying the promotion provides a positive incentive in an undeveloped and less competitive market.

NOTES

1. Besley and Case (1996) indicate that voters choose whether or not to reelect officials based on their performance while in office, using neighboring jurisdictions to evaluate the performance of the incumbent based on tax competition.

2. Although many SOEs are listed on the stock market, some or all of their state assets or shares are non-transferable. The restrictions on trading shares means that businesses are less subject to market forces.

3. In China, personnel control is centralized in the hands of the Communist Party of China (CPC) and the government. The State-owned Assets Supervision and Administration Commission (SASAC), authorized by the CCP at the state or local level and the government, takes responsibility for this as an investor of state-owned assets on behalf of the central or local government, and one of its tasks is to select and appoint the management of state-owned enterprises (please refer to the Web page of the SASAC at www.sasac.gov.cn for more details).

4. Since the mid-1990s, China's private sector, which is relatively free of the Party's control, has grown into a large employer in the labor market, and there is thus a possibility for officials to quit the government and be employed by private firms.

5. The chairman of the board of an SOE may be promoted to a leading position in the local or central government, such as Vice Mayor, Vice Province Governor, or State Secretary.

6. By analyzing 247 mayors of 1986 in China, Li and Bachman (1989) find that more than 80 percent have worked in industrial fields and taken the superior position such as factory director. They state that elites will be co-opted to serve in various formal organizations and will be expected to defend and advance institutional interests.

7. Chen, Li, and Zhou (2005) find that the turnover of provincial leaders hinges on provincial economic performance relative to their immediate predecessors.

8. More precisely, under the Chinese political hierarchy, the State Assets Supervision and Administration Commission (SASAC) governs China's SOEs on behalf of the state or local government. SOEs officially report their operational performance to the SASAC in their respective jurisdiction, and the SASAC at the local level reports directly to the administrative level of the SASAC directly above it. The SASAC of the State Council reports directly to the State Council.

9. The SASAC's mandate includes the drafting of laws and regulations regarding state-owned assets, the management of state assets, and the hiring and firing of the top executives of SOEs.

10. The four direct-ruled municipalities are Beijing, Shanghai, Tianjing, and Chongqing. The 22 provinces are Heibei, Shanxi, Liaoning, Jilin, Heilongjiang, Jiangsu, Zhejiang, Anhui, Fujian, Jiangxi, Shandong, Henan, Hubei, Hunan, Guangdong, Hainan, Sichuan, Guizhou, Yunnan, Shanxi, Gansu, and Qinghai. The five autonomous regions are Inner Mongolia, Guangxi, Tibet, Ningxia, and Xinjiang.

11. The industrial HHI is calculated by squaring the market share of each firm competing in an industry and then summing the resulting numbers. It is expressed as $HHI = s1^2 + s2^2 + s3^2 + \cdots + sn^2$, where sn is the market share of the ith firm in the industry. The closer a market is to being a monopoly, the higher its level of ownership concentration (and the weaker its competition). If, for example, there were only one firm in an industry, then that firm would have a 100% market share, and the HHI would equal 10,000 (100^2), indicating a monopoly. In contrast, if there were thousands of firms competing in an industry, then each would have a nearly 0% market share, and the HHI would be close to zero, indicating near perfect competition.

12. There are several layers of government ownership: central, provincial, municipal, and county (please see details in Appendix). Save for the central level, the other levels are called local government ownership. As central government ownership of such companies as energy or defense-related firms is considered key to national security, the central government maintains significant absolute or relative controlling stakes in these enterprises, and central government ownership occupies a substantial share of the economy.

13. According to the *Government Yearbook*, China is partitioned into six administrative areas: North, which consists of five provincial units (Beijing, Tianjing, Heibei, Shanxi, and Inner Mongolia); Northeast, which consists of three provincial units (Liaoning, Jilin, and Heilongjiang); East, which consists of seven provincial units (Shanghai, Jiangsu, Zhejiang, Anhui, Fujian, Jiangxi, and Shandong); Central, which consists of six provincial units (Henan, Hubei, Hunan, Guangdong, Guangxi, and Hainan); Southwest, which consists of five provincial units (Chongqing, Sichuan, Guizhou, Yunnan, and Tibet); and Northwest, which consists of five provincial units (Shanxi, Gansu, Qinghai, Ningxia, and Xinjiang). The less developed areas are poorer, with a lower GDP.

14. Stock market capitalization is the number of shares times the market price per share (if the state shares are non-tradable, then the market price of tradable shares is used as the market price per share).

15. The regional HHI is calculated by squaring the market share of each firm competing in a region or provincial unit, and then summing the resulting numbers. It is expressed as $HHI = s1^2 + s2^2 + s3^2 + \cdots + sn^2$, where sn is the market share of the ith firm in a region or provincial unit. The closer a market is to being a monopoly, the higher its level of ownership concentration (and the weaker its competition). If, for example, there were only one firm in a region or provincial unit, that firm would have a 100% market share, and the HHI would equal 10,000 (100^2), indicating a monopoly. In contrast, if there were thousands of firms competing, then each would have a nearly 0% market share, and the HHI would be close to zero, indicating near perfect competition.

ACKNOWLEDGMENTS

Thanks to discussants and participants at 2008 American Accounting Association annual meeting and the 18th Annual Conference on Pacific Basin Finance, Economics, Accounting, and Management (PBEAM) at Beijing.

REFERENCES

Aggarwal, R. K., & Samwick, A. A. (1999). Executive compensation, strategic competition, and relative performance evaluation: Theory and evidence. *Journal of Finance, 54,* 1999–2043.

Agrawal, A., Jaffe, J. F., & Karpoff, J. M. (1999). Management turnover and governance changes following the revelation of fraud. *Journal of Law and Economics, 43*(April), 309–342.

Alchian, A. (1965). Some economics of property rights. *Il Politicao, 30,* 816–829.

Antle, R., & Smith, A. (1986). An empirical investigation of the relative performance evaluation of corporate executives. *Journal of Accounting Research, 24,* 1–39.

Ball, R., Kothari, S. P., & Robin, A. (2000). The effect of international institutional factors on properties of accounting earnings. *Journal of Accounting and Economics, 29,* 1–51.

Ball, R., Robin, A., & Wu, J. (2003). Accounting standards, the institutional environment and issuer incentives: Effect on timely loss recognition in China. *Asia Pacific Journal of Accounting and Economics, 7,* 71–96.

Banker, R. D., & Datar, S. M. (1989). Sensitivity, precision, and linear aggregation of signals for performance evaluation. *Journal of Accounting Research, 27,* 21–39.

Barro, J. R., & Robert, J. B. (1990). Pay, performance, and turnover of bank CEOs. *Journal of Labor Economics, 8,* 48–481.

Berry, T. K., Bizjak, J. M., Lemmon, M. L., & Naveen, L. (2006). Organizational complexity and CEO labor markets: Evidence from diversified firms. *Journal of Corporate Finance, 12,* 797–817.

Besley, T., & Case, A. (1996). Does electoral accountability affect economic policy choices? Evidence from gubernatorial term limits. *The Quarterly Journal of Economics, 110*(3), 769–798.

Brickley, J. A. (2003). Empirical research on CEO turnover and firm-performance: A discussion. *Journal of Accounting and Economics, 36,* 227–233.

Bushman, R., Chen, Q., Engel, E., & Smith, A. (2004). Financial accounting information, organizational complexity and corporate governance systems. *Journal of Accounting and Economics, 37*(2), 167–201.

Bushman, R., & Piotroski, J. D. (2006). Financial reporting incentives for conservative accounting: The influence of legal and political institutions. *Journal of Accounting and Economics, 42,* 107–148.

Cannella, A. A., Fraser, D. R., & Lee, D. S. (1995). Firm failure and managerial labor markets evidence from Texas banking. *Journal of Financial Economics, 38,* 185–210.

Chang, E. C., & Wong, S. M. L. (2004). *Chief executive officer turnovers and the performance of China's listed enterprises.* Hong Kong Institute of Economics and Business Strategy Working Paper No. 1113.

Chen, Y., Li, H., & Zhou, L. (2005). Relative performance evaluation and the turnover of provincial leaders in China. *Economics Letters, 88*, 421–425.

DeFond, L. M., & Park, C. W. (1999). The effect of competition on CEO turnover. *Journal of Accounting and Economics, 27*, 35–56.

Diamond, D. W., & Verrechia, R. E. (1982). Optimal managerial contracts and equilibrium security prices. *Journal of Finance, 37*, 275–287.

Dye, R. (1992). Relative performance evaluation and project selection. *Journal of Accounting Research, 30*, 27–52.

Engel, E., Hayes, R. M., & Wang, X. (2003). CEO turnover and properties of accounting information. *Journal of Accounting and Economics, 36*, 197–226.

Fama, E. F., & Jensen, M. C. (1983). Separation of ownership and control. *Journal of Law & Economics, 26*(2), 301–325.

Fan, J. P. H., Wong, T. J., & Zhang, T. (2007). Politically connected CEOs, corporate governance, and Post-IPO performance of China's newly partially privatized firms. *Journal of Financial Economics, 84*(2), 330–357.

Fan, J., & Wong, T. J. (2002). Corporate ownership structure and the informativeness of accounting earnings in East Asia. *Journal of Accounting and Economics, 33*, 401–425.

Garvey, G. T., & Milbourn, T. (2003). Incentive compensation when executives can hedge the market: Evidence of relative performance evaluation in the cross-section. *Journal of Finance, 58*(4), 1557–1582.

Gibbons, R., & Murphy, K. (1990). Relative performance evaluation and chief executive officers. *Industrial and Labor Relations, 43*(Special issue), 30–51.

Gibbs, M. (1996). *Promotion and incentives.* Chicago, IL: Mimeo, University of Chicago.

Gilson, S. C. (1990). Management turnover and financial distress. *Journal of Financial Economics, 25*, 241–262.

Groves, T., Hong, Y., McMillan, J., & Naughton, B. (1995). China's evolving managerial labor market. *Journal of Political Economy, 103*, 873–892.

Holmstrom, B. (1979). Moral hazard and observability. *Bell Journal of Economics, 10*, 74–91.

Holmstrom, B. (1982). Moral hazard in teams. *Bell Journal of Economics, 13*, 324–340.

Holmstrom, B., & Milgrom, P. (1991). Multitask principal-agent analyses: Incentives contracts, asset ownership, and job design. *Journal of Law, Economics and Organization, 7*, 24–52.

Huang, Y. (1998). *The industrial organization of Chinese government.* Harvard University Working Paper No. 99-076.

Huson, M. R., Malatesta, P. H., & Parrino, R. (2004). Managerial succession and firm performance. *Journal of Financial Economics, 74*, 237–275.

Janakiraman, S., Lambert, R., & Larcker, D. (1992). An empirical investigation of the relative performance evaluation hypothesis. *Journal of Accounting Research, 30*, 53–69.

Jensen, M., & Meckling, W. (1976). Theory of the firm: Managerial behavior, agency costs and ownership structure. *Journal of Financial Economics, 3*, 305–360.

Jensen, M., & Meckling, W. (1979). Rights and production functions: An application to labor-managed firms and codetermination. *Journal of Business, 52*, 469–506.

Kale, J. R., Reis, E., & Venkateswaran, A. (2009). Rank-order tournaments and incentive alignment: The effect on firm performance. *Journal of Finance, 64*(3), 1479–1512.

Kaplan, S. N., & Minton, B. A. (1994). Appointments of outsiders to Japanese boards: Determinants and implications for managers. *Journal of Financial Economics, 36*, 225–258.

Karpoff, J. M., & Rice, E. M. (1989). Organizational form, share Transferability, and firm performance. *Journal of Financial Economics, 24*, 69–105.

Kato, T., & Long, C. (2006). CEO turnover, firm performance and enterprise reform in China: Evidence from new micro data. *IZA Discussion Paper No. 1914.*

La Porta, R., Lopez-de-Silanes, F., Shleifer, A., & Vishny, R. W. (1997). Legal determinants of external finance. *Journal of Finance, 52*(3), 1131–1150.

La Porta, R., Lopez-de-Silanes, F., Shleifer, A., & Vishny, R. W. (2000). Investor protection and corporate governance. *Journal of Financial Economics, 58*(1–2), 3–27.

Laffont, J. (1994). The new economics of regulation ten years after. *Econometrica, 62,* 507–537.

Lazear, E. P., & Rosen, S. (1981). Rank-order tournaments as optimum incentive contracts. *Journal of Political Economy, 89*(5), 841–864.

Li, C., & Bachman, D. (1989). Localism, elitism, and immobilism: Elite formation and social change in post-mao China. *World Politics, 42*(1), 64–94.

Li, H., & Zhou, L. (2005). Political turnover and economic performance: The incentive role of personnel control in China. *Journal of Public Economics, 89,* 1743–1762.

Li, S., Park, S. H., & Li, S. (2004). The great leap forward: The transition from relation-based governance to rule-based governance. *Organizational Dynamics, 33*(1), 63–78.

Maskin, E., Qian, Y., & Xu, C. (2000). Incentives, scale economies, and organization forms. *Review of Economic Studies, 67,* 359–378.

Matsumura, E. M., & Shin, J. Y. (2006). An empirical analysis of an incentive plan with relative performance measures: Evidence from a postal service. *The Accounting Review, 81*(3), 533–566.

Montinola, G., Qian, Y., & Weingast, B. (1995). Federalism, Chinese style: The political basis for economic success in China. *World Politics, 48,* 50–81.

Murphy, K. J., & Zimmerman, J. L. (1993). Financial performance surrounding CEO turnover. *Journal of Accounting and Economics, 16,* 273–315.

Oi, J. (1992). Fiscal reform and the economic foundations of local state corporatism in China. *World Politics, 45,* 99–126.

Opper, S., & Brehm, S. (2007). *Networks versus performance: Political leadership promotion in China.* Working Paper, Lund University.

Qian, Y. (2000). *Government control in corporate governance as a transitional institution: Lessons from China.* Working Paper, University of Maryland.

Qian, Y., & Weingast, B. (1997). Federalism as a commitment to preserving market incentives. *Journal of Economic Perspectives, 11,* 83–92.

Qian, Y., & Xu, C. (1993). Why China's economic reforms differ: The M-form hierarchy and entry/expansion of the non-state sector. *Economics of Transition, 1,* 135–170.

Shleifer, A. (1985). A theory of yardstick competition. *The RAND Journal of Economics, 16*(3), 319–327.

Shleifer, A., & Vishny, R. W. (1986). Large shareholders and corporate control. *Journal of Political Economy, 94,* 461–488.

Smith, C., & Watts, R. (1992). The investment opportunity set and corporate financing, dividend and compensation policies. *Journal of Financial Economics, 32,* 263–292.

Stigler, G. J. (1971). The theory of economic regulation. *The Bell Journal of Economics and Management Science, 2*(1), 3–21.

Sun, P., & Zhang, Y. (2006). *Is there penalty for crime: Corporate scandal and management turnover in China.* EFA 2006 Zurich Meetings Paper, Peking University.

Weisbach, M. S. (1988). Outside directors and CEO turnover. *Journal of Financial Economics, 20,* 431–460.

APPENDIX: THE CHARACTERISTICS OF CHINESE BUREAUCRATIC LAYERS (SOURCE: CHINESE GOVERNMENT YEARBOOKS)

From the bottom to top, there are four layers of administration of SOEs based on the jurisdictions. The provincial units are basic jurisdictional partitions.

County Level

This level is under the jurisdiction of the county level and consists of around 2,148 counties and 48,697 townships.

Municipal Level

This level is under the jurisdiction of the municipal level and consists of around 333 municipalities/cities.

Provincial Level

This level consists of 22 provinces including Heibei, Shanxi, Liaoning, Jilin, Heilongjiang, Jiangsu, Zhejiang, Anhui, Fujian, Jiangxi, Shandong, Henan, Hubei, Hunan, Guangdong, Hainan, Sichuan, Guizhou, Yunnan, Shanxi, Gansu, and Qinghai; the five autonomous regions including Inner Mongolia, Guangxi, Tibet, Ningxia, and Xinjiang; as well as the four "directly ruled municipalities" of Beijing, Tianjin, Shanghai, and Chongqing (Chongqing was affiliated with Sichuan Province before 1997 but has been one of the "directly ruled municipalities" since then).

Central Level

The central level is the ultimate level and the Central Government (guided by the Communist Party) holds the ultimate control rights.

PART III
CONTROL AND OWNERSHIP IN
THE CORPORATE SECTOR

DOES GOVERNMENT CONTROL ALWAYS REDUCE FIRM VALUE? THEORY AND EVIDENCE FROM CHINA

Ping He, Kun Wang and Xing Xiao

ABSTRACT

Purpose — *The goal of this paper is to investigate the relationship between government control and firm value in China.*

Design/methodology/approach — *Government might extract social or political benefits from a state-controlled firm, thus decreases firm value. However, government's monitoring on firm management reduces managers' agency problem, which increases firm value. We first build a game-theoretic model to prove the existence of optimal government control given these two roles of government, and we then employ the OLS regression method to test the theory predictions using the length of intermediate ownership chains connecting the listed state-owned enterprises to their ultimate controllers as the measure of government control.*

Findings — *We find that firm values first increase then decrease as government control weakens. Moreover, we find that government usually*

The Political Economy of Chinese Finance
International Finance Review, Volume 17, 151–187
ISSN: 1569-3767/doi:10.1108/S1569-376720160000017012

*retains a stronger control over state-owned enterprises than the optimal
level. In addition, we show that government control can be further weakened in firms with good corporate governance mechanisms, which serve
as a substitution of government monitoring.*

Social implications − *Our results demonstrate that government control
in China is still a necessary but costly mechanism to mitigate agency
costs, especially when corporate governance system is underdeveloped.*

Originality/value − *We identify the substitution effect between
government control and corporate governance using a unique measure
of government control.*

Keywords: Government control; state-owned enterprises; agency
problem; corporate governance

INTRODUCTION

It is a central issue in political economics studies how government should
function in the economy. Besides providing a legal framework and public
goods, conducting fiscal and monetary policies, etc., government also gets
involved in firm management when owning shares of enterprises. La Porta,
Lopez-de-Silanes, and Shleifer (1999) find that about one fifth of the firms
in 27 wealthy economies are ultimately controlled by government.[1] Despite
of the wide existence of government ownership through state-owned enterprises (SOEs), how government control affects firm performance has been
under debate for a long time.

A broad literature on privatization has argued that government control
reduces firm value. In contrast to this argument, Qian (1995, 1996) proposes
that government monitoring could mitigate management agency costs and
increases firm value, which could be necessary in a typical developing economy where corporate governance mechanisms have not been established.
Some other empirical studies on China's SOEs document the existence of
benefits or costs of government influence (Jiang, Laurenceson, & Tang,
2008; Lu, Tao, & Yang, 2010; Xu, Zhu, & Lin, 2005). Most previous studies
document only one side effect, either good or bad, of government control,
and the evidences are inconclusive.

In this paper, we take into consideration of both benefits and costs of
government control and prove in theory the existence of a non-monotonic

relationship between government control and firm performance. Using hand-collected data on the strength of government control, we provide empirical evidence consistent with Qian's (1995, 1996) conjectures. In particular, we show the existence of an optimal level of government control which balances benefits and costs of government control. Therefore, SOEs under the optimal government control have the highest firm value among SOEs, which is comparable to the firm value of private firms. In contrast, other SOEs under stronger or weaker control of government suffer a significant firm value loss than that of firms under the optimal control. Moreover, our theory results and empirical evidences show that the government would likely choose a suboptimal (for firm value) level of control, which contributes to an overall inferior SOE performance to private firms.

We first construct a simple model of initial public offering (IPO), in which the government decides how much control of an SOE to retain. We include both the grabbing effect and the monitoring effect as a result of government control and analyze how their interactions affect firm performance. There is a higher cost for the government to grab from the firm under a weaker control, which improves firm value. At the same time, however, it becomes more difficult for the government to monitor firm managers when control is weakened, and this reduces firm value. We show that without the monitoring effect, the government would choose a weak control as a commitment of grabbing less in exchange for a high fraction of retained shares and a high firm value. However, when both grabbing effect and monitoring effect are present, there exists an optimal level of government control that maximizes firm value. In addition, due to the misalignment of government's payoff and firm value, government has an incentive to retain more control over SOEs than the optimal level.

We then provide empirical evidences for the model prediction of a non-monotonic relationship between government control and firm value. A paper closely related to ours is Tian and Estrin (2008), which studies the effect of government ownership on firm value. They use total state-share proportion of listed companies that are directly controlled by their state shareholders (most state shareholders are SOEs) as the key explanatory variable in the empirical tests, which reflects both incentive and capability of government to intervene firms' management, either in a good way or in a bad way. In this paper, we focus on government's capability to intervene firms' decision making, and we test its effect on firm value. In particular, we use a unique measure of government control which reflects only the capability side of government control, and examine its impact on firm value while controlling for the shareholding of the state.

Moreover, Tian and Estrin (2008) look at the agency problem between the controlling shareholder (representing the ultimate controller, government) and other shareholders without considering managers' agency problem. In comparison, we argue that a strong government control allows government to monitor managers of firms closely and thus reduces agency problem between the shareholders and managers. At the same time, strong control of government, under which government may grab benefits from firms for social objectives such as employment rate, exacerbates the agency problem between government and other shareholders. The interaction of these two agency problems generates a non-monotonic relationship between government control and firm value.

Specifically, we measure the government control based on the length of intermediate ownership chains connecting the state-owned listed companies to their ultimate controllers – government, defined as "LAYER".[2] Among 1,500 Chinese listed companies, we first identify firms that are ultimately controlled by Chinese government either directly or through several intermediate corporations. When a government agency directly holds the majority shares of the listed company, the layer value is defined as 1. Layer increases as the number of intermediate companies on the ownership chain between the government and the listed companies goes up. The existence of intermediate ownership reduces the government's control over the listed company, due to increased information asymmetry between managers of the listed companies and government agencies (see, e.g., Aghion & Tirole, 1997) and/or other associated agency problems. Although the value of layer ranges from 1 to 9, more than 60% of listed firms are controlled by government agencies through one intermediate corporation, that is, the layer equals 2.

When listed companies are controlled by ultimate government through more layers of intermediate companies, due to the additional transaction costs, information asymmetry, agency costs, etc., the government controlling strength is weaker. Tian and Estrin (2008) assume those intermediate state-controlled firms that control the listed firm fully represent the interests of the ultimate owner, that is, government, and only shareholding matters. For example, Tian and Estrin (2008) treat the strength of government control the same whenever the government shareholder owns more than 50% of shares (i.e., *pricontrol*, the measurement of government control, equals 0 in any listed company that satisfies this criteria). However, our measure differentiates the strength of control based on layers of intermediate companies even though the ownership is the same. In China, the state shares that government retains are not freely transferable and highly concentrated, but decentralization can be effectively achieved through adding intermediate corporations (Fan, Wong, & Zhang, 2007a, 2007b).Using layer to proxy for government control, we identify a hump-shaped relationship between layer and firm value after controlling for state ownership and other factors related to firm performance. Our results indicate that firms with a layer of 4 have the highest firm value than other state-owned listed companies. It is also evident that government chooses a stronger level of control, since mean and median of realized layer are significantly smaller than optimal level at which firm value is maximized. More interestingly, we find that although SOEs perform worse than private firms in a full sample test, performance of those firms under the optimal government control (i.e., with a layer of 4) is comparable to that of private firms. We also find that firms with 3 layers perform similarly as those with 4 layers when corporate governance is poor. This confirms that government control is more beneficial for firms with underdeveloped corporate governance.

Last, we conduct a series of sensitivity tests. We identify a negative relationship between layer and over-employment and a positive relationship between layer and management over-expenditure. Following the existing literature (see, e.g., Chen, Chen, & Wan, 2005; Dong & Putterman, 2003), over-employment and management over-expenditure proxy for government grabbing and manager agency cost, respectively. Therefore, these findings are consistent with our interpretation of the benefits and costs of government control. We use multinomial logit regression model to control for endogeneity or reverse causality between level of government control and firm performance. The results indicate that the choice of government control for Chinese listed companies is not significantly influenced by the company's operating performance at the time of IPO and so reverse causality does not appear to be a problem. Our evidence is consistent with Aivazian, Ge, and Qiu (2005) and Chen, Firth, and Xu (2009).

This study contributes to the literature in two ways. First, related to the literature on government control, our findings indicate that government control of SOEs is a necessary, but costly, way of improving firm performance, especially in transition economies without effective corporate governance mechanisms. Good corporate governance can substitute for government monitoring of SOEs and provide an incentive for the government to choose a weaker control, and this reduces grabbing and improves firm efficiency. Accordingly, policy implication from our results is that privatization might not be the only optimal choice for SOE reform, and within the government control, SOEs could actually perform equally well as or even better than private firms. SOEs' reform could aim at improving corporate governance to fill in the government's monitoring role and decentralizing control of listed companies to reduce costs of grabbing.

Secondly, our study contributes to the literature on ownership structure. Compared to pyramid ownership of family-controlled firms in Southeast Asia (Claessens et al., 2000), the use of cross-shareholdings and pyramidal structure in China's state-owned listed companies is not widespread.[3] Government maintains ultimate ownership in more than 70% of partially privatized firms, either directly or indirectly, through SOEs. This allows us to empirically analyze the effect of government control on firm performance across firms with different level of government control, measured by the length of the intermediate ownership chain, which naturally captures the government's administrative power. With this unique ultimate ownership structure of state-owned listed companies in China, which was almost completely unexplored in prior studies, our work provides complementary results to previous findings in this area (see, e.g., Chang & Wong, 2004; Li, 2000; Qian, 1996; Xu et al., 2005).

The remainder of the paper is structured as follows. The next section provides the institutional background in China and literature review. The third section presents the model, in which we take into account both monitoring effect and grabbing effect arising from government control. Fourth section describes our sample and the methodology we use to construct our data on government control. We also provide several examples of government control structure in this section. The fifth section analyzes the empirical relationship between layer and firm value, and corporate governance's effect on layer and firm value. The penultimate section checks the robustness of our results, and the final section concludes the paper.

INSTITUTIONAL BACKGROUND AND LITERATURE REVIEW

Before the economic reform began in 1978, Chinese SOEs were solely state-owned proprietorships directly controlled by industry-specific government agencies at various administrative levels. The SOE reform decentralized operating decision rights from government agencies to firm management and expanded enterprise autonomy without a fundamental change of state ownership (Qian, 1995). Following a period of improved productivity in the 1980s, firm performance steadily deteriorated during the 1990s, which has led to a new focus of SOE reform: privatization and corporatization. Privatization was mostly used to sell small SOEs to private entrepreneurs (Cao, Qian, & Weingast, 1999). The main strategy, corporatization, turns SOEs into limited liability shareholding companies owned by the state and non-state investors, such as institutions, foreign companies, individuals, or employees (Xu et al., 2005; Zhu, 1999). With autonomous investment decision rights, SOEs set up joint ventures and subsidiaries and operate as business groups.

After the stock markets were opened in Shenzhen and Shanghai in 1990, the government allowed SOEs to sell a small portion of the firm shares to individual investors to maintain the government's controlling stake. Government agencies are prohibited from selling their shares to prevent the erosion of government control of the SOEs.[4] If an SOE (or the major part of an SOE) is restructured to be listed, a government agency serves as the direct controlling shareholder. If some parts or subsidiaries of an SOE are listed, the original SOE serves as the direct controlling shareholder. In both cases, the listed firms are ultimately controlled by government agencies, directly or indirectly, through intermediate layers of corporations.

With the ownership structure described above, it is not difficult to understand why government control remains pervasive in Chinese listed companies. Government retains a certain degree of authority over decision making in firms under its control, such as decisions relating to key personnel, investment, and labor deployment. Thus government may intervene in firms' decision making to pursue political or social objectives, and government control can therefore be detrimental to firm performance (Boycko, Shleifer, & Vishny, 1996; Shleifer & Vishny, 1994, 1998). Consistent with this argument, Dong and Putterman (2003) document excess employment in Chinese SOEs. Fan et al. (2007b) find that the listed companies where the CEOs are current or former government officers perform worse than others in both stock return and accounting performance.

When government reduces control over listed companies, however, managers may abuse their power to pursue personal gains or private ventures at the expense of the shareholders (Qian & Stiglitz, 1996). The development of private business provides opportunities for diverting state assets from SOEs to managers' private entities (Qian, 1995, 1996). Although the Chinese government attempts to reduce agency problems through the establishment of corporate governance mechanisms, it takes time to develop market-oriented economic and legal institutions conducive to effective corporate governance in a transitional economy (Shleifer & Vishny, 1997).

Therefore, government control is presently a mechanism of checks-and-balances to mitigate agency costs, especially in firms without effective corporate governance mechanisms. For example, Xu et al. (2005) document a negative relationship between operating autonomy (excluding labor deployment flexibility) and firm performance, suggesting serious agency problems in SOEs.

However, direct empirical investigation of the relationship between government control and firm performance is limited because of the difficulty in measuring the extent of government control. Two general approaches are taken to obtain such measurements. The first approach is to capture, mostly using surveys, whether or to what extent government control interferes in firms' decision making. For example, Chang and Wong (2004) constructed indices of average political decision-making power pertaining to 63 decisions based on survey data. Since politicians' influence over firms' decision making is multifaceted and often obscure, this measure cannot accurately describe the overall level of government influence. In addition, using a survey may lead to perception biases and non-replicability. The second approach is to measure government control by the proportion of shares held by state blockholders, that is, the cash flow rights (e.g., Wang, 2005; Xu & Wang, 1999). However, ownership could be an imperfect measure of government control because a substantial proportion of the government authorities over China's state-owned listed firms do not change with cash flow rights as long as the firms are controlled by the state. For example, the government retains ultimate decision rights concerning mergers and acquisitions, the disposal of shares and assets, as well as decision rights on the appointment of CEOs, for all firms when government is ultimate controller. Therefore, ownership is a measure for incentive as well as for capability, as used in Tian and Estrin (2008).

In this paper, we measure the level of government control based on the unique ownership structure of state-owned listed companies in China. In particular, we use "layer", defined as the length of intermediate ownership chains connecting the listed companies to government agencies. In China, decentralization of government control is effectively achieved through adding intermediate corporations (see, e.g., Fan et al., 2007a, 2007b) as the ownership structure of Chinese SOEs are usually highly concentrated and the state-owned shares are not freely transferable. As more layers are added, it becomes increasingly more difficult for the government to intervene in the business decisions of the firms either ex ante or ex post. As a result, more layer that connects listed companies to ultimate government controller enables credible decentralization of decision rights from the government to the management of the listed firms (Fan et al., 2007a, 2007b). We argue that these intermediate corporations on the controlling chain reduce government control over listed companies, possibly due to the information asymmetry created between the firms' managers and government agencies (Aghion & Tirole, 1997; Fan et al., 2007a) and/or other associated agency costs.[5] Consistently, anecdotal evidence suggests that government control is more intense in firms with fewer layers. For example, the "Regulation on Stock Option Plans of State Controlled Listed Companies" enacted by the Central State Asset Management Bureau (SAMB) and the Ministry of Finance in 2006 requires the listed company to submit its stock option plan to the government agency that ultimately controls the company for *approval* before it is discussed at a shareholders' meeting. However, if the number of layers between the government agency and the listed company increases to three or more, the stock option plan of the firm is only submitted for the government's *record*.

A MODEL OF GOVERNMENT CONTROL

Model Setup

We construct a model of government decision on IPO of a SOE, to explain the impact of government control on firm performance. In making the decision to go public, the government has two choices: (i) set up a new subsidiary of the existing non-public firm to go public; and (ii) let the existing non-public firm go public directly as it is. The outside investors will bid competitively for the IPO shares based on the government's decision on firm structure (whether a new subsidiary is set up). After IPO, the government chooses the level of social/political burden to impose on the listed firm at its own best interest. Here setting up a subsidiary to go public adds another "layer" to the government controlling pyramid.

Let us denote E as the cost to firm value for the realized social/political burden when the firm goes public. Thus, we can write the post-IPO firm market value as $V - E$, where V is the firm value free of grabbing. Assume that the IPO firm will need to raise I units of capital for the new investment. Therefore, the government will retain $\alpha_g = 1 - I/(V - E)$ fraction of the firm. Let e be the target level of social/political burden that the government wants to resolve, and, given the realized level of social/political burden, E, the government needs to expend additional cost $G(E) = (\gamma/2)(e - E)^2$ to meet the target. Let $b > 0$ measures how difficult the government can achieve the social/political goal within the firm. We can now write out the payoff to the government as:

$$V_g = (V - E)\alpha_g - bE - \frac{\gamma}{2}(e - E)^2 \tag{1}$$

Now let us discuss how E is determined. It is a two-stage game played between the government and the outside investors:

i. At the first stage, given the investment level, I, the government brings either the original firm or a subsidiary of the firm to go public. The investors bid competitively based on their expectation about the level of social/political burden imposed by the government on the new listed firm;
ii. Given the retained fraction of the firm, the government chooses an optimal level of social/political burden to impose on the listed firm.

The *sequential optimality* requires that the price bid by investors at the first stage needs to be consistent with the level of social/political burden chosen by the government at the second stage.

To simplify our analysis, assume $e > (1 + b)/\gamma$ and $V - (e - b/\gamma) > I,$[6] and, with some algebra, the equilibrium E chosen by the government is given by:[7]

$$E = \frac{V + e - (1+b)/\gamma - \sqrt{[V - e + (1+b)/\gamma]^2 - 4I/\gamma}}{2} \tag{2}$$

Dual Agency Problems and Optimal Government Control

When a new subsidiary is set up, the government's control on the firm is weakened with an extra layer of control, thus it becomes more difficult for the government to impose social burden on the firm. At the same time, adding a new layer also weakens the government's ability to monitor the manager's behavior, thus increases the agency cost. In our model, the first effect is reflected by a larger value of b, and the second one, a smaller value of V.

There are two lines of moral hazard problem in the corporate finance literature involved here. The first moral hazard problem is between the majority shareholder, the government, and the minority shareholders, the outside investors; the second moral hazard problem is between the manager and all shareholders. These two effects, intertwined with each other, determine the government's decision in going public as well as the firm value.

The following lemma addresses the first moral hazard problem.

Lemma 1 Assuming that the pre-grabbing firm value V does not depend on the government control, when the government retains a weaker control, the cost of grabbing increases, the government will impose a smaller social or political burden on the listed firm, and the payoff for the government increases.

Proof See Appendix. ∎

With a higher cost of grabbing, that is, it becomes more difficult for the government to impose social or political burden on the listed firm, the government will choose a lower E. For the government, though the marginal cost of imposing social or political burden on the firm increases, but that is covered by the gain from retaining more shares (as the firm market value, $V - E$, increases when E is smaller). Therefore, we can conclude that, if there is no other cost involved with a weaker control, that is, V remains constant; it is the best interest of the government to set up a subsidiary to go public. A higher marginal cost of "grabbing" with a subsidiary serves as a commitment device for the government to "grab" less.

The next lemma states the effect on firm value of the second moral hazard problem.

Lemma 2 A lower pre-grabbing firm value, caused by a weaker government control, leads to a lower firm market value, a higher social or political burden imposed by the government on the listed firm, and a lower payoff for the government.

Proof See Appendix. ∎

The above lemma says that both firm value and government payoff increases with the pre-grabbing firm value V. When the government retains a weaker control, the moral hazard problem between the government (shareholder) and firm manager leads to a lower pre-grabbing firm value V, and a lower market value, $V - E$, given other conditions fixed. At the same time, a weaker control leads to a higher cost of grabbing, which reduces the level of grabbing and increases firm market value. Therefore, we can expect that there exists an optimal level of government control that maximizes firm market value.

Theorem 1 If pre-grabbing firm value V is increasing with the government control, the government will choose an optimal layer, L_g, that maximizes its own payoff. At the same time there also exists an optimal layer, L, that maximizes the firm value, or the payoff to the outside investors.

Proof From Lemma 1 and Lemma 2, we can see that, as the layer increases, the government gains from a higher cost of grabbing, b, but loses from a lower pre-grabbing firm value, V. It is easy to show that when b is very large, the government will simply choose the level of social or political burden E to be 0 at the boundary, that is, the marginal gain from large b for the government is zero when b is large. This prevents the government from choosing an infinitely long layer, and this also implies the existence of a finite layer that maximizes the firm value.

We can see that government control could damage firm performance because of the grabbing hand, and, at the same time, it could also improve firm value due to the monitoring by the controlling shareholder, here, the government. There exists an optimal layer of government control that maximizes the firm value.

Next, we will discuss the relationship between the government-optimal layer, L_g, and the firm-value-optimal layer, L. To facilitate our analysis later, we summarize some results in the following lemma.

Lemma 3 Both the government payoff and the firm market value suffer from a lower pre-grabbing firm value, V, but the firm market value suffers more; the government payoff and the firm market value benefit from a higher cost of grabbing, b, but the firm market value gains more.

Proof We only need to show $\frac{d(V-E)}{dV} > \frac{dV_g}{dV} > 0$ and $\frac{d(V-E)}{db} > \frac{dV_g}{db} > 0$, which is algebra, and omitted here.

The asymmetry in the impact of V and b generates misalignment in the government's payoff and the firm's value, and it could happen that, setting up a subsidiary increases firm market value but it is not at the best interest of the government. To see this, let $\Delta V = V_1 - V_0 < 0$ denote the difference between the pre-grabbing firm value with a subsidiary (V_1) and that without a subsidiary (V_0), and let $\Delta b = b_1 - b_0 > 0$ denote the difference between the grabbing cost with a subsidiary (b_1) and that without a subsidiary (b_0). With Taylor's expansion, we have:

$$\Delta V_g \approx \frac{dV_g}{dV} \Delta V + \frac{dV_g}{db} \Delta b$$

$$\Delta(V - E) \approx \frac{d(V - E)}{dV} \Delta V + \frac{d(V - E)}{db} \Delta b \tag{3}$$

We can show the following theorem.

Theorem 2 Due to the misalignment of the government's payoff and the firm market value, there exist parameter values under which the firm goes public directly instead of splitting out a subsidiary for IPO even though the firm market value is maximized with a subsidiary.

Proof See Appendix. ∎

The proof in the above theorem also implies that, if we only look at the first-order effect, it is not possible to have a case in which $\Delta V_g > 0$ but $\Delta(V - E) < 0$, that is, it is not possible that setting up a subsidiary benefits the government but lowers the IPO firm market value. Indeed, there are four cases in total, which we summarize below:

(a) $\Delta V_g > 0$ and $\Delta(V - E) > 0$;
(b) $\Delta V_g > 0$ and $\Delta(V - E) < 0$;
(c) $\Delta V_g < 0$ and $\Delta(V - E) > 0$;
(d) $\Delta V_g < 0$ and $\Delta(V - E) < 0$.

Except case (b), all other cases are feasible for equilibrium outcome. The impossibility of case (b) is an empirically testable result, that is, there should be many firms with the number of controlling "layer" below the optimal level (for firm market value), but there are relatively few firms with the number of controlling "layer" above the optimal level (for firm market value). Actually it is the "layer diversity" due to the existence of firms with suboptimal "layer" that makes the empirical comparison feasible. To recapitulate the analysis in this subsection, our model predicts a hump-shaped relationship between government control and firm performance. In addition, we conjecture that government chooses to control SOEs stronger than the optimal level due to misalignment of government's payoff and firm market value.

Discussions for Empirical Implications

The first-order condition for Eq. (1) with respect to E gives us the equilibrium choice of the social/political burden in terms of the fraction of shares by the government, α_g, and the cost of imposing social/political burden within the firm, b:

$$E = e - \frac{\alpha_g + b}{\gamma} \tag{4}$$

Tian and Estrin (2008) assume the cost of grabbing, b, is a decreasing function of retained fraction of shares, α_g (or equivalently, the capability of grabbing is an increasing function of retained fraction of shares), and they test how firm market value change with the retained fraction of shares. From Eq. (4), we can see that the total amount of grabbing, E, is a function of α_g and b, and as b is also a function of α_g, E is ultimately a function of α_g. Furthermore, as Tian and Estrin (2008) argued, when α_g is low, the government has high incentive to grab, but high cost (low capability) to grab, therefore, the government will grab little, which leads to a high firm market value; and when α_g is high, the government has little incentive to grab, but low cost (high capability) to grab, therefore, the government will also grab little, which again leads to a high firm market value. Therefore, we would observe a U-shape relationship between firm market value and retained fraction of shares.

On the contrary, in this paper, we assume retained fraction of shares, α_g, is an endogenous variable, as a function of the cost of grabbing, or equivalently, the magnitude of government control, and we test how firm market value changed with government control, measured by "layer", defined as the length of intermediate ownership chains connecting the listed companies to government agencies. In Eq. (4), we have characterized the level of grabbing (the social or political burden imposed on the SOEs by the government), E, as a function of the cost of grabbing, b, and we show in Lemma 1, the level of grabbing is decreasing with the cost of grabbing as a result of the agency problem between the controlling shareholder and the minority shareholders, which implies that firm market value is a decreasing function of government control. At the same time, we assume that pre-grabbing firm value is an increasing function of government control due to the agency problem between the shareholders and the firm manager. Therefore, the interaction of these two moral hazard problems leads to a hump shape (inverse "U"-shape) relationship between firm market value and government control.

To summarize, our paper involves dual agency problems rather than just one agency problem as in Tian and Estrin (2008), and we test directly the impact of "capability" on firm market value instead of both "incentive" and "capability". Moreover, in our set up, "incentive" is an endogenous variable as a function of "capability".

DATA AND SAMPLE STATISTICS

Starting from 2004, the China Security Regulatory Committee (CSRC) required all listed companies to disclose their ultimate controllers in the annual reports.[8] The ultimate controller is defined as the ultimate owner who has substantial voting rights in listed companies, either directly or indirectly through a chain of holdings. The ultimate controller could be an individual investor, government agency, or other organization (e.g., universities, labor unions, etc.). Meanwhile, listed companies are required to disclose complete ownership and control structures between themselves and their ultimate controllers.

We manually collected data on ultimate controllers and controlling structures of listed companies from 2004 to 2009. The detailed information is provided in the "profile of shareholders and ultimate controller" section of each company's annual report. We first identify our sample as all the listed companies that are ultimately controlled by government agencies[9] and then collected the following data: (1) Name of the ultimate controller; (2) The identify of ultimate controller: Whether the ultimate controller is the SAMB or other government branches such as Ministry of Finance; whether the ultimate controller belongs to central government or provincial (local) government; (3) How does the ultimate controller maintain the control, including length of intermediate ownership chains, ultimate cash flow rights and control rights. Based on the complete ownership structure between the ultimate controller and the listed company, we construct the variables related to the ultimate control structure. In particular, layer is defined as the length of intermediate ownership chains connecting the listed companies to government agencies. In line with La Porta et al. (1999) and Claessens et al. (2000), we define cash flow right as the product of the ownership stakes along the controlling chain and voting right as the weakest ownership in the controlling chain.

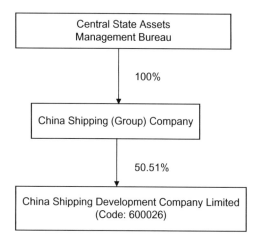

Fig. 1.   Sample SOE Control Structure: China Shipping Development Company
Limited (600026). *Note*: China Shipping Development Company Limited (600026)
is a state-owned listed company, which is ultimately controlled by central SAMB.
The central SAMB controls the listed company through a solely SOE, China
Shipping (Group) Company. *Source*: The 2004 annual report of China Shipping
Development Company Limited (600026).

Fig. 1 presents the most general control structure of state-owned listed
companies in China. The company presented in Fig. 1 is "China Shipping
Development Company Limited", which is listed on the Shanghai stock
market under the code 600026. The company is ultimately controlled by the
central SAMB, which reports to the State Council. From the control structure, it is clear that central SAMB controls China Shipping Development
Company Limited through one intermediate corporation, China Shipping
(Group) Company, which is a solely SOE. Therefore, the layer is 2. The cash
flow rights and voting rights of the ultimate controller are both 50.51%.
    When more than one ownership chain exists connecting the listed com-
pany and its ultimate controller, we identify all the chains and calculate
total cash flow rights and voting rights. We measure the layer based on the
chain with the most voting rights.[10] Take the company in Fig. 2 as an
example. China Fiberglass Company Limited (code 600176) is ultimately
controlled by the central SAMB. Central SAMB controls China National
Building Material Group Corporation, a solely SOE. The latter controls
China National Building Material Company Ltd., the controlling shareholder of China Fiberglass, through two chains: a direct control of 16.90%
ownership and an indirect control through Beijing New Building Material

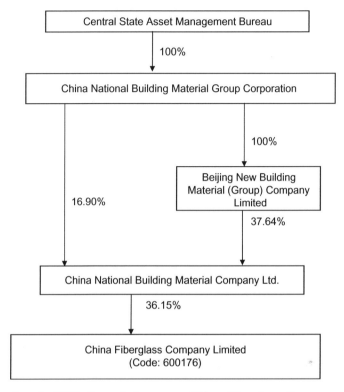

Fig. 2. Sample SOE Control Structure: China Fiberglass Company Limited (600176). *Note*: China Fiberglass Company Limited (600176) is a state-owned listed company, which is ultimately controlled by the central SAMB, which reports to the State Council. *Source*: The 2006 annual report of China Fiberglass Company Limited (600176).

(Group) Co. Ltd of 37.64% ownership. The layer value is thus 4 and is calculated using the indirect controlling chain, which conveys the most substantial voting right. The cash flow right held by the central SAMB is the total of the ownership products through both chains, which equals 19.71%. The voting right is the weakest ownership proportion through controlling chains, which equals 36.15% in this case.

In addition to above hand-collected data, we obtained other ownership data, financial data, and stock market data from the WIND database and the Shenzhen Genius Information Technology Company database (GENIUS). Table 1 provides definitions of all the variables used in this paper.

Table 1. Variables Definition.

Variable	Description
LAYER	Number of intermediate ownership chains connecting the listed companies to their ultimate controllers
Q1 (Q2, Q3)	Tobin's Q, measured as market value divided by total assets. Nontradable shares are valued at book value of equity per shares (stock price of tradable shares, 1 Yuan which is IPO price of nontradable shares)
Industry-adjusted Q1 (Q2, Q3)	Difference between Tobin's Q and the median of imputed Qs of its segments, where a segment's imputed Q is the industry median Q
LEVERAGE	Total liability divided by total assets
Total assets turnover	Sales divided by total assets
LOGAGE	The natural logarithm of firm age from the year of IPO
SIZE	The natural logarithm of the total assets
CAPX	Capital expenditure, defined as the cash outflow to fixed assets, deflated by the beginning balance of fixed assets.
Other blockholding	Sum of the direct shareholding of the second to tenth largest shareholders
Cash flow rights	Cash flow rights of the ultimate controller
STATESHR	Percentage of total shares held by government agencies
STATESHR2	Square of STATESHR
SAMB	Dummy variable that equals 1 if the ultimate controller is central or local SAMB, and 0 otherwise
LAYER1 (or 2, 3, 4, 5)	Dummy variable that equals 1 if the firm has 1 (or 2, 3, 4, or 5 and more) layer(s) in the ultimate controlling chain and 0 otherwise
Over-employment	Natural logarithm of industry median adjusted number of employee
Management expenditures	Industry-median adjusted (administration expense deflated by total assets)
STATE	Dummy variable that equals 1 if the firm is a state-owned firm, and zero otherwise
CGI	Corporate governance is comprehensively measured from the following aspects: management shareholding, whether CEO and chairman is the same person, foreign shareholders' ownership, percentage of independent directors in board, effectiveness of shareholding's annual meeting, and whether the company uses a big 10 CPA firm as its auditor. We calculate the CGI by adding the above measures together
CEO_GOV	Dummy variable that equals 1 if the CEO of the firm has the experience of working in government agent
GDP	Natural logarithm of the gross domestic product per capita
SID	Dummy variable that equals 1 if firm belongs to one of the five strategic industries (energy, iron and steel, oil refinery and petrochemicals, communications, and heavy machinery) and 0 otherwise

In Table 2, we provide summary statistics of our data, including the number of observations, layer, cash flow rights of ultimate controllers, controlling shareholders' ownership, state shareholding, and other blockholders' ownership. Our sample of the state-owned listed companies accounts for more than 70% of Chinese listed companies in all industries

Table 2. Summary Statistics of Government Control.

			Complete Sample	Firms with Central SAMB as Ultimate Owner	Firms with Central Government Bureau as Ultimate Owner	Firms with Local SAMB as Ultimate Owner	Firms with Local Government Bureau as Ultimate Owner
Mean layers			2.41	2.88	2.86	2.23	2.24
Observations with	1	layers	239	0	0	204	35
			(4.67)	(0.00)	(0.00)	(6.94)	(4.41)
	2		3,040	456	67	1,954	563
			(59.42)	(36.98)	(44.67)	(66.49)	(70.91)
	3		1,470	541	60	697	172
			(28.73)	(43.88)	(40.00)	(23.72)	(21.66)
	4		283	190	9	68	16
			(5.53)	(15.41)	(6.00)	(2.31)	(2.02)
	5		60	29	8	15	8
			(1.17)	(2.35)	(5.33)	(0.51)	(1.01)
	6		19	15	3	1	0
			(0.37)	(1.22)	(2.00)	(0.03)	(0.00)
	7		3	0	3	0	0
			(0.06)	(0.00)	(2.00)	(0.00)	(0.00)
	8		0	0	0	0	0
			(0.00)	(0.00)	(0.00)	(0.00)	(0.00)
	9		2	2	0	0	0
			(0.04)	(0.16)	(0.00)	(0.00)	(0.00)
Cash flow rights (mean, %)			37.80	38.99	26.97	37.74	38.22
Largest shareholding (mean, %)			41.26	44.52	34.45	40.53	40.19
STATESHR (mean, %)			43.60	45.89	39.81	42.68	44.21
Other blockholding (mean, %)			16.63	16.90	20.94	16.25	16.83
No. of observations			5,116	1,233	150	2,939	794

Notes: This table reports the characteristics of the ultimate controlling chains of state-owned listed companies. The complete sample includes all state-owned listed firms for which the ultimate owners can be clearly traced to government agencies. Both the statistics of the complete sample and that of subgroups by identity of ultimate owner: central SAMB, central government bureau, local SAMB, and local government bureau are reported. The percentages of the group are in parentheses. The variables are defined in Table 1.

except finance. The mean value of layer is 2.41 and is stable throughout our sample years. Sixty percent (60%) of the sample firms (3,040 out of 5,116) are controlled by government agencies through one intermediate SOE (layer equals 2); 29% (1,470 out of 5,116) are controlled through two intermediate SOEs (layer equals 3). The next largest subsample of firms is made up of those controlled through three intermediate SOEs (layer equals 4) and includes 5.5% of the whole sample. It is shown that ultimate government agencies own, on average, 38% of cash flow rights of listed firms. The direct ownership of controlling shareholders in listed companies is on average 41%, and total state shareholding is on average 43.6%.[11] Compared to the power of other blockholders which hold about 17% of shares, it is obvious why controlling shareholders could maintain a significant influence on the listed companies.

We then break the sample down into four subsamples according to the identity of the ultimate government controller. Of the 5,116 firm-year observations, 1,233 are ultimately controlled by central SAMBs; 150 are ultimately controlled by other central government agencies, such as the Ministry of Finance; 2,939 are ultimately controlled by provincial SAMBs; and 794 are ultimately controlled by other provincial government agencies. Central government-controlled firms have longer controlling chains compared to those of local government-controlled firms. The average values for layer are 2.88 and 2.86 in firms with the central SAMB and other central government agencies as the ultimate controllers, compared to 2.23 and 2.24 in firms that are ultimately controlled by local SAMBs and local government agencies. Consistently, most of firms have layer value of 3 when they are controlled by central government versus 2 by local government. In addition, we also report the ownership characteristics in each of subsample.

EMPIRICAL ANALYSIS

Government Control and Firm Characteristics

We first present descriptive statistics of firm characteristics for firms of different layer in Table 3. Following earlier studies on the relationship between ownership and performance, see, for example, Morck, Shleifer, and Vishny (1988), we use Tobin's Q — the ratio of the firm's market value to the replacement cost of its assets — as our dependent variable and interpret it as a measure of firm performance. The nontradable shares are

Table 3   Firm Performance and Characteristics for Different Layers.

	Total	Layer = 1	Layer = 2	Layer = 3	Layer = 4	Layer ≥ 5
Firm Performance						
Tobin's Q1	1.54	1.51	1.50	1.59	1.68	1.59
	(1.27)	(1.24)	(1.24)	(1.31)	(1.40)	(1.33)
Tobin's Q2	1.96	1.89	1.89	2.06	2.21	2.02
	(1.58)	(1.50)	(1.52)	(1.68)	(1.86)	(1.70)
Tobin's Q3	1.41	1.39	1.37	1.46	1.57	1.45
	(1.13)	(1.10)	(1.10)	(1.18)	(1.31)	(1.16)
Industry-adjusted Q1	0.09	0.14	0.07	0.12	0.18	0.06
	(−0.02)	(−0.01)	(−0.04)	(0.00)	(0.05)	(−0.01)
Industry-adjusted Q2	0.18	0.20	0.12	0.26	0.40	0.18
	(−0.05)	(−0.07)	(−0.09)	(0.01)	(0.16)	(0.00)
Industry-adjusted Q3	0.10	0.15	0.07	0.12	0.20	0.05
	(−0.03)	(−0.01)	(−0.05)	(−0.02)	(0.07)	(−0.04)
Firm Characteristics						
Total assets (million	7,510.00	4,220.00	9,290.00	5,360.00	3,420.00	3,900.00
Yuan)	(2,320.00)	(1,780.00)	(2,520.00)	(2,190.00)	(2,080.00)	(1,970.00)
LEVERAGE (%)	52.43	51.36	52.82	51.51	54.00	51.97
	(53.27)	(54.16)	(53.65)	(51.77)	(54.95)	(51.69)
Total assets turnover	0.73	0.53	0.72	0.77	0.90	0.60
	(0.59)	(0.47)	(0.59)	(0.62)	(0.78)	(0.49)
Over-employment	0.16	0.27	0.21	0.04	0.21	(0.09)
	(0.15)	(0.07)	(0.24)	(0.02)	(0.17)	(−0.18)
Management	4.72	4.78	4.49	5.04	5.16	5.40
expenditures (%)	(4.06)	(4.20)	(3.76)	(4.52)	(4.45)	(4.18)

Notes: This table provides means and medians (in parentheses) of firm performance and char-acteristics for complete sample and subsamples by layer. The variables are defined in Table 1.

valued at year-end book value of equity per share in Tobin's Q1. Tobin's Q2 is calculated on the basis of year-end market price for nontradable shares. Tobin's Q3 employs the face value per share (1 Yuan) for nontrad-able shares. To scale out industry effect, we also employ industry-adjusted Q, calculated as the difference between Tobin's Q and the median of imputed Qs of its segments, where a segment's imputed Q is industry-median Tobin's Q.

As Table 3 shows, no matter which Q is used to measure firm perfor-mance, it always achieves the highest level when layer equals 4. The descriptive statistics suggest that when government control is very strong or very weak, firm performance suffers. For example, the average industry-adjusted Q1 values are 0.14, 0.07, 0.12, 0.18, and 0.06, respectively, when the layer number increases from 1 to 5 or more. Perhaps surprisingly, firms with layer of 1 (i.e., firms held directly by the government agencies) perform better than those controlled by government agencies indirectly through one intermediate corporation (layer number equals 2). Moreover, firms with layer of 2 perform the worst in Tobin's Q and industry-adjusted Q. The results reflect that there is a substantial reduction in monitoring when a firm originally directly controlled by government agencies becomes indirectly controlled with an intermediate corporation. However, later on after we control for other factors that could affect firm value, the difference between layer 1 and layer 2 becomes insignificant with uncertain signs when different measures of firm value are used.

In Table 3, we also present descriptive statistics of total assets, leverage, total assets turnover, over-employment, and management expenditures for the whole sample and subsamples by layer. Firms with layer values of 4 have the smallest size as measured by total assets. The leverage ratio is on average 52% and does not differ significantly across subsamples. The total assets turnover is highest with a layer value of 4, indicating that the relationship between operating efficiency and layer number is similar to that between firm value and layer. More importantly, we show that over-employment reduces with a higher layer value, while management expenditures increase with a higher layer. These findings are consistent with our argument that government's control over listed companies is weakened when layer value becomes larger. Because of the weakened government control, firms are not burdened with over-employment. However, management's agency problem becomes severe since monitoring by government is reduced.

Government Control and Firm Value

We examine the effects of government control on firm performance using the following regression model:

$$\text{Tobin's } Q = \alpha + \beta X + \sum_n \gamma_n \text{LAYER}(n) + \varepsilon \tag{5}$$

On the right-hand side of the regressions, we measure government control by dummies specific to each number of layers instead of the number of layers to capture the non-linear relation between layer and firm value. The dummy variable LAYER(n) equals 1 if the number of layers is n and 0 otherwise. In the regression, we exclude the LAYER4 dummy. Because 4-layer firms perform the best compared with other groups of firms in univariate test as shown in Table 3, we consider their performance as a benchmark.[12] Therefore, the coefficient of other layer dummy variables represents the difference in firm value between those firms and 4-layer firms. For example, the coefficient of LAYER3 represents the performance difference between 3-layer firms and 4-layer firms. The ordinary least squares (OLS) results provide further quantification of the value effects of government control.

To control for state shareholding effect on firm value as found in Tian and Estrin (2008), we include STATESHR defined as all state-shares proportion of listed companies and its square STATESHR2. We also control for the type of ultimate government agency using a dummy variable SAMB, defined as 1 if firms are ultimately controlled by SAMB. Compared to other government branches, SAMB is more responsible to SOEs performance and professional in monitoring firm management. In addition, we also control firm size (SIZE), capital investment (CAPX), financial leverage (LEVERAGE), and firm age (LOGAGE). Explanation of these control variables are in Table 1. Year and industry fixed effects are controlled when we use Tobin's Q as dependent variable, and industry fixed effects are removed when industry-adjusted Q is used.

Table 4 contains the results of multivariate OLS regression of firm value on government control. In columns 1−3 (4−6), dependent variable is Tobin's Q1, Q2, and Q3 (industry-adjusted Q1, Q2, and Q3), respectively. The regression results are consistent with the univariate findings. Compared with firms with 4 layers, firms with either more or less layer valued significantly lower. For example, the coefficient of LAYER2 is negative 9.59% in the regression reported in column 1, statistically significant at 1%. It suggests that Tobin's Q1 increases by 9.59% when layer rises from 2 to 4. This finding remains qualitatively unchanged when other alternative performance measure is used as dependent variable. Taken together, these findings support the prediction of our theoretical model that an optimal level of government control exists. When government control is very strong or very weak, firms do not perform the best.

Consistent to the findings in Tian and Estrin (2008), coefficients on STATESHR and STATESHR2 are both negative and significant. More importantly, our results show that the layer effect on firm value is significant after controlling for state shareholding. Given the state shares held directly by controlling shareholders of listed companies, layer measures how government could influence listed companies as their ultimate

Table 4. The Effect of Government Control on Firm Performance.

	Dependent Variable = Firm Value					
	Firm value = Tobin's Q			Firm value = Industry-adjusted Q		
	Q = Q1 (1)	Q = Q2 (2)	Q = Q3 (3)	Q = Q1 (4)	Q = Q2 (5)	Q = Q3 (6)
INTERCEPT	4.8956***	7.3326***	5.2197***	2.5628***	4.3918***	2.9645***
	(33.66)	(29.10)	(32.59)	(18.95)	(18.83)	(19.60)
LAYER1	−0.1106**	−0.2394***	−0.1191**	−0.0936**	−0.2373***	−0.1062**
	(−2.31)	(−2.91)	(−2.22)	(−2.04)	(−3.06)	(−2.06)
LAYER2	−0.0959***	−0.2499***	−0.0964***	−0.0914***	−0.2615***	−0.0878***
	(−3.11)	(−4.82)	(−2.88)	(−3.02)	(−5.06)	(−2.64)
LAYER3	−0.0698**	−0.1797***	−0.0727**	−0.0621*	−0.1768***	−0.0632*
	(−2.18)	(−3.32)	(−2.09)	(−1.96)	(−3.25)	(−1.82)
LAYER5	−0.1602**	−0.2868***	−0.1955***	−0.1885***	−0.3164***	−0.2257***
	(−2.55)	(−2.78)	(−2.94)	(−3.08)	(−3.13)	(−3.47)
STATESHR	−0.7698***	0.0338	−1.0623***	−0.6407***	0.1035	−0.8683***
	(−7.80)	(0.22)	(−9.90)	(−6.70)	(0.68)	(−8.17)
STATESHR2	0.0371**	0.1008***	0.0477***	0.0516***	0.1312***	0.0635***
	(2.21)	(3.54)	(2.63)	(3.22)	(4.80)	(3.61)
SAMB	0.5550***	0.9294***	0.6715***	0.4353***	0.7032***	0.4909***
	(3.75)	(3.59)	(4.10)	(3.07)	(2.84)	(3.11)
SIZE	−0.1221***	−0.2176***	−0.1514***	−0.1058***	−0.1922***	−0.1334***
	(−18.46)	(−18.67)	(−20.47)	(−17.15)	(−17.65)	(−19.10)
CAPX	0.0349	−0.0896	−0.1117	0.1847	−0.0163	0.1595
	(0.27)	(−0.40)	(−0.80)	(1.59)	(−0.08)	(1.25)
LEVERAGE	−0.0037***	−0.0063***	0.0006	−0.0032***	−0.0053***	0.0007
	(−7.89)	(−7.85)	(1.21)	(−7.51)	(−7.20)	(1.39)
LOGAGE	0.0833***	0.1302***	0.1102***	0.0576***	0.1082***	0.0779***
	(7.09)	(5.69)	(8.59)	(5.23)	(5.23)	(6.44)
Year dummies	Controlled	Controlled	Controlled	Controlled	Controlled	Controlled
IND dummies	Controlled	Controlled	Controlled			
Region dummies	Controlled	Controlled	Controlled	Controlled	Controlled	Controlled
Observations	5,118	5,118	5,118	5,118	5,118	5,118
Adjusted R^2	0.49	0.43	0.49	0.13	0.12	0.15
F value	133.4893	115.8625	145.5732	42.3763	40.2862	47.7681

Notes: This table reports the results from OLS regressions of firm performance (Tobin's Q in columns (1)–(3) and industry-adjusted Q in columns (4)–(6)) on layer dummies. Standard errors are adjusted for heteroskadasticity and correlation among observations from the same year. In parentheses are the t-statistics. ***, **, and * denote signifi- cance at the 1%, 5%, and 10% levels, respectively. The variables are defined in Table 1.

shareholders. In Table 4, we also observe that firm size (SIZE) has a significantly negative effect on firm performance, indicating that larger firms tend to have relatively lower valuation in China. Firm age (LOGAGE) has significantly positive effects on firm performance. Consistent to the argument that SAMB is more professional in monitoring firm operation, we show a positive and significant relationship between SAMB and firm value.

To summarize, the empirical findings in this section suggest that ultimate control structures with layer value of 4 balance the costs of government grabbing and the benefits of government monitoring, thereby maximizing firm performance. Firms with a lower value of layer perform worse because of serious political costs resulting from excessive government grabbing. In contrast, firms with more than 4 layers suffer from excessive managerial agency problems due to weak government monitoring. In summary, our findings suggest that the appropriate level of government control balances government grabbing and monitoring. Neither very strong nor very weak government control over listed firms is optimal.[13]

Comparing the optimal layer value to the real layer distribution reported in Table 2, where the largest percentage of layer distribution is 2, it is not difficult to conclude that government tends to choose a tighter level of control, consistent with our theoretical prediction. If we take 4 as the optimal layer, only 5.53% of observations have a layer of 4, and 1.64% of observations have a layer greater than optimal number, the remained dominate fraction of sample firms (92.83%) have a layer smaller than 4. Government obtains benefits for political objectives by maintaining excessive control over SOEs, which destroy firm values and other shareholders' benefits.

We then use privately-owned firm as a benchmark and compare firm value of state-owned firms versus them. Results are presented in Table 5. Columns 1 and 3 of Table 5 report comparing statistics without separating state-owned firms of different layers. The dummy variable STATE equals 1 if the firm is a state-owned firm, and 0 otherwise. The coefficient of STATE measures the difference between firm value of all state-owned and private firms. We find that the coefficients of STATE when performance is measured by Tobin's Q1 or industry-adjusted Q1 are both negative and significant at 1%.[14] This indicates that overall performance of state-owned firms is worse than that of private firms.

Then we separate state-owned firms into five subgroups and compare their performance to that of private firms, respectively. Results are shown in Columns 2 and 4, with performance measured by Tobin's Q1 and industry-adjusted Q1. Following our previous definition of LAYER(n) dummies, their coefficients measure the difference between state-owned firms of each layer value and private firms. Table 5 shows that firms with optimal layer (i.e., layer equals 4) perform no worse than private firms, indicating that SOEs under government control can perform as well as private firms. SOEs performing worse than private firms as a group are mainly due to those under stronger government control. As the institutional environment is relatively underdeveloped and when law enforcement is capricious and weak, private firms' value is destroyed by serious agency problem

Table 5.   Performance Comparison between SOEs and Private Firms.

	Dependent Variable = Firm Value			
	Firm value = Q1		Firm value = Industry-adjusted Q1	
	(1)	(2)	(3)	(4)
INTERCEPT	3.4286***	2.1781***	5.0541***	5.4108***
	(31.97)	(32.32)	(50.24)	(45.80)
STATE	−0.0548***		−0.0633***	
	(−4.20)		(−5.08)	
LAYER1		−0.0725**		−0.1612**
		(−1.99)		(−2.30)
LAYER2		−0.0775**		−0.1452**
		(−2.25)		(−2.17)
LAYER3		−0.0700**		−0.1289*
		(−2.03)		(−1.91)
LAYER4		−0.0092		−0.0530
		(−0.25)		(−0.76)
LAYER5		−0.1553***		−0.2195***
		(−3.79)		(−2.84)
STATESHR	−0.7198***	−0.6345***	−0.7188***	−0.8264***
	(−9.69)	(−15.07)	(−10.01)	(−12.47)
STATESHR2	0.6557***	0.6548***	0.5404***	0.7427***
	(5.53)	(9.94)	(4.71)	(7.08)
SIZE	−0.1494***	−0.0926***	−0.1288***	−0.1454***
	(−29.51)	(−35.78)	(−26.95)	(−32.59)
CAPX	0.2645**	0.1789***	0.0878	0.1166
	(2.52)	(3.09)	(0.86)	(1.16)
LEVERAGE	−0.0019***	−0.0017***	−0.0033***	−0.0025***
	(−5.20)	(−9.47)	(−9.77)	(−8.03)
LOGAGE	0.0777***	0.0513***	0.0849***	0.0878***
	(7.78)	(9.25)	(8.81)	(9.36)
Year dummies	Controlled	Controlled	Controlled	Controlled
IND dummies	Controlled	Controlled		
Region dummies	Controlled	Controlled	Controlled	Controlled
Observations	7,694	7,694	7,694	7,694
Adjusted R^2	0.21	0.30	0.54	0.58
F value	128.6677	122.9554	533.1502	256.6959

Notes: This table reports the results from OLS regressions of firm performance (Tobin's Q1 and Industry-adjusted Q1) on firms' ownership identities. Standard errors are adjusted for heteroskadasticity and correlation among observations from the same year. In parentheses are the t-statistics. ***, **, and * denote significance at the 1%, 5%, and 10% levels, respectively. The variables are defined in Table 1.

between controlling shareholder and minority shareholders proved in prior literature (Claessens et al., 2000).

Corporate Governance and Government Control

The optimal level of government control depends on the tradeoff between benefits from reduced government grabbing versus agency costs due to weaker government monitoring. Therefore, it is not unique across SOEs with different corporate governance mechanisms which is a more effective solution to reduce agency costs, see, for example, Wong, Opper, and Hu (2004). The effective corporate governance can replace government in monitoring an SOE. That is, agency cost arising from reduced government control should be limited if firms have strong corporate governance, suggesting that the optimal level of government control over firms with effective corporate governance should be lower than that over firms without it.

To test this prediction, we divide our sample into two subgroups according to the presence of effective corporate governance mechanisms which could reduce managerial agency problems. Referring to Bai, Liu, Lu, Song, and Zhang (2004), corporate governance effectiveness is comprehensively measured from the following aspects: management shareholding, whether CEO and chairman is the same person, foreign shareholders' ownership, and percentage of independent directors on board. We also take participation rate of shareholding's annual meeting into consideration to measure efficiency of shareholders' annual meeting. We calculate the corporate governance index (CGI) by adding the above measures together for each firm and compare to the sample median. Firms with total CGI above the median are defined as "good" corporate governance firms, and others are "poor" corporate governance firms. We predict that the optimal level of government control is different between the subgroups. Specifically, we expect that the optimal level of government control for firms with poor corporate governance mechanisms is stronger, which suggests that the optimal value of layer is shorter. The empirical results on the effect of corporate governance on firm value and government control are presented in Table 6.

As shown in Table 6, firms with good corporate governance perform the best among others when layer value equals 4. In contrast, firms with 3 layers have the highest value in the poor corporate governance subsample. The difference in the optimal level of government control between subsamples suggests that stronger government control is more important for firms without effective corporate governance. Meanwhile, it suggests that with

Table 6. The Optimal Level of Government Control under Different Corporate Governance.

	Good corporate governance		Poor corporate governance	
	Q1 (1)	Industry-adjusted Q1 (2)	Q1 (3)	Industry-adjusted Q1 (4)
		Dependent Variable = Firm Value		
INTERCEPT	2.0926***	4.5678***	3.0263***	5.0162***
	(13.17)	(26.25)	(16.12)	(25.32)
SAMB	0.0304	0.0132	0.0483**	0.0629***
	(1.51)	(0.59)	(2.37)	(3.10)
LAYER1	−0.1166**	−0.1283**	−0.1267**	−0.1541***
	(−2.32)	(−2.19)	(−2.31)	(−2.85)
LAYER2	−0.0802**	−0.0931**	−0.0748*	−0.0756*
	(−2.27)	(−2.52)	(−1.79)	(−1.78)
LAYER3	−0.0713*	−0.1001***	0.0006	0.0063
	(−1.95)	(−2.64)	(0.01)	(0.14)
LAYER5	−0.1638***	−0.1765***	−0.1815*	−0.1570*
	(−2.74)	(−2.70)	(−1.95)	(−1.66)
STATESHR	−0.9554***	−1.1937***	−0.5299***	−0.6680***
	(−7.75)	(−8.99)	(−4.16)	(−5.04)
STATESHR2	0.6112***	0.8403***	0.5488**	0.6266***
	(3.76)	(4.71)	(2.45)	(2.76)
SIZE	−0.0811***	−0.1045***	−0.1365***	−0.1327***
	(−12.03)	(−13.81)	(−15.53)	(−14.81)
CAPX	0.0596	−0.1155	0.3545**	0.1470
	(0.45)	(−0.76)	(2.14)	(0.86)
LEVERAGE	−0.0032***	−0.0037***	−0.0023***	−0.0031***
	(−7.13)	(−7.33)	(−3.77)	(−4.81)
LOGAGE	0.0397***	0.0730***	0.0656***	0.0617***
	(3.29)	(5.35)	(4.09)	(3.70)
Year dummies	Controlled	Controlled	Controlled	Controlled
IND dummies	Controlled		Controlled	
Region dummies	Controlled	Controlled	Controlled	Controlled
Observations	2,813	2,813	2,305	2,305
Adjusted R^2	0.17	0.54	0.16	0.53
F value	31.2218	74.0850	24.9507	72.9624

Notes: This table reports the results from OLS regressions of firm performance (Tobin's Q1 and industry-adjusted Q1) on layer dummies of subsamples under good and poor corporate governance, respectively. Corporate governance is comprehensively measured from the following aspects: management shareholding, whether CEO and chairman is the same person, foreign shareholders' ownership, percentage of independent directors in board, effectiveness of shareholding's annual meeting, and whether the company uses big 10 CPA firms as its auditor. We calculate the CGI by adding the above measures together for each firm and compare to the sample median. Firms with total CGI above the median are defined as "good" corporate governance firms, and others are "poor" corporate governance firms. Standard errors are adjusted for heteroskadasticity and correlation among observations from the same year. In parentheses are the t-statistics. ***, **, and * denote significance at the 1%, 5%, and 10% levels, respectively. The variables are defined in Table 1.

the establishment of corporate governance mechanisms in SOEs, government should fade out from direct control further.

Robustness Check

The Specific Effects of Government Control

To better understand why the extent of government control affects firm value, we investigate how specific benefits and costs rise when layer increases. A typical cost induced by government control is over-employment in SOEs, since one of the key objectives of politicians is to maintain employment for society stability (Boycko et al., 1996; Dong & Putterman, 2003; Li, 2008). On the other hand, Chen et al. (2005) find that non-pecuniary compensation could measure managers' agency cost specifically especially in state-owned firms. In this section, we adopt these two proxies to test the specific effects of government controlling power. Follow the literature, over-employment is calculated by taking the natural logarithm of the number of employment and then subtracting industry-median. Management expenditure is measured by industry median adjusted administrative expenses deflated by total assets. We expect a negative (positive) relation between layer and over-employment (management expenditure) as additional evidence on how government control affects firm performance.

Table 7 reports the regression results for government control's impact on over-employment and management expenditures (deflated by total assets), respectively. Since the impact of layer may not be monotonic, we create a dummy variable (D_LAYER) which equals 1 if layer is greater than the median and 0 otherwise. We also include the following control variables: SIZE, measured by natural logarithm of total assets of listed companies; LEVERAGE, measured by debt over total assets; LOGAGE, natural logarithm of number of years after IPO; CASHR, government ultimate cash flow rights; ROA, return on total assets; and CAPX, capital expenditure measured by the cash outflow to fixed assets, deflated by the beginning balance of fixed assets.

Consistent with the performance results, the regression results confirm that firms with a higher value of layer have less over-employment problems but more management expenditures. The estimated coefficient between over-employment and D_LAYER is 9.58% (t-statistics is 3.72). In comparison, long-layer firms have significantly higher management expenditures than short-layer firms by 0.29% of firms total assets (which is about 22 million Yuan RMB per year), and significant at 1%. These findings

Table 7. The Effect of Government Control on Over-Employment and
Management Expenditure.

	Dependent Variable	
	Over-employment (1)	Management expenditures (2)
INTERCEPT	−11.9628***	0.0182***
	(−54.13)	(2.63)
D_LAYER	−0.0958***	0.0029***
	(−3.72)	(3.73)
SAMB	−0.1214***	0.0048***
	(−4.02)	(5.10)
STATESHR	0.0882	−0.0004
	(1.10)	(−0.18)
SIZE	0.5593***	−0.0009***
	(53.02)	(−2.61)
CAPX	1.5967***	−0.0274***
	(6.61)	(−4.03)
LEVERAGE	0.0002	−0.0001***
	(0.24)	(−4.20)
ROA	−0.0275***	−0.0009***
	(−10.06)	(−8.69)
LOGAGE	0.1167***	0.0042***
	(4.59)	(6.31)
Year dummies	Controlled	Controlled
Region dummies	Controlled	Controlled
Observations	5,118	5,118
Adjusted R^2	0.39	0.06
F value	282.5873	21.2843

Notes: This table reports the results from OLS regressions of over-employment and management expenditures on layer. Standard errors are adjusted for heteroskadasticity and correlation among observations from the same year. In parentheses are the t-statistics. *** denotes
significance at the 1% level. The variables are defined in Table 1.

confirm our conjectures that government control has two opposing effects.
When layer increases, it becomes costly and more difficult for government
to grab from firms as well as to monitor firm managers. These results
explain, at least partially, why firm value is maximized when government
control is neither too strong nor too weak.

Tests of Reverse Causality
A potential problem with our results is endogeneity or reverse causality if
the levels of government control are influenced by firm performance. To
address that whether initial level of government control is influenced by

firm value, we construct a sample of IPO firms that were listed before 2009, and examine whether pre-IPO firm performance affects layer value.[15] In addition, we assume ownership structure does not change and project the layer value to its IPO year for firms listed before 2004, as layer information is disclosed since 2004.[16] Number of observations adopted in regression is 966. We then use multinomial Logit regression models to explore whether firm value influences the initial choices of government control structure following Schmidt and Strauss (1975). Results are presented in Table 8.

Our results show that the coefficients on firm values are not significant. This indicates that the choice of initial layer of government control for state-owned firms is not influenced by the company's performance. In conjunction with the findings in Table 5, our findings suggest that the impact of government control on firm performance is not influenced by reverse causality problem. Our result is consistent with Aivazian et al. (2005), Wei, Xie, and Zhang (2005), and Chen et al. (2009) who, in different contexts, conclude that the Chinese government does not use profitability of SOEs as a criterion in deciding corporatization.

CONCLUSION

In this paper, we present a simple model and consistent empirical evidence on performance implications of government control based on a sample of Chinese state-owned listed companies. Unlike previous studies in which the degree of government control is measured by estimations from survey data or by the fraction of ownership directly held by state shareholders, our measurement, "layer", is based on the ultimate ownership structures of state-owned listed companies. This measure captures the effectiveness of the government's authority resulting from both its administrative power and ownership of assets.

We demonstrate a hump-shaped relationship between government control and firm performance, which suggests that neither very strong nor very weak government control is optimal for government-controlled firms. Government tends to exert excessive control on firms compared to optimal level. We further investigate corporate governance's impact on suboptimality caused by government excessive control. Our findings show that the optimal layer of government control is higher for firms with effective corporate governance.

Our results suggest that there is a tradeoff between government grabbing and government monitoring, both decrease when government control is

Table 8. Reverse Causality Checks.

	Dependent Variable = LAYER	
	Q = Q1 (1)	Q = Industry-adjusted Q1 (2)
INTERCEPT1	−5.9412**	−8.6883***
	(5.50)	(17.06)
INTERCEPT2	−1.8243	−4.6411**
	(0.52)	(4.96)
INTERCEPT3	0.3073	−2.5668
	(0.01)	(1.52)
INTERCEPT4	1.926	−0.9634
	(0.58)	(0.21)
INTERCEPT5	3.6462	0.7557
	(1.94)	(0.12)
Q	−0.3549	0.0745
	(1.30)	(0.07)
SAMB	−0.198	−0.1936
	(1.05)	(1.03)
SIZE	0.1665	0.2373**
	(2.55)	(5.85)
LEVERAGE	−0.1026	0.0274
	(0.03)	(0.00)
SID	0.0245	−0.1147
	(0.01)	(0.42)
Year dummies	Controlled	Controlled
IND dummies	Controlled	
Region dummies	Controlled	Controlled
Observations	966	966
Chi-Square	1337.68	968.72

Notes: This table reports the results from multinomial logit regressions of layer on pre-IPO firm performance (Tobin's Q1 and industry-adjusted Q1). Standard errors are adjusted for heteroskadasticity and correlation among observations from the same year. In parentheses are the Chi-square statistics. *** and ** denote significance at the 1% and 5% levels, respectively. The variables are defined in Table 1.

weakened. Taken together, we conclude that government control is still a necessary but costly mechanism of checks-and-balances to mitigate agency costs, especially for those firms with weak corporate governance. In the long run, SOE reform could aim at establishing effective corporate governance mechanisms as a substitution to government monitoring. More importantly, our results indicate that SOEs could actually perform as well as private firms with effective corporate governance and optimal government controlling structure.

NOTES

1. The proportion of firms ultimately controlled by government is slightly different when authors change definitions of control. The State controls 18% of firms using 20% definition of control and controls 20% of firms when control is defined by 10% of ownership.

2. We follow the definition of ultimate controller used in La Porta et al. (1999) and Claessens, Djankov, and Lang (2000). Therefore, the ultimate controllers of state-owned listed companies are various government agencies, for example, central and provincial (or local) State Assets Management Bureaus (SAMB), Finance Bureau, or industry-specific management bureaus.

3. For studies on firm ownership structure, see, for example, La Porta et al. (1999), Claessens et al. (2000), and Faccio and Lang (2002).

4. Subsequent to the primary offering, the shares held by government representatives can occasionally be transformed in blocks with government approval.

5. Private owners could reduce information asymmetry caused by layer through assigning their family members to listed companies or sit in the board for better monitoring. In contrast, government agencies have neither enough incentive nor ability to do so. Therefore, a higher layer implies lower government controlling power.

6. The condition $e > (1 + b)/\gamma$ guarantees the non-negativity of the optimal E, and the condition $V - (e - b/\gamma) > I$ guarantees that equilibrium E in Eq. (2) is real and feasible. These assumptions substantially simplify our discussion below.

7. To solve for equilibrium E, we first solve E in terms of α_g and then use $\alpha_g = 1 - I/(V - E)$ to get both E and α_g.

8. For more detail, refer to "Act No. 2 of information disclosure content and format for publicly listed firms" (Act No. 2), which was enacted by the China Security Regulatory Committee (CSRC) in 2004.

9. Except for government agencies, there are other types of ultimate owners: individuals (28%), universities and research institutions, labor unions (2.5%), financial institutions (0.7%). 2.5% of firms do not disclose ultimate owners clearly.

10. We also repeat our tests without multichain firms and results are consistent.

11. As our sample is all state-owned listed companies, largest shareholdings are state shares. The total state shareholding is larger than controlling shareholders' ownership due to the existence of other small state shareholders.

12. We repeat the tests with one-layer firms' performance as benchmark, the results are consistent. The t-statistics on layer dummies' coefficients are lower but remain significant.

13. Note that the sample includes firms controlled by ultimate owners through multiple ownership chains, we repeated our analysis on the sample excluding these firms and report the results in robustness tests and get similar results. In addition, we repeated the tests after winsorizing the top and bottom 1% of each of the variables to exclude the effect of outliers, and results were again similar.

14. We also repeat the tests using Tobin's Q2 and Q2 results are qualitatively consistent.

15. Since firm value and other characteristics are not available before IPO, we use IPO date value and year-end firm characteristics to proxy for them, respectively.

16. According to our descriptive statistics in Table 2 for a period of 2004–2006, government control structure does not change very frequently. Meanwhile, we repeat the test with firms listed in 2004–2006, results are consistent.

REFERENCES

Aghion, P., & Tirole, J. (1997). Formal and real authority. *Journal of Political Economy*, *105*(1), 1–29.

Aivazian, V., Ge, Y., & Qiu, J. (2005). Can corporatization improve the performance of state-owned enterprises even without privatization? *Journal of Corporate Finance*, *11*, 791–808.

Bai, C., Liu, Q., Lu, J., Song, F. M., & Zhang, J. (2004). Corporate governance and market valuation in China. *Journal of Comparative Economics*, *32*, 599–616.

Boycko, M., Shleifer, A., & Vishny, R. W. (1996). A theory of privatization. *Economic Journal*, *106*(435), 309–319.

Cao, Y., Qian, Y., & Weingast, B. R. (1999). From federalism, Chinese style to privatization, Chinese style. *Economics of Transition*, *7*(1), 103–131.

Chang, E. C., & Wong, S. M. (2004). Political control and performance in China's listed firms. *Journal of Comparative Economics*, *32*, 617–636.

Chen, D., Chen, X., & Wan, H. (2005). Regulation and non-pecuniary compensation in Chinese SOEs. *Economic Research Journal*, (in Chinese), *2*, 92–101.

Chen, G., Firth, M., & Xu, L. (2009). Does the type of ownership control matter? Evidence from China's listed companies. *Journal of Banking & Finance*, *33*, 171–181.

Claessens, S., Djankov, S., & Lang, L. H. P. (2000). The separation of ownership and control in East Asian corporations. *Journal of Financial Economics*, *58*(1-2), 81–112.

Dong, X., & Putterman, L. (2003). Soft budget constraints, social burdens, and labor redundancy in China's state industry. *Journal of Comparative Economics*, *31*(1), 110–133.

Faccio, M., & Lang, L. H. P. (2002). The ultimate ownership of Western European corporations. *Journal of Financial Economics*, *65*, 365–395.

Fan, J. P., Wong, T. J., & Zhang, T. (2007a). *Organized structure as a decentralization device: Evidence from corporate pyramids*. Manuscript, the Chinese University of Hong Kong.

Fan, J. P., Wong, T. J., & Zhang, T. (2007b). Politically connected CEOs, corporate performance, and Post-IPO performance of China's newly partially privatized firms. *Journal of Financial Economics*, *84*, 330–357.

Jiang, B., Laurenceson, J., & Tang, K. K. (2008). Share reform and the performance of China's listed companies. *China Economic Review*, *19*, 489–501.

La Porta, R., Lopez-de-Silanes, F., & Shleifer, A. (1999). Corporate ownership around the world. *Journal of Finance*, *54*, 471–518.

Li, D. (2000). *Insider control vs. government control: A study of China's state enterprise reform*. Manuscript, Hong Kong University of Science and Technology.

Li, L. (2008). Employment burden, government ownership and soft budget constraints: Evidence from a Chinese enterprise survey. *China Economic Review*, *19*, 215–229.

Lu, J., Tao, Z., & Yang, Z. (2010). The costs and benefits of government control: Evidence from China's collectively-owned enterprises. *China Economic Review*, *21*, 282–292.

Morck, R., Shleifer, A., & Vishny, R. W. (1988). Management ownership and market valuation: An empirical analysis. *Journal of Financial Economics, 20*, 293–315.

Qian, Y. (1995). Reforming corporate governance and finance in China. In M. Aoki & H. K. Kim (Eds.), *Corporate governance in transitional economics: Insider control and the role of banks*. Washington, DC: The World Bank.

Qian, Y. (1996). Enterprise reform in China: Agency problems and political control. *Economics of Transition, 4*(2), 427–447.

Qian, Y., & Stiglitz, J. (1996). Institutional innovations and the role of local government in transition economies: The case of Guangdong province of China. In J. McMillan & B. Naughton (Eds.), *Reforming Asian socialism: The growth of market institutions*. Ann Arbor, MI: University of Michigan Press.

Schmidt, P., & Strauss, R. P. (1975). Estimation of models with jointly dependent qualitative variables: A simultaneous logit approach. *Econometrica, 43*(4), 745–756.

Shleifer, A., & Vishny, R. W. (1994). Politicians and firms. *Quarterly Journal of Economics, 109*(4), 995–1025.

Shleifer, A., & Vishny, R. W. (1997). A survey of corporate governance. *Journal of Finance, 52*, 737–783.

Shleifer, A., & Vishny, R. W. (1998). *The grabbing hand: Government pathologies and their cures*. Cambridge, MA: Harvard University Press.

Tian, L., & Estrin, S. (2008). Retained state shareholding in Chinese PLCs: Does government ownership always reduce corporate value? *Journal of Comparative Economics, 36*, 74–89.

Wang, C. (2005). Ownership and operating performance of Chinese IPOs. *Journal of Banking & Finance, 29*, 1835–1856.

Wei, Z., Xie, F., & Zhang, S. (2005). Ownership structure and firm value in China's privatized firms: 1991–2001. *Journal of Financial and Quantitative Analysis, 40*(1), 87–108.

Wong, S. M. L., Opper, S., & Hu, R. (2004). Shareholding structure, depoliticization and enterprise performance: Evidence from China's listed firms. *Economics of Transaction, 12*(1), 29–66.

Xu, L. C., Zhu, T., & Lin, Y. (2005). Political control, agency problems and ownership reform. *Economics of Transaction, 13*(1), 1–24.

Xu, X., & Wang, Y. (1999). Ownership structure and corporate governance in Chinese stock companies. *China Economic Review, 10*(1), 75–98.

Zhu, T. (1999). China's corporatization drive: An evaluation and policy implications. *Contemporary Economic Policy, 17*(4), 530–539.

APPENDIX

Proof for Lemma 1 All we need to show is $\partial E/\partial b < 0$ and $\partial V_{\mathrm{g}}/\partial b > 0$. Write $\delta = V - e + (1 + b)/\gamma$, and we have:

$$\frac{\partial E}{\partial b} = -\frac{1}{2\gamma}\left(1 + \frac{\delta}{\sqrt{\delta^2 - 4I/\gamma}}\right) < 0$$

At the same time, we have:

$$\frac{\mathrm{d}V_{\mathrm{g}}}{\mathrm{d}b} = \frac{\partial V_{\mathrm{g}}}{\partial \alpha_{\mathrm{g}}}\frac{\partial \alpha_{\mathrm{g}}}{\partial b} + \frac{\partial V_{\mathrm{g}}}{\partial E}\frac{\partial E}{\partial b} + \frac{\partial V_{\mathrm{g}}}{\partial b} = -(V - E)\left[\gamma\frac{\partial E}{\partial b} + 1\right] - E$$

and some algebra gives us:

$$\frac{\mathrm{d}V_{\mathrm{g}}}{\mathrm{d}b} = \frac{4I^2/\gamma^2}{\left(\delta + \sqrt{\delta^2 - 4I/\gamma}\right)^2 \sqrt{\delta^2 - 4I/\gamma}} > 0$$

∎

Proof for Lemma 2 All we need to show is $\partial E/\partial V < 0$, $\partial (V - E)/\partial V > 0$, and $\partial V_{\mathrm{g}}/\partial V > 0$. Write $\delta = V - e + (1 + b)/\gamma$, we have:

$$\frac{\partial E}{\partial V} = -\frac{2I/\gamma}{\left(\delta + \sqrt{\delta^2 - 4I/\gamma}\right)\sqrt{\delta^2 - 4I/\gamma}} < 0$$

$$\frac{\partial (V - E)}{\partial V} = 1 - \frac{\partial E}{\partial V} = 1 + \frac{2I/\gamma}{\left(\delta + \sqrt{\delta^2 - 4I/\gamma}\right)\sqrt{\delta^2 - 4I/\gamma}} > 0$$

and

$$\frac{\mathrm{d}V_{\mathrm{g}}}{\mathrm{d}V} = \frac{\partial V_{\mathrm{g}}}{\partial \alpha_{\mathrm{g}}}\frac{\partial \alpha_{\mathrm{g}}}{\partial V} + \frac{\partial V_{\mathrm{g}}}{\partial E}\frac{\partial E}{\partial V} + \frac{\partial V_{\mathrm{g}}}{\partial V} = -(V - E)\gamma\frac{\partial E}{\partial V} - \alpha_{\mathrm{g}}$$

$$= \frac{4I^2/\gamma}{\left(\delta + \sqrt{\delta^2 - 4I/\gamma}\right)^2 \sqrt{\delta^2 - 4I/\gamma}} + 1 > 0$$

∎

Proof for Theorem 2 We first show $\frac{dV_g/dV}{dV_g/db} > \frac{d(V-E)/dV}{d(V-E)/db} > 0$. With $\delta = V - e + (1+b)/\gamma$, some algebra shows that:

$$\frac{dV_g/dV}{dV_g/db} = \frac{1}{\left[\delta - \sqrt{\delta^2 - 4I/\gamma}\right]^2}$$
$$\times \left[\left(\delta + \sqrt{\delta^2 - 4I/V}\right)^2 \sqrt{\delta^2 - 4I/V} \times 16I^2/\gamma^2 + 64I^4/\gamma^3\right]$$

and

$$\frac{d(V-E)/dV}{d(V-E)/db} = \frac{1}{\left[\delta - \sqrt{\delta^2 - 4I/\gamma}\right]^2} \times 64I^4/\gamma^3$$

The result is immediate. This result says, *relatively*, the effect of V on the government's payoff is higher than on the firm value. Intuitively, when b increases, the government's gain from choosing a lower level of social burden, E, is partially offset by a higher cost of grabbing, thus the effect of V is larger, relative to the effect of b, in comparison with the effects of these two variables on firm value. Therefore, when layer increases, the government's payoff peaks before the firm value peaks, and this can occur as long as:

$$\frac{dV_g/dV}{dV_g/db} > \frac{\Delta b}{-\Delta V} > \frac{d(V-E)/dV}{d(V-E)/db}$$

As $\frac{dV_g/dV}{dV_g/db} > \frac{d(V-E)/dV}{d(V-E)/db} > 0$, we know the parameter space that satisfies the above condition is not empty. ■

INTERNAL CONTROL, CORPORATE LIFE CYCLE, AND FIRM PERFORMANCE

Haiyan Zhou, Hanwen Chen and Zhirong Cheng

ABSTRACT

Purpose — *In this paper, we investigate whether internal control and whether corporate life cycle would affect firm performance in the emerging markets of China.*

Methodology/approach — *We use Chen, Dong, Han, and Zhou's (2013) internal control index on the effectiveness of internal control and Dickinson's (2011) definition on firm life cycle. We use multivariate regression analysis.*

Findings — *We find that the internal control improves corporate performance. When dividing firm life cycle into five stages: introduction, growth, mature, shake-out and decline, we find that the impacts of internal control on firm performance vary with different stages. The positive impact of internal control on firm performance is more significant in maturity and shake-out stages than other stages.*

Research limitations/implications — *Our findings would have implications for the regulators and policy makers with regards to the importance*

The Political Economy of Chinese Finance
International Finance Review, Volume 17, 189–209
Copyright © 2016 by Emerald Group Publishing Limited
All rights of reproduction in any form reserved
ISSN: 1569-3767/doi:10.1108/S1569-376720160000017013

of internal control in corporate governance and the effectiveness of implementing standards and guidelines on internal control in public firms.

Practical implications − *In addition, our findings on the various roles of internal control at different stages of firm life cycle would help managers and board of directors find more focus in risk management and board monitoring, respectively.*

Originality/value − *Although the prior literature have examined the link between internal control, information quality and cost of equity capital (Ashbaugh-Skaife, Collins, Kinney, & LaFond, 2009; Ogneva, Subramanyam, & Raghunandan, 2007), our study would be the first attempt to investigate the link between internal control and firm performance during different stages of firm life cycles.*

Keywords: Internal control; corporate life cycle; firm performance

INTRODUCTION

In September 1992, COSO Committee issued *Internal Control-Integrated Framework*, referred to COSO report, which defines the internal control as a process for assuring achievement of an organization's objectives in operational effectiveness and efficiency, reliable financial reporting, and compliance with laws, regulations and policies. Recently, the Chinese government issued similar regulations to enhance corporate governance. The five government agencies − the Ministry of Finance, the China Securities Regulatory Commission, the National Audit Office, the China Banking Regulatory Commission, and the China Insurance Regulatory Commission, jointly issued the *Basic Standards for Enterprise Internal Control (Basic Standards)* on May 22, 2008 and *Implementation Guidelines for Enterprise Internal Control* on April 26, 2010. According to these standards and implementation guidance, internal control is a process designed to achieve control objectives which is implemented by the board of directors, supervisors, managers and staff. The goal is to provide reasonable assurance of enterprise management, legal compliance, asset security, reliability, and completeness of financial reports and related information, to improve operational efficiency and effectiveness, and to promote the achievement of development strategies. Thus, both COSO Report and *Basic Standards* emphasize the goal of internal control, which is to improve the efficiency and effectiveness of operating, financing, and investment activities.

Internal control could help improve efficiency and effectiveness of operating activities and thus firm performance. On the first hand, effective internal control would indicate the effectiveness of its five elements – effective control environment, effective risk assessment, effective control activities, effective information communication, and effective monitoring. In an effective control environment, it is easy to understand and identify factors that help promote the efficiency and effectiveness of operating activities, such as human resources policy. Effective risk assessment can help managers limit risks within the affordable range, avoid operating losses, obtain investment opportunities, and increase profitability. Effective control activities, in particular, those in asset safeguards, proper authorization of transactions and activities, and performance evaluation, have direct effects on efficiency and effectiveness of firm activities. The reliability of information is crucial for decision-making of managers.

On the other hand, effective internal control could enhance information quality, which would help managers make better decisions. The literature shows important impacts of the effectiveness of internal control on information disclosure. Information can directly affect not only the effectiveness of corporate investment analysis and decision-making, but also executive pay performance sensitivity (Sloan, 1993). The latter could help improve the performance of executives, align the interests of shareholders and managers, reduce opportunism behaviors and reduce the company's business risk. The increase in the quality of accounting disclosure can also be used to detect incompetent executives, so a company can replace incompetent managers as soon as possible to reduce the company's business risk.

Although the prior literature have examined the link between internal control, information quality and cost of equity capital (Ashbaugh-Skaife, Collins, Kinney, & LaFond, 2009; Ogneva, Subramanyam, & Raghunandan, 2007), none of these studies have investigated the link between internal control and firm performance. Factors that influence operating activities could be complicated, varying from background, environment, scale, and the degree of complexity of the business. Moreover, it is difficult to find an accurate and quantitative measure of internal control. Some researchers believe that internal control will reduce investment efficiency of enterprises, because it sets a series of rules to control and restrict managers' decision making as managers may be more reluctant to take risks with more constrains on their power (Bargeron, Lehn, & Zutter, 2010).

In this study, we investigate whether the impact of internal control on firm performance vary in different life cycle stages. Firms are confronted with different information asymmetry and agency problems in different stages of its life cycle and these problems significantly affect internal controls in different ways (Abdulsaleh & Worthington, 2013). We test such a relationship using the data from the emerging markets of China. The emerging markets provide unique settings to investigate the different information asymmetry and agency problems reflected in the effectiveness of internal control in different stages of firm life cycle. First, due to weak shareholder protection in China, the effect of internal control on firm performance should be substantial and more readily detectable than developed market such as in the United States. A similar argument is made in the literature regarding the effectiveness of internal control on cash holdings (Chen, Chen, Schipper, Xu, & Xue, 2012). Second, disclosure regulations in China require a continuous measure of internal control effectiveness. This allows for greater granularity than analyses using U.S. data, where only the small subset of firms with ineffective internal control provide granularity on their underlying problems. This also allows us to distinguish between the existence of internal controls and the effectiveness of internal control (Ge, Li, Liu, & McVay, 2016).

Using Chen, Dong, Han, and Zhou's (2013) internal control index on the effectiveness of internal control and Dickinson's (2011) definition of firm life cycle based on cash flow patterns, we find that internal control has a significant and positive impact on corporate performance. When dividing firm life cycle into five stages: introduction, growth, mature, shake-out and decline, we find that the impacts of internal control on firm performance vary with different stages. The positive impact of internal control on firm performance is more significant in maturity and shake-out stages than other stages.

The remainder of the study proceeds as follows. The next section reviews the related research and develops hypotheses for the study. Models and empirical testing are discussed next. After this, reports the data collection and results are discussed, and the last section concludes the paper.

LITERATURE REVIEW AND HYPOTHESIS

The literature shows important impacts of the effectiveness of internal control on information disclosure. For instance, Ashbaugh-Skaife, Collins, and Kinney (2008) investigate the effect of internal control deficiencies and their remediation on accrual quality of U.S. firms. They find that firms reporting internal control deficiencies have lower quality accruals as measured by accrual noise and absolute abnormal accruals than firms not reporting internal control problems. They also find that firms that report internal control deficiencies have significantly larger positive and larger negative abnormal accruals than other firms, indicating internal control weaknesses are more likely to lead to unintentional errors and thus accrual noises. Third, firms whose auditors confirm remediation of previously reported internal control deficiencies have an increase in accrual quality.

Similarly, Doyle, Ge, and McVay (2007) examine the relation between accruals quality and internal control in U.S. firms and find that firms with internal control weaknesses are associated with poorly estimated accruals, measured by discretionary accruals, average accruals quality, historical accounting restatements, and earnings persistence. Further, they find that this relation between weak internal control and lower accruals quality is driven by weakness disclosures that relate to overall company-level controls, which may be more difficult to be detected.

The literature also documents important impacts of the effectiveness of internal control on cost of capital. However, the evidence is mixed so far. For instance, Ogneva et al. (2007) examine the association between cost of equity and internal control effectiveness for U.S. firms that filed Section 404 reports to the SEC. Although they find marginally higher cost of equity for firms disclosing material weakness in internal control than firms disclosing no material weaknesses, such differences in cost of equity disappear after controlling for firm characteristics. In contrast, Ashbaugh-Skaife et al. (2009) examine how changes in internal control quality influence firm risk and cost of equity. After controlling for other risk factors, they find that firms with internal control deficiencies have higher idiosyncratic risk, systematic risk, and cost of equity than other firms. They also find that changes in internal control effectiveness are followed by significant changes in cost of equity, indicating internal control can affect investors' risk assessments.

Although prior literature have examined the link between internal control, information quality and cost of equity (Ashbaugh-Skaife et al., 2009), none of these studies have investigated the link between internal control and firm performance. Different from prior studies, we argue that internal control could affect information quality, and therefore it would affect firm performance.

Internal control could affect firms' information quality both intentionally and unintentionally (Ashbaugh-Skaife et al., 2009). On one hand,

unintentional misstatements could result from the lack of adequate policies, training, or diligence by firm employees. Such examples include physical
inventory taking and pricing errors that misstate ending inventory and cost
of goods sold. The effect of these misstatements on financial reporting could
be random as it could either overstate or understate firm performance. On
the other hand, *intentional* misstatements could be non-random misstatements, which typically overstate current earnings, although in some settings
"big bath" write-offs can understate current earnings. Examples include
managers' discretion on contingent liabilities, and allowance for uncollectible
bad debts. In addition, employee fraud – misappropriation of assets – is
made possible by inadequate segregation of internal control duties. Thus the
effectiveness of internal control is an important determinant of disclosure
quality, which, in turn, can directly affect the decision-making of managers
and outside investors and creditors. That is, companies with deficiencies in
internal control tend to have lower quality of accounting information, which
not only lead to poor management decisions, but also make it difficult for
outside investors to efficiently monitor the managers' behavior (Healy &
Palepu, 2001).

The literature further documents that internal control could also affect
executive pay performance sensitivity (Sloan, 1993). Walsh and Seward
(1990) argue for a high degree of synergy between the effectiveness of internal control and the sensitivity of executive pay. The effectiveness of internal
control, via the pay performance sensitivity, could help stimulate the performance of executive, align the interests of shareholders and managers,
reduce opportunism behavior and reduce a firm's business risk. The
increase in the quality of accounting disclosure can also be used to identify
incompetent executives, so a company can replace them as soon as possible
to reduce the company's business risk. Therefore, we expect a direct link
between the effectiveness of internal control and firm performance.

However, some researchers also believe that internal control could
reduce investment companies' efficiency, because it set a series of rules
which could discourage managers from taking investment opportunities
(Bargeron et al., 2010). For instance, Ge and McVay (2005) examine the
disclosure of internal control deficiencies of U.S. firms and find a significant
negative correlation between deficiencies in internal control and firm's profitability. Thus, it remains an empirical question whether internal control
would help improve firm performance. Based on the discussion above, we
propose the following hypothesis:

H1. Internal control is positively related to firm performance.

Information asymmetry risk and agency cost vary in the different stages of life cycle, and so is the effectiveness of corporate governance mechanism to assure efficient resource allocation (Abdulsaleh & Worthington, 2013). The literature typically classifies firm life cycle into five stages — introduction, growth, mature, shake-out and decline (Dickinson, 2011). In the introduction period, innovation and entrepreneurship is important to a firm (Adizes, 1979; Greiner, 1997; Quinn & Cameron, 1983), and internal control typically would focus on cash flow controls and sufficient segregation of duties. Moreover, the decision making and action taking follow the pattern of trial-mistake-retrial due to the informal organization structures and procedures. In growth stage, internal control would focus on internal control activities, approval and authorization, and information communication. In maturity stage, internal control would focus on dealing with agency problems and internal crisis and a balance can be achieved between control and flexibility, because the management has accumulated rich experience over the history of a firm. During shake-out period, although some firms might still perform great, the organization structure has lost its flexibility and creativity. In the decline stage, internal control would focus mostly on risk management but most rules and policies are not effective. To restart a life circle, companies should re-design organization structure, and reform human resource management. The different focuses and functions of internal control at different stages of a firm's life cycle thus could have different influences on its operating activities and performance. Therefore, we develop the following hypotheses:

H2. In the different stages of life cycles, internal control have different impacts on firm performance.

RESEARCH DESIGN AND SAMPLE SELECTION

Measurement of Variables

Firm Life Cycle Stages
Following Gort and Klepper (1982), Dickinson (2011) constructed a firm life cycle based on cash flow patterns in operating investment and financing activities. Cash flow can be either positive or negative, which results in eight possible patterns. The eight patterns are classified into five stages — introduction, growth, maturity, shake-out, and decline stages as in Appendix A.

Besides Dickinson's (2011) cash flow approach on firm life cycle, other methods include financial ratios approach and trend curve approach. For instance, prior studies use variables such as firm age, sales growth, capital expenditures, dividend payout, or some combinations of these variables to estimate life cycle stage (Anthony & Ramesh, 1992; Black, 1998). When the trend shows a significant upward direction, the firm is classified as in a growth stage. When the curve shows a downward trend, the firm is classified as in a decline stage. Otherwise, the firm is classified as in a mature stage. With corporate characteristics and financial indicators such as profitability ratios, firm size and firm age, the drawback of these life cycle methods is that they assume a linear relationship between these variables and firm life cycle stages. However, such a relationship can be nonlinear. The combination of cash flow patterns to determine firm life cycle stages can solve the linear assumption issue (Dickinson, 2011).

In addition, an obvious advantage of using cash flow pattern proxy is that it uses the full information set contained in operating, investing, and financing cash flows rather than a single metric (or a composite of these items) to determine firm life cycle (Dickinson, 2011). This helps resolve the assumption issue of using financial ratio approach which assumes a uniform distribution of life cycle stages across firms. Moreover, using cash flow proxy addresses the assumption of size and age proxy that a firm moves monotonically through its life cycle. This assumption arises because product life cycles are featured as forward progression from introduction stage to decline stage. However, a firm normally produces multiple products at a different product life cycle stage. Thus, organization restructure, substantial product innovations, and expansion into new markets could change the firm life cycle status. Additionally, firms can enter the decline stage from any of the other four stages. Therefore, in this study, we use Dickinson (2011) cash flow pattern approach to define the life cycle of a firm.

Internal Control Effectiveness
In this paper, the effectiveness of internal control is measured by the internal index developed by Chen et al. (2013) (hereinafter referred to as the index) for the publicly listed companies in China. This index identifies five COSO elements, including the control environment, risk assessment, control activities, information and communication, and internal monitoring. The evaluation of each element is composed of a series of indicators. The overall evaluation system consists of a total of four levels and 144 indicators, based on COSO five elements framework: *Basic Standards of Internal Control (2008), Implementation Guidelines (2010), Internal Control Guidelines for Public Companies Listed in Shenzhen Stock Exchange,*

Internal Control Guidelines for Public Companies Listed in Shanghai Stock Exchange, Corporate Governance Guidelines, Company Law, Securities Law, and other relative guidelines. The metrics to calculate the index is presented in Chen et al. (2013). The index was first developed for all public firms in China in 2007 and released to the public annually via major newspaper.

Model Specification

Following Yu (2013), we use ROA to measure performance.[1] Following previous studies (Fairfield & Yohn, 2001; Nissim & Penman, 2001; Soliman, 2008), we also control for the effects of operating efficiency (TURNOVER). Following Sami, Wang, and Zhou (2011), we control for firm size (SIZE), capital structure (LEV), duality of CEO and Chair (DUALITY), ownership of largest stake shareholder (SHARE1), and capital intensity (CAPINT). As management ownership could help resolve agency problem to a certain degree, and improve firm performance (Mehran, 1995), we also include a control variable on management ownership (SHARE2). Book to market ratio (BM) is included as investors incorporate this factor in estimating firm value (Beaver & Ryan, 2000). The models are presented as following:

$$
\text{ROA} = \begin{aligned} &\beta_0 + \beta_1 \text{IC\_INDEX} + \beta_2 \text{SIZE} + \beta_3 \text{LEV} \\ &+ \beta_4 \text{TURNOVER} + \beta_5 \text{CAPINT} + \beta_6 \text{BM} + \beta_7 \text{SHARE1} \\ &+ \beta_8 \text{SHARE2} + \beta_9 \text{DUALITY} + \beta_k \text{YEAR DUMMIES} \\ &+ \beta_j \text{INDUSTRY DUMMIES} + \varepsilon \end{aligned} \quad (1)
$$

$$
\text{ROA} = \begin{aligned} &\beta_0 + \beta_1 \text{IC\_INDEX} + \beta_2 \text{LCIRCLE} + \beta_3 \text{IC\_INDEX} * \text{LCIRCLE} \\ &+ \beta_4 \text{SIZE} + \beta_5 \text{LEV} + \beta_6 \text{TURNOVER} \\ &+ \beta_7 \text{CAPINT} + \beta_8 \text{BM} + \beta_9 \text{SHARE1} + \beta_{10} \text{SHARE2} \\ &+ \beta_{11} \text{DUALITY} + \beta_k \text{YEAR DUMMIES} \\ &+ \beta_j \text{INDUSTRY DUMMIES} + \varepsilon \end{aligned} \quad (2)
$$

where

ROA = return on assets, calculated as net income/total assets;
IC_INDEX = Chen et al. (2013) internal control index;

LCIRCLE = firm life cycle proxy based on Dickinson (2011) cash flow
pattern. We further use GROWTH, MATURITY, SHAKEOUT, and
DECLINE dummy variables that denote growth, mature, shake-out
and decline stages of firm life cycle, respectively;
SIZE = Logarithm of total assets;
LEV = Total liabilities/total assets;
TURNOVER = asset turnover ratio, calculated as operating income/
total assets;
CAPINT = capital intensity, calculated as fixed assets/total assets;
BM = Book value/Market value;
SHARE1 = Percentage of shares owned by the largest shareholder;
SHARE2 = Percentage of shares owned by managers;
DUALITY = a dummy for the CEO-Chair duality, coded as 1 if a firm's
CEO is also its board chairman and zero otherwise.

The detailed definitions of the variables are shown in Table 1.

Sample Selection

Since the internal control index data became available in 2007, our sample
period covers the period of 2007–2012. The internal control index data are

Table 1. Definition of Variables.

Variables	Calculation	Description
ROA	Net income/Total assets	Total assets ratio
IC_INDEX	Chen et al. (2013) internal control index	Internal control effectiveness
LCIRCLE	Dickinson (2011) cash flow pattern	Firm life cycle stage
SIZE	Logarithm of total assets	Size
LEV	Total liabilities/Total assets	Capital structure
TURNOVER	Operating income/Total assets	Assets turnover
CAPINT	Fixed assets/Total assets	Capital intensity
BM	Book value/Market value	Book/market ratio
SHARE1	Proportion of largest shareholders	Proportion of largest shareholders
SHARE2	Proportion of managements	Proportion of managements
DUALITY	Coded as 1 if a firm's CEO is also its board chairman and 0 otherwise	Dummy for CEO-Chair duality

Table 2. Sample Selection and Sample Distribution.

Sample	N		2007	2008	2009	2010	2011	2012
Initial sample	11,602	Introduction	170	182	168	367	488	362
		Growth	476	489	523	706	719	700
Less: Financial firms	657	Mature	419	556	557	579	596	944
and firms with missing		Shake-out	199	182	237	174	280	261
observations		Decline	103	94	87	102	114	111
Final sample	10,945	Total	1,367	1,503	1,572	1,928	2,197	2,378

obtained from Chen (2010, 2011, 2012, 2013). We collect the financial data from China Stock Market & Accounting Research (CSMAR) Database. Our sample selection starts with all listed A-share companies in Shenzhen Stock Exchange and Shanghai Stock Exchange, including the motherboard, the Small and Medium Enterprise (SME) board and the Growth Enterprise Market (GEM), a total of 11,602 firm year observations. We further exclude 657 firm year observations on financial companies as they may have different characteristics than other firms, and observations with missing data. Our final sample includes 10,945 firm year observation.

As shown in Table 2, there is an increase of listed companies in the Chinese stock markets from 2007 to 2012. More companies are located in introduction, growth and maturity stages of firm life cycle in more recent years, showing an upward trend over time. There is no clear trend for firms in shake-out and decline stages. In the whole sample, the majority of companies are in the growth and mature stage, accounting for 66.4% of the total sample, while fewer companies are in the decline stage, accounting for 5.6% of the total sample. The distribution of the sample is similar with Dickinson (2011). To avoid the influence of outliers, all continuous variables are winsorized at 1% and 99% levels.

EMPIRICAL RESULTS

Descriptive Statistics

Panel A of Table 3 presents the descriptive statistics. The mean of internal control index (IC_INDEX) is 39.145 (out of 100), indicating that firms have low effectiveness in internal control in the emerging markets.

Table 3.   Descriptive Statistics.

	N	P25	Mean	Median	P75	Std.
Panel A. Descriptive Statistics of Pooled Sample						
IC_INDEX	10,945	32.135	39.145	39.313	45.893	10.169
ROA	10,945	0.015	0.040	0.040	0.068	0.064
SIZE	10,945	20.796	21.668	21.504	22.362	1.271
LEV	10,945	0.291	0.470	0.470	0.630	0.253
TURNOVER	10,945	0.358	0.683	0.567	0.858	0.483
CAPINT	10,945	0.105	0.246	0.209	0.356	0.178
BM	10,945	0.208	0.398	0.338	0.528	0.267
SHARE1	10,945	0.240	0.364	0.347	0.479	0.154
SHARE2	10,945	0.000	0.088	0.000	0.022	0.185
DUALITY	10,945	0.000	0.207	0.000	0.000	0.405

	2007	2008	2009	2010	2011	2012
Panel B Descriptive Statistics by Year						
N	1,367	1,503	1,572	1,928	2,197	2,378
IC_INDEX	28.695	35.677	38.354	39.935	42.559	44.072
ROA	0.044	0.026	0.033	0.048	0.046	0.040
SIZE	21.474	21.516	21.645	21.684	21.740	21.809
LEV	0.511	0.516	0.519	0.455	0.434	0.432
TURNOVER	0.734	0.738	0.658	0.667	0.682	0.648
CAPINT	0.284	0.282	0.271	0.230	0.217	0.223
BM	0.216	0.565	0.267	0.289	0.469	0.507
SHARE1	0.361	0.366	0.366	0.364	0.364	0.365
SHARE2	0.034	0.042	0.045	0.096	0.128	0.133
DUALITY	0.154	0.156	0.169	0.213	0.246	0.254

	Introduction	Growth	Mature	Shake-out	Decline
Panel C: Descriptive Statistics by Firm Life Cycle Stage					
N	1,737	3,613	3,651	1,333	611
IC_INDEX	39.456	40.502	39.284	36.812	34.499
ROA	0.025	0.045	0.051	0.030	0.011
SIZE	21.744	21.935	21.581	21.285	21.220
LEV	0.517	0.465	0.438	0.462	0.575
TURNOVER	0.672	0.645	0.763	0.637	0.557

Table 3.   (*Continued*)

	Introduction	Growth	Mature	Shake-out	Decline
CAPINT	0.178	0.273	0.282	0.199	0.161
BM	0.410	0.419	0.392	0.373	0.335
SHARE1	0.367	0.372	0.371	0.332	0.339
SHARE2	0.132	0.098	0.079	0.057	0.026
DUALITY	0.259	0.212	0.191	0.191	0.162

Note: See definitions of variables in Table 1.

The average return on assets (ROA) is 4%. As our sample period covers 2007−2008 financial crisis, which might be a reason for the low ROA. The average shareholding ratio of largest shareholder (share1) is 36.4%, indicating the dominance of large shareholders in the emerging markets of China, which is the state (Sami et al., 2011). In addition, 20.7% of the sample firms have their CEOs act as board chairmen at the same time.

Panel B presents the statistic description of variables by year. The sample size increase from 1367 firms in 2007 to 2378 firms in 2012, which is consistent with the upward trend of IPOs in Chinese stock markets. The average effectiveness of internal control increases from 28.695 in 2007 to 44.072 in 2012, which reflects the consequence of recent regulations on corporate internal control. The minimum ROA appears in 2008, showing that financial crisis had a significant effect on the emerging economy. The book value to the market ratio (BM) reaches its lowest in 2009, and financial leverage LEV declines after 2009. The asset turnover ratio (TURNOVER) from 2007 to 2012 shows a downward trend. Management ownership and duality of chairman and CEO show an upward trend. Moreover, the launch of the GEM, and the increasing number in listed firms whose stakeholders are non-state owned enterprises, largely attribute to the increase in the duality of chairman and CEO.

Panel C presents the statistic description of variables by the stages of firm life cycle. Most companies are in the growth and maturity stage, accounting for 66.4% of the total sample. The index is slightly low in shake-out and decline stages, indicating that when companies enter into a recession, their internal control systems begin to collapse. The distribution of the sample is similar to Dickinson's (2011) sample. Firm profitability shows an inverse U shape curve across different stages; financial leverage keeps declining from introduction period to shake-out period. However, firm's debt to asset ratio in recession has rebounded, which is similar to

Dickinson (2011). Capital intensity has higher values in growth and maturity stages. It is worth noting that the duality of the chairman and CEO reaches highest in introduction stage, and lowest in decline stage, which could be explained by the recent opening of the GEM.

Table 4 shows the results of Spearman (top) and Pearson (lower) correlation matrix. Internal control index is positively and significantly correlated with ROA, firm size (SIZE), the largest shareholder ownership (SHARE1), and management ownership (SHARE2). On the contrary, the index is significantly and negatively correlated with financial leverage (LEV). Firm size (SIZE) and BM are highly correlated with a Pearson coefficient of 0.474. ROA and LEV are negatively correlated with a Pearson coefficient of −0.418, and so are SHARE1 and LEV, with a Pearson coefficient of −0.365. None of other independent variables have a correlation coefficient higher than 0.30.

Regression Results Analysis

Table 5 shows regression results on the link between internal control and firm performance with ROA as the dependent variable. Column (1) presents the regression results without considering firm life cycle stages, controlling for industry fixed effect and year fixed effects. The estimated coefficient of internal control index (IC_INDEX) is 0.0006, at the 1% significance level, indicating the overall performance is positively related to the effectiveness of internal control. Consistent with the literature (Sami et al., 2011), firm size (SIZE), asset turnover ratio (TURNOVER), the largest shareholder ownership (SHARE1), the management ownership (SHARE2) have significant and positive impacts on firm performance, while financial leverage (LEV), capital intensity (CAPINT), and the book to market ratio (BM) have significant and negative impacts on firm performance.

Column (2) presents the regression results with dummy variables on firm life cycle stages, controlling for industry fixed effect and year fixed effects. The estimated coefficient of internal control index (IC_INDEX) is 0.0004, positively significant at 5% level, indicating that increase of internal control can promote firm performance. The estimated interaction (IC_INDEX × growth) coefficient is not significant, indicating there is no significant difference in the impact of internal control on firm performance between growing business and new business. The estimated coefficient on the interaction term between internal control and maturity stage (IC_INDEX maturity) is 0.0003, positively significant at 10% level, indicating that increase of internal control in

Table 4. Spearman (Up) and Pearson (Down) Correlation Matrix.

	IC_INDEX	ROA	SIZE	LEV	TURNOVER	CAPINT	BM	SHARE1	SHARE2	DUALITY
IC_INDEX		0.163	0.252	-0.107	0.075	-0.062	0.274	0.122	0.158	0.034
ROA	0.180		-0.003	-0.454	0.121	-0.177	-0.179	0.118	0.221	0.092
SIZE	0.319	0.075		0.391	0.078	0.078	0.425	0.243	-0.161	-0.187
LEV	-0.139	-0.418	0.249		0.138	0.134	-0.036	0.009	-0.301	-0.194
TURNOVER	0.064	0.089	0.088	0.131		0.146	-0.041	0.094	-0.031	-0.067
CAPINT	-0.061	-0.170	0.121	0.159	0.029		0.063	0.025	-0.173	-0.107
BM	0.267	-0.078	0.474	-0.067	-0.030	0.100		0.080	0.017	-0.058
SHARE1	0.124	0.118	0.288	-0.020	0.081	0.031	0.084		-0.191	-0.046
SHARE2	0.128	0.155	-0.249	-0.365	-0.093	-0.206	-0.054	-0.087		0.212
DUALITY	0.023	0.046	-0.181	-0.167	-0.065	-0.110	-0.078	-0.052	0.260	

Note: Correlation coefficient is in bold if it is significant at <10% level. See definitions of variables in Table 1.

Table 5. Regression Results.

| | (1) | | (2) | |
| | ROA | | ROA | |
	Estimate	t-Value	Estimate	t-Value
Intercept	−0.2158***	−10.42	−0.2097***	−9.8
IC_INDEX	0.0006***	9.22	0.0004**	2.56
GROWTH			0.0201***	2.88
MATURITY			0.0068	0.85
SHAKEOUT			−0.0118	−1.11
DECLINE			−0.0124	−0.88
IC_INDEX × GROWTH			−0.0001	−0.65
IC_INDEX × MATURITY			0.0003*	1.91
IC_INDEX × SHAKEOUT			0.0005*	1.9
IC_INDEX × DECLINE			0.0003	0.95
SIZE	0.0146***	16.69	0.0141	16.32
LEV	−0.1203***	−19.7	−0.1139	−18.5
TURNOVER	0.0211***	13.74	0.0193	12.61
CAPINT	−0.0438***	−8.83	−0.0543	−10.74
BM	−0.0639**	−20.94	−0.0618	−20.36
SHARE1	0.0145***	4.21	0.0132	3.88
SHARE2	0.0143***	5.29	0.0149	5.47
DUALITY	−0.0014	−1.05	−0.0011	−0.78
Year fixed effect	Yes		Yes	
Industry fixed effect	Yes		Yes	
N	10,945		10,945	
Adjusted R^2	0.3284		0.3424	
F	51.04		50.09	

Notes: GROWTH, MATURITY, SHAKEOUT, and DECLINE are dummy variables that denote growth, mature, shake-out, and decline stages of firm life-cycle, respectively. See definitions of other variables in Table 1.
*, **, *** indicates significance at 10%, 5%, 1% level, respectively.

mature companies can promote firm performance more significantly than new firms. The overall effect is 0.00070 (0.0004 + 0.0003), which almost double the effect of internal control on firm performance for new firms. The estimated coefficient of the interaction term between internal control and shake-out (IC_INDEX × shakeout) is 0.0005, positively significant at 10% level, indicating that the increased influence of internal control in shake-out companies can promote firm performance more significantly than new firms. The overall coefficient is 0.0009 (0.0004 + 0.0005), more than twice the impact of internal control in introduction stage and higher than the effect in maturity stage. When companies are in a shake-out period with the emergence of various internal unrests, internal control plays a more important role in this stage, although firm performance is worse than that of growth and maturity stages. The estimated coefficient of the interaction term between internal control and decline stage dummy(IC_INDEX × decline) is insignificant, indicating promoting internal controls works on firm performance no more than in introduction stage, but it is worth noting that, even in a recession, internal control has no negative impact on firm performance.

We further perform sensitivity tests to address the following issues: (1) measurement of firm performance, (2) definition of firm life cycle stages, and (3) endogenous relationship between internal control and firm performance. To test the robustness of using ROA as a proxy for firm performance, we also use Tobin's Q, CROA, ROE and EPS, the results are substantially similar to what are reported. As an alternative definition of firm life cycle, we use sales growth, capital spending growth rate and firm age to redefine firm life cycle, and the results are consistent with those reported earlier. Finally, firms with good performance could have more resources to establish and maintain effective internal control, and thus endogeneity problem may exist when using ROA, ROE and other performance indicators. In robustness test, we use a two-stage least square approach; the results obtained are consistent with primary tests.

CONCLUSIONS

In this paper, we explore the relationship between internal control and corporate performance at different stages of firm life cycle. One key objective of internal control is to improve effectiveness and efficiency of all activities. Therefore, one would expect a significant link between internal control and firm performance. However, the effect of internal control on firm performance is not clear at different firm life cycle stages.

We investigate whether internal control would affect firm performance and whether corporate life cycle would affect firm performance in the emerging markets of China. Using Chen et al.'s (2013) internal control index to measure the effectiveness of internal control and Dickinson's (2011) definition on firm life cycle, we find that the internal control improves corporate performance. When dividing firm life cycle into five stages: introduction, growth, mature, shake-out and decline, we find that the impacts of internal controls on firm performs vary with different stages. The positive impact of internal control on firm performance is more significant in maturity and shake-out stages than other stages.

In summary, internal control has significant and positive effects on corporate performance in the emerging markets. Our findings would have implications for the regulators and policy makers with regards to the importance of internal control in corporate governance and the effectiveness of implementing standards and guidelines on internal control in public firms. In addition, our findings on the various roles of internal control at different stages of firm life cycle would help managers and board of directors find more focus in risk management and board monitoring, respectively. In particular, our findings of more positive impact of internal control on firm performance in maturity and shakeout stages than other stages suggest that management needs to pay more attention to the function of internal control when firms are in these life cycle stages.

NOTES

1. Alternative measures of firm performance include RNOA and ROE. For instance, Baik, Chae, Choi, and Farber (2013) use RNOA (Return on net operating assets) to investigate the relationship between operational efficiency and company performance. Banker, Darrough, Huang, and Plehn-Dujowich (2013) use ROE as a performance measure to investigate the interaction between performance and executive compensation. We perform sensitivity tests using alternative measures and the results are qualitatively the same as reported.

ACKNOWLEDGMENTS

Hanwen Chen would like to acknowledge the financial support from the National Natural Science Foundation (Project No. 71332008), and the Key Research Base Fund for Humanities and Social Sciences from Ministry of Education of China (Project No. 10JJD630003).

REFERENCES

Abdulsaleh, A. M., & Worthington, A. C. (2013). Small and medium-sized enterprises financing: A review of literature international. *Journal of Business and Management, 8*(14), 36–54.

Adizes, I. (1979). Organizational passages—Diagnosing and treating lifecycle problems of organizations. *Organizational Dynamics, 8*(1), 3–25.

Anthony, J., & Ramesh, K. (1992). Association between accounting performance measures and stock prices. *Journal of Accounting and Economics, 15*, 203–227.

Ashbaugh-Skaife, H., Collins, D., Kinney, W. R., Jr., & LaFond, R. (2009). The effect of SOX internal control deficiencies on firm risk and cost of equity. *Journal of Accounting Research, 47*(1), 1–43.

Ashbaugh-Skaife, H., Collins, D. W., & Kinney, W. R., Jr. (2008). The effect of SOX internal control deficiencies and their remediation on accrual effectiveness. *The Accounting Review, 83*(1), 217–250.

Baik, B., Chae, J., Choi, S., & Farber, D. (2013). Changes in operational efficiency and firm performance: A frontier analysis approach. *Contemporary Accounting Research, 30*(3), 996–1026.

Banker, R. D., Darrough, M. N., Huang, R., & Plehn-Dujowich, J. (2013). The relation between CEO compensation and past performance. *The Accounting Review, 88*(1), 1–30.

Bargeron, L. L., Lehn, K. M., & Zutter, C. J. (2010). Sarbanes-Oxley and corporate risk-taking. *Journal of Accounting and Economics, 49*(1), 34–52.

Beaver, W. H., & Ryan, S. G. (2000). Biases and Lags in book value and their effects on the ability of the book-to-market ratio to predict book return on equity. *Journal of Accounting Research, 38*(1), 127–148.

Black, E. L. (1998). Life-cycle impacts on the incremental value-relevance of earnings and cash flow measures. *Journal of Financial Statement Analysis, 4*, 40–56.

Chen, H. (2010). Internal control index for public firms in China (2007–2009): Development, analysis and comments. *China Securities Journal*, June 11.

Chen, H. (2011). Internal control index for public firms in China (2007–2009): Development, analysis and comments. *Securities Times*, September 6.

Chen, H. (2012). Internal control index for public firms in China (2011): Development, analysis and comments. *Shanghai Securities Journal*, August 16.

Chen, H. (2013). Internal control index for public firms in China (2012): Development, analysis and comments. *Securities Times*, September 26.

Chen, H., Dong, W., Han, H., & Zhou, N. (2013). *A comprehensive and quantitate internal control index: Construction, validation and impact*. Working Paper. Xiamen University.

Chen, Q., Chen, X., Schipper, K., Xu, Y., & Xue, J. (2012). The sensitivity of corporate cash holdings to corporate governance. *Review of Financial Studies, 25*(12), 3610–3644.

COSO. *Internal control – Integrated framework*. Retrieved from www.coso.org

Dickinson, V. (2011). Cash flow patterns as a proxy for firm life cycle. *The Accounting Review, 86*(6), 1969–1994.

Doyle, J. T., Ge, W., & McVay, S. (2007). Accruals effectiveness and internal control over financial reporting. *The Accounting Review, 82*(5), 1141–1170.

Fairfield, P. M., & Yohn, T. L. (2001). Using asset turnover and profit margin to forecast changes in profitability. *Review of Accounting Studies, 6*(4), 371–385.

Ge, W., Li, Z., Liu, Q., & McVay, S. (2016). *When does internal control over financial reporting curb corporate corruption? Evidence from China.* Working Paper. University of Washington. Retrieved from http://ssrn.com/abstract=2704663

Ge, W., & McVay, S. (2005). The disclosure of material weaknesses in internal control after the Sarbanes-Oxley Act. *Accounting Horizons, 19*(3), 137–158.

Gort, M., & Klepper, S. (1982). Time paths in the diffusion of product innovation. *Economic Journal, 92,* 630–653.

Greiner, L. E. (1997). Evolution and revolution as organizations grow. *Harvard Business Review, 76*(3), 55–60.

Healy, P., & Palepu, K. (2001). Information asymmetry, corporate disclosure, and the capital markets: A review of the empirical disclosure literature. *Journal of Accounting & Economics, 31,* 405–440.

Mehran, H. (1995). Executive compensation structure, ownership, and firm performance. *Journal of Financial Economics, 38*(2), 163–184.

Nissim, D., & Penman, S. (2001). Ratio analysis and equity valuation: From research to practice. *Review of Accounting Studies, 6*(1), 109–154.

Ogneva, M., Subramanyam, K. R., & Raghunandan, K. (2007). Internal control weakness and cost of equity: Evidence from SOX section 404 disclosures. *The Accounting Review, 82*(5), 1255–1297.

Quinn, R. E., & Cameron, K. (1983). Organizational life cycles and shifting criteria of effectiveness: Some preliminary evidence. *Management Science, 29*(1), 33–51.

Sami, H., Wang, T., & Zhou, H. (2011). Corporate governance and operating performance of Chinese listed firms. *Journal of International Accounting, Auditing and Taxation, 20*(1), 106–114.

Soliman, M. T. (2008). The use of dupont analysis by market participants. *The Accounting Review, 83*(3), 823–853.

Sloan, R. G. (1993). Accounting earnings and top executive compensation. *Journal of Accounting and Economics, 16*(1–3), 55–100.

Walsh, J. P., & Seward, J. K. (1990). On the efficiency of internal and external corporate control mechanisms. *The Academy of Management Review, 15*(3), 421–458.

Yu, M. (2013). State ownership and firm performance: Empirical evidence from Chinese listed companies. *China Journal of Accounting Research, 6*(2), 75–87.

APPENDIX A

Table A1. Dickinson's (2011) Firm Life Cycle.

	1 Introduction	2 Growth	3 Mature	4 Shake-Out	5 Shake-Out	6 Shake-Out	7 Decline	8 Decline
Cash flows from operating activities	−	+	+	−	+	+	−	−
Cash flows from investing activities	−	−	−	−	+	+	+	+
Cash flows from financing activities	+	+	−	−	+	−	+	−

THE EFFECT OF PRIVATIZATION PROCESSES AND THE *SPLIT-SHARE STRUCTURE REFORM* ON THE MARKET REACTION TO THE ANNOUNCEMENTS OF *TRANSITIONAL NON-TRADITIONAL SHARES*[☆]

Aysun Ficici, Bo Fan, C. Bülent Aybar and
Lingling Wang

[☆] In this paper, the concept of *transitional non-traditional shares* refers to once *non-traditional shares* becoming *traditional shares* when they are announced to be listed in the capital market. They mainly become *split shares* through declaration of stock split by the firm, which is usually done to infill liquidity and to make shares afford-able for investors who could not afford to purchase previously.

The Political Economy of Chinese Finance
International Finance Review, Volume 17, 211–240
Copyright © 2016 by Emerald Group Publishing Limited
All rights of reproduction in any form reserved
ISSN: 1569-3767/doi:10.1108/S1569-376720160000017014

ABSTRACT

Purpose — *This paper attempts to explore the interrelationships between the* split-share structure reform *and privatization processes in light of the interplay between the listing announcements of the* non-traditional shares *of the Chinese firms within the steel industry and market reaction to these listed shares, as well as to analyze the value gained by the firms due to the privatization processes.*

Methodology/approach — *The paper examines market reaction to the listing announcements of* non-traditional shares *as traditional shares by employing* event-study methodology. *To determine the success of privatization process and value creation to the firm, the paper utilizes* multivariate analysis.

Findings — *The exogenous factors emphasized in a topographical order, explicitly profitability, efficiency, and leverage, are related to the privatization processes and* split-share structure reform *that impact the market. The study supports that market reacts positively to the listing announcements of* non-traditional shares. *Being listed improves value to the firm.*

Research limitations/implications — *The limitation of this study is the lack of data on country, industry, and firm factors; and this study merely relates to one specific industry and one country.*

Originality/value — *The paper fills a gap in the literature by articulating the impact of privatization and* split-share structure reform *on both market reaction and firm value. It focuses on the impact of a dynamic process rather than the impact of a static constituent on market reaction and firm value, as the previous studies have been concentrating on. The research shows that there is an accelerated privatization process of state-owned firms in Chinese steel industry and their integration in capital markets.*

Keywords: Chinese privatization reform/split-share structure reform; Chinese steel industry; emerging market SOEs; market reaction and event-study; non-traditional shares and traditional shares; shareholders' wealth

INTRODUCTION

The global steel industry has been going through significant changes since the 1970s. Although the changes are interconnected with various global factors, there are mainly two factors, which are predominant within this vital industry. The first predominant factor is related to structural attributes and price-production dynamics that overrule the worldwide output and distribution of steel. The second predominant factor is associated with macro aspects, such as geographical and strategic forces in the international arena.

When the first factor is considered, it becomes prevalent that there are mainly two interrelated dimensions: (1) The structural changes, which the global steel industry has been experiencing since 2010, and supply chain processes that gave way to structural changes; and (2) Short-term pricing in iron-ore contracts. Notably, during 2008 and 2009, the short-term contracts on iron-ore prices became exposed to spot market and hence, global steel prices experienced a sharp increase in 2010 (The Smart Cube, 2012). These changes were largely due to the fact that the supply of iron-ore — the main material for steel production began to be controlled by only a few global firms.

During this time, the second dynamic, namely the geo-strategic factor began to illustrate a seen, in which various emerging market countries initiated a crucial act in the role they took part in within the vibrant developments of the global steel industry. Due to the high manufacturing cost of steel production, only a few number of large global players were able to perform in this high-fixed industry. Among these large players, China became powerful with an estimation of 600 steel mills and a large output of about 1 million tons per year. Henceforth, China has emerged as a major producer and a consumer as well as the world's biggest importer of iron in 2003.

However, with the coming of the financial crisis in 2008, the global behavior of the steel industry in the market place began to illustrate a trend toward a notable decrease in consumption and production, and an increase in steel prices. Although the world was experiencing a decline within the steel industry, China continued to be the biggest steel importer in 2008 with its steel imports accounted for 60 percent of total global imports. In addition, Chinese iron-ore prices rapidly increased by 42 percent during this time. This increase triggered a dramatic rise in input costs of steel manufacturers (Tang, 2010).

One of the main reasons for China being a global leader and sustaining its leadership in this industry is the privatization processes that it has been experiencing since 2005. Between 2005 and 2006, China went through structural reforms and liberalization procedures that enhanced China's economy on the way to privatization, making the country the front-runner in the global market. As reported by the World Bank, 1,835 transactions of privatization with a total amount of US$452,682 million were completed in 101 countries within the period of 2000–2008 (World Bank, n.d.). China has taken a large portion of the total transactions by incorporating not only economic reforms, but institutional developments as well; and by linking liberalization processes within the steel industry in line with the new trends and acceleration in worldwide privatization processes of high-fixed cost industries. Since steel industry strategically experienced a rapid expansion of steel output during the early 2000s, most countries, including emerging markets, such as China[1] became impacted by the privatization trend of this industry. Hence, iron- ore, namely steel industry began to play a key role in privatization processes in China. In addition, this sector became an essential player in building the infrastructure in various geographic areas in China.

Since iron-ore is the major raw material in both semi-finished and finished steel products, it has the irreplaceable effect on building the essential infrastructure of a modern society. The application of steel is broad and varies from capital goods industries (e.g., construction, machinery, heavy transport, oil and gas) to consumer goods industries (e.g., automotive, home appliance, packaging). In terms of volume of steel consumed, the automobile and construction industries lead the mission in most countries.

Although the steel industry is a leading industry, it does not come free of challenges, as there are stringent national regulations and trade barriers. For example, subsidies – whether direct or indirect – overshadow nationwide and global processes and create major difficulties in this industry. This has been especially true for those countries that went through intensive privatization processes. During its transition of market reforms and privatization processes, which were employed in several stages, China became one of the main countries that faced specific challenges, such as impractical structural problems. This was mainly due to the existence of the predominance of state-owned enterprises (SOEs), mostly owned 100 percent by the Chinese government. China's steel industry has been and still is affected by various structural problems that stem from the dominant role of the chronically underperforming SOEs in this industry. The major reason for SOEs to have a strong presence in the steel industry is that the industry is still perceived by the Chinese authorities as a *pillar industry*[2] that is crucial for China's economic development.

For China to be a leader in the steel industry and to sustain its leadership role is also due to other structural reforms and liberalization processes in the financial sector. With the creation of stock markets in Shanghai and Shenzhen in 1991, enterprises became able to raise capital through trading their collectively owned shares (Fan & Fan, 1996). Although many steel producers were converted into shareholding enterprises by initial public offerings (IPOs) during the late 1990s, the vast majority of the listed enterprises still remain under control of either central or local governments. In this process, capital markets were used primarily by the Chinese government as a means of gradual reform, in which only about 30 percent equity of listed firms sold to the public were tradable, 60 percent of them were maintained under the ownership of the government, and the remaining proportion of 10 percent of the SOEs were non-tradable (Jiang, Laurenceson, & Tang, 2008). This is still the case within the capital structure of SOEs, where SOE sales are associated with various stringent rules and regulations.

Yet, there is an existence of an unparalleled feature of ownership structure in China — *non-traditional shares*. The ownership of *non-traditional shares* provides both the majority and minority shareholders with equal voting and dividend rights of traditional shares. Nevertheless, the concept of *non-traditional shares* is considered as a feature of the first stage of Chinese privatization reform, which represents a major hurdle to domestic financial market development and firm performance due to the Chinese government's insistence of controlling and managing it. The gradual reforms in traditional shares and *non-traditional shares* in China have been employed in a different manner than that of what is typically practiced by transition economies of the Eastern European countries, where privatization processes were introduced as a *shock therapy*. In China this process has been applied by pragmatic means, enabling the Chinese government and local authorities to maintain the control over SOEs and to maximize the proceeds gained from IPOs by managing and decreasing the supply of capital and increasing the stock prices. However, with the introduction of the *split-share structure reform*,[3] a proposed unprecedented political and economic mechanism was launched by the Chinese central government in 2005. The obstacle of controlling and managing *non-traditional shares* by the government began to lessen gradually, and the evolution as well as the progress of Chinese market economy started to take a more prosperous path.

As it is stated above, the Chinese privatization processes were structured in two stages. In the first stage, the privatization of SOEs was predominantly partial with government being the majority shareholder. In the second stage, although it was still partial, privatization of SOEs was less stringent on government holdings, as in 2015 the Chinese government only required to hold minimum shares of the partially privatized SOEs. The main reason for government decision to have minority shares was mainly due to the fact that the shareholders of SOEs required to have more liquidity. At present time, Chinese central government does not impose any limitations on the ownership of non-government owned shares, meaning government does not require any minimum percentage of ownership for itself.

Overall, the privatization processes of SOEs in China were mainly initiated and encouraged by the *split-share structure reform* and hence, shares of SOEs in the steel industry began to be listed in the capital markets as *non-traditional shares* in 2005. With this progress, the once *non-traditional* and/or non-tradable shares of firms in the steel industry began to be listed as traditional and/or tradable shares in the secondary market in China.

Hence, the primary purpose of this paper is to explore the interrelationships between the *split-share structure reform* and privatization processes in light of the interplay between the listing announcements of the *non-traditional shares* of the firms within the steel industry and market reaction to these listed shares, as well as to analyze the value gained by the firms due to these privatization processes.

Deriving from the research statement mentioned above, the primary research question may be stated as follows: Have the privatization process and the *split-share structure reform* in Chinese steel industry been successful? In order to be able to address this question, the following secondary questions can be posited as follows: (1) How does the recently founded Chinese stock market, as a platform and as a major instrument of the Chinese privatization processes, react to the listings of once *non-traditional shares* and/or non-tradable shares of firms in Chinese steel industry, whence they are announced to be listed as traditional and/or tradable shares through *split-share structure reform*? (2) What are the exogenous factors related to the privatization process and *split-share structure reform* that impact the market to react to the listing announcements of these shares in a certain way? and (3) Do the listing of *non-traditional shares* as traditional shares create or improve value to the firm?

In order to be able to objectively address the research question and sub-questions, the paper first focuses on the market reaction to the announcements of the listings by employing *event-study methodology*. Second, to determine the overall success of privatization process and the creation of value to the firm, firm performance is evaluated by utilizing *multivariate analysis*. It is important to note here that firm performance is the measure chosen in this paper in evaluating both the success of privatization and firm value. Hence, the hypotheses are generated in a topographical order by emphasizing profitability, efficiency, and leverage factors of the firm.

The data explored for this purpose are as follows: (1) The listed firms in Chinese steel industry are extracted from both the Chinese securities trading platform *Cinda* security and the *GF* security; (2) Stock market prices are collected from *Datastream*; and (3) The listing announcement dates of the *transitional non-traditional shares* by SOEs in Chinese steel industry during the 2005–2006 period are obtained from *Wind data*.

The paper is organized in the following order: the background and *split-share structure reform* are introduced in the next section. After this, the relevant literature and hypotheses are presented. In the next section, the data, model, and the methodology are illustrated. Following this, the empirical results are discussed. Finally, the conclusion is provided.

ISSUES OF SPLIT-SHARE STRUCTURE

With the rapid growth of Chinese economy and development of its financial markets, the government and regulatory authorities of China recognized the problems created by the predominance of *non-traditional shares* and the government ownership of SOEs, and hence launched *split-share structure reform*. In this way, shortcomings of the state ownership could begin to diminish. Hence, in order to make sense of the reforms and other developments of the Chinese privatization processes, it is important to identify these shortcomings.

One of the main shortcomings has been the existence of primary ownership of the Chinese government, in which SOEs structure was viewed as a problem, as the holders of traditional shares were mostly minority shareholders with limited power to influence management decisions. As stated by Megginson (2005), government ownership ensures that business enterprises balance social and economic objectives, such as maintaining employment rate, paying above-equilibrium wages, offering lower price than that of market, and constructing factories in underdeveloped regions. These objectives are mostly prevalent in the structures of various SOE operations; and the explanation for these objectives may be associated with economic or non-economic perspectives, which are not necessarily rooted in the notion of pure profit maximization, but in social foundations and causes pursued by SOEs.

However, the involvement of governments, central or local, in the ownership of firms in specific industries has had negative impact on the economic growth in China over the years. This has become a concern for the International Business scholars since they consider governments pursuing non-economic objectives may create inefficiencies in the way SOEs operate (Shleifer & Vishny, 1994). Some of the inefficiencies may be caused by the lack of incentives under the government ownership, impacting competition negatively in the market economy. When SOE managers have less incentive than those of privately owned firms, they may work less diligently towards revenue maximization and cost minimization (Shleifer, 1998). This has been true in the case of China and its most industries.

Second, in China the limitation on the free float of capital has made the domestic market extremely illiquid, volatile and thus prone to market manipulation as well as insider trading. Third, the inefficiencies experienced within the domestic market forced many valuable Chinese firms to list their stocks in overseas capital markets and in Hong Kong,[4] which has become one of the most preferred destinations. However, this adversely affected domestic investors, who were prevented from investing in major firms in mainland China, as the stocks were listed in foreign capital markets. The investors were also restricted with holdings in the less performing local firms.

LITERATURE AND HYPOTHESES

Market Reaction

Previous literature in the area of market reaction related to privatization focuses on firm performance. For example, Otchere (2002) analyzes stock price reaction of 314 firms to the privatization announcement by 121 firms that are divested via share offering in order to infer the expected impact of privatization on the performance of firms in 28 industries from 29 developed and developing countries. He discovers that rivals reacted negatively to privatization announcements, losing 1.72 percent (1.64 percent) of their value over the three-day (five-day) period surrounding the announcement, and that the reaction of rivals to a full privatization announcement was larger than that of a partial privatization announcement.

In line with this study, but more specifically focusing on a single country, Bortolotti and Beltratti (2006) examine 368 Chinese firms that successfully reformed their *non-traditional shares* into traditional shares. Particularly, they investigate the price effect of this reform during specific event periods. For example, during a 10-day interval, investors are informed, their feedback are collected, and the listing announcement dates of *transitional non-traditional shares* are agreed upon during the registration period. The authors find that the abnormal returns continue to increase throughout the reform process until the beginning of the registration or the record date.

Stemming from the previous literature in this concentration and based on the efficient markets hypothesis, a stock price is equal to the expectation of the future fundamentals.

Therefore, the following hypothesis may be proposed:

H1. No price change is associated with the listing announcements of transitional non-traditional shares and the implementation of the split-share structure reform for a given listed firm.

Profitability

Studies in this area are also focused in other areas rather than just market reaction. One of these angles is profitability related. For instance, Boardman and Vining (1989) examine the economic performance of the 500 largest non-U.S. firms in 1983, classified by ownership structure as state-owned, privately owned, or mixed-ownership enterprises. Employing four profitability ratios, they find that state-owned and mixed-ownership firms are significantly less profitable than privately owned firms. Similarly, Megginson, Nash, and Randenborgh (1994) analyze the significance of median changes in post-versus pre-privatization period by comparing three-year average post-privatization financial and operating performance ratios to the three-year pre-privatization values for 61 firms from 18 countries and 32 industries during 1961–1989. Their findings suggest that through economic and statistical evidence privatization improves firm performance, and that post-privatization increases profitability and efficiency significantly.

Similarly, Boubakri and Cosset (1998) apply the same methodology used by Megginson et al. (1994), by focusing on different industry charac-teristics and country data to examine firm performance post-versus pre-privatization, and find greater improvement in all sectors including operating efficiency and profitability. This effect is also stated by D'souza and Megginson (1999), who empirically document significant post-privatization increases in operating efficiency and profitability.

Comparison of pre- versus post-privatization performance is also examined by Dewenter and Malatesta (2001), in which 63 large, high-tech firms that divested during 1981−1994 period. Their comparison of the relative performance of a large sample of state and privately owned firms indicates significant increases in profitability and significant decreases in leverage over both short and long-term comparison. Research done by Laurin and Bozec (2001) also compares profitability of firms by focusing on two large Canadian rail carriers and their performances before and after the 1995 privatization of Canadian National Rail. Their research demonstrates that private ownership brings superior performance to both of these large carriers. Similarly, a study conducted by Liao, Liu, and Wang (2014) shows that SOE performance is positively correlated with the privatization processes in China during the *split-share structure reform*.

Based on the suggestions of the previous research in this area, the following hypothesis may be presented:

H2. The listing of the non-traditional shares as traditional shares creates value to the firm by impacting positively on firm profitability − conveying a positive signal to the market, and hence increasing shareholder wealth.

Efficiency

In consistent with efficiency research, Boardman and Vining (1989) employ two measures of efficiency, and find that both state-owned and mixed-ownership firms are significantly less productive than privately owned firms. Furthermore, they reveal that mixed-ownership firms are no more profitable than purely state-owned firms. Their research suggests that full private ownership may enhance efficiency in firms' operations. In another study, Vining and Boardman (1992) apply performance model to their empirical study and utilize 500 largest non-financial Canadian firms that include 12 state-owned and 93 mixed-ownership firms to test whether ownership "matters" in determining the efficiency of state-owned, mixed-owned and privately owned firms. Their findings suggest that privately owned firms are significantly more profitable and efficient than state-owned and mixed-ownership firms.

In line with previous studies, other research analyzes the differences of efficiency among state-owned, mixed-owned, and privately owned firms in India by using aggregate, industry-level survey data, where the findings support superior efficiency of privately owned and mixed-ownership firms over state-owned firms (Ficici, 2005; Majumdar,1998). Furthermore, Bartel and Harrison (2005) scrutinize whether inefficiencies in public sector are primarily created by the agency problem or by the industrial structure within the operating environment of state-owned firms. By utilizing panel data of all public and private manufacturing firms in Indonesia for the period of 1981–1995, the author illustrates that ownership structure along with environmental factors cause inefficiencies in state-owned firms (Bartel and Harrison, 2005).

On the other hand, a contrasting study of Feng, Sun, and Tong (2002) explores financial and operating performance of 31 Singaporean firms and posits that efficiency deteriorates after privatization. Here, the authors state that the Singaporean state-owned firms are unusually well managed before privatization, and illustrate that privatization may negatively impact firms' efficiency.

Similarly, Bottasso and Sembenelli (2004) explore the relationship between the identity of ultimate owners and the technical efficiency of firms by applying firm-level panel data for 12 Italian manufacturing firms for the period of 1978–1993, and reveal that state-owned firms are significantly less efficient than other two alternative ownership structures. Likewise, Ros (1999) examines the effects of competition and privatization on network expansion and efficiency of firms by employing International Telecommunications Union data in 110 countries over the period of 1986–1995. Their study that uses panel data regression methodology indicates that both privatization and competition increase efficiency. However, it also suggests that only privatization is positively associated with network expansion (Bottasso & Sembenelli, 2004).

Based on the prior studies in this area, the following hypothesis can be constructed:

H3. The listing of the non-traditional shares as traditional shares creates value to the firm by impacting positively on firm efficiency – conveying a positive signal to the market, and hence increasing shareholder wealth.

Leverage

In considering leverage, various studies illustrate significance of privatization. Although some studies illustrate increase in leverage after privatization, most

studies find that leverage decreases post-privatization. In the study of
Maquieira and Zurita (1996), an increase in leverage is shown, in which a
comparison of pre- versus post-privatization performance of 22 Chilean
firms that were privatized during the period of 1984–1989. They apply the
same methodology employed by Megginson et al. (1994).

Other studies as well show a decrease in leverage. For instance, Boubakri
and Cosset (1998) in their empirical study find that leverage decreases during post-privatization period. In agreement with Boubakri and Cosset
(1998), D'souza and Megginson (1999) study the significance of median
changes in ratio values, such as leverage, in 78 firms from 10 developing and
15 developed countries in post-versus pre-privatization periods during the
years of 1990–1994, by comparing a three-year average post-privatization
financial ratios. Their study, as well, indicates that the leverage substantially
decreases during post-privatization period. Similarly, Dewenter and
Malatesta (2001) examine private ownership and debt relationships by
focusing on the debt levels of 500 largest non-U.S. state-owned firms during
the years of 1975, 1985, and 1995. Their findings reveal that private ownership has significantly less debt and less labor-intensive production processes.

In addition, Dewenter and Malatesta (2001) find a significant decrease in
leverage as they compare pre- versus post-privatization performance of 63
large high-tech firms over both short and long-term comparison. Empirical
studies further support similar results. For example, Omran (2002) tests
performance changes in 69 Egyptian firms privatized between 1994 and
1998, and reveals that leverage declines significantly after privatization.

Based on the literature that concentrates on leverage, the following
hypothesis may be suggested:

H4. The listing of the non-traditional shares as traditional shares creates
value to the firm by impacting positively on firm leverage – conveying a
positive signal to the market, and hence increasing shareholder wealth.

DATA AND METHODOLOGY

Data

The data explored for this research are as follows:

1) The listed firms in Chinese steel industry are extracted from both the
   Chinese securities trading platform *Cinda* security and the *GF* security;
2) Stock market prices are collected from *Datastream*. Each firms' stock
   prices, local market price indexes around listing announcement dates,

three financial variables (profitability measured as ROE, efficiency measured as assets per employee, and leverage measured as total debt to total assets) are collected from *Datastream*.
3) The listing announcement dates of the *transitional non-traditional shares* by SOEs in Chinese steel industry during the period of 2005–2006 are obtained from *Wind data*.

Although originally the number of listed firms illustrated a large sample, due to lack of SOE ownership, listing date, and financial data, the number of sample firms was reduced to 31. The sample was further reduced by 2 more firms due to lack of reliable data on the announcement date of the listings and that there was also an inconsistency on the records of the 2 SOEs during the period of 2005–2006.[5] Consequently, the number of SOEs in Chinese steel industry became 29 in the analysis (Fig. 1).

Methodology 1

Event-Study
In this study *event-study methodology* is employed. The *event-study methodology* inspired by the efficient market hypothesis that capital markets are efficient instruments to evaluate and process the impact of new information available on firms (Fama, Fisher, Jensen, & Roll, 1969). The principal logic of the method is the credence that investors in the capital markets oversee publicly available information on firms to assess the impact of firms' activities on their current performances and forecasted future performance.

Model

$$R_{it} = LN\left(\frac{P_{it}}{P_{i(t-1)}}\right); R_{mt} = LN\left(\frac{P_{mt}}{P_{m(t-1)}}\right) \tag{1}$$

$$AR_{it} = R_{it} - \alpha_i + \beta_i R_{mt} \tag{2}$$

$$CAR_i = \sum_{T_1}^{T_2} AR_{it} \tag{3}$$

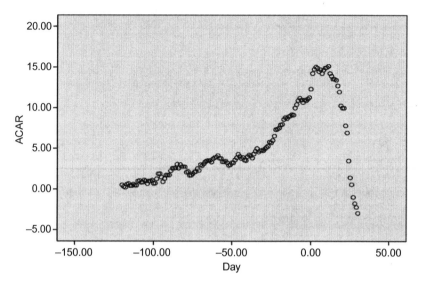

Fig. 1. Average Cumulative Abnormal Returns. *Notes*: The figure graphs the average cumulative abnormal return from day −120 to day +30. The trend of ACAR is obviously increasing until the peak on day +11 (15.13%). Noticeable, there are few big jumps during the period from day −23 (6.54%) to day −22 (7.33%), from day −11 (9.13%) to day −10 (9.98%), and from day −1 (11.26%) to day 0 (12.31%) and from day 0 (12.31%) to day 1 (14.21%)). Then it decreases sharply.

$$\text{SCAR}_{i(T_1,T_2)} = \frac{\text{CAR}_i}{\text{SD}_i} = \frac{\sum\limits_{T_1}^{T_2} \text{AR}_{it}}{\text{SD}_i} \tag{4}$$

AR_{it}: Abnormal return for firm i on day t.
CAR_i: Cumulative abnormal return for firm i from day T_1 to T_2.
$\text{SCAR}_{i(T_1,T_2)}$: Standardized cumulative abnormal return for firm i from day T_1 to T_2.
$P_{it}, P_{i(t-1)}$: Share price for firm i on day t and $t-1$, respectively.
$P_{mt}, P_{m(t-1)}$: Local market price index on day t and $t-1$, respectively.

Daily share returns and market returns are computed as logarithm of price on day t divided by price on day $t-1$ demonstrated in Eq. (1). Eq. (2) is estimated by using a 255 days estimation time-period from day −11 to day −265, where day 0 is the event day. In our analysis, we define the windows as 10 days prior the event day and 10 days post the event day. Twenty-one daily abnormal returns (ARs) for a firm are calculated by subtracting the local market returns.[6] Adding ARs together for a specific period around the event date yields the cumulative abnormal return (CAR) for that window. CAR is standardized based on the suggestion from Coutts, Mills, and Roberts (1995), by using SCAR for longer event windows to correct serial correlation of daily event AR for the same firm, we report the SCARs for the subsequent windows as follows:

SCAR (−10, + 10), SCAR (−5, + 5), SCAR (−10, + 5), SCAR (−1, + 1), SCAR (−2, + 1), SCAR (−1, 0), SCAR (0, + 1), SCAR (−1, + 2), and SCAR (−5, + 10).

Methodology 2

Multivariate Analysis

As discussed in the previous literature section, the transition of ownership from state-owned to privately owned could improve firm performance in terms of profitability, and efficiency, and leverage. In order to explore how these three factors impact on the value creation of the ownership transition, we conduct a cross-sectional analysis on firm cumulative abnormal returns, which are converted into standardized cumulative abnormal returns (SCARs).[7]

Model

We adopt the following multivariate model:

$$SCAR_{i(T_1,T_2)} = \alpha_i + \beta_1(CAROE)_i + \beta_2(CAAPE)_i + \beta_3(CATDTA)_i + \varepsilon_{i(T_1,T_2)} \quad (5)$$

where:

$$CAROE_i = \frac{AROE_{i(t_1,\, t_3)} - AROE_{i(t_{-1},\, t_{-3})}}{AROE_{i(t_{-1},\, t_{-3})}} \times 100 \quad (6)$$

$CAAPE_i$ and $CATDTA_i$ are calculated similarly.

CAROE is cumulative abnormal return on equity.

ROE is return on equity (Profitability Ratio, Annual Item), world scope code WC08301 [(Net Income before Preferred Dividends – Preferred Dividend Requirement)/Last Year's Common Equity * 100]

AROE represents the three-year average of firm i's ROE post to the *transitional non-traditional shares* announcement year.[8]

CAAPE is cumulative abnormal assets per employee.

APE is assets per employee (Asset Utilization Ratio, Annual Item), world scope code WC08406 (Total Assets/Employees)

CATDTA is cumulative abnormal total debt over total assets.

TDTA is total debt/total assets (Leverage Ratio, Annual Item), world scope code WC08236 [(Short-Term Debt and Current Portion of Long Term Debt + Long-Term Debt)/Total Assets * 100]

ANALYSIS AND RESULTS

Results of Even-Study/Market Reaction Analysis

First, the parameter estimates and estimation period statistics output in Table 1, display that each of the residual standard deviation of the 29 firms' announcements is quite small with minimum 0.0128 percent, and maximum 0.0329 percent, and with the mean value of 0.0229 percent. In other words, the model is statistically a good fit. Another indicator, the autocorrelation, is small as well, with minimum −0.1109, and maximum 0.2452, with the mean value of 0.0249, indicating that there is no serial correlation between return of firm stock price and return of market index.

Second, daily abnormal returns from the listing announcements of *transitional non-traditional shares* show that there is a statistically significant abnormal return at 1 percent on the announcement day with mean abnormal return at 1.10 percent. A total of 23 out of 29 firms report positive abnormal return, which equals to 79 percent (see Table 1). The mean of abnormal return increases to 1.95 percent on day +1, and its abnormal return is statistically significant at 0.1 percent level. However, prior to the announcement day, for example, on day −10 and −8, the abnormal returns are statistically significant at 1 percent and 10 percent levels, and the mean of abnormal return decreases from 0.89 percent to 0.54 percent.

The interpretation of the results shows that if there are no errors on these events' days, the local stock market is efficient. Since the market, in term of stock price, reacts immediately and in a short time-period, it

Table 1. Parameter Estimates and Estimation Period Statistics.

Ticker	Even Data	Mean Total Return	% of Raw Return	Alpha	Beta	Market Model Residuals > 0 (%)	Total Return Variance	Residual Standard Deviation	Autocorrelation
BAGF	June 28, 2005	-0.00179	36.22	-0.00157	0.73	55.91	0.00024	0.0128	0.0927
SGSS	July 27, 2005	-0.00175	38.58	-0.00155	1	53.15	0.0004	0.01557	-0.0605
FDTG	July 27, 2005	-0.00021	37.80	-0.00003	0.94	53.54	0.00058	0.02115	0.0713
PGGF	October 11, 2005	0.00121	39.37	0.00044	0.91	44.49	0.00042	0.01708	-0.0539
XXZG	October 11, 2005	-0.00155	40.16	-0.00251	1.13	59.45	0.0009	0.02644	0.0969
WGGF	October 17, 2005	-0.00119	44.88	-0.00248	0.91	56.30	0.00078	0.02548	-0.1109
SGGF	October 19, 2005	-0.00091	44.49	-0.00204	0.74	57.09	0.00074	0.02541	-0.01
AGFU	October 31, 2005	0.00033	42.52	-0.00097	1.07	54.33	0.00069	0.02203	-0.0435
TGGU	November 14, 2005	-0.00054	37.40	-0.00163	0.87	53.15	0.001	0.02928	0.0914
DYTG	December 5, 2005	0.00183	38.58	0.00042	1.11	40.16	0.00089	0.02551	0.01
HLGT	December 14, 2005	-0.00022	39.76	-0.00126	0.76	57.87	0.00074	0.02517	0.0865
HGGF	December 16, 2005	-0.00082	42.13	-0.00206	0.83	53.54	0.00059	0.02131	0.1139
BYGT	January 5, 2006	-0.00225	43.31	-0.00318	0.98	54.33	0.00083	0.02568	-0.0165
NXHL	January 11, 2006	0.00036	46.46	-0.00089	1.4	47.24	0.00112	0.02772	-0.0549
LGGF	January 11, 2006	-0.00182	44.49	-0.00262	0.91	53.94	0.00061	0.02148	0.0473
MGGF	January 25, 2006	-0.00172	38.98	-0.00283	0.91	56.69	0.00091	0.02767	0.0696
BGBC	February 7, 2006	-0.00059	44.09	-0.00206	0.87	50.39	0.00075	0.0251	-0.0049
BGGF	February 10, 2006	0.00007	38.98	-0.00146	0.81	53.15	0.0008	0.02643	0.0592
FSTG	February 14, 2006	-0.00013	53.15	-0.00227	1.23	52.76	0.00133	0.03293	-0.0253
TGBX	February 17, 2006	0.0022	41.34	0.00029	1.09	41.73	0.00055	0.01878	-0.0071
FERS	February 22, 2006	0.00209	50.79	-0.00016	1.34	48.43	0.00079	0.02244	-0.016
XNTG	February 22, 2006	0.00092	48.03	-0.00154	1.46	49.61	0.00103	0.02624	-0.0029
GGGF	March 8, 206	0.00071	41.73	-0.00086	1.11	49.21	0.00073	0.02329	0.2452
JGHX	March 14, 2006	-0.00032	38.98	-0.00137	0.74	53.15	0.00044	0.01891	-0.0166
JNGT	March 20, 2006	-0.00114	37.80	-0.00247	0.98	53.54	0.00067	0.02291	0.0182

Table 1. (Continued)

Ticker	Even Data	Mean Total Return	% of Raw Return	Alpha	Beta	Market Model Residuals > 0 (%)	Total Return Variance	Residual Standard Deviation	Autocorrelation
AYGT	April 19, 2006	−0.00042	39.37	−0.00147	1.02	48.43	0.00054	0.02037	−0.0754
GSGF	June 9, 2006	0.00041	46.83	−0.00271	1.01	53.17	0.00033	0.01421	0.1217
XGGF	August 28, 2006	0.0005	40.31	−0.00272	0.88	57.65	0.00079	0.02532	−0.0305
NGGF	September 21, 2006	0.00069	44.38	−0.00142	0.61	56.74	0.00041	0.01835	0.1284
Mean		−0.00021	42.10	−0.00155	0.98	52.38	0.00071	0.02293	0.0249
Median		−0.00022	41.34	−0.00155	0.94	53.17	0.00074	0.02329	−0.0029

reflects the significant information of these listing announcements of *transitional non-traditional shares*. Moreover, since in all the six events statistically significant market reactions are positive, the positive market reaction predominates cross 21-day window, indicating that these listing announcements of *transitional non-traditional shares* create value for shareholders in Chinese steel industry. Overall, the existence of two statistically significant positive abnormal returns prior to the listing announcement day is interpreted as there may be some information leakages[9] from the privileged insiders prior to the listing announcements day of *transitional non-traditional shares*. There may even be some other endogenous or indigenous events causing abnormal returns prior to or close to the listing announcements day of *transitional non-traditional shares* (Table 2).

Finally, daily and standardized cumulative abnormal returns (CARs) gained from the listing announcements of *transitional non-traditional shares* are shown in Table 3, which suggest that the cumulative abnormal returns during windows $(-1, 0)$, and $(-5, + 10)$ are statistically significant at 1 percent level. Similarly, CARs during windows $(-10, + 10)$, $(-5, + 5)$, $(-10, + 5)$, $(-1, + 1)$, $(-2, + 1)$, $(0, + 1)$, and $(-1, + 2)$ are statistically significant at 0.1 percent level. The results of mean and median cumulative abnormal returns for all listing announcements of *transitional non-traditional shares* done by these 29 firms in Chinese steel industry disclose a significant positive market reaction at different window intervals. Unlike the results in the daily ARs output, the positive market reaction remains strong for almost all short-term and long-term CARs. All of these statistically significant windows are dominated by positive market reaction.

In addition, positive market reaction persists through a longer pre- and post- announcement day period, which ranges from 2 to 21 days around announcement day. The results indicate a certain pattern that along the time approaching the announcement day; the CAR of each stock return is increasingly and statistically significant long after the announcement day. However, highly statistically significant CARs are mostly concentrated on days closed to the announcement. In sum, it is suggested that potential benefits expected from compensation through the *transitional non-traditional shares* outweigh various costs associated with *split-share structure* that are realized and recognized by the market, and it is concluded that firms' listing announcements of *transitional non-traditional shares* in Chinese steel industry create value for shareholders of firms in 2006–2007 sample time-period.

When examining the firms' cumulative abnormal returns in Chinese steel industry in a longer time-period, namely around the listing announcements of *transitional non-traditional shares*. The Fig. 1 shows the average

Table 2. Daily Abnormal Returns from the Listing Announcements of Transitional Non-Traditional Shares.

Day	N	Mean Abnormal Return (%)	Median Abnormal Return (%)	Positive: Negative	Patell: Z	StdCsect Z	CSectErr Z	Generalized Sign Z	Rank Test Z	Signed Rank	Running CAR (%)
-10	29	0.89	0.46	23:6$^>$	2.419**	2.999**	3.035**	2.903**	2.612**	150.500***	0.89
-9	29	0.46	0.20	19:10	1.262	1.589$	1.677$	1.416$	1.373$	60.500$	1.35
-8	29	0.54	0.25	19:10	1.289$	1.854*	1.824*	1.416$	1.373$	83.500*	1.89
-7	29	0.32	0.24	20:9$^>$	0.9	1.987*	2.108*	1.788$	1.316$	91.500*	2.22
-6	29	-0.18	-0.04	14:15	-0.505	-1.041	-1.117	-0.443	-0.735	-18.5	2.03
-5	29	-0.24	0.10	15:14	-0.491	-0.932	-1.242	-0.071	-0.92	-35.5	1.79
-4	29	0.34	0.21	17:12	0.864	1.551$	1.404$	0.672	0.71	54.5	2.14
-3	29	-0.03	0.10	16:13	-0.167	-0.349	-0.164	0.301	-0.266	-0.5	2.10
-2	29	0.27	0.04	17:12	0.946	1.071	1.026	0.672	0.208	15.5	2.38
-1	29	0.25	0.24	19:10	0.565	0.967	1.029	1.416$	0.763	52.5	2.62
0	29	1.10	0.45	17:12	2.865**	2.244$	2.105*	0.672	1.452$	71.500$	3.72
1	29	1.95	1.57	19:10	4.225***	1.634$	1.963*	1.416$	2.974**	93.500*	5.67
2	29	0.57	0.43	19:10	1.383$	1.434$	1.349$	1.416$	1.360$	60.500$	6.24
3	29	0.34	0.12	15:14	1.703*	1.147	0.63	-0.071	0.229	16.5	6.58
4	29	-0.06	-0.13	14:15	-0.06	-0.069	-0.173	-0.443	-0.611	-21.5	6.52
5	29	-0.43	-0.16	12:17	-1.261	-1.421$	-1.345$	-1.187	-1.594$	-59.5	6.09
6	29	0.29	0.31	17:12	0.571	0.992	1.175	0.672	1.175	73.500$	6.38
7	29	-0.44	-0.18	11:18(	-1.155	-1.747*	-1.509$	-1.558$	-1.251	-62.500$	5.95
8	29	0.48	0.04	16:13	1.071	1.366$	1.339$	0.301	0.551	29.5	6.43
9	29	0.31	0.15	18:11	0.677	1.552$	1.638$	1.044	0.858	77.500*	6.74
10	29	0.10	-0.03	14:15	0.207	0.359	0.406	-0.443	-0.323	-11.5	6.85

The symbols $, *, **, and *** denote statistical significance at the 0.10, 0.05, 0.01, and 0.001 levels, respectively, using a generic one-tail test. The symbols (<,) and > correspond to $, * and show the direction and generic one-tail significance of the generalized sign test. The table presents the daily abnormal returns of 29 firms from the listing announcements of *transitional non-traditional shares* in Chinese steel industry over the period 2005–2006. Daily cumulative abnormal returns are computed from the market model as prediction errors. Day 0 refers to the listing announcements day of *transitional non-traditional shares* as reported in the Wind data. Z-statistics (Petell test) is used to test for the statistical significance of mean abnormal returns.

Table 3. Daily and Standardized Cumulative Abnormal Returns from the Listing Announcements of Transitional Non-Traditional Shares.

Interval	N	Mean CAR (%)	PreCSIon on Weighted CAAR (%)	Median CAR (%)	Positive: Negative	Patell Z	StdCsect Z	CSectErr t	Generalized Sign Z	Rank Test Z	Signed Rank Z
(−10, + 10)	29	6.85	7.09	7.67	26:3>>>	3.657***	6.415***	7.467***	4.019***	2.456**	206.500***
(−10, + 5)	29	6.09	6.53	7.40	24:5>>>	3.894***	5.901***	6.686***	3.275***	2.561**	195.500***
(−5, + 10)	29	4.81	4.89	6.20	26:3>>>	2.920**	4.128***	4.225***	4.019***	1.329$	166.500***
(−5, + 5)	29	4.06	4.33	3.87	22:7>>	3.143***	3.972***	3.894***	2.532**	1.298$	148.500***
(−2, + 1)	29	3.57	3.52	4.75	24:5>>>	4.314***	3.753***	3.841***	3.275***	2.698**	147.500***
(−1, + 1)	29	3.30	3.13	3.77	23:6>>	4.427***	3.082**	3.335***	2.903**	2.996**	132.500**
(−1, + 2)	29	3.87	3.70	4.97	24:5>>>	4.519***	3.207***	3.232***	3.275***	3.274***	132.500**
(−1, 0)	29	1.34	1.41	0.25	18:11	2.423**	2.349**	2.242*	1.044	1.566$	74.500$
(0, + 1)	29	3.05	2.90	3.90	22:7>>	5.034***	2.905**	3.142***	2.532**	3.129***	128.500**

The symbols $, *, **, and *** denote statistical significance at the 0.10, 0.05, 0.01 and 0.001 levels, respectively, using a generic one-tail test. The symbols (<,), and > correspond to $, * and > and show the direction and generic one-tail significance of the generalized sign test. The table presents the daily cumulative abnormal returns (CARs) of 29 firms from the listing announcements of *transitional non-traditional shares* in Chinese steel industry over the period 2005–2006. Daily cumulative abnormal returns (CARs) are computed from the market model as prediction errors. Day 0 refers to the listing announcements day of *transitional non-traditional shares* as reported in the Wind data. Z-statistics (Petell test) is used to test for the statistical significance of mean CARs.

cumulative abnormal return from day −120 to day +30. The trend of ACAR is noticeably increasing until the peak, on day +11, to 15.13 percent. Hence, it can be observed that there are a few large increases during specific intervals. For example, during the interval of (−23, −22), there is an increase from 6.54 percent to 7.33 percent. During the interval of (−11, −10), there is an increase from 9.13 percent to 9.98 percent. During the interval of (−1, 0), there is an increase from 11.26 percent to 12.31 percent. In addition, during the interval of (0, 1), there is a large increase from 12.31 percent to14.21 percent, before decreasing back down sharply, and achieving negative cumulative abnormal return along the timeline. One possible explanation for this may be that speculations rather than firm level factors drive the movement in share prices.

Results of Multivariate Analysis

The empirical results presented in Table 4 illustrate that the estimated coefficient sign of CAROE is statistically significant at a 10 percent level for windows (−2, +1), (−1, +2) and (−1, 0), and statistically significant at a 5 percent level for windows (−1, +1) and (0, +1), and hence estimated coefficient sign of CAROE is consistent with H_2. The estimated coefficient sign of CATDTA is statistically significant at a 10 percent level, and for window (−5, +5), and statistically significant at a 5 percent level, for the following windows (−2, +1), (−1, +2), (−1, +1) and (0, +1). Although the significance levels for the estimated coefficient sign for CATDTA are low, the coefficient has some consistency with H_4. However, when CAAPE is considered, none of the estimated coefficients of CAAPE are statistically significant at any windows, indicating that the efficiency variable does not have an impact on SCARs gained during the listing announcements of *transitional non-traditional shares*, which may not give a clear indication of consistency with H_3.

The significance of the estimated coefficient change in CAROE suggests that the expectation of an increase in firms' profitability promoted by the *split-share structure reform* may have a positive impact on firm stock price. This reflects increasing shareholder wealth, and confirm that transition of ownership from state-owned to privately owned may have positive effect on firms' profitability, conveying a positive signal to the market and increasing shareholder wealth.

When other variables remain constant and with a 1 percent increase in the three-year average profitability in terms of return on equity, the

Table 4. Cross-Sectional Regression: Standardized Cumulative Abnormal Returns of Chinese Iron and Steel Industry (CISI) Firms.

Independent Variable	Dependent Variable								
	SCAR (−10, +10)	SCAR (−10, +5)	SCAR (−5, +10)	SCAR (−5, +5)	SCAR (−2, +1)	SCAR (−1, +2)	SCAR (−1, +1)	SCAR (−1, 0)	SCAR (0, +1)
Linear regression									
Intercept	0.636351	0.708628	0.388349	0.438495	0.510426	0.576433	0.465670	0.824676	0.491792
	0.0004	*0.0005*	*0.0372*	*0.0379*	*0.0736*	*0.0999*	*0.1785*	*0.0029*	*0.2273*
CAROE	0.018856	−0.001036	0.108029	0.103730	0.202037*	0.236003*	0.255955**	0.182674*	0.335447**
	0.7387	*0.9873*	*0.1041*	*0.1657*	*0.0525*	*0.0655*	*0.0464*	*0.0549*	*0.0285*
CAAPE	−0.057950	−0.180034	0.159381	0.056894	0.243124	−0.025716	0.201095	−0.607217	0.271470
	0.8047	*0.5058*	*0.5539*	*0.8517*	*0.5599*	*0.9600*	*0.6947*	*0.1190*	*0.6539*
CADTA	0.077209	0.091681	0.135711	0.168277*	0.280087**	0.376675**	0.387662**	−0.078330	0.478640**
	0.3081	*0.2930*	*0.1230*	*0.0932*	*0.0435*	*0.0290*	*0.0246*	*0.5212*	*0.0194*
Adjusted R-squared	−0.071243	−0.058140	0.086397	0.060704	0.169914	0.158372	0.194106	0.138408	0.227878
No. of observations	29	29	29	29	29	29	29	29	29

The table presents the results of OLS regressions. The variable CAROE used in the model is the percentage changes of the three years' average of firm *i*'s ROE post and prior to the split distribution announcement year. The variable CAAPE is the percentage changes of the three years' average of firm *i*'s APE post and prior to the split distribution announcement year. The variable CADTA is the percentage changes of the three years' average of firm *i*'s debt ratio post and prior to the split distribution announcement year. *P*-values are reported in the italics below the coefficient estimates. ***, **, * denote statistical significance at the 1%, 5%, and 10% levels, respectively. Dependent variable in the regression is the standardized cumulative abnormal return (SCAR) of CISI firms engaged in the Split-share Structure Reform over 2005–2006. SCARs are defined over various event windows around the split distribution announcement.

shareholder of the firm will gain 20.20 percent standardized cumulative abnormal return during the interval of (−2, +1), a four-day time frame.

The following increases are also accurate: (1) an increase of 23.6 percent standardized cumulative abnormal return for the interval of (−1, +2), a four-day time frame; (2) an increase of 25.60 percent standardized cumulative abnormal return for the interval of (−1, +1), a three-day time frame; and (3) an increase of 33.54 percent standardized cumulative abnormal return for the interval of (0, +1), a two-day time frame. It is clearly observed that the shorter the time-period around the announcement day, the greater is the percentage gain for shareholder wealth.

Although the sign of the estimated coefficient CATDTA has low consistency with H_4, the interpretation of this is not hard to understand after analyzing the firm's capital structure. Since the sample of firms in our analysis is from steel industry, which has a characteristic of capital-intensive structure, it is important to state that firms of this type of industry have higher proportion of tangible assets (fixed assets) compared with high-tech firms. Hence, the inconsistency may not necessarily mean that there is a negative impact on leverage.

Moreover, tangible assets can be used as collateral by firms to borrow funds from creditors. Here, the cost of debt is cheaper than that of equity because the risk for shareholder is more than that of the creditor. Therefore, a capital-intensive industry would be easier to be seen with high debt ratio than high-tech industry and hence, the higher the debt ratio, the higher the shareholder wealth. This becomes more apparent, if we analyze the firm value by recalling the evaluation formula of future cash flow discount at weighted average cost of capital (WACC). It is also important to point out here that the higher leveraged firms' WACC is smaller than that of the relative low leveraged firms. However, this does not necessary mean that purely funded debt is the best capital structure since bankruptcy risk should be taken into account as well. Therefore, all other things being equal, among firms with less fluctuated future cash flow and smaller WACC, the higher the firms' intrinsic value, which leads to higher stock price and high abnormal return.

From the investor perspective, the transition of ownership from state-owned to privately owned, would give investor more confidence in the improvements in corporate governance, which would generally lead to better monitoring of management and more transparent and efficient decisions to boost profitability and dividends, and to reduce curbing risk (Aybar & Ficici, 2009; Bortolotti & Siniscalco, 2004; Megginson & Netter, 2001). This, in turn, would increase creditability and decrease costs.

The significance of the estimated coefficient of (t) profitability change in CATDTA suggests that the expectation of an increase in firm's leverage, specifically in capital-intensive industry promoted by the *split-share structure reform*, has a positive impact on firm stock price as it increases shareholder wealth, confirming that the transition of ownership change from state-owned to privately owned has positive effect on capital-intensive firms' leverage.

This also conveys a positive signal to the market and increases shareholder wealth. When other variables remain constant and a 1 percent increase in the three-year average leverage in term of debt ratio occurs, the shareholder of the firm gains 16.82 percent standardized cumulative abnormal return during the interval of (-5, $+5$), a 11-day time frame; 28 percent standardized cumulative abnormal return during the interval of (-2, $+1$), a four-day time frame; 37.67 percent standardized cumulative abnormal return during the interval of (-1, $+2$), a four-day time frame; 38.76 percent standardized cumulative abnormal return during the interval (-1, $+1$), a three-day time frame; and 47.86 percent standardized cumulative abnormal return during the interval (0, $+1$), a two-day time frame. Hence, the shorter the time-period around the announcement day, the greater is the percentage gain on shareholder wealth (Ficici, 2005).

CONCLUSION

Our empirical event analysis shows that the structural reform that had taken place in the Chinese stock market has statistically significant positive effect on stock prices of Chinese steel industry firms in our sample. Such positive effect does not only appear around the listing announcements of *transitional non-traditional shares* in a short time frame, but also appears prior to the announcement day (e.g., 10-day prior to the announcement). The market reacts positively to the listing announcements of *transitional non-traditional shares* when the firm informs its investors and shareholders, confirming the statement that the transition of ownership from state ownership to private ownership would give market more confidence in expecting improvements in corporate governance structure of the firm. This would lead to better monitoring of management and more transparency and efficiency in Chinese steel industry, which in turn would boost profitability and dividends as well as curbing risk.

In examining a longer time-period window, we find that even though the momentum of increase is temporary and disappears within the following 10 days, overall reform promotes the shareholder wealth in appearance of abnormal return, which is consistent with the findings of Bortolotti and Beltratti (2006). Hence, our hypothesis supportsH_1: *No price change is associated with the listing announcements of transitional non-traditional shares and the implementation of the split-share structure reform for a given listed firm.*

In the *multivariate analysis* that integrates three key factors (profitability, efficiency, and leverage) in the process of privatization, we find that increase on firms' profitability promoted by the *split-share structure reform* has positive impact on firm stock price – increasing shareholder wealth, and confirming that the transition of ownership from state-owned to privately owned has positive effect on firms' profitability. This conveys a positive signal to the market and increases shareholder wealth, as well as increasing capital-intensive firms' leverage, specifically in capital-intensive industry promoted by the *split-share structure reform*. Our results supportsH_2: *The listing of the non-traditional shares as traditional shares creates value to the firm by impacting positively on firm profitability – conveying a positive signal to the market, and hence increasing shareholder wealth.* Our findings also support H_4: *The listing of the non-traditional shares as traditional shares creates value to the firm by impacting positively on firm leverage – conveying a positive signal to the market, and hence increasing shareholder wealth.*

Findings also illustrates that the *split-share structure reform* seemed to have produced a significant wealth effect for shareholders, and that efficiency factor gives positive results – showing statistically significant effects on shareholders' wealth. Consequently, our findings support H_3: *The listing of the non-traditional shares as traditional shares creates value to the firm by impacting positively on firm efficiency – conveying a positive signal to the market, and hence increasing shareholder wealth.* Our findings are consistent with previous literature, such as the study done by Feng et al. (2002) in which they conduct an empirical study test whether privatization improves financial and operating performance of 31 Singaporean firms divested through public share offerings between 1975 and 1998, and find significant improvements in financial and operating performance.

The results support thesis questions presented in the introduction section of the paper. They specifically illustrate that the privatization process and the *split-share structure reform* in the Chinese steel industry has been successful. The recently founded Chinese stock market, as a platform and as a major instrument of the Chinese privatization process, positively react to the listings of once *non-traditional* and/or non-tradable shares of Chinese steel industry firms, whence they are announced to be listed as traditional and/or tradable shares through *split-share structure reform.*

Overall conclusion supports that the exogenous factors emphasized in a topographical order, explicitly profitability, efficiency, and leverage, related to the privatization processes and *split-share structure reform* impact the market and the market reacts positively to the listing announcements of *non-traditional shares* as traditional shares create and improve value to the firm.

However, there are some limitations to this research. More specifically, the limitations circle around country, industry, and firm factors related to the lack of data. In addition, this study merely relates to one specific industry and one country. Future research should pay attention to these factors and take a multi-industry and as well as a multi-country path.

Finally, the contribution of this research to the field can be stated as the following: This paper looks at the impact of privatization and *split-share structure reform* on both market reaction and firm value. Hence, it focuses on the impact of a dynamic process rather than the impact of a static constituent on market reaction and firm value, as the previous studies have been concentrating on. In addition, the research shows that there is an accelerated privatization of state-owned firms in Chinese steel industry and their integration in capital markets.

NOTES

1. According to FTSE's (2015) classification, China is categorized as a secondary emerging market country. A secondary emerging market is classified as a country that adheres to the monitoring of the market and regulatory environment and the formal stock market by regulatory authorities (e.g., SEC, FSA, SFC). No objection to or significant restrictions or penalties applied to the investment of capital or the repatriation of capital and income. In terms of custody and settlement, there is sufficient competition to ensure high quality custodian services and clearing & settlement. In terms of dealing landscape, high quality brokerage is ensured with high quality broker services. Market liquidity is established to support sizeable global investment. Transaction costs − implicit and explicit, are reasonable and competitive. Transparency on market depth information is visible for timely trade reporting process (FTSE, 2015).

2. Historically in China, the auto, construction, mechanical, electrical and petrochemical sectors were considered pillar industries. In recent years, the Chinese government has been identifying the new pillar industries as energy conservation and

environmental protection, new-generation information technology, bio-tech indus-try and high-end equipment manufacturing.

3. The *split-share structure reform* took place during the 2005–2006 period to challenge the control of central government and to enhance the privatization process.

4. Although Hong Kong is considered a separate entity from China by the inter-national rating agencies, it has been a part of China since 1997. Hong Kong was occupied and ceded by England in 1842 with the First Opium War.

5. Chinese Securities Regulatory Commission (CSRC) Act set the date December 30, 2006, as the deadline for the firms to be listed. First 64 firms were announced gradually. A total of 759 firms, which, account for 97.8 percent firms that were to be reformed and listed in Shanghai stock exchange either completed their reforma-tion period, or in the process of reforming. Only in 11 firms *split-share structure* has not been applied yet, which account for 3.24 percent of the total market value of Shenzhen stock exchange.

6. The market index return used in the analysis is Shanghai composite index return. A total of 11 out of 29 firms listed in the Shenzhen stock exchange. The corre-lation coefficient of the two market composite indexes amounts to a high 98 percent. Therefore, we adopt Shanghai composite index as the local market index.

7. As stated by Coutts, Mills, and Roberts (1995), using SCARs for longer event windows could correct the serial correlation of daily event period abnormal returns for the same firm.

8. $AROE_{i(t_1,t_3)}$ represents the three-year average of firm i's ROE post to the *transi-tional non-traditional shares* announcement year; $AROE_{i(t_{-1},t_{-3})}$ represents the three-year average of firm i's ROE prior to the *transitional non-traditional shares* announcement year. t_0 is the announcement year.

9. There is possibility that the information leakage maybe coming from a 10-day period where investors are informed by firms.

REFERENCES

Aybar, B., & Ficici, A. (2009). Cross-border acquisitions and firm value: An analysis of emerging-market multinationals. *Journal of International Business Studies, 40*(8), 1317–1338.

Bartel, A. P., & Harrison, A. E. (2005). Ownership versus environment: Disentangling the sources of public-sector inefficiency. *Review of Economics and Statistics, 87*(1), 135–147. doi:10.1162/0034653053327595

Boardman, A. E., & Vining, A. R. (1989). Ownership and performance in competitive environ-ments: A comparison of the performance of private, mixed, and state-owned enter-prises. *Journal of Law & Economics, 32*, 1.

Bortolotti, B., & Beltratti, A. (2006). *The non-tradable share reform in the Chinese stock market*. SSRN eLibrary. Retrieved from http://papers.ssrn.com/sol3/papers.cfm?abstract_id=944412

Bortolotti, B., & Siniscalco, D. (2004). *The challenges of privatization: An international analysis (OUP Catalogue)*. Oxford: Oxford University Press. Retrieved from http://econ papers.repec.org/bookchap/oxpobooks/9780199249343.htm

Bottasso, A., & Sembenelli, A. (2004). Does ownership affect firms' efficiency? Panel data evidence on Italy. *Empirical Economics*, *29*(4), 769–786. doi:10.1007/s00181-004-0210-z

Boubakri, N., & Cosset, J.-C. (1998). The financial and operating performance of newly privatized firms: Evidence from developing countries. *Journal of Finance*, *53*(3), 1081–1110.

Coutts, J. A., Mills, T. C., & Roberts, J. (1995). Misspecification of the market model: The implications for event studies. *Applied Economics Letters*, *2*(5), 163–165. doi:10.1080/135048595357528

Dewenter, K. L., & Malatesta, P. H. (2001). State-owned and privately owned firms: An empirical analysis of profitability, leverage, and labor intensity. *The American Economic Review*, *91*(1), 320–334.

D'souza, J., & Megginson, W. L. (1999). The financial and operating performance of privatized firms during the 1990s. *Journal of Finance*, *54*(4), 1397–1438.

Fama, E. F., Fisher, L., Jensen, M. C., & Roll, R. (1969). *The adjustment of stock prices to new information*. SSRN eLibrary. Retrieved from http://papers.ssrn.com/sol3/papers.cfm?abstract_id=321524

Fan, C., & Fan, L. (1996). The embryonic development of a stock exchange in communist China: The Shanghai securities exchange, advances in Pacific Basin Business. *Economics and Finance*, *2*, 33–42.

Feng, F., Sun, Q., & Tong, W. H. S. (2002). *Do government-linked companies necessarily under-perform?* Citeseer. Retrieved from http://citeseerx.ist.psu.edu/viewdoc/download?doi=10.1.1.199.1877&rep=rep1&type=pdf

Ficici, A. (2005). *Value implications of emerging market multinationals' cross-border expansion patterns: An analysis of M&As, JVs and SAs*. Retrieved from http://academicarchive.snhu.edu/handle/10474/1803

FTSE. (2015). *FTSE country classification process*. Retrieved from http://www.ftse.com/products/downloads/FTSE_Country_Classification_Paper.pdf

Jiang, B.-B., Laurenceson, J., & Tang, K. K. (2008). Share reform and the performance of China's listed companies. *China Economic Review*, *19*(3), 489–501.

Laurin, C., & Bozec, Y. (2001). Privatization and productivity improvement: The case of Canadian National. *Transportation Research Part E: Logistics and Transportation Review*, *37*(5), 355–374.

Liao, L., Liu, B., & Wang, H. (2014). China's secondary privatization: Perspectives from the split-share structure reform. *Journal of Financial Economics*, *113*(3), 500–518.

Majumdar, S. K. (1998). Assessing comparative efficiency of the state-owned mixed and private sectors in Indian industry. *Public Choice*, *96*(1), 1–24. doi:10.1023/A:1004941023587

Maquieira, C., & Zurita, S. (1996). *Privatizaciones en chile: Eficiencia y politicas financieras*. Repositorio Académico – Universidad de Chile.

Megginson, W. L. (2005). *The financial economics of privatization*. Oxford: Oxford University Press. Retrieved from http://books.google.com/books?hl=en&lr=&id=TdcwG6n_I24C&oi=fnd&pg=PR7&dq=%E2%80%9CThe+Financial+Economics+of+Privatization%E2%80%9D.+Oxford+University+Press&ots=QB2EcfMWm5&sig=xocqgOFb9SO2BOyqsHHqSOkPsSs

Megginson, W. L., Nash, R. C., & Randenborgh, M. V. (1994). The financial and operating performance of newly privatized firms: An international empirical analysis. *The Journal of Finance, 49*(2), 403. doi:10.2307/2329158

Megginson, W. L., & Netter, J. M. (2001). From state to market: A survey of empirical studies on privatization. *Journal of Economic Literature, 39*(2), 321–389.

Omran, M. (2002). *The performance of state-owned enterprises and newly privatized firms: Empirical evidence from Egypt.* Citeseer. Retrieved from http://citeseerx.ist.psu.edu/viewdoc/download? doi=10.1.1.19.4423&rep=rep1&type=pdf

Otchere, I. K. (2002). *Intra-industry effects of privatization announcements: Evidence from developed and developing countries.* SSRN eLibrary. Retrieved from http://papers.ssrn.com/sol3/papers.cfm?abstract_id=363881

Ros, A. J. (1999). Does ownership or competition matter? The effects of telecommunications reform on network expansion and efficiency. *Journal of Regulatory Economics, 15*(1), 65–92. doi:10.1023/A:1008048924876

Shleifer, A. (1998). State versus private ownership. *Journal of Economic Perspectives, 12*(4), 133–150.

Shleifer, A., & Vishny, R. W. (1994). Politicians and firms. *The Quarterly Journal of Economics, 109*(4), 995–1025. doi:10.2307/2118354

Tang, R. (2010). *China's steel industry and its impact on the United States: Issues for Congress.* Retrieved from http://digitalcommons.ilr.cornell.edu.ezp-prod1.hul.harvard.edu/key_workplace/756/?utm_source=digitalcommons.ilr.cornell.edu%2Fkey_workplace%2F756&utm_medium=PDF&utm_campaign=PDFCoverPages

The Smart Cube. (2012, December 22). *Changing dynamics in the global steel industry – The trend towards short-term, flexible contracts.* Retrieved from http://www.thesmartcube.com/insights/sourcing/item/changing-dynamics-in-the-global-steel-industry-the-trend-towards-short-term-flexible-contracts. Accessed on November 21, 2015.

Vining, A. R., & Boardman, A. E. (1992). Ownership versus competition: Efficiency in public enterprise. *Public Choice, 73*(2), 205–239. doi:10.1007/BF00145092

World Bank. (n.d.). *Privatization dataset 2000–2008.* Retrieved from siteresources.worldbank.org/EXTFINANCIALSECTOR/Resources/PrivatizationData00_08.xls?resourceurlname=PrivatizationData00_08.xls. Accessed on November 21, 2015.

PART IV
RISK, REGULATION, AND FINANCIAL MARKETS

REGULATORY RISKS AND STRATEGIC CONTROLS IN THE GLOBAL FINANCIAL CENTRE OF CHINA

Artie W. Ng and Wallace Tang

ABSTRACT

Purpose — *This study explores the interrelationship between regulatory risks and strategic controls within the financial supervision architecture of an emergent global financial centre of China that embraces innovation as part of its strategic objectives.*

Methodology/approach — *This paper employs a longitudinal case study approach to examine the institutional dynamics of the key financial regulators in connection with the regulated financial institutions in Hong Kong before and after the financial tsunami of 2008.*

Findings — *First, this study reveals an organic development of a specialised financial regulatory architecture that resists transforming itself structurally despite the significant impact of externalities. Second, in this post-financial crisis analysis, regulated financial institutions swiftly respond by strengthening their risk controls through compliance with the*

The Political Economy of Chinese Finance
International Finance Review, Volume 17, 243–270
ISSN: 1569-3767/doi:10.1108/S1569-376720160000017015

guidelines imposed by the regulator. Institutional dynamics in influencing the implementation of risk controls through a top-down interactive mechanism are observed. Such dynamic and pertinent rapid responses induce the pursuit of optimal risk management within a regulatory framework.

Originality/value – *This paper provides a longitudinal case study to reveal regulatory risks and strategic controls of the global financial centre of China. It unveils mitigating risk control measures in the aftermath of the global financial crisis. The study demonstrates how regulatory institutions strive to take precautionary, coercive measures such that the regulated institutions mimic and implement prudent mechanisms.*

Keywords: Financial regulation and compliance; institutional dynamics; regulatory risk; risk management; strategic control

INTRODUCTION

The Hong Kong Special Administrative Region (Hong Kong) of China has emerged as a prominent global financial centre in the Asia Pacific region over the past decades. As articulated in a study by IMF, Hong Kong possesses the '*first-mover*' advantage as China's financial system continues to integrate with the rest of the world (Leung & Unteroberdoerster, 2008). With a well-functioning legal and financial regulatory system, Hong Kong has also been a platform for raising capital and for facilitating cross-border financial transactions among emerging Chinese multinationals. Despite Hong Kong's past success, Hong Kong needs to sustain its competitive edge on skills, legal and institutional infrastructure, as well as regulation, so as to maintain an environment that promotes both stability and innovation (Leung & Unteroberdoerster, 2008). The emergence of China as a significant economy of the world has instituted attempts to simulate its financial regulatory practice with that of the global standards (Walter, 2010). Hong Kong continues to strengthen its status as the global financial centre for China with timely adoption of internationally accepted financial regulatory standards.

Nevertheless, the collapse of Lehman Brothers (LB) in the United States had a significant impact on the financial regulatory system of Hong Kong, as the local investors in LB 'Minibonds' incurred severe losses and criticised the effectiveness and accountability of the two major regulators — the Hong Kong Monetary Authority (HKMA) and the Securities and Futures Commission (SFC).[1] While both the HKMA and the SFC have completed reviews on the need to strengthen their effectiveness through reforms of the current supervision architecture and the establishment of an integrated or 'twin-peak' approach (HKMA, 2008; Securities and Futures Commission [SFC], 2008), there are scepticisms over such potential reforms in dealing effectively with systemic risk. The regulated financial institutions face a fundamental dilemma of how to generate targeted returns while the cost of compliance continues to rise.

The major challenges today are about the extent of implementation needed to address regulatory risks, associated with failures of regulation, as well as strategic controls in both local and international dimensions. By examining the experiences of Hong Kong's financial institutions exposed to global systemic risk, this paper explores the underlying regulatory risk controls that have been seemingly reemphasised and optimally implemented within the unique developmental experience of Hong Kong's financial regulatory system. It begins with a literature review of interdisciplinary studies regarding global financial regulations and neo-institutionalism as well as contemporary knowledge about corporate risk management and strategic control. Conducting a case study of Hong Kong, this study further reveals the organic development of Hong Kong's financial supervision architecture under its unique governance system and provides evidence regarding the dynamics among policy objectives, regulators and regulated institutions in response to the externalities of unprecedented systemic risk and the resulting control failures. Such responses are formulated as an array of risk control measures that are embraced by the overall strategic objectives within the financial regulations as embedded in the financial supervision architecture. The increased risk controls are presented as institutional isomorphism among the regulated financial institutions contingent on the adverse impacts of a global financial crisis. A conceptual framework is proposed to explain an optimisation of strategic risk controls is devised.

GROWING CONCERNS OVER GLOBAL FINANCIAL REGULATIONS

With respect to the global financial system, there have been concerns about the growing systemic risk across borders, and there have been suggestions to establish a global regulatory system to address such risk. As noted by D'Apice and Ferri (2010), although financial instability can be traced back to the 1930s, it has become increasingly widespread during the past 25 years due to different forms of bailouts. The problem of systemic risk became a significant concern among public policy-makers, bank regulators and central banks after the Asian financial crisis in 1998 and the Russian and Latin American crises in the 1990s (Alexander, Dhumale, & Eatwell, 2006). Davis and Green (2008) note that there could be emerging turbulence in the financial market given the interconnectedness among the markets; however, it can also be argued that the existing international regulatory system was ineffective and required strong mechanisms of crisis management. It is further noted that the highly diversified investment banking groups, hedge funds and other innovative initiatives in the capital markets complicated the regulatory environment (Davis & Green, 2008).

In a recent banking industry survey conducted by the Center for the Study of Financial Innovation (CSFI), the results showed the greatest threat to the regulated financial institutions lies in the strong *regulation* and *political interference* that has taken place against banks in reaction to the recent financial crisis. These risks were ranked No. 1 and No. 2, respectively, out of a field of 28 risks in the survey. The findings were based on responses from more than 650 bankers, regulators and close observers of the banking scene in 59 countries. This study revealed concerns about over-regulation concentrated in Europe and North America. The Asia Pacific region, including China, sees regulation as a worry but less so than globally (Center for the Study of Financial Innovation [CSFI], 2014).

As a result, there are advocates for strengthening the global regulatory framework to more effectively regulate these increasing cross-border financial activities. Such proposed reform could build on frameworks such as the emerging International Financial Reporting Standards, the Basel standards and the Financial Stability Forum (now Financial Stability Board). For instance, the Basel II and Basel III standards being adopted by various regulators of the world are considered initiatives that could both enhance and complicate the role of risk management in international banks (Wahstrom, 2009).

Despite the insight about the need to strengthen cross-border regulations, there are practical concerns regarding the implementation of regulations given the variations in legal and political systems among the countries of the world. For example, there are, at the present time, various regulatory structures across the world. As noted by Pellegrina and Masciandro (2008), both the politicians and the central bank of a country have significant roles to play in shaping the domestic financial supervision architectures. The authors indicate that a country has either a single authority – a specialised model or a hybrid model of supervision architecture. For instance, a unified model could be associated with good governance, judicial efficiency and the absence of corruption. The study further suggests that it would be rather unrealistic to pursue uniform, optimal supervision architecture through a simple traditional cost-benefit analysis because of the specific political factors within each country (Pellegrina & Masciandro, 2008). Because of these local issues, there exist differences in supervision architecture as well as strengths and weaknesses among these different architectures when dealing with regulatory risks.

NEO-INSTITUTIONALISM

Institutional Isomorphism

To study the dynamics of the financial institutions involved in the regulations, institutional theory is perceived to be of increasing relevance. In particular, neo-institutionalism notes that institutions are typically influenced by the broader environment in which their main goal is to survive. DiMaggio and Powell (1983) noted that institutions must establish political power and legitimacy and that such institutional effects are diffused throughout organisations by coercive (constraining), mimetic (cloning) and normative (learning) mechanisms. Institutional isomorphism has been described as a constraining process that forces one institution to resemble another institution facing similar environmental conditions without necessarily becoming more efficient. As such, three types of institutional forces have been found to be more significant to government organisations than to organisations in the business and non-profit sectors (Frumkin & Galaskiewicz, 2004).

Financial Regulations and Institutions

In examining the globalisation of financial markets, Carruthers, Babb, and Halliday (2001) unveiled the widespread deregulation and globalisation of capital markets where formerly regulated financial markets were unrestrained. With respect to the development of central banks and bankruptcy law, the study suggested that while international convergence in regulations had occurred among nations, divergence in practice had occurred among institutions in different countries.

Merton and Bodie (2005) argued that neoclassical theories provide limited prescription for the institutional structure of financial systems and, therefore, incomplete guidance to understand the process of institutional change. Specific types of financial intermediaries, markets, and regulatory bodies evolve in response to underlying changes in technology, politics, demographics and cultural norms as a result of the continued innovations in financial firms. An analytical framework that treats functions rather than institutions as the conceptual anchors would enhance the study of the dynamics of financial systems.

In a more recent study regarding the role of institutions in facilitating economic development and the growth of the state, Fligstein and Choo (2005) noted that institutional components of national corporate governance can work together as a system that includes institutional features of property law, financial market regulations and labour law. Accordingly, the successful importation of another country's corporate governance institutions would likely require existence of an integrative system.

Fligstein and Choo (2005, p. 79) suggested that it would be unrealistic to have a single model for different jurisdictions and explained possible paths for such studies, '*First, we think that comparative studies in institutions and economic growth must be analyzed longitudinally within countries, as they evolve over time. ... Such research will also begin to untangle the kinds of feedback that are possible between institutions and economic actors. As societies develop and new interest groups appear, for example, such developments may alter institutions. We also know that institutions that exist set up the possibilities for new institutions. It seems useful to tease out such **trends and dynamics** over long historical periods*'.

RISK MANAGEMENT AND STRATEGIC CONTROLS

Dealing with Financial Crises

In a prior study, it is pointed out that the financial crises are intertwined with a series of dynamic processes influenced by the '*mechanisms of the capitalist economy*' leading to financial instability if regulated ineffectively (D'Apice & Ferri, 2010). In an older study by Minsky (1975) regarding financial instability, a model was adopted to illustrate the irrational exuberance within the financial sector caused by economic expansions and contractions over a period of time. Given the on-going issues with the global financial crisis, there are increasing concerns among the public regarding the adverse impacts caused by the financial institutions, as these institutions are expected to be regulated effectively. New management control systems are needed for the financial services industry because the systems were rapidly changing as a result of the on-going consolidation and deregulation of the industry (Middaugh, 1988); the regulators must bear the fiduciary responsibility and be accountable for managing risks associated with regulatory failures.

Risk management is particularly critical for public-sector organisations that are accountable to a broad range of external stakeholders (Ng & Mitchell, 2009; Woods, 2009). A balance between performance and risk management must be maintained for an organisation's sustainable development when considering its strategic objectives. Carbo (2010) noted that the difficulties in balancing financial innovation and regulation in Spain after the financial crisis of 2008. The need to achieve balance between financial innovation strategy and financial risk management remains as a challenge to both the regulatory and the regulated institutions. A more recent study regarding the effects of financial regulations on the global financial crisis suggested that financial innovation could have contributed to the banking crisis (Kim, Koo, & Park, 2013).

Optimal policy development is a possible solution for achieving such a balancing act. The application of scientific methods, such as optimisation models, was long advocated to assist in public-sector planning because of the methods' ability to produce planning alternatives and to facilitate the evaluation and elaboration of insights (Brill, 1979). In this relation, the implementation of strategic controls could be adopted as an interactive process driven by the overall strategy adopted by an institution. Management control system in a public-sector entity was found to be an interactive process (Ittner & Larcker, 1997; Kober, Ng, & Paul, 2007). The challenge for the regulatory body to implement such a monitoring system is, however, to maintain the system's dynamism in measuring the relevant indicators given the exposures to externalities (Henri, 2010).

Normative Development of Risk Management and Controls

A financial regulatory institution's concern about the negative externalities of the financial system could be well beyond its control. Precautionary policy measures can be taken to examine the possibilities for and the potential impacts on the public at large (Barrieu & Sinclair-Desgane, 2006). In the United Kingdom, it was advocated that the Financial Services Authority (FSA) should act as a risk-based regulator that allocates resources for supervision and enforcement action in priority areas (Burger, 2006).

Contingency theory is considered essential when studying the overall effectiveness of the public-sector organisation with respect to pertinent policy setting and effective information and communication measures and with respect to the size of the entities involved (Woods, 2009). In another recent study, Bhimani (2009) revealed the significance and interconnection among corporate governance, risk management and management controls. Accordingly, institutions are expected, by their stakeholders, to strengthen risk management and to convey related information for improved legitimacy (Bhimani, 2009; Oliveira, Lima Rodrigues, & Craig, 2011).[2]

Increasingly normative developments are observed among professional communities as they seek a common understanding of the enterprise risk management approach. As derived by the Institute of Risk Management, the Association of Insurance and Risk Managers and the National Forum for Risk Management in the Public Sector, a set of risk management standards may be adopted by the public-sector organisation (Institute of Risk Management, 2002). This standard identifies the importance of governance in creating the environment and the structures for risk management to operate effectively. Similar standards, such as the COSO framework, have been gaining acceptance among the accounting and finance professions (Ng & Mitchell, 2009). Out of the 17 internal control principles by internal control component as presented in COSO's 2013 Framework, Principle No. 1 states that organisation should demonstrate a commitment to integrity and ethical values (McNally, 2013).

CONCEPTUAL FRAMEWORK AND RESEARCH APPROACH

Conceptual Framework of Strategic Controls for the Financial Services Industry

As noted by Kober et al. (2007), there is an underlying interrelationship between management control mechanisms and strategy, as the management control mechanisms are bounded by the overall strategic objectives of an organisation. However, the significance and interconnections among corporate governance, risk management and management controls should also be recognised (Bhimani, 2009). As stakeholders expect institutions to strengthen risk management, management must implement controls for improved legitimacy (Bhimani, 2009). This phenomenon is observed when there are extended public interests at stake.

Due to constraints on institutions to maintain legitimacy, as explained by DiMaggio and Powell (1983) as well as North (1990), there may be resistance in imposing reforms on an existing regulatory architecture bounded by strategic objectives. The regulators, when facing such a risk management dilemma, attempt to optimise strategic control measures to attain a degree of legitimacy while imposing new strategic controls bounded by the overall strategic objectives.

Research Questions

Despite concerns over the increasing systemic risk on a global basis, study regarding risk management and policy among financial regulators has not been extensive. This paper employs a longitudinal case study approach, as advocated by Fligstein and Choo (2005), to examine the institutional dynamics of the key financial regulators (or regulating institutions) in connection with the regulated financial institutions in Hong Kong before and after the financial tsunami of 2008. It examines the mitigating measures in the form of strategic controls taken to address systemic risk that is influenced by such institutional dynamics within an established financial supervision architecture. It explores the relationship between strategies and management control mechanisms within the financial supervision architecture of an emergent international financial centre that embraces innovation as part of its strategic objectives.

Case Study Approach

The case study approach is adopted as the research methodology for this study. Yin (1994) noted that the case study approach was adopted in a number of studies that explored new knowledge at the individual, group, organisational, social and political levels as well as other related phenomena. It is suggested that the case study method enables investigators to embrace the 'holistic and meaningful characteristics of real-life events'. The case study strategy is considered effective when there is no requirement of the control of behavioural events but rather a focus on contemporary events. Moreover, as posited by Fligstein and Choo (2005), studies of institutional trends and dynamics may be extended over a period of time using the case study approach.

The data collected for this study consist of archival reports, issued financial regulations, published guidelines and circulars distributed by regulators. A total of 12 structured interviews were conducted with individuals who had worked in the regulated financial institutions involved in selling and administration of financial products during the time of the study, that is, between 2008 and 2012.

CASE IN POINT

Organic Development of Hong Kong's Financial Regulatory System:
Two Main Authorities

The Securities and Futures Commission (SFC) is an independent non-governmental statutory body outside the civil service and is responsible for regulating the securities and futures markets in Hong Kong. The SFC was established following the initial enactment of the Securities and Futures Commission Ordinance (SFO) in 1989, subsequent to the October 1987 stock market crash, which resulted in the four day closure of both the Hong Kong stock and stock index futures markets (Ho, Scott, & Wong, 2004). The SFC has a broad mandate to promote fairness, efficiency and competitiveness in the securities industry while also providing protection and education to public investors, minimising related crime and reducing industry risks. In contrast, the Hong Kong Monetary Authority (HKMA) is a government authority in Hong Kong that is responsible for maintaining monetary and banking stability. The HKMA was established in 1993 by merging the Office of the Exchange Fund with the Office of the Commissioner of Banking. Two of the HKMA's main policy objectives are (a) to maintain currency stability within the framework of the Linked Exchange Rate system and (b) to promote the stability and integrity of the financial system, including the banking system. The HKMA is described as the 'de facto' central bank of Hong Kong (Ho et al., 2004). The two key

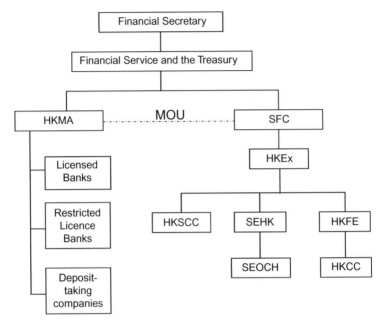

Fig. 1. Key Statutory Bodies in the Financial Supervision Architecture of Hong Kong.

statutory bodies within the financial supervision architecture of Hong Kong are illustrated in Fig. 1.

As a regulatory body, the HKMA's main functions and responsibilities are governed by the Exchange Fund Ordinance and the Banking Ordinance. Moreover, the HKMA acts as the frontline supervisor of registered institutions — banks that intend to engage in securities business. When a bank or an authorised institution (AI) applies to become a registered institution, the HKMA advises the SFC whether the bank is fit and proper to execute the regulated activities for which it seeks registration. To facilitate the necessary coordination, the HKMA and the SFC signed a memorandum of understanding (MOU) in December 2002 that detailed their respective roles and responsibilities. However, their respective roles and responsibilities in regulating these banks have been criticised for being convoluted and for failing to segregate the responsibilities between the two regulatory institutions.[3] A summary of the division of responsibilities between the HKMA and the SFC in regulating the AIs is provided in Table 1.

Table 1. Summary of Segregation of Duties between HKMA and SFC
HKMA (2008).

Segregation of Responsibilities for Regulating Securities Business under the Memorandum of
Understanding between the HKMA and the SFC

	HKMA	SFC
Regulatory processes and supervisory functions	• Responsible for making guidelines under the BO • Consulting the SFC in so far as such guidelines apply to registered institutions • Frontline supervisor of registered institutions • Responsible for the day-to-day supervision of registered institutions	• Responsible for making rules and publishing codes and guidelines under the SFO • Consulting the HKMA on rules, codes and guidelines • Consult the HKMA before exercising its powers of supervision under s.180 of the SFO in relation to an AI
Handling complaints	• Referring complaints to the SFC whenever they are considered by the HKMA to be relevant to a matter that the SFC can investigate under s.182 of the SFO (e.g. an offence under the SFO or market misconduct) or to relate to the SFC's functions under the SFO	• Referring to the HKMA complaints concerning any registered institution, any executive officer of a registered institution, any member of the management of a registered institution, and any relevant individual
Conducting investigations and sharing of results	• Opening a case for investigation • Keeping the SFC informed of the progress • Reporting any related matter to the SFC before completing the investigation when considered appropriate	• Consulting the HKMA before exercising its power to initiate an investigation under s.182(1)(e) of the SFO • Sharing the investigation findings with the HKMA

Pressure to Reform under a Financial Crisis

In 2008, Lehman Brothers Holdings Inc. (LB) filed for bankruptcy protection under Chapter 11 of the US Bankruptcy Code and its regional headquarters in Hong Kong proceeded to liquidate. It was revealed that Hong Kong had been designated to arrange for a particular type of structured product – a callable credit-link note that LB distributed under the name of 'Minibond', which, in fact, contained complex derivative arrangements (HKMA, 2008). The investing public made investments in 'Minibond' products that were spread across a number of retail banks in Hong Kong.

Reportedly, these products lost a significant part of their value upon the collapse of LB.

In response to such losses, the regulatory system in Hong Kong came under pressure from the victims seeking compensation for their losses. In particular, the HKMA was questioned as the frontline supervisor of the securities business of authorised institutions to oversee their governance and internal controls in accordance with standards established by the SFC to ensure the proper conduct of their regulated activities under the SFO. As of the end of 2008, the HKMA received almost 20,000 complaints regarding the sale by AIs of LB-related investment products, which involved approximately US $2.6 billion (HKMA, 2008). The SFC reported an additional 7,000 complaints from the public involving at least 16 licensed banks in Hong Kong (SFC, 2008).[4]

Vulnerability in the Regulatory System

As Hong Kong has been positioned to become the international financial centre for Asia, one of the most significant objectives of the SFO was to enhance financial innovation while promoting a fair, orderly and transparent market. Banks attempt to diversify their portfolio of offerings with 'innovative investment products'. Accordingly, there evolved a mimetic mode of profit-seeking across the authorised institutions despite the risks involved in innovative, derivative financial products. There is still an inexplicable reward system for bankers that incentivises risk-taking. The complexity of incentives is a risk − incentives are not a priori a bad thing, but they need to be transparently and fairly structured (CSFI, 2014).

Subsequent to the outbreak of the LB Minibond incident, the regulators responded with a clarification of their roles and responsibilities. The SFC, as the leader in regulating securities businesses, emphasised the disclosure-based approach within the regulatory regime over investment products distributed throughout the retail operations of banks in Hong Kong (SFC, 2008). While these investment products have been reviewed by the SFC with respect to their adequacy of disclosure on the risks involved, the majority of the affected investors purchased these LB-related investment products through their financial service providers, including banks.

Nonetheless, the disclosure-based approach enables a wide range of possibilities for the innovation of financial products, but it also implies potential complexity of a structured investment product being linked with the underlying global systemic risk pertinent to an overseas capital market.

Were the retail investors informed of the underlying risks related to a complex derivative product? Who would be capable of explaining such systemic risk when selling these products driven by sales commissions?

The HKMA is tasked with the responsibility of supervising registered institutions to ensure that they follow the standards set by the SFC. As prescribed in the MOU between the two regulators, any complaints relating to the regulated activities of registered institutions are to be handled by the HKMA (2008). The stated regulatory coordinating activities, however, seem to be circular between the two regulators, and the effectiveness and timeliness of monitoring of the securities business operations is questionable. Other criticisms over the existing MOU arrangement between regulators include its informality, lack of legitimacy and operational ineffectiveness (Yiu, Chan, & Wong, 2009).

In fact, the focus of inquiry in the aftermath of the LB collapse is related to the possibility of inappropriate selling practices by banks to retail investors. Under the current investigation of the LB debacle, the regulators have concentrated on responding to the inquiries regarding the adequacy of the regime to protect the retail investors in Hong Kong, as not all of these investors are qualified to invest in these high-risk products (HKMA, 2008; SFC, 2008). Internally, it is questionable whether the banks selling these products have adequate internal control procedures in place to appropriately monitor the frontline sales activities. Did they ensure that their frontline sales persons possessed the professional knowledge and integrity to market and sell these investment products? Was there a performance measurement system that balanced short-term sales performance and proper conduct integrated with the overall banking culture?

Mitigating Measures

While the regulators have examined various options of reform, including a unified system similar to the UK structure, as suggested by Carse (2008), the authorities have thus far expressed their confidence in the existing regulatory system that has developed organically over the past two decades. As reported by Yiu et al. (2009), Joseph Yam, former chief executive of the HKMA, however indicated that no major restructuring of the system is necessary; he reemphasised the effectiveness of the existing regulatory system in Hong Kong despite the consent regarding potential areas of improvement.

While political stakeholders, including the legislative council members, criticised the lack of responsible actors in the system, the officials in Hong Kong and Beijing emphasised their support for and belief in the stability of Hong Kong's financial system — thus, no structural reform was deemed necessary (Pauly, 2011). After a series of investigations, the SFC and the HKMA and 16 distributing banks jointly announced that they had reached an agreement in relation to the repurchase of LB Minibonds from eligible customers in July 2009.

Using powers under SFO, the SFC led the effort to arrange for the repurchase scheme along with the HKMA for 16 Minibond distributing banks in the best interests of the investing public, which was allegedly to have received a high level of investor acceptance, according to the following deliberations among key regulators:[5]

> '*Strong markets, like Hong Kong's, need strong regulations. This agreement will provide substantial benefits for the vast majority of customers holding Minibonds that would not otherwise be received by them and, given the number of Banks and customers involved, the agreement is a watershed in the regulation of financial services in Hong Kong*', stated the SFC's Chief Executive Officer, Mr. Martin Wheatley.

> Mr. Y K Choi, Deputy Chief Executive of the HKMA, said, '*The HKMA welcomes and supports the repurchase scheme and considers it to be practical, reasonable and in the interests of the great majority of Minibond investors. The HKMA encourages eligible customers to consider the repurchase offer by the Banks*'.

Substantial assistance from the HKMA in the investigation of these cases was acknowledged by the SFC. However, the investigation was criticised, as justice for the victims had not been attained because the matters were now resolved outside of the courts.[6]

Proposed Changes through 'Add-On' Mitigations

Subsequently, the SFC solicited public comments on proposals to fine-tune regulations governing the sale of retail investment products to the public. In 2010, the Financial Services and the Treasury Bureau under the Hong Kong Government proposed the creation of an Investor Education Council (IEC) and a Financial Dispute Resolution Center as enhancements to the existing regulatory framework. These initiatives, considered 'add-ons' to the existing architecture, aim to prevent the public from entering into improper investment schemes and to mitigate legal issues as a result of on-going pertinent disputes within the financial institutions. However, no major reform of the HKMA or the SFC has been proposed. It is likely that these aftermath mitigating mechanisms will be quite different from the 'twin peaks' approach that would refine the specific roles and responsibilities of the HKMA and the SFC in regulating the banks' securities business. As such, the specialised model in Hong Kong would continue to be implemented similar to certain jurisdictions in the world, noted in the study by Pellegrina and Masciandro (2008).[7]

Normative Development among the Regulated

Coercive Force from the Regulators

Although no major reform was made to the current financial supervision architecture, the regulators provided a number of guidelines for the licensed banks to implement. It is significant that subsequent to the HKMA's Report on Issues Concerning the Distribution of Structured Products Connected to LB, a detailed list of recommendations by the HKMA was issued to authorised banking institutions requiring them to implement proper control procedures within a specific time frame (HKMA, 2008).[8]

Nevertheless, there is not much restriction on similar types of financial products sold through these networks – in other words, financial innovation has not been discouraged. The banks are, however, advised to establish risk management measures on approval of financial products to be sold through their networks. As reflected by an interviewee, '*To meet our customers' needs to diversify their investments, we continue to carry a wide range of products from more conservative savings instruments, bonds to a variety of structured investment-linked products with better returns. However, we now are conscious about the risk-profile of a customer – that means we would rather sell more conservative products to those who are less prepared to do so*'.

Mimic – Cloning of 'Add-Ons' Risk Control Measures

As the incident related to the LB investment products had certain adverse implications on the customers' confidence with respect to acquiring investment products and services through banks in Hong Kong, more prudent measures imposed by the regulators are reflected in banks' daily operations. Banks proactively scrutinised their operation guidelines after the LB incident to strengthen customer protection and to re-establish customer trust. Major areas of practice and reinforced implementations after the financial crisis are summarised in Table 2.[9]

Table 2. Summary of Key Implementations in Internal Control Practice.

Areas of Practice	Reinforced Implementations
Audio recording requirement pertaining to sales of investment products	Audio recording throughout the process of conducting customer risk-profile assessment and sales of investment products to retail investors
Access to customers' information and profiles	Staff only allowed to utilise clients' deposit-related information for providing investment or wealth management services with written consent
Cooling-off period on selling investment products	When buying applicable unlisted structured investment products, investors may exercise the right to cancel their order or unwind the transaction and receive a refund within a defined period
Commissions, fees and other benefit disclosure	Requirement to disclose any monetary benefits or trail commission from product providers for each investment product sold/invested in by clients before sale
Mystery shopping programme regarding banks' sales practices	Augmented activities by the regulators to look into the sales practices of intermediaries with respect to selling practices
Physical segregation of retail securities business activities from ordinary banking business at branches	All investment activities take place in distinct 'investment corners' to provide a physical differentiation between traditional deposit-taking and retail securities activities
Statement for derivative products traded on an exchange	Increased efforts to ascertain clients' knowledge of derivatives, clients must read the statement for derivative products prior to confirmation
Sufficient understanding of products and disclosure of product information	Stronger emphasis on providing professional training to frontline staff to ensure they have the necessary knowledge about the investment products. The information about investment products should be presented in a manner that is appropriate to the target investor and in a format that can be easily understood
Suitability obligations	Increased efforts to ensure there is clear understanding about a client's financial situation, investment experience, objectives, knowledge and horizon together with risk tolerance, etc.

Another interviewee working in a local bank noted, '*There are definitely more procedures imposed throughout the past two years. Although similar procedures were in place before, we are now asked to follow through more detailed procedures and paperwork when handling marketing and sales of our investment products .... I feel the audio recording requirement now required throughout the selling process is fairly tedious but we have to follow through these requirements*'.

Normative — Learning from the Past and from Peers
Although the new operation procedures appear time-consuming for investors and bank staff when dealing with investments, these new procedures,
as implemented in 2010, are intended to improve the effectiveness of the
regulatory regime over the wide range of investment products and to
improve the relevant conduct and selling practices of intermediaries.

As observed by the interviewees, the intermediaries are required to dis-
charge their duties with due skill, care, and diligence as they assess the suit-
ability of the products for the customer. The new procedures further ensure
that investors can obtain the latest and most accurate information and
complete product disclosure without misinterpretation due to misleading or
unfair practices. The alleged advantage is that the investors are able to
make an informed judgement regarding their investment, thereby sufficiently protecting the interests of the investors. Apparently, such procedures enhance the protection for the investing public while strengthening
Hong Kong's position as an international financial centre.

Training and development activities regarding these enhanced internal
control procedures were also increased in the period following the LB debacle. Another local bank staff expressed, *'We now have to attend regular
training arranged by our human resources department. These courses are
largely related to compliance requirements as well as technical knowledge
about structured financial products — some of them are fairly complicated
concepts .... All newly joined employees are required to take up additional
commencement sessions'.*

DISCUSSION

Organic Development and Externalities

The Hong Kong financial supervision architecture has been demonstrated
to be similar to the specialised model as prescribed by Pellegrina and
Masciandro (2008) in that it has characteristics similar to those of other
specialised-model regulators in the world that are influenced by a strong
'central bank' and by the government's 'grabbing hand' (GH) approach.
As posited by Pellegrina and Masciandro (2008), *'It is possible that the GH
policymaker will preserve the central bank's supervisory tasks, although mitigated by the presence of other supervisors. The reason for mitigation is that
this kind of policymaker can also dislike the central bank involvement in*

supervision, since she/he fears the creation of an overly powerful bureaucratic agency that can reduce his/her possibilities to design policies aimed at pleasing, time to time, all vested constituencies'.

Institutional Isomorphism and Dynamics

Despite the material impact on the financial services sector, the two key financial regulators in Hong Kong have neutralised the critics regarding the necessary reforms over the existing financial supervision architecture. Despite the increasing dynamics and challenges in the global financial centre and contrary to Merton and Bodie (2005), neither regulatory reform nor restructure was considered as a preferred approach by the regulators. As noted by DiMaggio and Powell (1983), institutional isomorphism is the result of a constraining process that forces one unit or entity to become like another unit under similar environmental conditions, without necessarily becoming more efficient. Although the SFO's objectives remain the same, similar investment products are allowed to be sold based on the product disclosure approach with measurable enhancements on risk control procedures. From a macro policy perspective, the regulators in Hong Kong are inclined to seek an optimal risk management approach to mitigate such inherent deficiencies. New guidelines pinpointing operational risk management are required to be implemented among the regulated banks.

Seeking Optimal Risk Management through Strategic Control Measures

The LB Minibond incident reflected the fact that the organic development experience in Hong Kong reform would likely not be accommodated due to the rapid global financial innovation and the complexity in investment product development linked with implausible risk exposures (Fig. 2). As regulated financial institutions, banks' increased involvement in the securities business was unanticipated during such organic development. The question arises, did the regulated financial institutions make adequate assumptions regarding the underlying innovation risks when initially designing the supervision architecture and during subsequent reviews? Were the new mitigation procedures good enough to put these financial institutions into their 'comfort zone'?

If appropriate responses were to be made, the regulators would have to consider a comprehensive approach to risk management within the existing

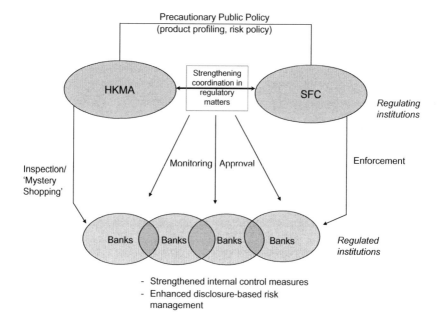

Fig. 2. Optimising Strategic Controls in a Financial Supervision Architecture.

architecture, as stipulated (Ng & Mitchell, 2009; Woods, 2009). First, there should be precautionary measures in light of the increasing complications with global systemic risk. Relevant policy should be in place to prevent any implausible risk exposures for the public at large. Second, the ineffectiveness within the existing financial supervision architecture needs to be reviewed with enhanced operationalisation of monitoring and control systems rather than relying on a convoluted MOU and procedures established between the HKMA and the SFC. Timely information and communication enabled through an interactive management system are critical if regulators are to reveal information about any problematic practices among the regulated institutions (Woods, 2009). Third, other preventive measures include utilising 'mystery shoppers', strengthening routine enforcement and on-site inspections or audit activities imposed upon the regulated financial institutions.[10]

Moreover, especially for the sizable banks involved in securities business, these regulated financial institutions are cautiously reminded to implement effective enterprise-wide performance measurements and integrated risk management systems in alignment with the regulatory requirements.

Proper internal control procedures are urged to be in place, and any control weaknesses must be identified and properly addressed in a timely manner. Proper disclosures regarding financial products are not only printed in the brochures but must also be clearly explained to the investor. Frontline staff members are given thorough training on pertinent regulatory issues and compliance procedures under a relatively more risk-averse culture than in the past. Subsequent to the financial crisis, both formal and informal constraints appear to be imperative for the regulated institutions to improve their legitimacy operating in the emerged global financial centre (DiMaggio & Powell, 1983; North, 1990).

The above measures constitute strategic controls implemented within the established financial supervision architecture. In this sense, the overall policy to sustain financial product innovation has not been abolished, as Hong Kong continues its strategic positioning as the international financial centre not only for Asia but also, more critically, for China.[11] While this strategic objective is to continue for the foreseeable future, risk control measures have been developed and implemented more extensively and prudently within the system. This system includes the array of licensed banks that are involved in handling securities business. These strengthened control and compliance procedures are in turn meant to reduce the risk of similar incidents occurring in an extensive manner given Hong Kong's policy strategy as global financial centre.

CONCLUDING REMARKS

An Organic Financial Regulation Architecture

In conclusion, this study reveals an organic development of a specialised financial regulatory architecture that resists transforming itself despite the significant impact of externalities. Further, this study reinforces the prior studies regarding similar dynamics in other jurisdictions (Pellegrina & Masciandro, 2008). Radical reform of such architecture seems remote, even under the intense pressure to change. Furthermore, the concept of institutional isomorphism is contemplated for its relevance in explaining the need to retain legitimacy within a regulatory system (Oliveira et al., 2011). Such legitimacy is attempted through the incorporation of new measures to mitigate the inherent risk. Nevertheless, this study does not find the necessary reform initiatives in a financial regulatory system within a dynamic environment of economic growth, as suggested by Merton and Bodie (2005). Institutions in this case maintain their legitimacy through defending, rationalising and strengthening their existing roles with organic developments.

In a report presented to the Legislative Council of Hong Kong by Carse (2009), *'There is no perfect model of an integrated regulator. All the various options have their pros and cons, the balance between which can only be determined by the particular circumstances of each jurisdiction'*. Despite the pros and cons, this study reveals that the regulators could still upgrade risk management for feasible improvement through dynamic risk control measures at the policy, compliance and operational levels. This phenomenon reflects a mode of strategic controls within such a regulatory system in response to the systemic risk instigated under a global financial system. Such strategic control measures are both interactive and responsive to externalities (Ittner & Larcker, 1997; Kober et al., 2007). Nevertheless, this case study further suggests that induced strategic controls are bounded by the overall strategic objectives that constrain the range of mitigating risk control measures as well as a radical reform of the existing architecture.

Institutional Dynamics in Regulatory Risk and Strategic Controls

In this post-financial crisis analysis, regulated financial institutions swiftly respond by strengthening their risk controls through compliance with the guidelines imposed by the regulator. These strengthened strategic controls, however, appear to be contingent on significant adverse impacts on the existing regulatory system and the resulting demands from the stakeholders. This situation suggests that contingency theory as used in the study of risk management and related controls should consider such adverse external incidents (Woods, 2009).

Moreover, in this case, institutional dynamics in influencing the implementation of risk controls through a top-down interactive mechanism are observed. Such dynamic and pertinent rapid responses induce the pursuit of optimal risk management within a regulatory framework. Mitigating risk control measures are strengthened in the aftermath of a financial crisis. Having experienced such a significant adverse impact, regulatory institutions attempt to take precautionary, coercive measures such that the regulated institutions mimic and implement prudent mechanisms. Mitigating measures are instituted by the regulators, who attempt to balance continuing financial innovation and increased risk management for the market as a whole (Carbo, 2010), as there are trade-offs between these two opposing policies.

This case also reflects that risk management guidance in response to a crisis is developed by the regulator for the regulated to follow and implement. The implication is that the regulator with exposure to extended public stakeholders is encouraged to take a proactive and optimal approach in policy-making before another crisis occurs (Barrieu & Sinclair-Desgane, 2006; Brill, 1979). This study also demonstrates that the regulator has the power to institute risk management through a top-down method of strategic control and related risk control measures (Bhimani, 2009; Ng & Mitchell, 2009).

In reflection, to prevent and minimise such adverse impacts on the investing public stakeholders at large, a periodic review of the effectiveness of the overall risk controls would be crucial when anticipating systemic risk. It becomes critical to identify any unrecognised risks that could be more likely to emerge after rather than before positioning as an international financial centre under a global economy. Precautionary risk control measures must be formulated as the public's confidence in investing may not be restored solely through risk mitigating measures with investor education and aftermath dispute resolution mechanisms.

Strategic Responses by the Regulators

On 6 June 2012, the Legislative Council of Hong Kong released its investigation report on the LB Minibond incident. The former chief executives of the HKMA and the SFC were criticised for the leadership's failure to detect and rectify widespread non-compliance among banks. In response, both regulators indicated that various significant mitigating measures had been taken to settle with the affected investors and to strengthen the existing regulatory framework. As released by the HKMA, '*Learning from past experience and having regard to evolving market conditions and practices, the HKMA has since September 2008 implemented a series of measures to enhance the regulation of sales of investment products by banks ....These measures have been operating effectively in the past few years ... The HKMA has also enhanced its supervisory framework with increased resources devoted to banking conduct supervision and enforcement so as to protect the interests of investors*'.[12]

Similarly, the SFC responded, '*The SFC also implemented a package of enhanced investor protection measures in 2010 to strengthen the regulatory regime governing the offering of investment products and will set up an Investor Education Center (IEC) in the fourth quarter of this year to take up broader investor education responsibilities covering the entire financial services sector*.[13]

The Hong Kong government suggested that the measures taken by the two regulators would foster investor protection and financial stability in the future as it was noted that *'the scope and magnitude of the global financial crisis in 2008 exceeded the expectations of all parties and the ramifications were cross-sectoral, cross-border and far-reaching'*.[14] However, there was no mention of how the balance between financial product innovation and stability would be optimised, nor was there mention of how stronger collaboration between the two prime regulators would be enhanced. In the meantime, a substantial effort being made to potentially reduce and transfer of pertinent regulatory risks to individual investors through education under the regime of IEC – a newly established institution as a subsidiary of the SFC that takes a holistic approach to improving financial literacy in Hong Kong.

NOTES

1. According to Hong Kong Monetary Authority [HKMA] (2008), Minibonds are credit-linked notes, arranged by Lehman Brothers Asia Limited, with payment of interest and redemption payout at maturity linked to the credit of specified entities for each series of Minibonds. Minibonds are subject to certain early redemption conditions. The interest coupon varies from series to series but is, generally above the prevailing HIBOR/LIBOR at the time of issue.

2. Such incremental changes in an institutional environment for legitimacy can be complicated by informal constraints that would alter the game by increasing or decreasing cooperative outcomes, as explained by North (1990). It is useful to test what types of informal constraints, namely corporate culture, would produce cooperative behaviour under a model of wealth-maximising norms within a game theoretic context.

3. Despite the defined responsibilities of the two regulators, there are allegedly overlapping roles in regulating banks involved in securities businesses. Under current practice, the SFC registers banks that undertake securities business that are constituted as regulated activities under the Securities and Futures Ordinance (Cap 571) (SFO) re-established in 2003. Financial institutions registered for this purpose are referred to as registered institutions. Because the SFC is the lead regulator for the securities industry, any entity with an intention to conduct a business in activities regulated under the SFO must be licensed or registered by the SFC. The SFC is the authority that establishes the standards, through rules, codes and guidelines

issued under the SFO, with which financial intermediaries are required to comply when conducting regulated activities.

4. The public outcry called for the accountability and responsibility of regulating the sales of such high-risk investment products to retail-level investors. These investors were considered unqualified as they lacked the necessary understanding to acquire such investments. Moreover, there were complaints about misrepresentation regarding the risk profile of the 'Minibond', which was unlikely to be suitable for some senior citizens who had little knowledge about the underlying derivative arrangement and the investment risk involved. The confidence in the financial regulatory system was damaged, and the public at large questioned the effectiveness of the existing regulatory measures.

5. This report is based on the press release by the SFC on 22 July 2009, titled 'SFC, HKMA and 16 banks reach agreement on Minibonds'.

6. For instance, as reported by Ng and Ng (2011), 'Democratic Party lawmaker Kam Nai-wai, who supports the investors, believed those who choose not to take the ex-gratia payment would continue to make claims against the banks. He said the amount of the ex-gratia payment was insufficient to reflect the banks' responsibility'.

7. In addition to the HKMA and the SFC, the two main specialised financial regulators in Hong Kong, the Office of the Commissioner of Insurance and the Mandatory Provident Fund Schemes Authority, are responsible for regulating the insurance industry and the retirement fund investment schemes, respectively.

8. This notification was issued by the HKMA on 25 March 2009 as a circular to the authorised banking institutions.

9. This summary of reinforced implementations is referenced in the documents released to the public by the SFC and the HKMA between 2010 and 2012. These implementations are corroborated in semi-structured interviews conducted with practitioners who have worked in the regulated financial institutions during the specific period of time.

10. According to the HKMA (2008), since 2005, an increasing number (50 for 2008) of large, complex or active registered institutions (including all the active retail banks) have been required to commission only annually an independent unit (e.g. their compliance department) to review the institution's compliance with the regulatory requirements of the SFC and the HKMA concerning regulated activities. The units' reports are reviewed jointly by the institutions' case officers and the Securities Supervision Team. Common issues arising from the assessment of the reviews from 2005 to 2007 included inadequate controls for ensuring the accuracy of relevant individuals' registration details and breaches of the Securities and Futures (contract notes, statements of accounts and receipts) Rules. A few registered institutions reported control deficiencies in relation to the marketing of investment products.

11. Hong Kong is now considered an offshore, international financial centre for handling Chinese Yuan settlement.

12. 'Statement of the Hong Kong Monetary Authority on the Report of the Legislative Council Subcommittee to Study Issues Arising from Lehman Brothers-related Minibonds and Structured Financial Products', Press Release by HKMA 6th June 2012.

13. 'Subcommittee report on Lehman Brothers Minibonds and structured financial products', Press Release by SFC 6th June 2012.

14. 'Investment regulation upgraded', Press Release by HKAR Government 6th June 2012.

ACKNOWLEDGEMENTS

An earlier version of this paper was presented at the International Symposium on Management Accounting and Control in the Age of Globalization Conference 2012 held at Cardiff University, UK. The authors would like to express their sincere thanks for the valuable comments provided by Professor Kent Matthews of the Cardiff Business School and other reviewers.

REFERENCES

Alexander, K., Dhumale, R., & Eatwell, J. (2006). *Global governance of financial system: The international regulation of systemic risk*. New York, NY: Oxford University Press.

Barrieu, P., & Sinclair-Desgane, B. (2006). On precautionary policies. *Management Science*, *52*(8), 1145–1154.

Bhimani, A. (2009). Risk management, corporate governance and management accounting: Emerging interdependencies. *Management Accounting Research*, *20*, 2–5.

Brill, E. D. (1979). The of optimization models in public-sector planning. *Management Science*, *25*(5), 413–422.

Burger, R. (2006). FSA enforcement process review. *Journal of Financial Regulation and Compliance*, *14*(1), 14–23.

Carbo, S. (2010). Financial crisis and regulation: The case of Spain. In R. R. Bliss & G. G. Kaufman (Eds.), *Financial institutions and markets – The financial crisis: An early retrospective* (pp. 127–146). New York, NY: Palgrave Macmillan.

Carruthers, B. G., Babb, S. L., & Halliday, T. C. (2001). Institutionalizing markets, or the market for institutions? Central bank, bankruptcy law and the globalization of financial markets. In J. L. Campbell & O. L. Pedersen (Eds.), *The risk of neoliberalism and institutional analysis* (pp. 94–126). Princeton, NJ: Princeton University Press.

Carse, D. T. R. (2008, July). *Review of the Hong Kong Monetary Authority's Work on Banking Stability*, 1–49.

Carse, D. T. R. (2009). *The future structure of financial regulation in Hong Kong*. Hong Kong Legislative Council Paper No. 1-11.

Center for the Study of Financial Innovation. (2014). *Banking banana skins survey report*, 4-32.

D'Apice, V., & Ferri, G. (2010). *Financial instability: Toolkit for interpreting boom and bust cycles*. New York, NY: Palgrave Macmillan.

Davis, H., & Green, D. (2008). *Global financial regulations*. Cambridge: Polity Press.

DiMaggio, P. J., & Powell, W. W. (1983). The iron cage revisited: Institutional isomorphism and collective rationality in organizational fields. *American Sociological Review, 48,* 147–160.

Fligstein, N., & Choo, J. (2005). Law and corporate governance. *American Sociological Review, 1,* 61–84.

Frumkin, P., & Galaskiewicz, J. (2004). Institutional isomorphism and public sector organizations. *Journal of Public Administration Research and Theory, 14*(3), 283–307.

Henri, J. (2010). The periodic review of performance indicators: An empirical investigation of the dynamism of performance measurement systems. *European Accounting Review, 19*(1), 73–96.

Ho, S. S. M., Scott, R. H., & Wong, K. A. (2004). Overview of financial institutions and markets and their regulation. In S. S. M. Ho, R. H. Scott, & K. A. Wong (Eds.), *The Hong Kong financial system: A new age.* New York, NY: Oxford University Press.

Hong Kong Monetary Authority. (2008, December). *Report of The Hong Kong Monetary Authority on Issues Concerning the Distribution of Structured Products Connected to Lehman Group Companies,* 1–83.

Institute of Risk Management. (2002). *A risk management standard,* 1-17.

Ittner, C., & Larcker, D. F. (1997). Quality strategy, strategic control systems, and organizational performance. *Accounting, Organizations and Society, 22*(3/4), 293–314.

Kim, T., Koo, B., & Park, M. (2013). Role of financial regulation and innovation in the financial crisis. *Journal of Financial Stability, 9*(4), 662–672.

Kober, R., Ng, J., & Paul, B. J. (2007). The interrelationship between management control mechanisms and strategy. *Management Accounting Research, 18*(4), 425–452.

Leung, C., & Unteroberdoerster, O. (2008). *Hong Kong SAR as a financial center for Asia: Trends and implications.* International Monetary Fund: Working Paper No. 1-17.

McNally, J. S. (2013). The 2013 COSO framework & SOX compliance. *Strategic Finance,* June Issue, 5.

Merton, R. C., & Bodie, Z. (2005). Design of financial systems: Towards a synthesis of function and structure. *Journal of Investment Management, 3*(1), 6–28.

Middaugh, J. K. (1988). Management control in the financial services industry. *Business Horizons, 31*(3), 79–86.

Minsky, H. P. (1975). *John Maynard Keynes.* New York, NY: Cambridge University Press.

Ng, A. W., & Mitchell, B. (2009). Developing knowledge capital in an integrated enterprise risk management system: Framework and structured gap analysis for public sector organizations. *International Journal of Learning and Intellectual Capital, 6*(1–2), 170–184.

Ng, K., & Ng, J. (2011). HK banks agree extra Lehman Minibond payouts. *South China Morning Post,* March 29.

North, D. (1990). *Institutions, institutional change and economic performance.* New York, NY: Cambridge University Press.

Oliveira, J., Lima Rodrigues, L., & Craig, R. (2011). Voluntary risk reporting to enhance institutional and organizational legitimacy: Evidence from Portuguese banks. *Journal of Financial Regulation and Compliance, 19*(3), 271–289.

Pauly, L. W. (2011). Hong Kong's financial center as a regional and global context. *The Hong Kong Journal,* July, 21.

Pellegrina, L. D., & Masciandro, D. (2008). Politicians, central banks, and the shape of financial supervision architectures. *Journal of Financial Regulation and Compliance, 16*(4), 290–317.

Securities and Futures Commission. (2008, December). *Issues raised by the Lehman Minibonds Crisis: Report to the financial secretary, 1–105.*

Wahstrom, G. (2009). Risk management versus operational action: Basel II in a Swedish context. *Management Accounting Research, 20,* 53–68.

Walter, A. (2010). Chinese attitudes towards global financial regulatory co-operation: Revisionist or status quo. In E. Helleiner, S. Pagliari, & H. Zimmermann (Eds.), *Global finance in crisis: The politics of international regulatory change.* London: Routledge.

Woods, M. (2009). A contingency theory perspective on the risk management control system within Birmingham city council. *Management Accounting Research, 20,* 69–81.

Yin, R. Y. (1994). *Case study research: Design and methods.* Thousand Oaks, CA: Sage.

Yiu, E., Chan, M., & Wong, A. (2009). Monetary authority chief defends regulatory system. *South China Morning Post,* January 11, p. A3.

BANK INTERNATIONALISATION: AN EXAMINATION OF THE ROLE OF GOVERNMENT AND HOME INSTITUTIONS IN EMERGING ECONOMIES

Weijing He, Patrick Ring and Agyenim Boateng

ABSTRACT

Purpose − *Over the past decade internationalisation by banks from emerging market economies has accelerated. The purpose of this study is to examine the role of government and home country institutions in the international expansion process of Chinese commercial banks (CCBs).*

Methodology/approach − *By employing qualitative research method, data was collected via interviews from 30 senior managers based on a sample of 10 CCBs involved in international expansion over the 2001−2013 period.*

Findings − *The study finds that the Chinese government and home institutions play an important role in motivating CCBs' internationalisation.*

The Political Economy of Chinese Finance
International Finance Review, Volume 17, 271−293
Copyright © 2016 by Emerald Group Publishing Limited
ISSN: 1569-3767/doi:10.1108/S1569-376720160000017016

Evidence from this research illustrates the effect institutional factors have in emerging economy firms' internationalisation.

Practical implications − *The managerial implication of these findings is that CCBs could take great advantage of government policy by developing proper internationalisation strategies and capabilities that would enhance CCBs' competitiveness in global market. On the institutional front, removal of the institutional constraints imposed on Chinese banking industry is required. Using market-oriented management and regulatory rules rather than imposing administrative restrictions could therefore accelerate CCBs' adaption and integration in the international market and enhance their competitive power.*

Keywords: Bank internationalisation; government; home institutions; emerging economy; Chinese commercial banks

INTRODUCTION

The internationalisation of firms from emerging economies (EEs) has increased rapidly in the last few decades (Clarke, Cull, Peria, & Sanchez, 2003; Lehner & Schnitzer, 2008; UNCTAD, 2013). Hoskisson, Eden, Lau, and Wright (2000) and UNCTAD (2006) note that recent economic liberalisation and other reforms in BRIC (i.e., Brazil, Russia, India and China) countries have not only attracted high investment inflows but have also motivated firms from these countries to invest abroad. It is therefore not surprising that a growing theoretical literature on emerging economy multinational enterprises (EEMNEs) has been devoted to their internationalisation strategies (Anderson & Sutherland, 2015; Cui & Jiang, 2012; Luo & Tung, 2007). These studies (e.g., Cui & Jiang, 2012; Luo, Xue, & Han, 2010) have documented that emerging country governments are behind the rise in firm internationalisation by EEMNEs. Yet relatively little attention has been given to the nature of the role of government and home country institutions on firm internationalisation, particularly, in the banking sector.

Understanding the role of government in bank internationalisation is important because EEMNEs are unlikely to possess ownership advantages which can be exploited in the developed country (Demirbag, Tatoglu, & Glasister, 2009). As latecomers in the international market, EEMNEs not only lack ownership advantages in terms of strategic resources and international experience but also face institutional constraints which increase the cost of going abroad (Du & Boateng, 2015; Hitt, Ahlstrom, Dacin, Levitas, & Svobodina, 2004). Government involvement therefore becomes an important means to circumvent institutional barriers and ownership disadvantages of EEMNEs internationalisation (Child & Rodrigues, 2005; Hitt et al., 2004). As a result, EEMNEs may pursue compromise strategies which exploit government-related advantages in order to compensate for their entrepreneurial weaknesses (Luo et al., 2010; Rugman & Verbeke, 1992; Wang, Hong, Kafouros, & Boateng, 2012).

It is therefore argued that, due to the high state involvement in businesses and the incomplete market-based reforms in the home country, the internationalisation of service firms from EEs may not necessarily be explained by the asset exploitation perspectives which suggest that firms go abroad to exploit unique firm-specific assets or ownership advantages to take advantage of market imperfections (Dunning, 1993; Wright, Filatotchev, Hoskisson, & Peng, 2005). The purpose of this paper, therefore, is to examine the role of government and home institutions in bank internationalisation by looking, in particular, at the effect of government policy on the Chinese commercial banks' (CCBs) international expansion.

The idiographic features of CCBs are important considerations in justifying the worthiness of the research in terms of the specific nature of a transitional country and an EE. CCBs were historically owned and controlled by the Chinese government. Even after the reform of the banking system, the influence of government remains significant on CCBs (Boateng, Huang, & Kufuor, 2015). The Chinese commercial banking sector is dominated by five very large state-owned banks known as the 'Big Five' — Bank of China (BOC), China Construction Bank (CCBank), Agricultural Bank of China (ABC), Industrial and Commercial Bank of China (ICBC) and Bank of Communication (BOCOM), which together account for about 75% of industrial assets; more than 90% of the banking sector assets of the state-owned banks (CBRC, 2013). The other commercial banks are wholly or partly owned by different tiers of government or/and stated-owned enterprises and/or private firms (CBRC, 2013). Inside the banking sector, the lack of an explicit identity of ownership, alongside government interference, has restricted the pace of development of Chinese banks (Chen & Shi, 2004). These features make CCBs' international expansion distinctive compared to banks from developed market economies, and these features justify research to shed light on what drives the internationalisation of CCBs.

The focus on CCBs' internationalisation during the 2001–2013 period as an empirical context for this study has two key motivations. First, China is the largest EE and the past decade has witnessed a significant growth of CCBs in international markets. The dramatic development of the Chinese economy has brought CCBs great opportunities to expand internationally. Chinese banks have been ranked among the top banks in the world (Alexander, 2010) and now have a presence in every continent and in all major financial centres. Second, Chinese government policies towards outward foreign direct investment (OFDI) and banking reforms, such as 'Go Abroad' initiated in 2000, have largely prompted CCBs' internationalisation.

The rest of the chapter is organised as follows. Next section briefly reviews the institutional theory with respect to firm internationalisation. This is followed by the research methodology used in this study. The penultimate section provides the findings and discussion. The final section provides a conclusion and implications of the study.

THEORETICAL FRAMEWORK

Institutional Theory and Bank Internationalisation

Institutional theory is a widely accepted theoretical perspective that emphasises the importance of rational myths, isomorphism and legitimacy (Scott, 2008). Scott (1995) asserts that institutions are social structures composed of cultural-cognitive (shared social beliefs and values), normative (established norms and professionalisation) and regulative (the legal system and its enforcement) elements. These three pillars work together to help constitute a country's institutional profile. Operating within the context of these three pillars, organisations have to adapt to a variety of institutional pressures when making strategic choices (Child, 1972, 1997).

Institutional theory identifies two sets of constraints in an institutional environment. One set is categorised as formal constraints and refers to economic, political and legal factors. The other set consists of informal constraints, including culture and ideology in a society (North, 1990). Both sets of institutional elements are argued to exert enormous influence on firms' behaviour and performance. According to institutional theory, firms' strategic choices are not merely driven by the industry-specific and firm-specific resources that traditional strategic research emphasises (Barney, 1991). Rather strategic decisions may also be the result of, or a response to, the formal and informal constraints of the particular institutional environment in which a firm is embedded (Scott, 1995). Institutional theory suggests that firms' internationalisation is facilitated or constrained by social, political or legal factors, which either promote or hinder the enhancement of a firm's existing resources and capabilities.

In such a context, non-market relationships, such as relationships with government, play an important role. This is particularly the case for EE firms, whose internationalisation has taken place in a variety of political and institutional contexts (Cantwell, Dunning, & Lundan, 2010), the nature of which suggest that an institutional approach is significant in any analysis of EE firms' internationalisation (Gaur & Kumar, 2010). Combining resource-based and institutional-based views enables the examination of the inclination and ability of EE firms' to internationalise; generally found to be a result of coordination of the resources the firms possess in the context their response to regulatory, normative and cultural-cognitive pressures (Hong, Wang, & Kafouros, 2015). Strategic choices become the outcome, underlining the importance of strategic research concerning the institution-based view (Peng, 2002).

The Role of Government and Internationalisation of EE Firms

Previous studies have suggested that the institutional framework of a firm's home country, especially in EEs, has a strong influence in shaping that firm's internationalisation strategy (Meyer & Peng, 2005; Peng, Wang, & Jiang, 2008; Rui & Yip, 2008). These studies specifically indicate that EE governments and their institutions play an important role in a firm's international expansion decisions (Hoskisson et al., 2000). The recent empirical literature has shown that the introduction of supportive and straightforward regulatory policies by home country governments will encourage firms to engage in international expansion Buckley et al. (2007), while a poor institutional environment in the home country, which may include obstacles such as regulatory uncertainty and governmental interference, may also push the firm into pursuing overseas development (Luo et al., 2010).

Governments can influence firm internationalisation mainly in two ways: policymaking and ownership. Luo et al. (2010) point out that government creates policies and regulations affecting the business environment to facilitate internationalisation of EE firms. Such policies could be tax rebates, foreign exchange assistance and financial support. On the other hand, government can also exert regulatory and coercive pressures to limit firm's international expansion.

Due to increasing global competition in the past decade, EE firms have gradually realised the importance and dynamic nature of international markets and global business systems. As a result, both EE governments and firms believe an increasing presence in international or global business systems is imperative, and EE governments have attempted to help their national firms to play an active part on the global market. Government can support EE firms to strengthen their competitive position in international markets or compensate for their competitive disadvantages by employing its resources and institutional power (Wang, Hong, Kafouros, & Wright, 2012). EE governments can also promote OFDI as an efficient way to strengthen the competitiveness of their enterprises and nations by bringing vital resources such as technological and managerial know-how from advanced countries to their home country and hence help improve the efficiency and best practices of their countries (Luo et al., 2010). Therefore, taking full advantage of home government support is very important and helpful to EE firms' international efforts.

More specifically, it has been argued that state ownership can significantly influence the internationalisation of EE firms (Hong et al., 2015). Certain types of ownership can be a vital institutional advantage to an EE firm (Wang, Hong, Kafouros, & Wright, 2012). This is consistent with the Dunning's eclectic paradigm (OLI model). Though the original OLI model posits that ownership advantage is an economic agent (Dunning, 1993) rather than an embeddedness in an environment, Dunning and Lundan (2008a) re-conceptualised ownership advantage in relation to institutional advantage including firm-specific norms and values and the institutional environment in which the firm is embedded. Institutional advantage is seen as being made up of home-country-specific advantages that can be leveraged in the course of internationalisation even by a firm with weak firm-specific advantages (Hong et al., 2015).

Particularly, a government may affect a firm's inclination towards international expansion by exerting normative pressures on enterprises, in particular state-owned ones. EE firms tend to comply with the objectives of the state by implementing state policy, an activity known as 'show(ing) the national flag' (Deng, 2009; Wang, Hong, Kafouros, & Wright, 2012). Meanwhile, since market mechanisms in EEs are often under-developed, the ability of EE firms to internationalise is also influenced by government, or more precisely by state ownership, because state ownership comes with advantages, such as market protection, financial support and control over important assets, all of which can offset the ownership disadvantages such firms face in foreign markets (Dunning & Lundan, 2008b). Therefore, firms with a high degree of state ownership may be more likely to pursue a strategy of internationalisation.

It is noteworthy that a high level of government involvement may lead to firms experiencing further reliance on government support and therefore reduce their motivation to become more competitive by developing internal capabilities (Wang, Hong, Kafouros, & Boateng, 2012). Yet, these internal capabilities are important in terms of absorbing and understanding the value of external knowledge if firms are to take advantages of resources and knowledge once they have entered an overseas market (Kafouros & Buckley, 2008).

Wang, Hong, Kafouros, and Wright (2012) argue that government involvement influences both the willingness and ability of EE firms to internationalise through influencing 'their strategic objectives and decisions; the availability and cost of various resources; the way in which these resources are used; their capabilities; the provision of valuable knowledge, information and intermediary services; and transaction costs associated with cross-border expansion' (Wang, Hong, Kafouros, & Wright, 2012, p. 4). For example, the Chinese government plays an active role in shaping and encouraging Chinese enterprises' (CEs) OFDI. Chinese government guides the direction of OFDI by providing information and assessment of overseas investment by CEs and offers guidance for investors undertaking business connected with favoured government policies, meaning that investments consistent with these guidelines will enjoy favourable financial supports, exchange rates, taxation and other favourable treatment (Luo et al., 2010).

On the other hand, government also imposes regulations and restrictions on EE firms which constrain their international expansion, such as China's approval system in relation to firms' OFDI. It is argued that, in these circumstances, undesirable institutional interference in strategic decision-making through state ownership (Shleifer & Vishny, 1994) may increase the cost of doing business (Michailova & Ang, 2008). Government influence, the so-called 'visible hand', can exercise tight control over firms both in the home market and in overseas markets (Rosenzweig & Singh, 1991), remaining a powerful force in relation to firms' internationalisation in EEs like China (Hong et al., 2015; Luo et al., 2010; Rasiah, Gammeltoft, & Jiang, 2010; Wang, Hong, Kafouros, & Wright, 2012). In attempting to create an overseas presence, firms may face costs in coping with these institutional restraints.

METHODOLOGY

As this study seeks to understand and explain the nature and effect of home country institutional, and in particular the Chinese government's influence upon CCBs' internationalisation, a qualitative approach using interviews was employed to collect data.

Sample Selection

The population of interest is CCBs that have participated in internationalisation activities by establishing overseas institutions over a period from 2001 to 2013, a time span which starts at China's entry into the WTO to the time of data collection. Therefore, it was required that the target banks should:

- be CCBs which have adopted strategies of internationalisation;
- belong to the first two tiers of Chinese banks; that is, play a main role in internationalisation activities and;
- be present physically and have operated virtually in at least one foreign market during the time period of this study, and for a period of at least two years in order to provide sufficient depth of experience.

These restrictions led to a total of 10 banks being selected for this study, including the Big Five state-owned commercial banks – ICBC, BOC, CCBank, ABC and BOCOM, which account for 92% of overseas institutions, and another five joint stock commercial banks – China Merchants Bank (CMB), China Minsheng Bank (CMBC), China Everbright Bank (CEB), Guangdong Development Bank (GDB) and China CITIC Bank (CNCB). A profile of the sample banks is provided in Appendix A.

Data Collection and Analysis

The data for this research was collected via 30 in-depth semi-structured interviews with senior managers, either working in China or in an overseas institution of the sample banks. The questions for the interviews were divided into two main parts as follows: (i) the first part related to the motivation and mode of entry choice used in the banks' internationalisation and (ii) the second part had questions on the effects of government and home country institutions on the internationalisation process. The relevant part of our interview questions is provided in Appendix B. Between March and November 2014, 30 in-depth and semi-structured interviews – 26.7% face-to-face and 73.3% telephone – were carried out with senior managers who are key decision makers of their bank's internationalisation. An examination of the job titles of the respondents revealed that: 70% of the interviewees were senior managers in international department at the banks' head offices; and 30% were senior managers of the overseas branches or subsidiaries who were involved in the internationalisation process. Regarding the sample, 18 interviewees (60%) were from big state-owned banks, namely, BOC, ICBC, BOC, CCBank, ABC and BOCOM. The other 12 interviewees (40%) were from small joint-stock banks, including CMB, CMBC, CEB, GDB and CNCB.

The length of the interviews varied from 30 to 60 minutes. As all of the interviews were conducted in Mandarin, transcripts were recorded in Chinese and were then translated into English. The translations were cross-checked by a professional translator in order to ensure their accuracy, and the analysis was undertaken based on the English transcripts. Secondary data covering the research period was collected from the sample banks' annual reports provided via their websites, internal documents, books, magazines, journals, published press releases giving internationalisation information of banks, industry reports and statistics from government departments.

The adoption of multiple sources of information enabled data triangulation and improves the reliability and validity of the results. Data from the two different sources were cross-checked in order to increase the reliability and validity of the analysis while also minimising both internal and external bias (Eisenhardt, 1989).

Content analysis is used as the data analytical approach for this study. In this study, a manually based system is applied to extract the key themes from the interview programme, as a manual system is workable in cases where all of the interviews have been undertaken over a relatively short period of time and by a single researcher.

FINDINGS AND DISCUSSIONS

Internationalisation Encouraged by Government Policies

According to the results, 70% of the interviewees cited encouraging government policies as a motivation for CCBs' internationalisation. The majority of them (18 out of 21 interviewees who hold this viewpoint) are from state-owned banks, indicating that the government policy has particular effect on state-owned banks. As two managers said:

(Going abroad) is related to national policies. (Interviewee, p. 10)

Government policies do have influences, because the (bank) leaders take the policies into account. (Interviewee, p. 5)

The findings are in line with the conclusion drawn by Buckley et al. (2007), who point out that specific policies introduced by home governments tend to encourage firms to go abroad.

As suggested by institutional theory, developing countries and transition countries like China are characterised by a heavy political and institutional involvement in their business systems (Child & Rodrigues, 2005; Dunning & Narula, 2003), which can either support firms' development or restrict it (Du & Boateng, 2015). Since the 1990s, the Chinese government and its agents have implemented a series of policies reducing restrictions and encouraging a more outward-oriented economy, popularly known as the 'Go Abroad' state policy, formally initiated in 2000. This policy has provided strong, national public endorsement for an institutional environment that fosters OFDI.

Based on this principal state strategy, a series of regulations were announced in the following several years and complex regulatory regimes were constructed (Luo et al., 2010). For example, foreign exchange rules concerning OFDI have been reformed to facilitate CEs' overseas investments. Rather than enforcing a limited quota on the use of foreign exchange, CEs were allowed to use self-owned foreign exchange, or purchase the foreign exchange by RMB, or apply for domestic and overseas foreign exchange loans, to invest abroad. This in turn had implications for the internationalisation of CCBs. As interviewee 27 indicated:

The 'Go Abroad' policy has encouraged many domestic enterprises entering into foreign markets around the world. As a result, we are expanding into international markets to follow them. (Interviewee, p. 27)

The Chinese government has also changed its role from regulator to being a supporter of OFDI (Luo et al., 2010). As well as providing financial support to firms going abroad, the Chinese government also introduced risk-safeguard mechanisms to reinforce immunity from risk for enterprises going abroad, through establishing promotion and mutual protection agreements with other countries. Moreover, in an attempt to aid CEs to overcome investment obstacles in overseas markets, the Chinese government provides an information service network which issues reports annually relating to obstacles faced by Chinese investors in foreign countries.

Most importantly, the Chinese government's guidance, in influencing the investment direction and location of CEs, has had significant effects on CCBs' international investment, in that the cost of collecting information relating to clients' overseas markets is reduced. The 'Go Abroad' policy and other policies which have been implemented along with it, such as Renminbi (RMB) internationalisation, have become tremendous push factors behind the rise of CEs' OFDI activities (Deng, 2007; Du & Boateng, 2015) which, in turn, forges the rationality of CCBs' decisions to follow their customers' activities. Moreover, as the main players undertaking RMB business in overseas markets, CCBs largely benefit from this policy, in terms of an increase in scale of RMB business worldwide.

Another important driver of CCBs' outward investment is that the Chinese government has tended to increase currency export and thereby reduce the pressure on the Chinese economy caused by massive foreign exchange transactions, appreciation of the Chinese currency RMB and excessive liquidity. This consideration was indicated by interviewees 21, 23 and 26, who commented that:

> *Government policy encourages outward investment because too much inward investment has caused high level of foreign exchange reserve. This results in weak finance policy. If the reserve from foreign exchange exceeds an acceptable level, it becomes a signal of financial weakness of the state. (Interviewee, p. 21)*

> *Over the last one or two years, the government has released many essential policies such as foreign exchange management and RMB internationalisation, which has not been thorough-going in the past but has been developing quickly in the last two years ... The internationalisation of banks is accordance with the degree and pace of our country's openness to the outside world. (Interviewee, p. 23)*

> *Because Chinese foreign exchange reserve is too large, the government encourages enterprises to invest abroad. (Interviewee, p. 26)*

This circumstance is almost exactly the same situation experienced by Japanese banks in the 1980s. At that time, the Japanese economy had grown very quickly and accumulated a massive current account surplus, leading to the prosperity of Japanese banks, which can been seen as an important driving force behind Japanese banks' internationalisation (Slager, 2004).

With China's membership of the WTO since 2001 and its decision to permit foreign banks' operations in the home market, catching up with the world's leading banks and becoming locally competitive to maintain market share have become urgent tasks for Chinese banks (Berger, Hasan, & Zhou, 2009). Encouraged by the state strategy and strong Chinese economic development, the Big Five, and even joint-stock commercial banks, aspire to become world-class banks by participating in the international market and building their own global brands. They are eager to become organisations like the world's giant banks, such as Citigroup and HSBC. Their growing overseas participation clearly demonstrates their ambition. This is especially the case for the Big Five banks, because government policy has a more direct influence on their development decisions with regard to their dominant status in China's financial system and their ownership type and state control. Interviewee 27 indicated that:

In terms of government policy, the big banks are more likely to be affected. They follow big state projects abroad, guided by government policy. (Interviewee, p. 27)

In relative terms, the Chinese government is less concerned about interfering with the operations of joint stock banks, as they are more market-orientated in the first place. Pursuing and maximising profits is, therefore, the most dominant strategic motivation for joint stock banks. More than one interviewee from the joint stock banks have indicated this point. For example, one manager stressed that:

Government guidance is not the main driving factor ... Joint stock banks focus more on making profits. (Interviewee, p. 18)

Interviewee 27, also from a joint stock bank, added that:

Joint stock banks are relatively small, so the state government has no special requirement for them. (Interviewee, p. 27)

Given the analysis above, the evidence suggests that Chinese government policies have a relatively stronger effect on state-owned banks' than joint stock banks' decisions regarding their international development. Though no unique government policy has been proposed specifically addressing CCBs' international expansion, government policy has heavily influenced CCBs' internationalisation, leading to a reduction of some of the previous restrictions on their OFDI by continual reform of the banking industry; for example, the gradual liberalisation of foreign exchange accounts (Jiang & Hu, 2015; Luo et al., 2010). It might be argued that, to this degree, government policy has attempted to provide a more favourable environment facilitating both state-owned and joint stock banks' international expansion.

Home Country Institutional Restrictions

Despite the evidence above, the interview data also suggests that institutional restrictions can have a significant impact on CCBs' international expansion. Administrative constraints put in place by government and its agencies have a strong influence on CCBs' decision-making. One-third of interviewees explicitly acknowledged this influence. For example, the establishment of overseas institutions and each acquisition proposal has to be approved first by government agents before implementation. Interviewee 25 explained that:

> *The establishment of all overseas institutions should be reported to and approved by the government and CBRC (China Banking Regulatory Commission), as well as agreed by the local market regulators. (Interviewee, p. 25)*

He continued that:

> *It (the government's management) mainly refers to administrative approval ... The government may have a blueprint for the bank industry. All the banks have to wait on the waiting list (for their international expansion). (Interviewee, p. 25)*

From the perspective of institutional theory, the approval system is likely to increase the costs incurred by banks in their international expansion. Although the Chinese government has been engaging in reducing restrictions on the domestic financial industry step by step over the last two decades, such as the progressive liberalisation of interest rates and foreign exchange rate marketization (Wu, Yang, & Ba, 2010; Yang, Wu, & Ba, 2011, 2012); there are still some restrictions on financial management in China, such as the procedures relating to the examination and approval system in OFDI. These include restrictions on foreign exchange and capital accounts, which have limited the speed of international development of CCBs (Chen & Shi, 2004). There are several political and regulatory institutions in China that guide and manage CCBs' OFDI, such as the Ministry of Finance of the People's Republic of China, the People's Bank of China, the Commission of Banking Regulation of China and the State Development and Reform Commission. CCBs have to wait for the approval of OFDI by the relevant departments in these institutions, which may result in delayed investment and raise the cost of CCBs' internationalisation. The constraint of approval is also indicated by interviewee 27:

> *The government would not allow banks to open many overseas outlets in a rush without exerting restriction. (Interviewee, p. 27)*

Moreover, in a non-fully market-oriented domestic market, CCBs are restricted by domestic institutional constraints. For instance, licences for commercial banking, insurance and security businesses are handled separately by the government in the home market, and conglomerates are thereby discouraged in the interests of reducing risks within the Chinese financial system. CCBs therefore have little chance to engage in the whole range of financial services including insurance business and security business, a situation which may impede CCBs' competitive power in the international market. Such restrictions force CCBs to undertake bancassurance or universal banking from outside Mainland China. As interviewee 16 indicates:

> We obtained ... a full banking license in foreign market by acquiring a local bank. Such a license is unavailable in home market because of the government regulation. (Interviewee, p. 16)

Under these circumstances, escaping from domestic institutional constraints could be a strategic consideration in CCBs' international expansion, once the government opens the door for Chinese banks to go abroad. Such considerations can, in fact, be found in the histories of American, German and Italian banks. During the second wave of bank internationalisation (which happened from 1960s through 1990s) the outward investments of these banks were designed to circumvent the domestic regulations and controls imposed by their respective monetary authorities (Slager, 2004).

Government involvement could be another institutional influence on CCBs' international expansion. Though it has adapted its economy towards a market system since 1979, China still remains a political economy (Child & Tse, 2001). This restricts economic freedom. In such a system, government involvement is more common in firms' decision-making, achieved both through ownership and through regulation (Peng, 2000). According to the interview data, the influence of government involvement on CCBs has two facets. One side is the positive encouragement of CCBs' internationalisation, as discussed in section 'Internationalisation Encouraged by Government Policies'. The other side negatively affects CCBs' international expansion by imposing restrictions on their decision-making. Interviewee 5 expressed the view that:

> It is hard to say (whether it is) good or bad. The good side is that the internationalisation can be promoted and accelerated by supportive policy; but the bad side is that policy places too much restriction on decision-making. (Interviewee, p. 5)

Although state ownership can empower big banks by giving them advantages through the provision of support and protection, on the other hand too many institutional constraints can impede CCBs' efficiency and performance (Lin & Zhang, 2009). The restrictions imposed by government in state-owned banks' management, such as the dominance and preferential promotion of top managers (Hawes & Chiu, 2007), have constrained CCBs' freedom of operation in the market. This paradox may suggest that Chinese banks might expect to internationalise by taking advantage of government support, but at the same time if they accept too much government interference it may weaken their international expansion plans.

In pursuing a global position, government restrictions mean that CCBs cannot follow the example of existing global banks, but must find their own path. One manager indicated that:

> *We have to make our own way rather than just follow and copy the strategies of others banks (i.e., the world's leading banks). Otherwise, the way ahead (for) our internationalisation will be more difficult, because they are far ahead of us, (we cannot catch-up them only by following and copying). Only if we have unique advantages and figure out our own way, can we reap something special. (Interviewee, p. 24)*

CONCLUSIONS

This discussion has investigated the role of government and home institutions on CCBs' internationalisation during the 2001–2013 period. The findings, drawn from a sample of 10 banks, offer insights for Chinese banks seeking opportunities and/or engaging in expanding overseas, as well as government policy makers.

First, our findings suggest that government policies are important in promoting the international expansion of Chinese banks, particularly the largest state-owned banks, which indicates that government policy has significant effect on state-owned banks' internationalisation more than joint stock banks. Compared to state-owned banks, joint stock banks may have more entrepreneurial freedom in making international development decisions as they have fewer real or psychic obligations in terms of following government directions closely. Rather than merely emphasising traditional firm resources such as technological assets, it has been argued that CCBs could take better advantage of government policy by developing internationalisation strategies and capabilities consistent with the institutional environment in China (Hong et al., 2015).

As well as a series of 'Go Abroad' policies from the Chinese government, some have argued that, more recently completed policies such as the

'One Belt and One Road' policy (which refers to the Silk Road economy belt and 21th century maritime Silk Road) proposed by government will largely further prompt the internationalisation of CCBs, and more international entry by CCBs, particularly with the intention of following the international investments of CEs and benefiting from the increasing cooperation between China and other counties (Jiang & Hu, 2015). Indeed, our study suggests that government support is as important as developing firm-specific resources for CCBs in particular, and for EE firms in general, when they seek to embark on internationalisation. In these circumstances, government supportive national policies, which are an institutional advantage, could also be considered as ownership advantage (Dunning & Lundan, 2008a, 2008b).

Secondly, this study suggests that CCBs need to find a compromise between balancing home institutional constraints and exerting entrepreneurial initiative when embarking on international expansion. The findings of this discussion show that the banking industry in China is still guided and influenced to a large extent by government. CCBs, especially state-owned banks, have to cope with many restrictions imposed by the government, which may handicap entrepreneurial initiative. Although our study emphasises the value of state ownership of CCBs in terms of employing government policy, institutional constraints caused by government interference in decision-making may limit the flexibility and efficiency of CCBs' internationalisation. Under such a unique institutional environment, in order to pursue success in new international ventures, CCBs may need to balance the bureaucratic governmental system and the utilisation of entrepreneurial logic (Zhang & Van Den Bulcke, 1996). That is, Chinese banks may, on the one hand, take advantage of government support to facilitate their international expansion, as, for example, where state ownership may enable them to gain a higher credit rating based on the strong development of China's economy; and on the other hand, they bear the restrictions imposed on them which constrain their freedom of management. The evidence in this paper also suggests that CCBs may, as a means of alleviating the effects of these constraints in the home market, establish overseas institutions via subsidiary or by M&A, so that some of the institutional constraints at home are no longer significant barriers to them.

Regarding the importance of government supportive policy, our study has implications for policy makers. Since the aim of Chinese government is to strengthen the global competitiveness of CCBs as well as the nation itself, more supportive policies facilitating CCBs' international expansion, such as promoting the realisation of RMB internationalisation, will be important in developing greater internationalisation, particularly given the current entrepreneurial weaknesses of CCBs. Meanwhile, as suggested by our findings, policymakers also need to be aware that policies may not work uniformly in relation to each bank. That is, the large state-owned banks are more likely to be influenced by government policy, while the joint stock banks may choose the way which they deem most favourable to their own strategic goals.

Another implication to be drawn from our results is that the institutional constraints imposed on the Chinese banking industry need to be lessened. Using market-oriented management and regulation rather than imposing administrative restrictions could therefore accelerate CCBs' adaption and integration to the international market and enhance their competitive power. By playing the role of the builder of formal institutions, the Chinese government might be expected to provide further support and direction rather than specific managerial interference in bank business.

At the firm level, reducing unnecessary government involvement in banks' operation through establishing a real market-oriented system and reducing restrictions on the banking industry could favour the internationalisation of Chinese banks. From the perspective of CCBs, although we find that state ownership could facilitate CCBs' internationalisation, continuing significant state-ownership is likely to result in prolonged non-market-oriented government interference. In turn, this may continue to constrain CCBs' competitive power in the international market because these restrictions inevitably hamper their flexibility of operation and competition. Therefore, the government may need to reduce the level of state ownership of CCBs and consequently relax the restrictions currently in place in the banking industry, in order to facilitate more market-oriented international development for CCBs. However, the reality is that, at the present stage and into the foreseeable future, CCBs have to bear the legacy of institutional dependence and remain subject to administrative approval (Child & Rodrigues, 2005), in a situation that Chinese government still remains a strong influence within Chinese banking industry.

In general, policymakers also need to be aware that though policies may work efficiently to CCBs' internationalisation, while establishing efficient market mechanisms more than emphasising government restrictions and regulations is very important in improving the institutional environment and increasing banks' capabilities and competitiveness. Long-term growth in the global market supported by sound mechanisms rather than speculation stimulated by temporary policy seems most likely to be able to assist the forging of world-class banks.

There has been a tendency, as China's social and economic development has continued, that the Chinese government has become less interfering and directing in relation to firms' outward FDI, allowing more entrepreneurial initiative (Luo et al., 2010). However, this reform process is expected to be carried out in a gradual step-by-step way. This has implications for CCBs' internationalisation. The Chinese financial system still needs to be controlled and protected in the view of the government. It is predictable that in the short run these institutional restrictions will continue to limit the international development of CCBs to some extent.

ACKNOWLEDGEMENT

The authors would like to thank the reviewer and the editors for valuable comments and suggestions on our earlier draft.

REFERENCES

Alexander, P. (2010). Top 1000 world banks 2010. *The Banker, 6*, 1–15.
Anderson, J., & Sutherland, D. (2015). Entry Mode and Emerging Market MNEs: An analysis of Chinese Greenfield and acquisition FDI in the United States. *Research in International Business and Finance, 35*, 88–103. doi:10.1016/j.ribaf.2015.03.008
Barney, J. (1991). Firm resources and sustained competitive advantage. *Journal of Management, 17*(1), 99–120. doi:10.1177/014920639101700108
Berger, A. N., Hasan, I., & Zhou, M. (2009). Bank ownership and efficiency in China: What will happen in the world's largest nation? *Journal of Banking & Finance, 33*(1), 113–130. doi:10.1016/j.jbankfin.2007.05.016
Boateng, A., Huang, W., & Kufuor, N. K. (2015). Commercial bank ownership and performance in China. *Applied Economics, 47*, 5320–5336.
Buckley, P. J., Clegg, L. J., Cross, A. R., Liu, X., Voss, H., & Zheng, P. (2007). The determinants of Chinese outward foreign direct investment. *Journal of International Business Studies, 38*(4), 499–518.
Cantwell, J., Dunning, J. H., & Lundan, S. M. (2010). An evolutionary approach to understanding international business activity: The co-evolution of MNEs and the institutional environment. *Journal of International Business Studies, 41*(4), 567–586. doi:10.1057/jibs.2009.95
CBRC. (2013). *2012 Annual Report*. Beijing, China: China Banking Regulatory Commission. Retrieved from http://www.cbrc.gov.cn/chinese/files/2013/4CF24B3E79704CEA85D330A7CC18CD7D.pdf
Chen, J., & Shi, H. (2004). *Banking and insurance in the new China: Competition and the challenge of accession to the WTO*. Cheltenham: Edward Elgar Publishing.

Child, J. (1972). Organisational structure, environment, and performance: The role of strategic choice. *Sociology, 6*(1), 1–22. doi:10.1177/003803857200600101

Child, J. (1997). Strategic choice in the analysis of action, structure, organisations, and environment: Retrospect and prospect. *Organisation Studies, 18*(1), 43–76. doi:10.1177/017084069701800104

Child, J., & Rodrigues, S. B. (2005). The internationalisation of Chinese firms: A case for theoretical extension? *Management and Organisation Review, 1*(3), 381–410. doi:10.1111/j.1740-8784.2005.0020a.x

Child, J., & Tse, D. K. (2001). China's transition and its implications for international business. *Journal of International Business Studies, 32*(1), 5–21. doi:10.1057/palgrave.jibs.8490935

Clarke, G., Cull, R., Peria, M. S. M., & Sanchez, S. M. (2003). Foreign bank entry: Experience, implications for developing economies, and agenda for further research. *The World Bank Research Observer, 18*(1), 25–59. doi:10.1093/wbro/lkg002

Cui, L., & Jiang, F. (2012). State ownership effect on firms' FDI ownership decisions under institutional pressure: A study of Chinese outward-investing firms. *Journal of International Business Studies, 43*(3), 264–284. doi:10.1057/jibs.2012.1

Demirbag, M., Tatoglu, E., & Glaister, K. W. (2009). Equity-based entry modes of emerging country multinationals: Lessons from Turkey. *Journal of World Business, 44*(4), 445–462. doi:10.1016/j.jwb.2008.11.009

Deng, P. (2007). Investing for strategic resources and its rationale: The case of outward FDI from Chinese companies. *Business Horizons, 50*(1), 71–81. Retrieved from http://www.researchgate.net/profile/Ping_Deng2/publication/222838233_Investing_for_strategic_resources_and_its_rationale_The_case_of_outward_FDI_from_Chinese_companies/links/0c96052a105fbdda7d000000.pdf

Deng, P. (2009). Why do Chinese firms tend to acquire strategic assets in international expansion? *Journal of World Business, 44*(1), 74–84. doi:10.1016/j.jwb.2008.03.014

Du, M., & Boateng, A. (2015). State ownership, institutional effects and value creation in cross-border mergers & acquisitions by Chinese firms. *International Business Review, 24*(3), 430–442. doi:10.1016/j.ibusrev.2014.10.002

Dunning, J. H. (1993). Trade, location of economic activity and the multinational enterprise: A search for an eclectic approach. *The Theory of Transnational Corporations, 1*, 183–218.

Dunning, J. H., & Lundan, S. M. (2008a). Institutions and the OLI paradigm of the multinational enterprise. *Asia Pacific Journal of Management, 25*(4), 573–593. doi:10.1007/s10490-007-9074-z

Dunning, J. H., & Lundan, S. M. (2008b). *Multinational enterprises and the global economy.* Cheltenham: Edward Elgar Publishing.

Dunning, J. H., & Narula, R. (2003). *Foreign direct investment and governments: Catalysts for economic restructuring.* London: Routledge.

Eisenhardt, K. M. (1989). Building theories from case study research. *Academy of Management Review, 14*(4), 532–550. Retrieved from http://www.jstor.org.gcu.idm.oclc.org/stable/258557

Gaur, A., & Kumar, V. (2010). Internationalisation of emerging market firms: A case for theoretical extension. *Advances in International Management, 23*, 603–627. Retrieved from http://www.researchgate.net/profile/Vikas_Kumar48/publication/228121977_Internationalization_of_Emerging_Market_Firms_A_Case_for_Theoretical_Extension/links/0c9605195244795f30000000.pdf

Hawes, C., & Chiu, T. (2007). Foreign strategic investors in the Chinese banking market: Cultural shift or business as usual? *Banking & Finance Law Review*, *22*(2), 203. Retrieved from http://search.proquest.com.gcu.idm.oclc.org/docview/218854260?pq-origsite=summon

Hitt, M. A., Ahlstrom, D., Dacin, M. T., Levitas, E., & Svobodina, L. (2004). The institutional effects on strategic alliance partner selection in transition economies: China vs. Russia. *Organisation Science*, *15*(2), 173–185. doi:10.1287/orsc.1030.0045

Hong, J., Wang, C., & Kafouros, M. (2015). The role of the state in explaining the internationalisation of emerging market enterprises. *British Journal of Management*, *26*(1), 45–62. doi:10.1111/1467-8551.12059

Hoskisson, R. E., Eden, L., Lau, C. M., & Wright, M. (2000). Strategy in emerging economies. *Academy of Management Journal*, *43*(3), 249–267.

Jiang, J., & Hu, H. (2015). The practice and thinking of Chinese banking's going abroad (in Chinese). *Globalisation*, Beijing, China: China Centre for International Economic Exchanges, *5*, 5–19.

Kafouros, M. I., & Buckley, P. J. (2008). Under what conditions do firms benefit from the research efforts of other organisations? *Research Policy*, *37*(2), 225–239. doi:10.1016/j.respol.2007.11.005

Lehner, M., & Schnitzer, M. (2008). Entry of foreign banks and their impact on host countries. *Journal of Comparative Economics*, *36*(3), 430–452. doi:10.1016/j.jce.2008.02.002

Lin, X., & Zhang, Y. (2009). Bank ownership reform and bank performance in China. *Journal of Banking & Finance*, *33*(1), 20–29. doi:10.1016/j.jbankfin.2006.11.022

Luo, Y., & Tung, R. L. (2007). International expansion of emerging market enterprises: A springboard perspective. *Journal of International Business Studies*, *38*(4), 481–498. doi:10.1057/palgrave.jibs.8400275

Luo, Y., Xue, Q., & Han, B. (2010). How emerging market governments promote outward FDI: Experience from China. *Journal of World Business*, *45*(1), 68–79. doi:10.1016/j.jwb.2009.04.003

Meyer, K. E., & Peng, M. W. (2005). Probing theoretically into central and Eastern Europe: Transactions, resources, and institutions. *Journal of International Business Studies*, *36*(6), 600–621. doi:10.1057/palgrave.jibs.8400167

Michailova, S., & Ang, S. H. (2008). Institutional explanations of cross-border alliance modes: The case of emerging economies firms. *Management International Review*, *48*(5), 551–576. doi:10.1007/s11575-008-0036-6

North, D. C. (1990). *Institutions, institutional change and economic performance*. Cambridge: Cambridge University Press.

Peng, M. W. (2000). *Business strategies in transition economies*. Los Angeles, CA: Sage.

Peng, M. W. (2002). Towards an institution-based view of business strategy. *Asia Pacific Journal of Management*, *19*(2), 251–267. doi:10.1023/A:1016291702714

Peng, M. W., Wang, D. Y., & Jiang, Y. (2008). An institution-based view of international business strategy: A focus on emerging economies. *Journal of International Business Studies*, *39*(5), 920–936. doi:10.1057/palgrave.jibs.8400377

Rasiah, R., Gammeltoft, P., & Jiang, Y. (2010). Home government policies for outward FDI from emerging economies: Lessons from Asia. *International Journal of Emerging Markets*, *5*(3–4), 333–357. doi:10.1108/17468801011058415

Rosenzweig, P. M., & Singh, J. V. (1991). Organisational environments and the multinational enterprise. *Academy of Management Review*, *16*(2), 340–361. Retrieved from http://www.jstor.org.gcu.idm.oclc.org/stable/258865

Rugman, A. M., & Verbeke, A. (1992). A note on the transnational solution and the transaction cost theory of multinational strategic management. *Journal of International Business Studies, 23*(4), 761–771. doi:10.1057/palgrave.jibs.8490287

Rui, H., & Yip, G. S. (2008). Foreign acquisitions by Chinese firms: A strategic intent perspective. *Journal of World Business, 43*(2), 213–226. doi:10.1016/j.jwb.2007.11.006

Scott, W. R. (1995). *Institutions and organisations.* Thousand Oaks, CA: Sage.

Scott, W. R. (2008). *Institutions and organisations: Ideas and interests.* Thousand Oaks, CA: Sage.

Shleifer, A., & Vishny, R. W. (1994). Politicians and firms. *The Quarterly Journal of Economics, 109*(4), 995–1025. Retrieved from http://www.jstor.org.gcu.idm.oclc.org/stable/2118354

Slager, A. (2004). *Banking across borders.* Rotterdam: Erasmus Research Institute of Management (ERIM), Erasmus University Rotterdam.

UNCTAD. (2006). *World investment report.* Geneva: United Nations.

UNCTAD. (2013). *World investment report.* Geneva: United Nations.

Wang, C., Hong, J., Kafouros, M., & Boateng, A. (2012). What drives outward FDI of Chinese firms? Testing the explanatory power of three theoretical frameworks. *International Business Review, 21*(3), 425–438. doi:10.1016/j.ibusrev.2011.05.004

Wang, C., Hong, J., Kafouros, M., & Wright, M. (2012). Exploring the role of government involvement in outward FDI from emerging economies. *Journal of International Business Studies, 43*(7), 655–676. doi:10.1057/jibs.2012.18

Wright, M., Filatotchev, I., Hoskisson, R. E., & Peng, M. W. (2005). Strategy research in emerging economies: Challenging the conventional wisdom. *Journal of Management Studies, 42*(1), 1–33. doi:10.1111/j.1467-6486.2005.00487.x

Wu, W. D., Yang, Z., & Ba, S. (2010). *Chinese bankers survey 2010.* PwC China and China Bank Association, Beijing, China.

Yang, Z., Wu, W. D., & Ba, S. (2011). *Chinese bankers survey 2011.* PwC China and China Bank Association, Beijing, China.

Yang, Z., Wu, W. D., & Ba, S. (2012). *Chinese bankers survey 2012.* PwC China and China Bank Association, Beijing, China.

Zhang, H., & Van Den Bulcke, D. (1996). International management strategies of Chinese multinational firms. In J. Child & Y. Lu (Eds.), *Management issues in China: International enterprises.* London: Routledge.

APPENDIX A

Table A1. Profile of Sample Banks.

Sample Banks	Ownership	Going International	Entry Mode	Location in World (Continent)
ICBC	State-owned	1992	Greenfield, M&A	Asia, Europe, America, Africa, Ocean
BOC	State-owned	1929; 1979	Greenfield	Asia, Europe, America, Africa, Ocean
CCBank	State-owned	1991	Greenfield, M&A	Asia, Europe, America
ABC	State-owned	1995	Greenfield	Asia, Europe, North America, Ocean
BOCOM	State-owned	1989	Greenfield	Asia, Europe, North America, Ocean
CMB	Joint stock	1998	Greenfield, M&A	Asia, Europe, North America
CMBC	Joint stock	2004	Greenfield	Asia
CEB	Joint stock	1992	Greenfield	Asia
CGB	Joint stock	1993	Greenfield	Asia
CNCB	Joint stock	2009	M&A	Asia, North America

APPENDIX B: INTERVIEW QUESTIONS

1. As far as your bank was concerned, what were the motivations for your bank to go abroad?
   a. How important is the role of Chinese government in the international expansion of your bank?
   b. If it is, how did government policy affect the internationalisation decision-making?
   c. If not, why?
2. As far as your bank was concerned, how important was the effect of ownership type (i.e., state ownership or private ownership) on the bank's decision to expand internationally?
   a. If yes, please indicates what they were (benefits and/or problems)? Could you please provide me with more details about this?
   b. If no, please indicate why?
3. What barriers did your bank face in the process of internationalisation?
   a. Is home institutions a barrier to your bank's international expansion?
   b. If yes, how did home institutions affect the internationalisation of your bank?
   c. If not, why?

CLIMATE CHANGE, CATASTROPHE RISK, AND GOVERNMENT STIMULATION OF THE INSURANCE MARKET: A STUDY OF TRANSITIONAL CHINA

Qihao He

ABSTRACT

Purpose — *Due to climate change and an increasing concentration of the world's population in vulnerable areas, how to manage catastrophe risk efficiently and cover disaster losses fairly is still a universal dilemma.*

Methodology — *This paper applies a law and economic approach.*

Findings — *China's mechanism for managing catastrophic disaster risk is in many ways unique. It emphasizes government responsibilities and works well in many respects, especially in disaster emergency relief. Nonetheless, China's mechanism which has the vestige of a centrally planned economy needs reform.*

Practical Implications — *I propose a catastrophe insurance market-enhancing framework which marries the merits of both the market and*

The Political Economy of Chinese Finance
International Finance Review, Volume 17, 295–340
Copyright © 2016 by Emerald Group Publishing Limited
All rights of reproduction in any form reserved
ISSN: 1569-3767/doi:10.1108/S1569-376720160000017017

government to manage catastrophe risks. There are three pillars of the framework: (i) sustaining a strong and capable government; (ii) government enhancement of the market, neither supplanting nor retarding it; (iii) legalizing the relationship between government and market to prevent government from undermining well-functioning market operations. A catastrophe insurance market-enhancing framework may provide insights for developing catastrophe insurance in China and other transitional nations.

Originality — First, this paper analyzes China's mechanism for managing catastrophic disaster risks and China's approach which emphasizes government responsibilities will shed light on solving how to manage catastrophe risk efficiently and cover disaster losses fairly. Second, this paper starts a broader discussion about government stimulation of developing catastrophe insurance and this framework can stimulate attention to solve the universal dilemma.

Keywords: Catastrophe risk; government stimulation; catastrophe insurance; transitional China

INTRODUCTION

Due to climate-related extremes, growing population in high-risk areas, and aging infrastructure but low levels of public and private investment in risk reduction measures, the world is more vulnerable to catastrophe disasters, and the losses are increasing significantly (Kunreuther & Michel-Kerjan, 2013, p. 517). How to manage catastrophe risk efficiently and cover disaster losses fairly is still a universal dilemma.

"Famine happens every three years, epidemic happens every six years, and natural hazard happens every twelve years" (Wei, Jin, & Wang, 2014, p. 289). This old saying is a perfect description of the natural disasters in China. Due to China's unusual size and regional diversity, as well as its distinctive history and current political-economic configuration of "socialism with Chinese characteristics,"[1] its approach to handling disaster challenges is in many ways unique (Perry, 2014, p. 5). The Chinese mechanism for managing catastrophe risks or challenges is known as the "Whole-Nation System" (*Juguo tizhi*), which generally refers to the government's effort to deploy and allocate the whole-nation's resources to fulfill a specific difficult task within a limited time and thus promote the nation's interest (Shi & Zhang, 2013, p. 111). In the field of natural disaster, the Whole-Nation System is a kind of emergency-driven management system and focuses on disaster emergency relief. While effective in delivering governmental relief in the short run, it is hardly sustainable in the long run due to inevitable government failures. Nonetheless, comparing it with possible alternatives is still illuminating and may provide important insights for its reform.

Insurance is traditionally regarded as a main mechanism to cover losses caused by disasters. Even though underwriting catastrophe insurance is susceptible to market failures because of both supply-side and demand-side barriers, it is still an attractive tool to deal with catastrophe risk, especially compared with government intervention, due to its advantages of lower transaction costs, lower adverse selection, and more efficiency as a result of competitive markets (Jaffee & Russell, 1997; Kunreuther, 1996; Priest, 1996).

In this paper, I begin to introduce the impact of climate change, and then assess the Chinese government's responsibilities under the Whole-Nation System, highlighting what is unique or unusual (for better or worse) in efforts to resolve the universal dilemma of catastrophe risks. Furthermore, I explore the Chinese government's responsibilities for embracing and developing catastrophe insurance (although cognizant of some market failures), and finally propose a catastrophe insurance market-enhancing framework which marries the merits of both private market and pubic government to address the universal dilemma of natural disasters.

CLIMATE CHANGE AND CATASTROPHE RISKS IN CHINA

Climate change is occurring on a significant scale, and its effects are occurring on all continents and across the oceans (IPCC, 2014). It is demonstrated that there is a clear link between climate change and many extreme weather-related catastrophes: "[A] changing climate leads to changes in the frequency, intensity, spatial extent, duration, and timing of extreme weather and climate events, and can result in unprecedented extreme weather and climate events" (IPCC, 2012).

The impact of climate change for China has closely followed the global trend. The range of warming and the affected areas are great. It is estimated that by 2020, the national average surface temperature could increase by 1.7 °C; by 2030, 2.2 °C; and by 2050, 2.8 °C (Qin et al., 2005). The affected areas of climate warming extend from south to north. The adverse consequences of climate change will be severe for China. More droughts will occur, the drought-prone area will continue to expand, and droughts will grow more intense. Except for the increased rainfall in the western part of the northwest, the northern and southern part of the northeast could become permanently dry (Qin et al., 2005). Meanwhile, floods, heavy rainfall, and landslides are likely to increase dramatically.[2]

China has the largest population in the world, and most of it lives in South China and East China, both of which are vulnerable to floods, typhoons, landslides/mudslides, and earthquakes. Furthermore, China has become a booming economy – the second biggest in the world in 2009, with a per capita GDP of $6,100 in 2012 (Lin, 2013). For example, the Pearl River Delta, a densely populated metropolitan area comprising Hong Kong, Guangzhou, and Shenzhen, is situated in one of the world's most disaster-prone regions. Floods and typhoons there put more people at risk than in any other metropolitan area in the world (Sundermann et al., 2013). As a consequence, the economic losses and the population affected by catastrophes are increasing significantly and causing much greater socioeconomic impacts, especially during the last decade (2003–2012). Relative to the period 1900–2012, China experienced the highest frequency of natural disasters during the last decade (2003–2012), accounting for 37.6 percent of total occurrences. The last decade also saw 55.5 percent of the economic losses and was responsible for 52.4 percent of the affected population (Table 1).

Data for almost the same time period (2004–2010) also shows that the occurrences of major natural disasters are quite frequent and losses caused by catastrophes have mounted (Table 2).

THE WHOLE-NATION SYSTEM AND HOW IT WORKS IN CHINA

The State has traditionally played the major role in covering risk and providing disaster relief in China (Zhou, 2008). After launching the project of "reform and opening" (*gaige kaifang*) in 1978, the disaster prevention, reduction, and relief mechanisms – collectively known as the "Whole-Nation System" – have been gradually established (Zou & Yuan, 2010). The Whole-Nation System is not the result of the failure of the catastrophe insurance market but rather the child of China's history, economy, and

Table 1. Natural Disasters of 2003−2012 in China, Relative to the Period 1900−2012 (Percent).

Drought	Occurrences	Deaths	Affected Population	Direct Economic Losses
	25.0	0.0	31.2	28.4
Earthquake	34.1	10.4	76.0	92.2
Flooding	53.0	0.1	35.6	38.8
Landslide	41.8	54.0	96.3	48.5
Local storm	39.0	18.6	19.8	68.7
Tropical cyclone	32.5	1.3	55.8	56.3
Average	37.6	14.1	52.4	55.5

Sources: EM-DAT: The OFDA/CRED International Disaster Database, www.emdat. be − Universite catholique de Louvain, Brussels (Belgium). Calculations and categorization performed by the author; Xu and Mo (2013).
Data include data up to January 31, 2012, "Past Decade" roughly refers to the period from 2003 to 2012.

Table 2. Occurrences of Major Natural Disasters in China, 2004−2010 (Xu & Mo, 2013).

Disasters	2004	2005	2006	2007	2008	2009	2010	Total	LOSS (bn $US)
Earthquake	5	2	6	1	1	2	5	28	86.79
Flood	9	11	20	12	7	7	5	71	35.29
Storm	7	14	8	6	9	10	6	60	26.37
Drought	0	2	1	0	1	2	0	6	6.74
Extreme temperature	1	1	0	0	2	0	0	4	21.10

Sources: EM-DAT: The OFDA/CRED International Disaster Database, www.emdat. be − Universite eatholique de Louvain, Brussels (Belgium). Calculations and categorization performed by the author; Xu and Mo (2013).

socialist political system. Before asking the question of what the content of the Whole-Nation System is and how it works, it is necessary to track the history of China's disaster policy.

Historical Review of the Whole-Nation System: The Transformation of Disaster Risk Management Since 1949

Natural disaster management has been a highly sensitive issue for thousands of years in China. For example, building dams to prevent floods and protect agricultural production was routinely regarded as a major function of the centralized government in ancient times (Wittfogel, 1957, pp. I–XIX). Since the founding of the PRC in 1949, disaster risk management policy has passed through two phases. The socialist government and a centrally planned economy were key features of the postrevolutionary order and had great influence on disaster policy in the first phase. This period (1949–1978) saw the setting up of centrally planned disaster policies, accompanied by the shutting down of private insurance markets. During this period, people had no opportunity to buy insurance to cover their catastrophe exposures. The centrally planned economic system, not the mere existence of market failures, is responsible for the disappearance of private insurance. According to the requirements of socialist planned governance, there is no need – at least in theory – for business insurance because the government will bear all risks and cover individuals' exposures. However, China was one of the poorest nations at that time. Even in 1978, the per capita annual income was only $154, less than one-third of the average in Sub-Saharan African countries (Lin, 2013). Worse still, political leaders prioritized the development of large, heavy, advanced industries as they started building the nation (Lin, 2013), but paid less attention to natural disaster relief.

The dawn of the Third Plenum of the Eleventh Party Congress in 1978 brought an entirely new set of socioeconomic reforms, including disaster risk management reform. The most significant feature of this period is the dramatically increased government intervention and expansion of disaster relief. The comparison between the Tangshan Earthquake happened in 1976 and the Great Sichuan Earthquake in 2008 clearly shows the expansion of government relief and its changing priorities for disaster relief. The Tangshan Earthquake, magnitude 7.5, killed 242,769 people. Central and local governments put RMB 4.3 billion into aid for disaster relief. In contrast, the Great Sichuan Earthquake, magnitude 8.0, caused 69,277 deaths, and central and local governments put RMB 128.7 billion into disaster relief, a thirtyfold increase (Hu, 2008).

The most convincing explanation for this change relates to China's miraculous success in economic growth since 1978, when China launched the project of "reform and opening." With GDP growing at an average of 9.8 percent per year, and international trade growing by 16.6 percent annually over the past 33 years, China is now an upper middle-income country, and more than 600 million people have escaped poverty (Naughton, 2014). Per capita GDP reached $6,100 in 2012 (Lin, 2013). With China's success in raising personal incomes and individuals' relative risk aversion increasing with wealth, protection against the loss of existing income apparently emerged as an increasingly significantly social objective. When the government began to obtain sufficient resources for disaster relief, disaster risk management became an important item on the nation's policy agenda.

The Content of the Whole-Nation System

The Whole-Nation System is a disaster-management system in which the government mobilizes, deploys, and allocates the nation's resources to cope with catastrophes, compensate victims, and conduct reconstruction, thus promoting the welfare of victims and the nation's interests. These interests extend beyond coping with a given disaster, including also promoting the government's image and fostering good relations between the various levels of government and the people (Wang, 2013, pp. 65−67). The 1998 Yangtze River flood and the 2003 Severe Acute Respiratory Syndrome (SARS) epidemic have been regarded as watershed events for the development of the Whole-Nation System. In 2007, the *Emergency Response Law* was promulgated. This law comprehensively stipulates emergency response plans, institutions, mechanisms, and legal systems, and emphasizes the dominant role of government in emergency response to natural disasters (Wang, 2007).

The Whole-Nation System is under the unified leadership of the State Council (the Central People's Government). The central government is responsible for the coordination and organization of catastrophic disaster risk management (ONCDR, 2012). At the national level, the system is headed by the National Committee for Disaster Reduction (NCDR) which consists of 33 disaster-related member agencies (Fig. 1).

A vice premier of the State Council serves as the director of NCDR, and the Minister of Civil Affairs acts as its secretariat. A board of experts serves as consultants for the NCDR. For specific disasters, the corresponding ministries or bureaus are responsible for governance and technical affairs. For example, the China Earthquake Administration takes charge of governance in the case of earthquakes, and the Ministry of Water Resources takes charge of governance in the case of floods and droughts. These coordinating bodies not only provide decision-making services for NCDR on disaster response and relief but also implement NCDR's decisions (Jiang, Wang, & Liu, 2008, p. 39). At the local level, corresponding organizations in accordance with the national level are also established.

Under the Whole-Nation System, the government occupies the dominant position and government fiscal support serves as the major capital

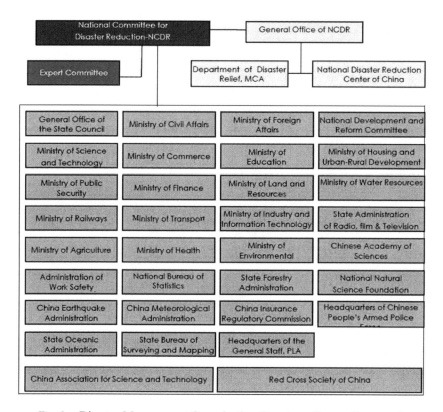

Fig. 1. Disaster-Management Organization Structure. *Source*: Jiang et al. (2008, p. 40).

source for disaster relief and postdisaster reconstruction (ONCDR, 2012). In practice, government intervention can be classified into predisaster and postdisaster arrangements.

- Predisaster arrangements
  These include conducting natural disaster risk investigation and zoning, establishing a natural disaster monitoring system and an early-warning system, pushing forward natural disaster prevention projects, establishing National Comprehensive Disaster Reduction Demonstration Communities, drawing people's attention to disaster prevention through designating May 12 as national Disaster Prevention and Reduction Day, and so on (ONCDR, 2012).

- Postdisaster arrangements
  These include rescuing victims; providing medical treatment to injured people; providing food and shelter for victims; engaging in water purification, sanitation, quarantine, and epidemic prevention; restoring transportation and other infrastructure for public interest; providing a three-month temporary living subsidy to disaster-affected people, compensation to victim's families, compensation to the injured, orphans, the elderly, and the handicapped, and subsidies to help farm workers reconstruct their houses; organizing counterpart aid (*duikou zhiyuan*) to help disaster-affected areas, implementing reconstruction plans, and so on (Dalen, Flatø, Jing, & Huafeng, 2012).

Unified leadership by the government is the foremost principle of the Whole-Nation System (Wang, 2013, pp. 65–67). For a transition state such as China, its legitimacy depends not only on its economic performance but also on its response and accountability to the people (Lazarev, Sobolev, Soboleva, & Sokolov, 2014). During the transition process, the Chinese government has come to prioritize disaster relief in its agenda. Since the early 1980s, China has promulgated more than 30 laws and regulations concerning disaster prevention, reduction, and relief (Zou & Yuan, 2010). These laws and regulations cover different aspects of disaster risk management. Besides laws and regulations, the Chinese government has also announced several national strategic plans relating to disaster risk management. As a recent example, in 2007, the Chinese government issued the National Plans for Comprehensive Disaster Reduction in the Eleventh Five-Year-Plan Period (Zou & Yuan, 2010). Although it is difficult to evaluate how well these laws, regulations, and plans are implemented, at least they reflect the government's concern for this issue. They stand for the government's willingness and efforts to prioritize disaster risk management on its agenda.

How the Whole-Nation System Works in Practice — A Case Study of the 2008 Great Sichuan Earthquake

The 2008 Great Sichuan Earthquake has shown how this system works. The earthquake caused 69,277 deaths, and the losses exceeded $100 billion (Hu, 2008). The Whole-Nation System played an essential role in coping with this catastrophic earthquake. According to three surveys conducted after the earthquake, government relief and the recovery process are viewed as successful by the public, particularly in the immediate aftermath of the earthquake (Dalen et al., 2012). The response of the government to the earthquake is regarded as both "close and timely":

> [M]ost damage caused by the earthquake was quickly repaired... households were able to resume economic activities relatively quickly, and ... education and healthcare systems continued to function under extraordinarily difficult circumstances, and resumed normal operations well before the end of the recovery period. In material terms, the recovery process did succeed in 'building back better' by providing new and improved public facilities, houses and infrastructure. (Dalen et al., 2012)

Undertaking Disaster Relief and Compensating Victims
Thanks to its economic power, the Chinese government has the ability to play a facilitating role in disaster relief. After 1995, social resources available to the government, particularly for the central government, grew enormously due to both overall economic development and fiscal reform. Tax revenues as a share of GDP illustrate this dramatic change (Fig. 2).

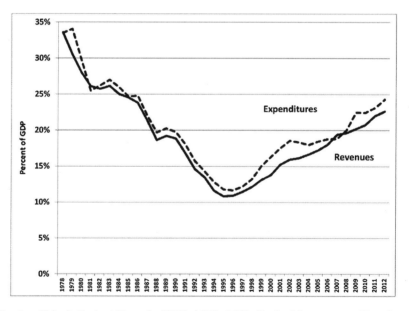

Fig. 2. China's Budget Share in GDP, 1978–2012. *Recited from source:* Naughton (2014).

Considering the rapid growth of the GDP itself, real budgetary revenues were almost 20 times in 2012 of what they had been in 1995.[3] In 2012, Chinese government revenues at $1.86 trillion were about equal to the US federal government on-budget revenues, which are estimated by the Congressional Budget Office at $1.97 trillion (excluding Social Security) (Naughton, 2014).

In the immediate aftermath of the Great Sichuan Earthquake, which occurred on May 12, the central government appropriated $83 million to victims that evening; within one week, the central government supplied more than $400 million in earthquake relief (Xinhua News Agency, 2008). Within four months, the government had created an emergency disaster relief fund in the amount of about $11 billion (Shi & Zhang, 2013, p. 109). On September 23, 2008, the State Council announced a "Notice on the State Council Overall Planning for Post-Great Sichuan Earthquake Restoration and Reconstruction" (hereinafter "the Plan"). According to the Plan, more than $157 billion was to be allocated for restoration work in the 51 disaster-affected counties in the provinces of Sichuan, Gansu, and Shaanxi (The State Council, 2008).

Direct payment to victims from government disaster relief funds is an important feature of the Whole-Nation System. Disaster relief funds were spent on victims mainly in the following ways. First, the funds were used to supply a three-month temporary living subsidy to earthquake-affected people. From May 20, this subsidy was about RMB 10 plus 0.5 kg of grain product every day to those affected people who had no residence and no income (Jiang et al., 2008, p. 23). Second, the fund supplied compensation to victims' families. The number of fatalities was more than 70,000, and the government provided each victim's family with RMB 5,000 (Jiang et al., 2008, p. 24). Third, it compensated the injured, orphans, the elderly living alone, and the handicapped (RMB 600 per month). The government launched a special mechanism to mobilize 375 hospitals from 20 provinces to treat more than 10,000 seriously injured victims, providing RMB 28,000 of medical subsidies for each injured person. For those with minor wounds, around 374,000 people, their medical treatment was free of charge (Jiang et al., 2008, p. 24). Fourth, it supplied subsidies to help farmers reconstruct their houses. In early June, the State Council decided that it would pay an average of RMB 10,000 per household to farmers whose houses collapsed or were severely damaged or who became homeless in the earthquake-affected region including Sichuan, Gansu, and Shaanxi provinces, for the purpose of reconstructing their houses (Jiang et al., 2008, p. 24).

Three years after the earthquake, when the recovery and reconstruction periods outlined in the Plan were over, the surveys of victims showed that most households' living conditions had indeed recovered to pre-earthquake levels or better (Dalen et al., 2012). For example, housing and employment goals, as the first two objectives of the Plan, had been largely fulfilled. Almost everyone in the earthquake-affected area lived in a permanent house, with only 0.6 percent of households still living in temporary houses or tents (Dalen et al., 2012). The employment rate was indeed relatively high, with the unemployment rate at only 2 percent, and household income increased considerably as well (Dalen et al., 2012).

Mobilizing Military Power for Emergency Disaster Relief
The Chinese People's Liberation Army (PLA) has a long history of involvement in disaster relief. As a developing country, China lacks sufficient civilian emergency management capacity compared with Western countries. The PLA is warmly welcomed and receives hardly any criticism in domestic disaster relief. This is in contrast to the United States where deploying military power for domestic disaster relief has been a subject of controversy (Anderson, 1970). The query "Where's the cavalry?" which arose after the failed response to Hurricane Katrina, illustrates this inherent tension (Kent, 2006). In recent years, the mounting frequency of natural catastrophes in China has placed increasing demands on the military to be deployed to domestic disaster relief under its powers to conduct "military operations other than war" (Banks, 2006). In 2005, the State Council and the Central Military Commission jointly promulgated "Regulation on the Army's Participation in Disaster Rescue," which designated the PLA as the "shock force" in national responses to catastrophic disasters.

Due to the central government's mobilization and the PLA's command-and-control structure, the PLA made significant contributions to the operation of the Whole-Nation System, especially in the emergency response to disasters. First, the military responded with unprecedented speed to the earthquake and made the best use of the golden hours of disaster rescue to save as many as lives as possible (Zhang, 2014, p. 79). Only thirteen minutes after the earthquake, the PLA activated the military plan for handling emergency incidents; Within ten hours, 12,000 PLA and People's Armed Police (PAP) soldiers arrived and undertook earthquake rescue; and on the next day, another 11,420 troops arrived by air transportation alone (Chen, 2008). Second, the civilian government made use of the military's vertical command-and-control structure to improve relief efficiency under the circumstance of catastrophic impacts and losses. Within the PLA, a three-tiered command system was quickly set up to oversee the military's relief operation, and these ad hoc institutions were also subject to the leadership of the civilian government at the corresponding level (Zhang, 2014, pp. 79–80). Third, the military undertook wide-ranging relief activities, counting on its huge numbers of troops. The PLA is the largest army in the world, and it can quickly mobilize a large number of soldiers to handle disasters, as it has throughout the PRC's history (Table 3).

As many as 146,000 troops were deployed, and they evacuated around 1.4 million people, provided medical treatment to 1.36 million injured people, and rescued 3,338 people (Zhang, 2014, p. 80). Furthermore, they also restored road transportation; provided food and shelter for victims; and engaged in water purification, sanitation, quarantine, and epidemic prevention, and the like (Zhang, 2014, p. 80). Even though the majority of PLA troops withdrew within three months of the earthquake, some engineering units stayed for another three months to assist with postearthquake reconstruction (Zhang, 2014, p. 80).

*Counterpart Aid (*Duikou Zhiyuan*): National "Pooling" of Catastrophe Risk among Provincial and Local Governments*
Pooling is a fundamental mechanism in both public risk management and private insurance. Its basic principle lies in combining and spreading a sufficient number of exposures across a group as large as possible (Moss, 2004, pp. 292–296; Vaughan & Vaughan, 2007, pp. 34–44). Counterpart

Table 3. Numbers of Soldiers that Participated in Major Disaster Relief Since 1998.

Year	Event	PLA and PAP Troops	Reserve and Militia
1998	Major flooding of the Yangtze, Songliua, and Nen Rivers	300,000	5,000,000
2002	Flooding in Sharrxi, Fujian, and 19 other provinces	20,000	170,000
2003	Flooding of the Huai River in Jiangxi, Hunan, and ShanKi provinces	48,000	410,000
2008	Snow and ice storms in 21 provinces	224,000	1,036,000
2008	Earthquake in Wenquan, Sichuan	146,000	75,000
2008	Security for the Olympics	131,000	na
2010	Earthquake in Yushu, Sichuan	16,000	na
2010	Mudslides in Zhouqu, Gansu	7,600	na

Source: Fravel (2011).

aid (*duikou zhiyuan*) is a mechanism that, under the central government's organization, requires some provinces which have stronger economic power to assist and support the reconstruction of disaster-affected areas (Zhao & Jiang, 2009). It is generally conducted on a one-to-one basis, under the principle of "one province helps one significantly affected county" (Wei et al., 2014, p. 295). The match criterion set up by the central government is that the richest donor provinces will contribute to the hardest-hit victim areas, while the less wealthy provinces will be asked to do less, and the least wealthy provinces will not be assigned any victim areas. According to the "Notice on the State Council Overall Planning for Post-Great Sichuan Earthquake Restoration and Reconstruction (2008)," 18 heavily affected counties in Sichuan Province were supported by 18 other provinces or municipalities. For example, Guangdong Province – the richest province measured by GDP – was responsible for the reconstruction of Wenchuan County, which was the epicenter of the earthquake and suffered the most severe losses. Shandong Province – the second richest province in 2008 – was responsible for and supported the reconstruction of BeiChuan County, which was the neighbor of Wenchuan County and was also heavily hit by the earthquake. Meanwhile, Gansu Province, Guizhou Province, and other less wealthy provinces had no responsibility for counterpart aid.

Under the framework of counterpart aid, supporting provinces are required to donate 1 percent of their fiscal revenue from the preceding year to supported counties for reconstruction in the next three years (Wei et al., 2014, p. 296). One percent is the minimum requirement of the central government, but the supporting province may increase the donation at its discretion. As a matter of fact, some provinces gave more than a 1 percent share (Table 4).

Under the authoritarian regime, political benefit is an important incentive for the supporting provinces' governors to increase the counterpart aid capital.[4]

In short, counterpart aid, to some extent, can be regarded as a special "pooling" of catastrophe risk because it spreads specific natural disaster risk across the whole-nation and improves the social welfare. This mechanism differs from a central fund, which would require every province to give 1 percent to a fund that can then be used across victimized areas. Counterpart aid linking donor and recipient areas in this way seems economically pointless, since it only imposes unneeded constraints on the flow of funds. However, due to China's unusual size and regional diversity, especially the huge economic imbalance among different provinces – for example, the GDP of the richest province in 2014 is 77 multiples of

Table 4. Performance of Some Supporting Provinces in Counterpart Aid in Response to the 2008 Great Sichuan Earthquake (Billion RMB).

Supporting Provinces or Municipalities	Fiscal Revenue (2007)	Required Counterpart Aid (1%)	Supported Counties	Counterpart Aid (2008)
Guangdong	278.526	2.785	Wenchuan	4.162
Jiangsu	223.666	2.236	Mianzhu	4.363
Zhejiang	164.949	1.649	Qingchuan	3.499
Shanghai	207.448	2.074	Dujiangyan	6.198
Beijing	164.964	1.649	Shifang	5.306
Liaoning	108.199	1.081	Anxian	2.6
Fujian	70.03	0.703	Pengzhou	3.318
Anhui	54.347	0.534	Songpan	1.889

Source: Hua (2010).

the poorest — requiring the richer provinces to contribute more in disaster relief emphasizes the concern for equality rather than the economic efficiency.

The Problems of the Whole-Nation System

Having reviewed how the Whole-Nation System works in dealing with catastrophes, it appears that China's government has done a reasonable job, at least in the immediate aftermath of a disaster. Though by no means a perfect risk manager, the Chinese government does take up the vacuum, as Nobel economist Kenneth Arrow suggested in another context, to "undertake insurance in those cases where [a private market for insurance], for whatever reason, has failed to emerge" (Arrow, 1963). Now we are ready to ask whether the Whole-Nation System can possibly do any better than private insurance, which has already demonstrated significant market failures in covering catastrophe risk. As will become clear, the answer is a resounding "yes" in theory but only a tantalizing "no" in reality. Just as even the best market systems confront "market failures," government solutions confront many obstacles and problems, collectively known as "government failures." The Whole-Nation System is no exception.

According to surveys conducted after the 2008 Great Sichuan Earthquake, the degree of satisfaction with all levels of government (except the central government) had declined since the quake (Dalen et al., 2012, p. 175) (Fig. 3).

The criticism of government relief grew over time.

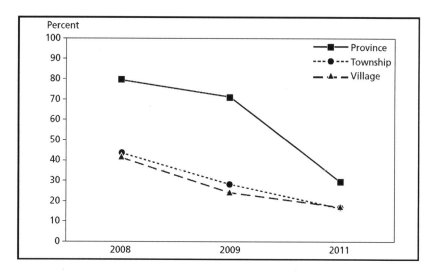

Fig. 3. Declining Satisfaction with Government Relief after the 2008 Great Sichuan Earthquake. *Source*: Dalen et al. (2012, p. 175).

Added to the above discussion of how the Whole-Nation System worked during the 2008 Great Sichuan Earthquake must be an examination of some of its many problems, especially in the long run.

Corruption Problems

Before the economic reform and opening, corruption tended to be visible and easy to prevent because officials normally had only a single income source under the planned economy (Lin, 2012, p. 19). However, corruption problems became more serious and rampant when China decided to transit from a planned to a market economy. While the government remains as powerful as it has always been, the market-oriented reforms create substantially greater rent-seeking opportunities.[5] As a result, officials at every level have found many sources of income beyond a single government salary.[6] Officials who implement the Whole-Nation System are not easily immunized from corruption problems. This system involving distributing large sums of money is vulnerable to dishonest contractors and corrupt officials.

The relief and reconstruction funds from the central government were allocated to local governments, and local governments were requested to take responsibility for implementation (Jiang et al., 2008, p. 51). In the early days after the disaster, almost all government relief programs were under the spotlight of the whole-nation, not only the central government

but also the media. Under these circumstances, it was difficult for local officials to divert disaster aid. However, as time passed and the media spotlight
shifted, national attention was diverted. As a result, although the total
accumulated capital for disaster relief was quite high, the central government leaders' focus on the disaster was short-lived (Moss, 2010).[7] Public
attention to disasters is in proportion to media coverage. As is common
throughout the world, media coverage surges upward in the immediate
aftermath of a disaster, throwing a bright spotlight on the victims, and
then the attention quickly dissipates (Moss, 2010). This short time horizon
weakens public and media supervision of local government disaster relief
work. When local officers are the only ones who know what is going on,
they may succumb to the temptation to abuse their power and exploit the
victims (Lin, 2012, p. 198). For example, the central government sent funds
to various agencies in Sichuan Province after the earthquake. Although
that money was intended for relief, significant amounts of it were used in
paying for government banquets and officials' bonuses (Wang, 2013,
pp. 92–93). According to the earthquake relief audit report of the National
Audit Office of the PRC, there were 146 of these cases in Sichuan in 2008,
totaling $220 million (Wang, 2013, pp. 92–93).

The Samaritan's Dilemma
The "Samaritan's Dilemma"[8] haunts governmental aid. According to
James Buchanan's definition, the Samaritan's Dilemma is created when the
government makes direct payments to individuals after a disaster, giving
them incentives not to take protective measures or purchase insurance but
instead to rely on government to bail them out (Buchanan, 1972). Even if
the government promises ex ante not to provide such relief, the promise is
not credible, because it will be in everyone's interests to offer such relief
after a disaster has struck (Buchanan, 1972). Therefore, more government
bailouts may cause more disaster losses because people are less likely to
take precaution measures.

The Whole-Nation System rouses the Samaritan's Dilemma. Often, a
government bailout is motivated by an admirable humanitarian impulse
which spurs redistributing wealth to those who have suffered loss from
those who have been spared (Priest, 2003). Political concerns are also
important under the Whole-Nation System. Although the Chinese central
government has no re-election constraints, governmental performance in
providing relief during and after the disaster impacts the support for the
authorities at all levels (Lazarev et al., 2014). However, this humanitarian
and political action ignores the fact that in some cases, the effect of the
redistribution will encourage future loss-causing activities that would not

otherwise have been undertaken (Priest, 2003). Some pure forms of government bailout, including ad hoc direct payment and compensation funds, provide insufficient incentives for risk prevention and loss mitigation (Van den Bergh & Faure, 2006). Therefore, individuals will be less inclined to protect against disaster when they believe the government will bail them out, which increases the magnitude of loss for the whole-nation.

In addition, the Chinese people have historically had a strong desire to rely on a governmental bailout in the wake of a catastrophe. Under the Whole-Nation System, the government is committed to restoring social and economic order after a disaster. Thanks to such a governmental commitment, individuals' personal experiences, and media reports of past catastrophes, it is perfectly rational for the Chinese people to fail to take adequate protective measures. Many residents admit that they are exposed to catastrophe risks, but they seldom transfer risks through insurance because they believe government will bail them out when catastrophes happen (Wang, 2013, p. 5). According to an empirical study on property and causality insurance in five Chinese provinces, there is a negative correlation between the amount of government relief and residents' investment in prevention measures such as purchasing insurance (Tian & Zhang, 2013).

The Regressive Effects of Counterpart Aid

Counterpart aid relies on the maxim that "one province helps one significantly affected county," requiring the richer provinces — not all provinces — to help disaster-affected areas and contribute more in disaster relief. However, when the disaster is a widespread catastrophe and many counties are affected, this "one province helps one significantly affected county" arrangement frequently leads to the situation in which not-that-rich provinces have to help reconstruct richer (by per capita fiscal expenditure) counties. For example, Hunan Province was responsible for the construction of Lixian County after the Great Sichuan Earthquake. However, the per capita fiscal expenditure of Hunan Province was only RMB 2,135 in 2007; of Sichuan Province, RMB 2,165; and of Lixian County, RMB 4,209 (Ni, Zhang, & Tongzhou, 2009). Similar per capita disparities existed in Jilin, Anhui, and Jiangxi provinces (Table 5).

Counterpart aid aims to realize the goal of "common prosperity" through richer provinces helping poorer ones. In practice, however, sometimes poorer provinces have to help richer ones. Adding to the problem is the fact that there are no legal provisions regulating counterpart aid, which means the obligations of supporting provinces are unclear and arbitrary and decided at the discretion of the central government (Zhao & Jiang, 2009).

Table 5. Comparison between Some Supporting Provinces and Supported Counties in per Capita Fiscal Expenditure Before the 2008 Earthquake (RMB).

Supporting Provinces or Municipalities	Per Capita Fiscal Expenditure (2007)	Supported Counties	Per Capita Fiscal Expenditure (2007)
Hunan	2,135	Lixian County	4,209
Jilin	3,237	Heishui County	4,149
Anhui	2,033	Songpan County	4,107
Jiangxi	2,072	Xiaojin County	3,056

Source: Ni et al. (2009).

Even when poor areas suffer from catastrophe losses, unfairness may also arise. For example, after the 2008 Great Sichuan Earthquake, Shandong Province, which ranked in the top three in GDP in 2007, was responsible for the reconstruction of BeiChuan County and donated RMB 12 billion (about $2 billon) (Zhao & Jiang, 2009). The per capita fiscal expenditure of Shandong Province was RMB 2,415 in 2007, while it was RMB 2,299 in Beichuan County (Ni et al., 2009). Five years later, however, after receiving the counterpart aid, BeiChuan County was much more prosperous than a lot of counties of the Shandong Province (Wang, 2013, p. 86). In 2012, the per capita fiscal expenditure of Shandong Province was around RMB 5,900, while it was about RMB 8,000 in Beichuan County (Beicuan County, 2012; Shandong Province, 2012).

As a matter of fact, counterpart aid does not eliminate risk but only distributes the burden of disaster losses across the taxpayers of supporting provinces. Therefore, counterpart aid emerges as an arguably unfair arrangement for the residents of the supporting provinces because the supporting provinces may treat their own residents "less favorably" than those in disaster areas. Under China's political selection system in which the central government has the final word rather than the residents (Zhou, 2014), governors of supporting provinces have strong incentives to deal with disaster-affected areas more favorably than they do with their own residents because the counterpart aid is politically favored by the central government.

Lack of Risk Financing

Risk financing is regarded as one of the three pillars of risk management and classically requires those who face risks to pay for coverage through risk-based premiums (Outreville, 1998, pp. 45−64; Thoyts, 2010, pp. 286–295).[9] Ex ante insurance with risk-based premiums provides incentives to accumulate reserves and mitigate losses before disasters, while ex post government aid may reduce incentives to reserve funds or carry out mitigation activities (Jaffee & Russell, 2013). However, the Whole-Nation System pays little attention to, and indeed, lacks the capability of risk financing through ex ante insurance markets to compensate victims, instead focusing on ex post relief.

Furthermore, aspects of the Whole-Nation System, such as counterpart aid, "crowd out" the establishment and development of risk financing markets by depressing the demand of individuals for catastrophe insurance. Individuals are less likely to purchase insurance to prefinance their potential disaster losses. According to general international experiences, a catastrophe insurance system is often established within two years after a disaster occurs. For example, in 1944, after the 1942 earthquake in New Zealand, an earthquake insurance system was established. California's experience was similar. However, five years after the 2008 Great Sichuan Earthquake, a catastrophe insurance market had not yet been officially established in China. The Whole-Nation System, which played a powerful role in earthquake relief, at least partially accounts for this.

Other Challenges and Remarks
Besides the above problems of the Whole-Nation System, there are other potential challenges. Disaster relief imposes burdens on public budgets and may hinder economic growth. In smaller and developing countries, a catastrophe event can result in higher public deficits and debt (Swiss Re, 2008). Although China is now the second largest economy in the world, the cost of the Whole-Nation System still imposes a considerable burden on the public budget. For example, the government spent approximately $166 billion after the 2008 earthquake in restoration and reconstruction.[10] Despite that, there is no consensus on whether disaster relief depresses or in fact enhances economic growth (Xu & Mo, 2013). A two-period equilibrium model indicates that direct payment of disaster relief funds may depress rather than enhance economic growth because disaster relief related to the loss of capital and the substitution effect of direct transfer payment depresses postdisaster labor supply (Barry, 2000). Such effects of disaster relief on growth have been tested using panel data on 31 Chinese provinces, municipalities, and autonomous regions over the period 2004–2010 (Xu & Mo, 2013). In addition, the Whole-Nation System as the ad hoc compensation tool for victims, leads to an unstable budget, which may dampen economic growth.

The extensive use of the military in disaster relief has been a double-edged sword because it could potentially displace the development of an effective civilian-based disaster-management system in the future (Zhang, 2014, pp. 70–72).

After considering the structure of the Whole-Nation System, how it works, and its problems, we may see that the Whole-Nation System has indeed played a valuable role in dealing with catastrophe losses in China. More important insights for the Whole-Nation System, however, suggest opportunities for improvement. Summarized in Fig. 4, the System's predisaster measures as ex ante mitigation actions are efficient policies to address catastrophe losses, and its postdisaster measures in emergency response are also efficient.

Fig. 4 also shows the problems of the Whole-Nation System. What the System did in predisaster measures is too little, not too much. For actions postdisaster, there should be a close examination of the methods of victims' compensation and counterpart aid.

The Whole-Nation System, in this limited context, seems to have performed reasonably well, but it is far from a totally efficient, sustainable, and long-term catastrophe risk management system. To deal with the risk

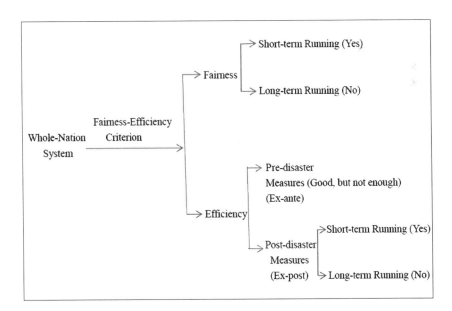

Fig. 4. Evaluation of the Whole-Nation System.

of natural disasters more effectively in China, there is an urgent need for the reform of the Whole-Nation System to integrate it with insurance and other market mechanisms.

GOVERNMENT STIMULATION OF CATASTROPHE INSURANCE MARKETS FOR DISASTERS

Having reviewed the performance of the Whole-Nation System – its achievements and problems – we are now ready to explore its reform and transition. Compared with the government-run Whole-Nation System, insurance is traditionally recognized as an important tool to deal with catastrophic disasters, through risk pooling and risk shifting, but also risk reduction and risk management (Ben-Shahar & Logue, 2012). Moreover, many law and economics scholars favor insurance as a private-market mechanism for distributing catastrophe risk, especially when compared to government-provided compensation. For example, Jaffee and Russell (1997), Faure and Heine (2011), Kunreuther (1968), Epstein (1996), Priest (1996), and Kaplow (1991) argue that insurance is better equipped to deal with catastrophe risks than government due to its advantages of lower transaction costs, lower adverse selection, and greater efficiency. Michel-Kerjan, Zelenko, and Cardenas (2011) provide a simplified view of different options that the state would typically choose: with the level of economic development improving, a public and private catastrophe insurance system is gradually developing in different countries (Fig. 5).

According to this simplified view, it seems that China should move from step 2 to step 3. It is consistent with our conclusion that catastrophe insurance could be a necessary and proper complement to the Whole-Nation System. Before the discussion of insurance's role in addressing catastrophe losses, however, the starting point should be how to create a catastrophe insurance market in China where, for whatever reason, it has still failed to emerge.

The Immature Catastrophe Insurance Market in China

In 1959, the Chinese government closed all domestic insurance companies, and the insurance business as a whole virtually disappeared from 1959 to 1978 (Wang, 2013, pp. 87–89). After the Third Plenum of the Eleventh

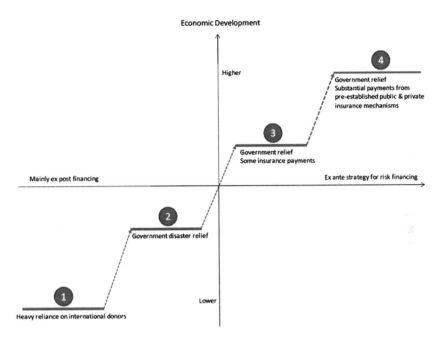

Fig. 5. A Simplified View of Governments' Responses to Financial Management of Natural Disasters. *Source*: Michel-Kerjan et al. (2011).

Party Congress, the process of institutional transformation toward a market-oriented economy began, and commercial insurance agencies also resumed doing business. In 1979, the State Council approved the "Notice on Restoration of the Domestic Insurance Business and Strengthening of the Insurance Agency" (*Guanyu Huifu Guonei Baoxian Yewu He Jiaqiang Baoxian Jigou De Tongzhi*), which allowed insurers to underwrite property insurance, vehicle insurance, marine insurance, and life insurance. Since 1989, the insurance industry has been one of the fastest growing industries in China, with nominal premium income growing at an annual average 30 percent (Chen, Luo, & Pan, 2013). China's insurance market ranked as the fourth largest in the world in 2013 (Xinhua News Agency, 2013).

Catastrophe insurance, however, has walked a much bumpier road than other lines in the insurance industry. In 1987, the Ministry of Civil Affairs launched the agricultural insurance pilot projects in Heilongjiang, Fujian, and Jiangsu provinces. It is worth noting that these agricultural insurance policies covered catastrophic risks such as droughts and floods. However, these pilot projects were closed after twelve years' experimentation (Shi, Tang, Liu, Chen, & Zhou, 2008). In 1996, floods, typhoons, and other natural disasters were all prescribed as exclusions by regulators in property insurance policies (People's Banks of China, 1996). Thus, these catastrophic exposures were excluded from coverage under standard-form policies. As a result, it should be no surprise that in the 1998 Yangtze River flood, insurance covered only about 1.25 percent of economic losses – $500 million coverage out of a total loss of $40 billion (Ministry of the Civil Affairs, 1998). In 2000, the China Insurance Regulatory Commission (CIRC) – the newly established insurance regulatory agency – prohibited insurers from underwriting earthquake insurance policies without its permission (CIRC, 2000).

This 2008 Great Sichuan Earthquake underscored the need for catastrophe insurance. In 2012, one of the main topics in the Fourth National Finance Working Conference was establishing a system of catastrophe insurance.[11] In 2013, "Regulation on Agriculture Insurance" was promulgated, which included government-subsidized agricultural catastrophe insurance. For example, Article 8 provides that the central government should establish subsidized agricultural catastrophe insurance, and local governments are encouraged to follow and contribute to the pool; Article 17 prescribes that any insurance company that wants to underwrite an agricultural insurance policy must include catastrophe coverage (No. 619, Decree of the State Council of the People's Republic of China 2013).[12] In 2014, catastrophe insurance program trials were launched in Shenzhen, in the Pearl River Delta (a densely populated metropolitan area and also one of the world's most disaster-prone regions), and in the Chuxiong region in the southwestern province of Yunnan, which is prone to earthquakes (Reuters, 2014). These pilot programs have yet to be evaluated. Overall, catastrophe insurance in China is still at a very immature stage and cannot yet meet the rising demand for disaster relief. It needs proper government intervention.

Theoretical Framework for Developing a Catastrophe Insurance Market: Overcoming the Market–Government Dichotomy and Looking for Customized Solutions

Generally speaking, there are three major theoretical frameworks for analyzing government responsibilities in market intervention: the laissez-faire theory, also called the market-friendly view; the public-interest theory, also called the developmental-state view; and the market-enhancing theory (Aoki, Murdock, & Okuno-Fujiwara, 1998; Bruggeman, 2010, pp. 193–195; Cummins & Mahul, 2009, pp. 84–85; Lewis & Murdock, 1999). How to develop an insurance industry generally falls into one of these three camps.

Laissez-Faire Theory
The laissez-faire theory of government policy believes that the efficient allocation of resources within the economy can be achieved through the market mechanism; even when markets alone are insufficient, other private-sector organizations will suffice, and the outcome still remains more efficient than government intervention (Bruggeman, 2010, pp. 193–195; Cummins & Mahul, 2009, pp. 84–85). According to this theory, private insurance markets can achieve efficient market equilibrium, and government's role is limited to providing a fair legal environment for market transactions (Aoki et al., 1998). In such an analysis, calling for government intervention in providing catastrophe insurance would be viewed as opportunistic "rent-seeking" attempts of special-interest groups to secure an ex ante wealth transfer from taxpayers (Cummins & Mahul, 2009, pp. 84–85).

In many respects, this theoretical framework has merits. In the absence of distortion-inducing government intervention, the outcome of the private insurance market may remain more efficient. The UK's private flood insurance scheme, developed about half a century ago, offers an example of how largely private markets could work (Huber, 2004). The British government merely sets standards and rules for flood protection, land-use, and flood warning, and it promises to guarantee the independence of privately run compensation "schemes" according to a gentleman's agreement which defines the rights and duties of state and industry (Huber, 2004). The UK private flood insurance scheme has remained largely unchanged since its emergence in 1961 and has proven to be efficient and sustainable (Huber, 2004).

However, the laissez-faire theory, in which government is considered as a black box usually unsuccessfully solving problems of markets, is largely inappropriate for dealing with the practical problems of economic development and social reform in transitional countries (Ahrens & Mengeringhaus, 2006). The theory confronts the "paradox of the adjusting state": on the one hand, "the government is required to withdraw from interventions into economic activities and to perform a more passive role"; on the other hand, "economic transition and development usually require nimble and robust political authorities to implement and enforce the new market-oriented policy directives due to existing market imperfections" (Ahrens, 2007).

Making the government more effective so that it can solve new challenges and perform new roles in facilitating private-sector coordination is of utmost importance for economic transformation and social reform (Ahrens, 2007).

Catastrophe insurance started only recently in China. Clear imperfections in the insurance market in China make it is easy to perceive why catastrophe insurance has not been quickly established since the Great Sichuan Earthquake. From the supply-side, insurers face a lot of obstacles to underwriting catastrophe insurance policies, such as lack of catastrophe data to identify, quantify, and estimate the chance of disasters and to set premiums; relatively low capacity of insurance industry; limited access to international reinsurance and capital markets; regulatory obstacles; and so forth. From the demand-side, consumers do not always behave rationally and maximize their expected utility to protect themselves from catastrophe losses. Their demand for catastrophe insurance has also been blunted by expectations of a government bailout. Therefore, following the guide of the laissez-faire theory, the catastrophe insurance market would both fail to develop soon in China and fail to play its potential role in mitigating and financing catastrophe losses.

Public-Interest Theory

Public-interest theory of government policy contests laissez-faire theory and requires government to act as a substitute for coordination in the private markets. It holds that government intervention targets market failures (such as externalities, imperfect competition, moral hazard, and adverse selection), and by solving the suboptimal allocation of resources, government intervention can improve social welfare (Cummins & Mahul, 2009, pp. 84–85). According to this theoretical framework, government intervention is often seen as a substitute for or complement to imperfect coordination in the private markets (Lewis & Murdock, 1999). Advocates consider government to have better information and judgment than private insurers and to be able to guide markets wisely (Aoki et al., 1998). For developing countries where market failure is more pervasive, government intervention is more urgently needed. Limitations on insurance market infrastructure, lack of liquid capital markets, information asymmetries, and other imperfections associated with the catastrophe insurance market necessitate the role of government in developing a private market (Cummins & Mahul, 2009, pp. 84–85). Even in the United States, where Americans have long believed in the gospel of free markets and antistatist logic, deep government intervention in the management of private-sector risks is really nothing new

(Moss, 2004, p. 17).[13] When private insurers have failed to emerge or withdrawn underwriting, in consideration of the public interest, government has chosen to secure continuing insurance markets.

Although market failure and the need for economies of scale are common justifications for the government to intervene in an insurance market, they are not alone sufficient (Korczyk, 2005, p. 1). On the contrary, a lot of public insurance programs have been shown to be inefficient. Take the US National Flood Insurance Program for example. The non-risk-based premiums tend to distort the market price signal and encourage policyholders to overinvest in risky areas and to take inadequate steps to mitigate losses (Scales, 2006).

Public-interest theory is not suitable for China's market-oriented transition and reform. Right now, China is still struggling through the transition from a centrally planned economy toward a market economy. No independent business sectors or free markets existed until 1978 (Wang & Yin, 2012). During the transition process, China adopted a gradual dual-track approach, rather than shock therapy, and moved gradually to a well-functioning market economy (Lin, 2013). The experience of the dual-track approach shows that the more energetic power is coming from private companies. The dual-track approach as the transitional arrangement can hardly serve as the permanent foundation for further development, and China needs to move from the dual tracks to a single-track market economy (Lin, 2012, p. 178). In addition, if China adopted the public-interest theory, the threat of a reunion of the government and the state-owned insurance enterprises would become reality and we would see the dual-track approach backslide to the single-track planned economy (Wang & Yin, 2012). The case of a collaborative rural house insurance system in the Zhejiang Province supplies a vivid example. In this program, initiated in 2006, insurance products are primarily designed by the government and marketed through administrative mobilization instead of market channels run by the People's Insurance Company of China (PICC; Zhejiang branch) – a state-owned insurance enterprise. However, a well-functioning market for insurance has not been established, and adequate financial protection to residents against natural disaster losses is still lacking (Wang & Yin, 2012).

Market-Enhancing Theory
Market-enhancing theory of government policy is different from both laissez-faire theory and public-interest theory and takes a middle position. It recognizes that market failure leads to suboptimal allocations of resources

and thus suggests government can facilitate more efficient coordination in the private sector and enhance the development of the private market; it also suggests government should not substitute or replace the private sectors and should especially avoid creating permanent new government institutions to substitute for private insurers (Cummins & Mahul, 2009, pp. 84–85). This theory was first applied to managing catastrophe disaster risk by Lewis and Murdock as early as the 1990s (Lewis & Murdock, 1996, 1999). It has been widely discussed by scholars and international financial institutions, such as the World Bank (Abousleiman, Calderón, Cordella, & Yeyati, 2007; Cummins & Mahul, 2009; Gurenko, Lester, Mahul, & Gonulal, 2006; Hellmann, Murdock, & Stiglitz, 1998; World Bank, 2008).

Market-enhancing theory represents a new kind of government intervention that helps facilitate the creation of private markets and assists private insurers to solve market failures. In contrast to the laissez-faire theory, this framework looks for the role of government in achieving more efficient market equilibrium. This is particularly true for transitional and developing countries where private institutions are more limited and presently unable to solve all market failures (Aoki et al., 1998). In contrast to the public-interest theory – the traditional government intervention – it promotes the decentralized decision making of private insurers and avoids creating bureaucracy. In other words, the provisions of catastrophe insurance policies should be left to private insurers (Lewis & Murdock, 1999). This is particularly important for transitional countries where, under the impact of a planned economy, government is still powerful and might be tempted to meddle in micromanagement of insurance activities. The government should create a legal environment to enhance private transactions rather than get involved in the details of setting premiums and underwriting policies.

This theoretical framework has many merits. It helps establish an effective and sustainable catastrophe risk financing system with collaboration between government and private insurers. The government avoids acting as a direct insurer, but it can act as a reinsurer or lender of last resort when private underwritings are unavailable or inadequate (Cummins & Mahul, 2009, p. 87). More importantly, this theoretical framework encourages public-private partnership, which could help facilitate access to international reinsurance and capital markets to generate affordable products for domestic insurers (Cummins & Mahul, 2009, p. 87). In practice, this market-enhancing theoretical framework has already attracted the attention of international financial institutions like the World Bank, which guides government intervention in catastrophe risk markets of low- and middle-income countries (Cummins & Mahul, 2009, pp. 8–9). In 2000, the Turkish Catastrophe Insurance Pool (TCIP) was established with the assistance of the World Bank in the aftermath of the Marmara earthquake.[14] The TCIP sold more than 4.8 million policies set at market-based premium rates in 2012, compared to 600,000 covered households when the pool was set up, and penetration rate rose to 29 percent nationwide (TCIP, 2012). A similar catastrophe pool is being developed in Romania, and there are now even multiple-country regional organizations, such as the Caribbean Catastrophe Risk Insurance Facility(Cummins & Mahul, 2009, p. 93).

Like many other areas of the economy, the developing catastrophe insurance market in China can draw lessons from the accumulated achievements of the ongoing socioeconomic reforms — the so-called Chinese miracle (Perry, 2014). What a coincidence! The essence of China's "miracle" is consistent with market-enhancing theory, rather than laissez-faire theory or public-interest theory.[15] The Chinese approach stresses the fundamental role of the market in resource allocation but also expects the government to play a facilitating role by addressing externalities, coordination, and many other market-failure issues.[16]

Considering the low-probability but high-consequence nature of catastrophe risk and the currently immature condition of the insurance market and economic development experiences, the market-enhancing theory could be the proper guiding theory to develop a catastrophe insurance market in China. In addition, market-enhancing theory conforms to the practice of catastrophe insurance pilot programs in China. Market-enhancing theory emphasizes the importance of local information and suggests that decentralized private agents can use locally available information to come up with market-based solutions that are significantly more efficient than those that could be imposed by a central authority (Lewis & Murdock, 1999).

By examining the laissez-faire theory, public-interest theory, and market-enhancing theory, I suggest that the market-enhancing theory might be a proper theoretical guide for the development of a catastrophe insurance market in China. As Ronald Coase said, "satisfactory views on policy can only come from a patient study of how, in practice, the market, firms, and governments handle the problem of harmful effects" (Coase, 1960). Such study indicates that devising a catastrophe insurance market system and enhancing insurance's role in addressing catastrophe losses become an urgent challenge.

*Principles for Government Intervention in the Catastrophe
Insurance Market*

Based on the above analysis of market-enhancing theory and the experiences of China's transitional development, I propose a catastrophe insurance market-enhancing framework to coordinate the role of government and market in catastrophe risk management in China. The content of this framework has three pillars:

- Sustaining a strong and capable government
- Enhancing the market, neither supplanting nor retarding it
- Legalizing the relationship between government and market to prevent the government from undermining well-functioning market operations

To efficiently apply the catastrophe insurance market-enhancing framework, and to help establish a well-functioning catastrophe insurance market and disaster compensation system,[17] I further propose three principles to facilitate government intervention in the catastrophe insurance market:

- Principle 1. Government should help solve market failures in catastrophe insurance and secure insurers' business operations using market mechanisms, rather than creating new government institutions to substitute or supplant private solutions.
- Principle 2. Government may establish a mandatory catastrophe insurance system through legislation and help solve the affordability problem at the same time.
- Principle 3. Government should reform the Whole-Nation System to avoid crowding-out private insurance and enhance the collaboration between the insurance industry and the government.

Government Responsibilities under Principle 1
Helping Insurers Fulfill the Insurability Requirements. Insurability of catastrophe risk is an important consideration for insurers when they decide whether to underwrite policies. Generally speaking, there are two agreed-upon requirements for insurability: (i) the insurer must have the ability to identify, quantify, and estimate the chances of disasters and the resulting losses; (ii) the insurer must have the ability to set and collect appropriate premiums for catastrophe risks (Kunreuther & Michel-Kerjan, 2007; Roth & Kunreuther, 1998, pp. 27–38). Due to insurability limits with catastrophe risk and the high potential losses of catastrophe exposures, insurers lack the capacity and appetite to sufficiently cover all such losses. To help

fulfill the insurability requirements, governments can assist insurers with risk assessment, mapping risk zones, information flows, and so on.

Risk assessment is used to discover the underlying actuarial costs of catastrophe risk and help set accurate risk-adjusted premiums (Cummins & Mahul, 2009, pp. 76–77). It requires data collection, catastrophe risk modeling, and other technical support. Government, for example, has the advantage in data collection of natural disasters due to its disaster-relief experiences. Mapping risk zones, in fact, can be regarded as a means of risk assessment because it depicts and summarizes specific hazard risks of properties or zones (Paudel, 2012). It could best be conducted through collaboration between governments and insurers (Paudel, 2012). For example, European countries were required to prepare flood hazard and flood risk maps before 2014 to abide by the 2007 European Flood Risk Management Directive (Van Alphen, Martini, Loat, Slomp, & Passchier, 2009). Insurance businesses are heavily dependent on information flows, which include information flowing from policyholder to intermediaries, from intermediaries to insurers, and from insurers to reinsurers (Cummins & Mahul, 2009, pp. 31–32). If information cannot flow smoothly and accurately, it will not only increase transaction costs but make it difficult for insurers/reinsurers to identify, quantify, and correctly estimate the chances of disasters and the resulting losses.

Increasing the Capacity of the Insurance Industry. Due to the highly correlated and aggregate nature of natural disasters, the potential losses of catastrophe risks are large and uncertain. China's insurers may still lack sufficient financial capacity to fully cover catastrophe losses. Indeed, the total capital of China's property insurance companies is much lower than the total amount of losses caused by natural disasters (Table 6).

As early as 1992, following Hurricane Andrew, insurers have known that outside capital is needed to supplement the industry's capacity (King, 2005). Government can enhance the marriage between insurance markets

Table 6. Capital of Main Chinese Property Insurers Compared to Natural Disaster Losses (Billions of US Dollars).

	2007	2008	2009	2010
Net capital of main insurers	5.5	5.1	6.9	9.0
Natural disaster losses	38.1	189.5	40.1	86.1

Source: CIRC (2008, 2009, 2010, 2011).

and capital markets with measures like proper deregulation and tax exemptions. This is particularly important for the Chinese government because its insurance/reinsurance market and capital markets are still in their infancy. To make the marriage work, government has the duty to facilitate its development by eliminating market barriers, reducing transaction costs, establishing a rule-of-law market, and more.

In addition, government may act as the reinsurer to help increase the capacity of the insurance industry. Indeed, effective and sustainable catastrophe risk financing solutions require collaboration between government and private insurers, especially in the case of extreme catastrophes when the private reinsurance market "hardens."[18] The designers of the government's role as a reinsurer may learn from the well-functioning TCIP. When earthquake losses exceed $80 million, the excess losses are transferred to the reinsurance market (Von Lucius, 2004). Turkish government covers "losses that would exceed the overall claims paying capacity of the TCIP, which is currently sufficient to withstand a 1-in-350 year earthquake" (GFDRR, 2011). TCIP is supported by the World Bank, which provided financial and technical assistance. TCIP serves as a good model for China since it has been the first national catastrophe insurance pool in World Bank-client countries.

Besides acting as a reinsurer of last resort to increase the capacity of the insurance industry, government may sell industry-level excess-of-loss contracts for insured disaster losses as a last resort, as proposed by Lewis and Murdock.[19] Furthermore, government funds or government guarantees could also be alternative considerations.

Promoting Risk Classification and Encouraging Risk-Based Premiums. Risk classification and risk-based premiums are the heart and lungs of a healthy insurance business (Abraham, 1985). Only by segregating policyholders into different risk pools can insurers charge different premiums for different pools; reduce adverse selection; and incentivize risk reduction by policyholders, and thus make profits (Avraham, Logue, & Schwarcz, 2014). However, government and government-run catastrophe insurance systems are unlikely to implement this basic principle when faced with political pressures (Paudel, 2012)[20] because risk classification is not always compatible with social solidarity objectives which promote equal treatment of all citizens (Cummins & Mahul, 2009, pp. 76–78). Therefore, government should neither create new institutions to supplant private solutions nor refrain premiums of insurance policies but should allow insurers to set the premiums to reflect risks. Even if there are concerns about the affordability of catastrophe insurance, it is better to take measures from the perspective of consumer demand (such as insurance vouchers, discussed below) than to refrain insurers' incentives to underwrite policies and distort risk signals provided by actuarially based premiums. As a Chinese proverb has it, "you can't expect the horse to run fast when you don't let it graze." Government cannot expect the insurers to underwrite policyholders' risks if it does not let them make profits.

Encouraging Disaster Mitigation Activities. Disaster mitigation activities can benefit both the policyholders and insurers because they decrease costs of the catastrophe insurance system in the long run. The government should encourage disaster mitigation policies which include but are not limited to conducting natural disaster risk investigation and zoning; establishing natural disaster monitoring systems and early-warning systems; implementing building code standards; pushing forward natural disaster prevention projects; and investing in public protection infrastructure (Paudel, 2012).

Government Responsibilities under Principle 2
Establishing a Mandatory Catastrophe Insurance System. Probably one of the most debated issues in establishing catastrophe insurance systems is whether they should be mandatory. Unlike private insurers, the government or lawmakers have the power to compel consumers to participate in insurance programs, no matter whether those programs are government-run or private-run insurance (Moss, 2004, pp. 49–50). Opponents and proponents both propose a lot of arguments to justify their propositions.[21] Generally speaking, the potential challenges associated with the mandatory catastrophe insurance system include (i) violating contract freedom, (ii) cross-subsidization, and (iii) anticompetition. In contrast, the potential benefits generally include (i) correcting irrational behaviors to justify violating contract freedom, (ii) managing adverse selection to justify cross-subsidization, (iii) enhancing national solidarity to justify anticompetition, and (iv) promoting damage mitigation. Although there are several (potential) challenges to a mandatory insurance system, the advantages often justify this system.

More importantly, due to the low-probability nature of catastrophe risks and the reliance on government bailouts under the Whole-Nations System, Chinese consumers have very weak incentives to purchase catastrophe insurance products. In addition, consumers everywhere do not always behave rationally and maximize their expected utility to protect themselves from catastrophe losses by buying insurance. As a result of myopic loss aversion, prior to a disaster, consumers believe that natural disasters will not happen to them (Benartzi & Thaler, 1995). Prospect theory also explains that consumers regard the premium as a certain loss which is more painful than possible future gains (Kahneman & Tversky, 1979).

Solving the Affordability Problem. When deciding to establish a mandatory catastrophe insurance system, there is an obvious tension between a high-risk-based premium and affordability, given the severity and spatial correlation of catastrophe losses (Kousky & Kunreuther, 2014). The pricing debate over the National Flood Insurance Program in the United States is a vivid example of this tension. On March 21, 2014, President Obama signed the Homeowner Flood Insurance Affordability Act of 2014, which responded to political complaints of "unaffordability" by repealing and softening certain provisions of the Biggert-Waters Flood Insurance Reform Act of 2012, which moved toward premiums reflecting risk (FEMA, 2014). As a developing country, the affordability problem is even more severe in China.

A government may provide basic coverage for residents. The basic coverage of catastrophe losses as part of social safety net programs could be justified because the public social insurance is insufficient in China (Cummins & Mahul, 2009, pp. 81−83). However, it should be implemented via ex ante catastrophe insurance rather than compensating victims directly via the ex post Whole-Nation System, which faces severe problems of many types. From this perspective, outsourcing coverage via purchasing insurance may be more efficient.

Ideally, coverage of catastrophe losses can be regarded as an integrated system consisting of different layers. Government coverage is just the first layer, and the remaining layers supplied by private insurers can cover broader exposures. In this instance, to solve the affordability problem of poor people, the government could supply insurance vouchers rather than traditional direct-premium subsidies to insurance buyers.[22] Direct-premium subsidies that depress premiums "tend to have highly distortional implications for the insurance markets and risk management behavior of the policyholders" (Cummins & Mahul, 2009, pp. 82−83). The US Crop Insurance Program and India's National Agricultural Insurance Scheme are two examples demonstrating the imperfection of direct-premium subsidy (Cummins & Mahul, 2009, pp. 82−83). The problems of direct-premium subsidies include criticisms that (i) they are untargeted and available to all policyholders, without distinction between low-income households and high-income households; (ii) they tend to become permanent, even though the government initially introduces them as temporary subsidies; (iii) they put an increasing fiscal burden on the government as the scope of the subsidy creeps up; and (iv) they mainly benefit policyholders located in high-risk zones (Cummins & Mahul, 2009, pp. 82–83).

In contrast, insurance vouchers that recipients can use like cash but only to buy qualifying insurance could help secure risk-based premiums, assure that insurers play their desired role, and also solve the affordability problem for low-income households (Kousky & Kunreuther, 2014; Kunreuther, 2008; Michel-Kerjan, Czajkowski, & Kunreuther, 2014). Unlike a direct-premium subsidy, means-tested insurance vouchers assure that recipients use the funds for obtaining insurance, without distorting the insurance premium reflecting risk (Kunreuther, 2008). The amount of voucher can be determined by using a sliding scale based on annual family income, and a voucher program could be coupled with mitigation requirements so as to reduce future disaster losses (Kousky & Kunreuther, 2014). In the United States, there are several kinds of well-functioning voucher programs, such as the Housing Choice Voucher Program, the Food Stamp Program, the Low-Income Home Energy Assistance Program, and the Universal Service Fund (Kousky & Kunreuther, 2014). The design of insurance vouchers can draw lessons from them.

Government Responsibilities under Principle 3
Principle 3 reflects the need to reform the current catastrophe disaster compensation arrangements under the Whole-Nation System to enhance the collaboration between the insurance industry and the government. Therefore, some arrangements of the Whole-Nation System should be reformed – such as counterpart aid – to avoid crowding-out private insurance.

How to coordinate the Whole-Nation System and market-based catastrophe insurance depends on whether relief under the Whole-Nation System crowds out private insurance transactions. Basic rational choice theory tells us that if individuals treat ad hoc relief from the Whole-Nation System as a substitute for insurance, they will underinsure or fail to insure at all (Kaplow, 1991; Kelly & Kleffner, 2003; Lewis & Nickerson, 1989; Raschky, Schwarze, Schwindt, & Zahn, 2013). According to the empirical studies on different postdisaster relief schemes comparing Austria, where governmental relief is certain but incomplete, and Germany, where governmental relief is uncertain but more complete, the results show that "expected governmental relief has a strong crowding-out effect on insurance demand and this effect is even more pronounced when governmental relief is more certain" (Raschky et al., 2013). In other words, the government relief scheme of Austria has a stronger crowding-out effect for market-based insurance because of its certainty. Unfortunately, China's Whole-Nation System is more like the Austrian than the German model. It means that, under the Whole-Nation System, even introducing market-based catastrophe insurance may not play an expected and desired role. Counterpart aid in the form of direct disaster grants to affected households is an example. This form of assistance is likely to crowd out private insurance markets, according to American data.

For example, an empirical study suggests that the direct disaster grants of the US Federal Emergency Management Agency (FEMA) have a statistically significant negative impact on average coverage per policy. Kousky et al. state, "A $1,000 increase in the average IA [Individual Assistance program] grant decreases average insurance coverage by roughly $6,400" (Kousky, Michel-Kerjan, & Raschky, 2014). However, the volume of Small Business Administration disaster loans has no significant effect (Kousky et al., 2014). In other words, government loans induce less crowd-out than direct grants (Kousky et al., 2014). Counterpart aid under the Whole-Nation System operates much like disaster grants from the IA program and thus would create substantial crowding-out of market-based insurance. Government loans, however, even at a low interest rate, will induce less crowding-out of insurance than direct disaster grants. Therefore, the form of counterpart aid could be changed into government loans rather than direct disaster grants.

CONCLUSION

Government is playing an expanding role in catastrophe disaster aid, relief, and compensation around the world. The spent money is sharply rising, and this trend is evident in the United States, European countries, and many others (Cummins, Suher, & Zanjani, 2010, European Commission, 2013). The same is happening in China, where government traditionally plays a fundamental role in dealing with catastrophe disasters.

Based on the above analysis, we may admit that the Whole-Nation System is necessary because it works well in the short run as emergency relief, especially in the absence of a catastrophe insurance market. In addition, the government continues this system because it helps the government gain support from the people.[23] When disaster provides a unique opportunity for the government to show its responsibility and accountability, it is not difficult to imagine that the Whole-Nation System, with its powerful capability, increases people's support for the government. If only for political expediency, it is hard to believe that the Chinese government will totally give up the Whole-Nation System, even if it has a lot of problems.

Nonetheless, the Whole-Nation System needs reform. It might be appropriate to combine the Whole-Nation System with catastrophe insurance to marry the merits of both private market and public government. It seems clear that the Whole-Nation System mainly works well in emergency relief. Beyond that, the government should encourage catastrophe insurance to be responsible for risk finance and loss compensation and support insurance in that role.

Alford once raised the question in *Prospects for the Professions in China* regarding "whether developing countries have a fateful choice: to embrace Western models of professional organization as they now exist, or to set off on an independent path, adapting elements of Western practices to their own historical and cultural situation?"(Alford, Kirby, & Winston, 2010, p. 2). Though the answer may be "blowing in the wind," I wish that the proposed catastrophe insurance market-enhancing framework could help capture some part of that answer. Hopefully, it could shed light on solving the universal dilemma of how to manage catastrophe risk efficiently and cover disaster losses fairly.

NOTES

1. "Socialism with Chinese characteristics" is a grand but marvelously vague expression. It was first raised by reformist politician Deng Xiaoping in 1984, and it stretches the acceptable ideological framework to allow the country to pursue policies that worked (Vogel, 2011, p. 465).

2. Based on the regression analysis of natural disaster occurrence and average global temperature from 1980 to 2010, the frequency of epidemics, extreme temperature, floods, and storms was projected to increase by 506 times per year if the average global temperature increases by 1 °C (Xubin, Danna, Xuejun, & Patton, 2011).

3. Budget revenues increased from 10.8 percent of GDP in 1995 to 22.6 percent of GDP in 2012, and the annual GDP growth average 9.8 percent over the period (Naughton, 2014).

4. Under China's authoritarian regime, the political selection of officers depends on a competitive political tournament. Therefore, the governors of provinces have

incentives to perform better in counterpart aid to attract the attention of the central government (Zhou, 2014).

5. China's economic transition process is known as the "dual-track system" which differs from "shock therapy." The dual-track system refers to the process of moving from a single track, planned economic system to a combination system and finally to the single track of a market system. Under the dual-track system, market prices of goods during the transition are obviously higher than the planned prices because planned prices are artificially suppressed by the government. Furthermore, the government regulates market access to placate "legacy" suppliers. These market distortions too often lead to rent-seeking and corruption (Lin, 2012, pp. 194–198).

6. For example, officials have the power to grant permits for a variety of businesses such as land acquisitions or construction. They may ask for direct payments but also share in the company, property at below market price, lavish dinners, and others. Such practices are so widespread, and so many officials and their family members are involved, that those corruption problems are extremely difficult to solve (Vogel, 2011, p. 712).

7. For example, then-premier Wen Jiabao arrived at the affected areas to command disaster relief just 8 hours after the 2008 Sichuan Earthquake. However, after less than a month, he had to go back to Beijing to deal with other national affairs and paid less and less attention to earthquake relief after the emergency work was accomplished (China News, 2008).

8. It is based on an old parable of the traveler from Samaria who helped a stranger whom he found beaten and robbed by the side of the road.

9. The other two are risk assessment [also known as risk analysis] and risk control.

10. The total fiscal revenues are around $1 trillion in 2008 (Jiang et al., 2008, p. 36).

11. The National Finance Working Conference is the supreme financial conference in China, which decides on the most important financial issues, such as establishing the China Insurance Regulation Commission (CIRC).

12. However, there are no details on how the government will establish the system, how much government will subsidize policyholders, how insurers should underwrite for the catastrophe events, or many other technical questions.

13. For example, The Deposit Insurance System and the U.S. Federal Deposit Insurance Corporation were established, in order to prevent the type of mass banking panic that crippled the American financial system in the early 1930s, and to protect depositors and maintain confidence in the banking system (Baker & Moss, 2009); The Federal Crop Insurance Program (FCIP), which is administered by the Federal Crop Insurance Corporation (FCIC), within the USDA's Risk Management Agency, was established in the face of potentially catastrophic weather risks (Barnett, 1999); The Terrorism Risk Insurance Act (TRIA) was passed in November 2002, which provided government reinsurance; and, the National Flood Insurance Program (NFIP) was established and sponsored by the federal government (Jaffee & Russell, 2013).

14. The TCIP is managed by a board of seven members; insurance companies cede 100 percent of all risk to the pool; the adjustment of claims is done by independent loss adjustors; and the full risk capital requirements of TCIP are funded

through commercial reinsurance, including Milli Re and Munich Re (Von Lucius, 2004).

15. Simply speaking, the main experiences of China's "miracle" development are: (i) well-functioning competitive markets, which are the precondition for developing a country's industries because only with such a market can prices reflect scarcities of production in the economy and propel firms to enter industries; (ii) a proactive, facilitating government, which is equally important because, for transitional countries, the government should seize and capture the advantages of late-comers through playing a role in information collection, coordination, and compensation for externalities (Lin, 2013).

16. The Chinese approach strives to institute a new hybrid system, which, indeed, is the market-enhancing approach. China does not follow shock therapy – a policy recommendation based on orthodox economic theory – promoting economic liberalization and privatization, which is more or less the application of the laissez-faire theory. The failure of Russian's transition, a typical example of shock therapy, however, reveals that the liberalization-cum-privatization approach does not automatically bring about efficient and sustainable market structures. China's success and Russia's failure prove that maybe for developed countries the government should interfere less, but for transitional countries, a minimalist government is not optimal. On the other hand, a strong, proactive and facilitating state could start and enhance genuine market-oriented reforms, because the leaders of China recognize that only genuine market reforms and sustained economic growth which benefits all strata of society – not only the political elite and big business – can supply their political legitimacy. Following this direction, it differs from the public-interest theory, which requires the government to act as a substitute for private sectors (Ahrens, 2007; Lin, 2011).

17. Based on the comparative analysis of types of systems in different countries, the ideal standard consists of the following features: (i) be financially sustainable, (ii) have adequate policies for preventing and mitigating risks, and (iii) be able to provide affordable insurance with low management expenses to a broad public in hazard-prone areas (Paudel, 2012; Skees & Barnett, 1999).

18. For example, in France and Japan, where catastrophe coverage is mandatory, all catastrophe insurance policies written by private insurers are reinsured by the government-run reinsurance company, which essentially serves as guarantor for all policies written. In the US, according to the requirement of Terrorism Risk Insurance Act in November 2002, the federal government agreed to provide a kind of reinsurance "backstop" for terrorism losses (Nektarios, 2011; Russell & Thomas, 2008).

19. "It is designed to complement existing private-sector insurance and reinsurance mechanisms by covering only layers of reinsurance currently unavailable in the private market" (Lewis & Murdock, 1999).

20. "In general, the fully public private insurance systems have not integrated risk-based premiums and financial incentives for mitigation."

21. A summary literature overview of the debate is as follows: Kunreuther proposed a mandatory model as early as 1968. This opinion was repeated by some other scholars, especially after Hurricane Katrina, and also received support from European scholars. See Kunreuther (1968), Kunreuther and Pauly (2006), and Telesetsky (2010). European scholarship includes: Schwarze and Wagner (2004),

Faure (2007), and Faure and Bruggeman (2008). On the other hand, some literature indicates the potential dangers to mandatory insurance system, such as regulatory paternalism, anticompetition, overgeneralization, etc. See Ogus (2005) and Harrington (2000).

22. Direct-premium subsidy is often an arrangement where 50% of the risk-based premium is paid by the policyholders and the rest may be paid by government (Cummins & Mahul, 2009, pp. 82–83).

23. The impact of natural disasters on support for authorities is conditional on governmental performance during and after the shock. For a transitional state like China, government's legitimacy depends on not only its economic performance but also its response and accountability to the people. A similar example presents in Russia. According to an empirical study conducted in the areas affected by the disaster over the course of the summer of 2011 in Russia, it indicates that active government performance and generous aid increase loyalty to the authorities among people directly affected by the disaster (Lazarev et al., 2014).

REFERENCES

Abousleiman, I., Calderón, C., Cordella, T., & Yeyati, E. L. (2007). *Country insurance: Reducing systemic vulnerabilities in LAC*. Washington, DC: World Bank Publishing.

Abraham, K. S. (1985). Efficiency and fairness in insurance risk classification. *Virginia Law Review, 71*, 403–451.

Ahrens, J. (2007). Governance in the process of economic transformation. *System Transformation in comparative perspective. Affinity and diversity in institutional, structural and cultural patterns*. Berlin: LIT Verlag. Retrieved from http://www.researchgate.net/publication/228858828_Governance_in_the_process_of_economic_transformation

Ahrens, J., & Mengeringhaus, P. (2006). Institutional change and economic transition: Market-enhancing governance, Chinese-style. *European Journal of Comparative Economics, 3*(1), 75–102.

Alford, W. P., Kirby, W., & Winston, K. (Eds.). (2010). *Prospects for the professions in China*. London: Routledge.

Anderson, W. A. (1970). Military organizations in natural disaster: Established and emergent norms. *American Behavioral Scientist, 13*(3), 415–422.

Aoki, M., Murdock, K., & Okuno-Fujiwara, M. (1998). Beyond the East Asian miracle: Introducing the market-enhancing view. *The role of government in East Asian economic development* (pp. 1–33). Oxford: Oxford University Press.

Arrow, K. J. (1963). Uncertainty and the welfare economics of medical care. *The American Economic Review, 53*, 941–973.

Avraham, R., Logue, K. D., & Schwarcz, D. (2014). Understanding insurance antidiscrimination law. *Southern California Law Review, 87*, 195–274.

Baker, T., & Moss, D. (I 2009). Government as risk manager. In D. Moss & J. Cisternino (Eds.), *New perspectives on regulation* (pp. 87–109). Cambridge, MA: The Tobin Project, Inc.

Banks, W. (2006). Who's in charge: The role of the military in disaster response. *Mississippi College Law Review, 26*, 75–105.

Barnett, B. J. (1999). US government natural disaster assistance: Historical analysis and a proposal for the future. *Disasters, 23*(2), 139–155.

Barry, F. (2000). Government consumption and private investment in closed and open economies. *Journal of Macroeconomics, 21*(1), 93–106.

Beicuan County. (2012). *Annual fiscal report of Beicuan county.* Retrieved from http://www.beichuan.gov.cn/html/2013/gsgg_0529/10227.html?cid=11

Ben-Shahar, O., & Logue, K. D. (2012). Outsourcing regulation: How insurance reduces moral hazard. *Michigan Law Review, 111*(2), 197–248.

Benartzi, S., & Thaler, R. H. (1995). Myopic loss aversion and the equity premium puzzle. *Quarterly Journal of Economics, 110,* 73–92.

Bruggeman, V. (2010). *Compensating catastrophe victims: A comparative law and economics approach.* Leiden: Kluwer Law International.

Buchanan, J. M. (1972). The samaritan's dilemma. *Altruism, morality and economic theory* (pp. 71–85). New York, NY: Russel Sage foundation.

Chen, S., Luo, Z., & Pan, X. (2013). Natural disasters in China: 1900–2011. *Natural Hazards, 69,* 1597–1605.

Chen, W. (2008). Zhijing! Xinshiqi zuikeai de ren [Pay tribute to the most beloved people in the new period]. *Dangshi Yanjiu [Journal of Party History], 8,* 1–5.

China News. (2008). *Wen Jiabao: Please remember the great Sichuan earthquake.* Retrieved from http://www.chinanews.com/gn/news/2008/05-24/1260997.shtml

CIRC. (2000). *The notice of regulating approving procedure of extended earthquake insurance in enterprise property insurance policy.* Retrieved from http://www.chinalawedu.com/news/1200/21829/21838/21979/2006/3/pa135912281516136024334-0.htm

CIRC. (2008). *China Insurance Regulation Committee (CIRC): The volumes of yearbook of China insurance 2008.* Beijing: Yearbook of China Insurance Press.

CIRC. (2009). *China Insurance Regulation Committee (CIRC): The volumes of yearbook of China insurance 2009.* Beijing: Yearbook of China Insurance Press.

CIRC. (2010). *China Insurance Regulation Committee (CIRC): The volumes of yearbook of China insurance 2010.* Beijing: Yearbook of China Insurance Press.

CIRC. (2011). *China Insurance Regulation Committee (CIRC): The volumes of yearbook of China insurance 2011.* Beijing: Yearbook of China Insurance Press.

Coase, R. H. (1960). The problem of social cost. *Journal of Law and Economics, 3,* 1–44.

Cummins, J. D., & Mahul, O. (2009). *Catastrophe risk financing in developing countries: Principles for public intervention.* Washington, DC: World Bank Publications.

Cummins, J. D., Suher, M., & Zanjani, G. (2010). Federal financial exposure to natural catastrophe risk. *Measuring and managing federal financial risk* (pp. 61–92). Chicago, IL: University of Chicago Press.

Dalen, K., Flatø, H., Jing, L., & Huafeng, Z. (2012). *Recovering from the Wenchuan earthquake. Living conditions and development in disaster areas 2008–2011.* Fafo-report 2012: 39. Oslo: FAFO.

Epstein, R. A. (1996). Catastrophic responses to catastrophic risks. *Journal of Risk and Uncertainty, 12*(2–3), 287–308.

European Commission. (2013). *Disaster risk reduction: Increasing resilience by reducing disaster risk in humanitarian action.* Retrieved from http://ec.europa.eu/echo/files/policies/prevention_preparedness/DRR_thematic_policy_doc.pdf

Faure, M., & Bruggeman, V. (2008). Catastrophic risks and first-party insurance. *Connecticut Insurance Law Journal, 15,* 1–52.

Faure, M., & Heine, K. (2011). Insurance against financial crises. *NYU Journal of Law and& Business, 8*, 117–150.

Faure, M. G. (2007). Insurability of damage caused by climate change: A commentary. *University of Pennsylvania Law Review, 155*, 1875–1899.

FEMA. (2014). *Homeowner flood insurance affordability act: Overview.* Retrieved from http://www.fema.gov/media-library-data/1396551935597-4048b68f6d695a6eb6e6e7118d3ce464/HFIAA_Overview_FINAL_03282014.pdf

Fravel, M. T. (2011). Economic growth, regime insecurity, and military strategy: Explaining the rise of noncombat operations in China. *Asian Security, 7*(3), 177–200.

GFDRR. (2011). *Turkish catastrophe insurance pool.* Retrieved from http://www.gfdrr.org/sites/gfdrr.org/files/documents/DFI_TCIP__Jan11.pdf

Gurenko, E., Lester, R., Mahul, O., & Gonulal, S. O. (2006). *Earthquake insurance in Turkey: History of the Turkish catastrophe insurance pool.* Washington, DC: World Bank Publications.

Harrington, S. E. (2000). Rethinking disaster policy. *Regulation, 23*, 40–47.

Hellmann, T., Murdock, K., & Stiglitz, J. (1998). Financial restraint and the market enhancing view. *IEA conference volume series* (Vol. 127, pp. 255–279). London: The Macmillan Press Ltd.

Hu, J. (2008). Zai Quanguo Kangzhen Jiuzai Zongjie Biaozhang Dahui Shangde Jianghua [Address on the National Earthquake Relief Summary Commendation Conference]. Beijing: People's Publishing House.

Hua, Z. (2010). Duikou Zhiyuan Cujin Jiben Gonggong Fuwu Zhundenghua Xiaoying Fenxi [The effects analysis of counterpart support to the equalization of basic public services – Taking earthquake-stricken areas of Sichuan as a case]. *Xi'an Caijing Xueyuan Xuebao [Journal of Xi'an University of Finance and Economics], 5*, 75–81.

Huber, M. (2004). Insurability and regulatory reform: Is the English flood insurance regime able to adapt to climate change? *Geneva Papers on Risk and Insurance Issues and Practice, 29*, 169–182.

IPCC. (2012). Summary for policymakers. In C. B. Field, V. Barros, T. F. Stocker, T. F. Qin, Dokken D. J., Ebi K. L., Mastrandrea M. D., Mach K.J., Plattner G.-K., Allen S.K., Tignor M., and Midgley P.M. (Eds.), *Managing the risks of extreme events and disasters to advance climate change adaptation* (pp. 3–21). Cambridge: Cambridge University (Special Report of Working Groups I and II of the Intergovernmental Panel on Climate Change).

IPCC. (2014). *Climate change 2014: Impacts, adaptation, and vulnerability.* Retrieved from http://www.ipcc.ch/report/ar5/wg2/

Jaffee, D., & Russell, T. (1997). Catastrophe insurance, capital markets, and uninsurable risks. *Journal of Risk and Insurance, 64*(2), 205–230.

Jaffee, D., & Russell, T. (2013). The welfare economics of catastrophe losses and insurance. *The Geneva Papers on Risk and Insurance – Issues and Practice, 38*(3), 469–494.

Jiang, L., Wang, J., & Liu, L. (2008). *People's Republic of China: Providing emergency response to Wenchuan earthquake (Technical assistance consultant's report).* Beijing: Ministry of Civil Affairs, People's Republic of China, and Asian Development Bank.

Kahneman, D., & Tversky, A. (1979). Prospect theory: An analysis of decision under risk. *Econometrica, 47*, 263–291.

Kaplow, L. (1991). Incentives and government relief for risk. *Journal of Risk and Uncertainty, 4*(2), 167–175.

Kelly, M., & Kleffner, A. E. (2003). Optimal loss mitigation and contract design. *Journal of Risk and Insurance, 70*(1), 53–72.

Kent, E. F. (2006). Where's the cavalry-federal response to 21st century disasters. *Suffolk University Law Review, 40*, 181–213.

King, R. O. (2005). *Hurricanes and disaster risk financing through insurance: Challenges and policy options.* Washington, DC: Congressional Information Service, Library of Congress.

Korczyk, S. M. (2005). *Insuring the uninsurable: Private insurance markets and government intervention in cases of extreme risk.* Indianapolis, IN: National Association of Mutual Insurance Companies.

Kousky, C., & Kunreuther, H. (2014). Addressing affordability in the national flood insurance program. *Journal of Extreme Events, 1*(01), 145–173.

Kousky, C., Michel-Kerjan, E. O., & Raschky, P. (2014). *Does federal disaster assistance crowd out private demand for insurance?* Retrieved from http://opim.wharton.upenn.edu/risk/library/WP201404_CK-EMK-PAR_Does-assistance-crowd-out-insurance.pdf

Kunreuther, H. (1968). The case for comprehensive disaster insurance. *Journal of Law and Economics, 11*, 133–163.

Kunreuther, H. (1996). Mitigating disaster losses through insurance. *Journal of Risk and Uncertainty, 12*(2–3), 171–187.

Kunreuther, H. (2008). Reducing losses from catastrophic risks through long-term insurance and mitigation. *Social Research: An International Quarterly, 75*(3), 905–930.

Kunreuther, H. C., & Michel-Kerjan, E. O. (2007). Climate change, insurability of large-scale disasters and the emerging liability challenge. *University of Pennsylvania Law Review, 155*, 1795–1842.

Kunreuther, H., & Michel-Kerjan, E. (2013). Managing catastrophic risks through redesigned insurance: Challenges and opportunities. In *Handbook of insurance* (pp. 517–546). New York, NY: Springer.

Kunreuther, H., & Pauly, M. (2006). Rules rather than discretion: Lessons from Hurricane Katrina. *Journal of Risk and Uncertainty, 33*(1–2), 101–116.

Lazarev, E., Sobolev, A., Soboleva, I. V., & Sokolov, B. (2014). Trial by fire: A natural disaster's impact on support for the authorities in rural Russia. *World Politics, 66*(04), 641–668.

Lewis, C. M., & Murdock, K. C. (1996). The role of government contracts in discretionary reinsurance markets for natural disasters. *Journal of Risk and Insurance, 63*, 567–597.

Lewis, C., & Murdock, K. C. (1999). Alternative means of redistributing catastrophic risk in a national risk-management system. In *The financing of catastrophe risk* (pp. 51–92). Chicago, IL: University of Chicago Press.

Lewis, T., & Nickerson, D. (1989). Self-insurance against natural disasters. *Journal of Environmental Economics and Management, 16*(3), 209–223.

Lin, J. Y. (2011). New structural economics: A framework for rethinking development. *The World Bank Research Observer, 26*, 193–221.

Lin, J. Y. (2012). Demystifying the Chinese economy. Cambridge: Cambridge University Press.

Lin, J. Y. (2013). *Demystifying the Chinese economy. Australian Economic Review, 46*(3), 259–268.

Michel-Kerjan, E., Czajkowski, J., & Kunreuther, H. (2014). Could flood insurance be privatized in the United States? A primer. *The Geneva Papers on Risk and Insurance-Issues and Practice, 39*, 651–667.

Michel-Kerjan, E., Zelenko, I., & Cardenas, V. D. T. (2011). *Catastrophe financing for governments: Learning from the 2009—2012 multicat program in Mexico.* Joint Working Paper OECD—Wharton Risk Center—World Bank Treasury. OECD Publishing.

Ministry of the Civil Affairs. (1998). *The statistics report of the civil affairs development.* Retrieved from http://cws.mca.gov.cn/article/tjbg/200801/20080100009419.shtml

Moss, D. (2004). *When all else fails: Government as the ultimate risk manager.* Cambridge, MA: Harvard University Press.

Moss, D. (2010). The peculiar politics of American disaster policy: How television has changed federal relief. In E. Michel-Kerjan & P. Slovic (Eds.), *The irrational economist: Making decisions in a dangerous world* (pp. 151–160). New York, NY: Public Affairs Press.

Naughton, B. (2014). China's economy: Complacency, crisis & the challenge of reform. *Daedalus, 143*(2), 14–25.

Nektarios, M. (2011). A catastrophe insurance system for the European Union. *Asia-Pacific Journal of Risk and Insurance, 5*(2), Art. 6, 1–22.

Ni, F., Zhang, Y., & Tongzhou, Y. (2009). Wenchuan Dadizhen Duikou Zhiyuan Chubu Yanjiu [Preliminary research on counterpart aid of Wenchuan Earthquake]. *Jingji Guanli Yu Yanjiu [Research on Economics and Management], 7,* 55–62.

Ogus, A. (2005). Regulatory paternalism: When is it justified? In *Corporate governance in context: Corporations, States, and markets in Europe, Japan and the US* (pp. 303–320). Oxford: OUP.

ONCDR (Office of National Commission for Disaster Reduction, P. R. China). (2012). China's natural disaster risk management. In *Improving the assessment of disaster risks to strengthen financial resilience* (pp. 121–131). Beijing: A Special Joint G20 Publication by the Government of Mexico and the World Bank.

Outreville, F. (1998). *Theory and practice of insurance.* New York, NY: Kluwer Academic Publishers.

Paudel, Y. (2012). A comparative study of public—private catastrophe insurance systems: Lessons from current practices. *The Geneva Papers on Risk and Insurance-Issues and Practice, 37*(2), 257–285.

People's Banks of China. (1996). *Notice on the term, rate and provision interpretation of <property basic insurance> and <property comprehensive insurance>.* Retrieved from http://law.baidu.com/000570240002206ed685b5a29b1feb0fd7ae84890045.html

Perry, E. J. (2014). Growing pains: Challenges for a rising China. *Daedalus, 143*(2), 5–13.

Priest, G. L. (1996). The government, the market, and the problem of catastrophic loss. *Journal of Risk and Uncertainty, 12*(2–3), 219–237.

Priest, G. L. (2003). Government insurance versus market insurance. *Geneva Papers on Risk and Insurance. Issues and Practice, 28,* 71–80.

Qin, D., Ding, Y., Su, J., Ren, J., Wang, S., Wu, R., ... Luo, Y. (2005). Assessment of climate and environment changes in China (I): Climate and environment changes in China and their projection [J]. *Advances in Climate Change Research, 1*(002), 4–9.

Raschky, P. A., Schwarze, R., Schwindt, M., & Zahn, F. (2013). Uncertainty of governmental relief and the crowding out of flood insurance. *Environmental and Resource Economics, 54*(2), 179–200.

Reuters. (2014). *China says testing catastrophe insurance system.* Retrieved from http://www.businessinsurance.com/article/20140820/NEWS04/140829990?AllowView=VDl3UXk1T3hDUFNCbkJiYkY1TDJaRUt0ajBRV0ErOVVHUT09#

Roth, R. J., Sr & Kunreuther, H. (Eds.). (1998). *Paying the price: The status and role of insurance against natural disasters in the United States.* Washington, DC: Joseph Henry Press.

Russell, T., & Thomas, J. E. (2008). Government support for terrorism insurance. *Connecticut Insurance Law Journal, 15,* 183−209.

Scales, A. F. (2006). A nation of policyholders: Governmental and market failure in flood insurance. *Mississippi College Law Review, 26,* 3−47.

Schwarze, R., & Wagner, G. G. (2004). In the aftermath of Dresden: New directions in German flood insurance. *The Geneva Papers on Risk and Insurance Issues and Practice, 29*(2), 154−168.

Shandong Province. (2012). *Annual fiscal report of Shandong province.* Retrieved from http://www.mof.gov.cn/zhuantihuigu/2013ssyshb/201302/t20130219_733742.html

Shi, P. J., Tang, D., Liu, J., Chen, B., & Zhou, M. Q. (2008). Natural disaster insurance: Issues and strategy of China. In *Asian catastrophe insurance* (pp. 79−93). London: Risk Books.

Shi, P. J., & Zhang, X. (2013). Chinese mechanism against catastrophe risk − The experience of great Sichuan earthquake. *Journal of Tsinghua University (Philosophy and Social Sciences), 28,* 96−113.

Skees, J. R., & Barnett, B. J. (1999). Conceptual and practical considerations for sharing catastrophic/systemic risks. *Review of Agricultural Economics, 21*(2), 424−441.

Sundermann, L., Schelske, O., Hausmann, P., Reichenmiller, P., Fehr, K., & Leimbacher, U. (2013). Mind the risk: A global ranking of cities under threat from natural disasters. Zurich: Swiss Reinsurance Company.

Swiss Re. (2008). Disaster risk financing: Reducing the burden on public budgets. Swiss Re Focus Report.

TCIP. (2012). *Turkish catastrophe insurance pool English annual reports.* Retrieved from http://www.tcip.gov.tr/content/annualReport/2012_Annual_Report_DASK.pdf

Telesetsky, A. (2010). Insurance as a mitigation mechanism: Managing international greenhouse gases through nationwide mandatory climate change catastrophe insurance. *Pace Environmental Law Review, 27*(3), 691−734.

The State Council. (2008). *Notice on the state council overall planning for post-great Sichuan earthquake restoration and reconstruction.* Retrieved from http://www.gov.cn/zwgk/2008-09/23/content_1103686.htm

Thoyts, R. (2010). *Insurance theory and practice.* London: Routledge.

Tian, L., & Zhang, Y. (2013). Woguo Juzai Baoxian Xuqiu Yingxiang Yinsu Shizheng Yanjiu: Jiyu Wusheng Bufen Baofei Shouru Mianban Yanjiu [Influence factors of catastrophe insurance demand in China − Panel analysis in a case of insurance premium income of five provinces]. *Wuhan University of Technology (Social Science Edition) [Wuhan Ligong Daxue Xuebao (Shehui Kexue Ban)],* 26(2), 175−179.

Van Alphen, J., Martini, F., Loat, R., Slomp, R., & Passchier, R. (2009). Flood risk mapping in Europe, experiences and best practices. *Journal of Flood Risk Management, 2*(4), 285−292.

Van den Bergh, R., & Faure, M. (2006). Compulsory insurance of loss to property caused by natural disasters: Competition or solidarity? *World Competition, 29*(1), 25.

Vaughan, E. J., & Vaughan, T. (2007). *Fundamentals of risk and insurance.* Hoboken, NJ: Wiley.

Vogel, E. F. (2011). *Deng Xiaoping and the transformation of China.* Cambridge, MA: Belknap Press of Harvard University Press.

Von Lucius, J. A. (2004). A reinsurer's perspective on the Turkish Catastrophe Insurance Pool (TCIP). *Catastrophe risk and reinsurance: A country risk management perspective* (pp. 217–224). Washington, DC: World Bank Publications.

Wang, F., & Yin, H. (2012). A new form of governance or the reunion of the government and business sector? A case analysis of the collaborative natural disaster insurance system in the Zhejiang province of China. *International Public Management Journal, 15*(4), 429–453.

Wang, H. (2013). *Research on catastrophe risk insurance mechanisms*. Beijing: China Financial Publishing House.

Wang, Y. (2007). *Legislative background and overall thinking on emergency response law*. Retrieved from http://www.gdemo.gov.cn/yjpx/ztjz/200712/t20071210_37179.htm

Wei, Y. M., Jin, J. L., & Wang, Q. (2014). Impacts of natural disasters and disaster risk management in China: The case of China's experience in the Wenchuan Earthquake. *Resilience and recovery in Asian disasters* (pp. 287–307). Japan: Springer.

Wittfogel, K. (1957). *Oriental despotism: A comparative study of total power*. New Haven, CT: Yale University Press; London: Oxford University Press.

World Bank. (2008). *The World Bank group's catastrophe risk financing products and services*. Washington, DC: World Bank Publishing.

Xinhua News Agency. (2008). *Central government appropriated $400 million to earthquake relief*. Retrieved from http://news.xinhuanet.com/newscenter/2008-05/15/content_8180172.htm

Xinhua News Agency. (2013). *China ranks no. 4 in the world for insurance premiums revenue*. Retrieved from http://www.gov.cn/xinwen/2014-07/09/content_2714415.htm

Xu, X., & Mo, J. (2013). The impact of disaster relief on economic growth: Evidence from China. *The Geneva Papers on Risk and Insurance-Issues and Practice, 38*(3), 495–520.

Xubin, P., Danna, S., Xuejun, D., & Patton, B. (2011). Natural disaster occurrence and average global temperature. *Disaster Advances, 4*(4), 61–63.

Zhang, J. (2014). The military and disaster relief in China: Trends, drivers and implications. In M. Sakai, E. Jurriëns, J. Zhang, & A. Thornton (Eds.), *Disaster relief in the Asia Pacific: Agency and resilience* (Vol. 79, pp. 69–85). London: Routledge.

Zhao, L., & Jiang, Y. J. (2009). Difang Zhengfu Duikou Zhiyuan Moshi Fenxi [Analysis of local government coordinated assistance modes]. *ChengDu Daxue Xuebao (Sheke Ban) [Journal of ChengDu University (Social Science Edition)]*, 2(4–7), 25.

Zhou, L. (2014). Xizheng Fabaozhi [Administrative subcontract]. *Shehui [Society]*, 6, 1–38.

Zhou, Y. (2008). *Speech at international catastrophe insurance fund management symposium*. Retrieved from http://insurance.hexun.com/2008/jzfx/index.html

Zou, M., & Yuan, Y. (2010). China's comprehensive disaster reduction. *International Journal of Disaster Risk Science, 1*(1), 24–32.

PART V
THE POLITICAL ECONOMY IN
THE EXTERNAL SECTOR

DETERMINANTS AND FLUCTUATIONS OF CHINA'S EXCHANGE RATE POLICY: NATIONAL INTERESTS AND DECISION-MAKING PROCESSES

Falin Zhang

ABSTRACT

Purpose — *Propose a more comprehensive explanation on the determinants and fluctuations of China's exchange rate policy in the past decade (2005–2015).*

Approach — *Case study on China's exchange rate policies in three respective stages since 2005 and then a comparative study on these three stages.*

Findings — *Put forward a two-pronged explanation on the determinants and fluctuations of China's exchange rate policy in the past decade and arrive at three specific conclusions. First, external pressure is only one factor among many influencing the formation of China's national interests (Guojia Liyi in Chinese) and the decision-making process on*

The Political Economy of Chinese Finance
International Finance Review, Volume 17, 343–369
Copyright © 2016 by Emerald Group Publishing Limited
ISSN: 1569-3767/doi:10.1108/S1569-376720160000017018

exchange rate policy. Second, national interest is the fundamental driving force and substratum for making China's exchange rate policy. Third, in the short term, the specific exchange rate policies in different periods were not always in accordance to the national interests (or Guojia Liyi), due to the influences of some factors on the decision-making environment.

Value — *The comprehensive view is conducive to better explaining the formation and fluctuations of China's exchange rate policy and consequently contributes to understanding and even predicting future policies.*

Keywords: China's exchange rate policy; national interest; *Guojia Liyi*; decision-making process

INTRODUCTION

China's growing economic might in the world economy and its incrementally important currency, the Renminbi (RMB or yuan), have made Chinese domestic exchange rate policy generate prodigious international spillover effects. The related literatures, therefore, have paid high attention to changes and determinants of China's exchange rate policy. Nonetheless, the mounting attention is not equal to a clearer comprehension in any sense. On the contrary, many voices have emerged, focusing on various aspects, including external pressures, domestic decision-making process and national interests and preferences.

External pressures have been considered as a key factor in forming China's exchange rate policy. Given the international spillover effects of China's exchange rate policy, such as on trade balance, employment and investment flow, major Western economies and international organizations (IOs), especially the United States and the International Monetary Fund (IMF or the Fund), have kept a close eye on China's exchange policies. Ample evidence shows that the United States has exerted pressure on China to reform its exchange rate regime. For example, the *2010 US House of Representatives Documents* denounced that China's undervalued exchange rate hurts the US economy and workers (Congressional Documents and Publications, 2010). Congressman Sander Levin, chairman of the House Ways and Means Committee, said that 'China's exchange rate policy is one of China's many mercantilist policies that distort trade and investment flows and place a drag on US economic growth and job creation' (Asia Pulse (Rhodes), 2010). Along with the Western economies, relevant IOs have also exerted pressure on China to reform its exchange rate regime towards what has been dubbed the 'Washington Consensus'. Among many IOs is the IMF, which, by and large, has claimed that the RMB is undervalued and that China's exchange rate regime needs to be reformed although the specific views of the Fund have altered in different periods. Following the 1997 Asian financial crisis during which China adopted a 'no devaluation' policy and until 2005 when the Chinese authorities launched an exchange rate reform, the IMF spoke only vaguely about the desirability of greater flexibility in the RMB's value (IMF, 2003). After China announced adoption of a managed floating exchange rate regime based on market supply and demand in 2005 and until the stagnation of this reform in 2008, the Fund lavished praise on China. From 2008 when the exchange rate reform stagnated mainly as a result of the 2008 global financial crisis to 2010 when China relaunched this reform, critical words, such as 'substantially undervalued' (IMF, 2009) or 'fundamentally misaligned' (Beattie, 2009), appeared in IMF documents or discussions assessing China's exchange rate policy. Since 2010 when China decided to return to a managed floating exchange system and further reform RMB exchange rate regime, the Fund changed its assessment on China's exchange rate from 'substantially undervalued' to 'undervalued' and recently to 'moderately undervalued' (IMF, 2012).

The continuous pressure from the United States and the related IOs and the concurrent exchange rate reform of China in the last decade lead to a plausible conclusion that international pressure drives China's exchange rate reform and compels China to be a status-quo power in global economic governance. For instance, Buckley (2012) argued 'the main factor pushing China toward RMB appreciation is US pressure, considering that China does not wish to jeopardize the stability resulting from lucrative trade with the US'. This argument, however, oversimplifies the reality. China's exchange rate policy is not a simple consequence following an antecedent. In the same vein, China cannot be categorized as a complete status-quo or revisionist power.

Another group of scholars explains China's exchange rate policies focusing on the policy-making mechanism. Specifically, the related studies mainly focus on, but are not limited to, formal and informal lobbying practices on China's exchange rate policy (Kennedy, 2009), cleavage between the Chinese Ministry of Commerce (MOFCOM) and the People's

Bank of China (PBC) (Freeman III & Yuan, 2011), influence of policy elites (Liew, 2004) and the exchange rate policy-making mechanism per se (Yi, 2007). These literatures indubitably contribute to understanding the determinants of China's exchange rate policy, but fail to put forward a comprehensive framework to explain the formation and changes of it. As Steinberg and Walter (2013, p. 27) argued, these numerous political factors, 'including the preferences of industries, policymakers, political parties as well as institutional arrangements, such as democracy, elections, the electoral system, the number of veto players and central bank independence', do not always matter, and many of them have different effects under different circumstances.

Against this backdrop, this paper puts forward a two-pronged explanation on the determinants and fluctuation of China's exchange rate policy in the past decade (2005–2015). First, drawing on the realist school of thought in international political economy (IPE), this paper argues that China's exchange rate policy is driven and determined by China's national interests (or *Guojia Liyi*[1] in Chinese) in the long run. In this period, China's *Guojia Liyi* and corresponding national objectives are to promote and maintain economic development by establishing and improving the socialist market economic system in China and enabling the market to fully play its role in resource allocation. In terms of exchange rate policy, a more specific national interest and objective is to establish and improve a managed floating exchange rate regime based on market supply and demand as well as keep the exchange rate of the currency yuan basically stable at an appropriate and balanced level. This *Guojia Liyi* is shaped by three major factors: domestic and international environment, state ideology and interpretation.

Second, from the perspective of policy analysis, in the medium or short term, specific domestic decision-making processes may conform to or violate the long-term *Guojia Liyi* due to the influence of a further set of factors, including lobbying of interest groups, institutional conflict, complexity of the issue, international pressures, emergent events and risk appetite of decision makers. Putting the two aspects together, the determinants and fluctuations of China's exchange rate policy are well explained.

The remainder of this paper proceeds in three sections. The first section examines the formation of the *Guojia Liyi* in reforming China's exchange rate regime. The following section explores the decision-making environment of China's exchange rate policy in three stages – 2005 reform, 2008 stagnation and 2010 relaunch. A final section concludes by offering implications.

FORMATION OF CHINA'S NATIONAL INTERESTS

The most important step of China's exchange rate reform in the new century is the establishment of a managed floating regime based on market supply and demand with reference to a basket of currency initiated in 2005 (PBC, 2010). As mentioned above, the United States and global financial governance institutions, particularly the IMF, had long called on China to reform its exchange rate regime. However, this reform in 2005 was not a direct result of these international pressures, but a deliberated move of the Chinese government considering China's national interest. The national interest (or *Guojia Liyi*) has prioritized economic development since the third Plenary Session of the 11th Communist Party of China (CPC) Central Committee in 1978. It has sought to promote and maintain economic development by establishing and improving the socialist market economic system while enabling the market to fully play its role in resource allocation (Xinhua, 2003). In terms of exchange rate regime, the *Decision of the Central Committee of the Communist Party of China on Some Issues Concerning the Improvement of the Socialist Market Economy* issued by the third Plenary Session of the 16th CPC Central Committee in 2003 unambiguously stipulated China's objectives as seeking to establish and improve a managed floating exchange rate regime based on market supply and demand as well as to keep the exchange rate of the currency yuan basically stable at an appropriate and balanced level. This specific *Guojia Liyi* in reforming China's exchange rate regime is determined by both material and ideational factors, mainly domestic and international political economic environment, state ideology and interpretation.

Domestic and International Environments

Domestic and international political economic environments make key policy elites realize the necessity and feasibility of exchange rate reform and exert pressure on the Chinese government to reform the problematic exchange system. The international environment and its influences on China's *Guojia Liyi* in exchange rate reform can be observed from the following three respects. First, international experiences on exchange rate reform provide key policy elites and the Chinese government both positive and negative examples and have urged China to reform. Chinese scholars widely studied successful and failed international exchange reforms,

including Asian-pacific countries like Japan (Zhu, 2007) and Australia
(Tang, 2005), some transition countries (Zhu, 2006), such as Poland, emerging countries like India (Lu & Cha, 2011), Thailand (Huang, 2006) and
Chile (Zhang, 2005) and even developed capitalist countries, such as
Germany (Liao, 2011). Poland, for example, actively launched a series of
exchange rate reforms, evolving from pegging to one single currency to a
basket of currencies and later to managed float or even free float.
Consequently, it avoided possible societal and economic instability after
the collapse of the Soviet Union. In sharp contrast, in the decade before
the 1997 Asian financial crisis, Thailand applied a pegged exchange rate
regime, in which the Exchange Equalization Fund (EEF) defended the
Baht value against the US Dollar, and was unwilling to reform the formation mechanism of its exchange rate. As a result, Thai economy had
suffered catastrophically from the 1997 Asian financial crisis. Second, as
the recovery of Asian economies from the 1997 Asian crisis, the 'no devaluation' policy that had been adopted by the Chinese government since
1997 as an expedient policy against the 1997 crisis became inappropriate
and needed to be changed.

Third and more importantly, the Chinese government faced huge pressures
from major Western countries, global financial governance institutions and
even international academia, as mentioned before. The 2005 *US Treasury
Department Report on International Exchange Rate Policies* asserted that
Chinese exchange rate policies 'are highly distortionary and pose a risk to
China's economy, its trading partners, and global economic growth', and,
without substantial alteration, 'China's policies will likely meet the statute's
(Omnibus Trade and Competitiveness Act of 1988) technical requirements
for designation'. In the 2003, 2004 and 2005 *IMF China Article IV
Consultation*, the Fund continuously expressed its desirability for a more flexible Chinese exchange rate. In addition, many scholars from central banks,
research institutes and academia, including but never limited to Eichengreen
(2004), Bernanke (2005) and Frankel (2005), enunciated their views on
China's exchange rate policy, most of which concur with the US government's view (Laurenceson & Qin, 2006). Although these international factors
influenced China's decision to reform its exchange rate regime to some extent,
according China's exchange rate reform to these factors, especially international pressures, is simplistic and misleading (Goujon & Guérineau, 2005).
Domestic factors, as governor of the PBC Zhou Xiaochuan remarked, are
key factors in making China's currency policy (Xinhua, 2010).

The domestic environment is the principal determining factor of China's
national interests or *Guojia Liyi* that guided China's exchange rate reform

particularly from 2005 onward. On the one hand, as Broz and Frieden (2008, p. 591) observed, national states' cooperation and coordination in international monetary system 'rest on the foundation of national currency policies', which 'involve trade-offs with domestic distributional implication' and 'electoral implication'. In China's case, the electoral implication of China's currency policy is minimal, considering the authoritative nature of China's political system. On the other hand, the (potential) distributional implication changed China's domestic environment, which mainly refers to the domestic pressures on and pre-conditions for reforming. The former includes pressures of changing the long-time 'twin surpluses', mitigating inflationary expectation and increasing the independence of currency policy. According to economic theories, under a free-floating exchange rate regime, the sum of current account and capital account should be zero, while under a fixed exchange rate regime, imbalances between capital account and current account can be adjusted through foreign exchange reserves. By 2005 China had been running twin surpluses in current account and capital account for 15 years, a world record (Yu, 2006). The influx of huge foreign currency pressed the RMB to appreciate. To maintain a fixed exchange rate the Bank of China had to purchase foreign currencies and, as a result, increased tremendously the funds outstanding for foreign exchange. This huge amount of money would result in inflation in the goods market and asset bubble in the capital market, which would hurt the macro economy of China.

As the famous 'Impossible Trinity' (Mundell, 1963) stipulates, an economy cannot simultaneously maintain a fixed exchange rate, free capital movement and an independent monetary policy. Independent monetary policy is treated as part of the state sovereignty by the Chinese government. Free capital movement is the long-term objective of China's financial system reform. Therefore, the fixed exchange rate has to be changed in order to maintain or achieve independent monetary policy and free capital movement, and exchange reform became urgent. As Hersh (2014, p. 2) observed, 'leaders and top economic policy-makers have set clear intentions to open China's capital account and to halt direct policy interventions in setting interest rates, the exchange rate, and prices for other assets and financial services'. The Chinese government's strategy to handle this 'Impossible Trinity' trilemma, as pointed out in the 2014 China International Balance of Payments Report issued by the State Administration of Foreign Exchange (SAFE), is to further improve the market-based exchange rate formation mechanisms of the RMB, enhance the government's capability of coping with increased capital mobility and ensure the independence of China's monetary policy (SAFE, 2015).

In addition to these domestic pressures, the 2005 exchange rate reform was based on some pre-conditions. Zhou Xiaochuan summarized these pre-conditions as bank sector reform, decreasing unnecessary controls on foreign exchange transaction and foreign market development (Xinhua, 2005). He noted that China's banking system had been reformed by 2005 and that 70–80% banks had stepped into a virtuous development circle; some unnecessary constraints on capital account transaction had been cancelled and capital market had been further opened up; financial system had been reformed and financial market was more mature. These changes and development provided a material basis for the formation of China's *Guojia Liyi*.

State Ideology

The Chinese modern state ideology centred on the Socialism with Chinese characteristics and the scientific outlook on development has embedded the idea of market economy in the mind of key policy elites and prompted the state to redefine the boundary between the government and the market. The exchange rate reform since 2005 reflects this market economy idea and is a crucial step to redefine the government–market boundary. In the late 1970s, Deng Xiaoping's economy-centred 'reforms and opening' policy replaced Mao's revolution-oriented and politics-centred domestic and foreign policies. Deng's idea prioritized economic development and launched the creation of Socialism with Chinese characteristics, a combination of socialism with market economy. As Deng said in the famous South Tour speech (People's Daily, 2012):

> Planning and market forces are not the essential difference between socialism and capitalism. A planned economy is not the definition of socialism, because there is planning under capitalism; the market economy happens under socialism, too. Planning and market forces are both ways of controlling economic activity.

Following this view, China started to construct its socialist market economy. The exchange rate reform is a vital part of the construction. The subsequent generations of political leaders have largely inherited the ideology and aimed at developing a socialist market economy in China. In the official documents of the Chinese government, 'accelerating the improvement of the socialist market economy' are highly frequent wordings and have been treated as the pivotal of China's economic development. For example, in Hu's (2012) report at the 18th Congress, a whole section is about 'Accelerating the Improvement of the Socialist Market Economy and the Change of the Growth Model'.

As the proceeding of the socialist market economy construction, many social issues have emerged, particularly environment degradation, unbalanced development and absence of human rights. Consequently, the government proposed the scientific outlook on development to improve the growth model. The new development ideology, on the one hand, changes the definition of development from GDP growth to social and human development, and, on the other hand, continues to redefine the boundary between the state and the market. The exchange rate reform initiated in 2005 aims to delegate more power to the market that had been defined as a 'basic' role in allocating resources since the initiation of the market economy construction in 1992. Recently, the 'basic' role was even enhanced to be a 'decisive' role in the third Plenary Session of the 18th CPC Central Committee. The market-oriented exchange rate reform is both important content and premise of completing China's market economy mechanism.

Interpretation

The structuring effects of the domestic and international environments and state ideology on *Guojia Liyi* are through the interpretation of great people, key policy elites and/or people and the judgment of the incumbent government. Interpretation here mainly refers to political decision makers' and government's understanding of the domestic and international environments based on the state ideology. In the medium term, the reform legacy of the great people Deng Xiaoping and the consequent Socialism with Chinese characteristics have provided the subsequent political leaders a thinking pattern in making domestic and international policies. Confined by the state ideology, in the short term, policy elites may have their own understanding of the domestic and international environments and make policies based on their understanding. As far as the exchange rate regime is concerned, key policy elites's interpretation on the domestic and international environments and state ideology espouses a market-oriented reform as a long-term objective.

The most important person in China's exchange rate reform in the past decade is Zhou Xiaochuan. Zhou, a scholar official, has been in charge of the PBC as governor since late 2002. In March 2013, he was reappointed unconventionally to the same position, which makes him the longest-serving central bank governor since the founding of the new China in 1949. The basic academic view of this western-educated governor strongly advocates establishing a more free-floating and flexible exchange rate regime. Therefore, since his inauguration in the PBC, Zhou has been prompting the exchange rate reform towards a market-oriented mechanism. Consequently, Zhou is called an 'arch-reformer' (Xia, 2004) and 'Mr. RMB'. Moreover, Yu Yongding, a financial expert for the Monetary Policy Committee, is another important policy elite, whose formulation of a gradual style of modest appreciation was adopted in 2005 reform (He, 2011). In addition, many high-level officials and advisers of the PBC who received PhD degrees in universities from the United States, such as Yi Gang, Zhou Qiren, Li Daokui and so on, favour currency reform (Freeman III & Yuan, 2011).

The identity and ideology of the government and the internal cause and external pressures together form the judgment of the government that exchange rate reform in the medium or long term is imperative for China's sustainable development. As mentioned before, under the guidance of the Socialism with Chinese characteristics and considering the domestic and international situation, the Chinese government treats the exchange rate reform as a crucial step to redefine the boundary between the state and the market and finally to complete the market economy. Despite some short-term side effects, a market-oriented foreign exchange reform has been a long-term objective of the Chinese government. A reform plan from the Chinese government released following the Third Plenum of the 18th CPC Central Committee clearly demonstrates this long-term objective, saying that the Chinese government vows to 'improve the market-based yuan exchange rate formation mechanism and speed up the marketisation of interest rates'. Some scholars even predict that China may achieve the long-term objective with foreign exchange reform as well as interest rate and capital account reforms by 2020 (Li & Shi, 2013).

In sum, from a long-term perspective, China's exchange rate reform is in favour of economic development, construction of socialist market economy and the flourishing of socialism with Chinese characteristics. Therefore, the 2005 exchange rate reform, on the one hand, met the expectation of the international community inadvertently, especially the major Western countries and IOs like the IMF, while, on the other hand and more importantly, it was motivated by the *Guojia Liyi* determined largely by domestic and international environments, state ideology and interpretation of key policy elites.

HOW THE DECISION-MAKING ENVIRONMENT MATTERS

China's exchange rate policymaking under different administrations has varied slightly. Under the Hu-Wen administration (2003–2012), several policy organs and elites played crucial roles in making China's exchange rate policy. The Central Politburo Standing Committee of the CPC (PSC) has been standing at the centre of China's exchange rate policymaking, supported by some functional units like the General Office that provides administrative and logistical support (Yuan, 2012). Another body that is directly accountable to the PSC and crucial in making the exchange rate policy is the Financial and Economic Affairs Leading Small Group (FEALSG). Wen Jiabao, former Chinese Premier and chair of the FEALSG, was the key policy elite in exchange rate policymaking. Hua Jianmin, deputy secretary-general of the FEALSG, and Ma Kai, deputy secretary-general of the State Council, were key assistants of Wen in evaluating policy alternatives and making final decisions. The PBC became the most influential exchange rate policy inputs after the China Banking Regulatory Commission (CBRC) was formed in 2003 to take over the supervision responsibilities on China's banking sector. Zhou Xiaochuan, governor of the PBC, was and remains one of the most influential policy elite in the exchange rate policymaking in the past decade. In addition, Yi Gang, director of the PBC monetary policy department, is also influential in exchange policy formulation due to his monetary economics expertise. The MOFCOM, which was formed in 2003 in response to China's accession to the WTO, was also important in providing input for China's exchange rate policy. Consequently, Bo Xilai, former Minister of Commerce, had a certain influence on the China exchange rate policymaking under the Hu-Wen administration.

These policy organs and elites made the final decision to transform China's exchange rate regime to be a managed floating exchange rate regime based on market supply and demand with reference to a basket of currency in 2005. This policy output accords with the *Guojia Liyi* and corresponding policy objectives mentioned above. In 2008 and 2010 respectively, however, similar policy organs and elites made different decisions related to China's exchange rate policy. This difference and fluctuation were not due to changes of China's *Guojia Liyi*, which has virtually favoured exchange rate reform in China in the long run, but due to the different influences of six key factors on the decision-making environment, which are lobbying of interest groups, institutional conflict, complexity of the issue, international pressures, emergent events and risk appetite of decision makers. The following section explores how the six factors influence the decisions on 2005 exchange rate reform, 2008 reform stagnation and 2010 reform relaunch.

2005 Reform

Lobbying of interest groups opposing the 2005 reform and the consequent appreciation of the RMB, especially the export sector, was comparatively weak. What must be pointed out first is that interest groups can also influence exchange rate policy in authoritarian states. Many recent quantitative analyses verify the influence of political regime type on exchange rate policy, arguing that non-democratic governments are more insulated from domestic societal pressures (Steinberg & Shih, 2012). Many scholars have falsified this idea by exploring the multiple ways in which interest groups exert influence on and even change China's exchange rate policy (Yuan, 2012). Steinberg and Shih (2012, p. 1407) argue that 'interest groups have multiple points of access in non-democratic regimes, and autocrats have strong incentives to keep the exchange rate at a level that is supported by powerful domestic interest groups to ensure their political survival'. As far as China's exchange rate policymaking is concerned, the lobbying consists of two layers – lobbying of interest groups on related government agencies and lobbying of government agencies on the central leadership. The latter specifically appears as the institutional conflicts between the PBC and the MOFCOM, which will be discussed subsequently. Here the lobbying particularly refers to the export sectors' influence on the central exchange policy, which was both direct and indirect. The direct manner was to lobby the MOFCOM through provincial and local level Chambers of Commerce, which serves as a middleman to pass along the concerns of the export sectors, especially big export companies, to the MOFCOM. The indirect way mainly refers to the manipulation of the media (Yuan, 2012).

The lobbying of the export sectors against the 2005 reform and the consequent RMB appreciation was not strong enough to impede the reform. The fundamental reason is that the interest of most export sectors had not been substantially damaged because of the limited RMB-appreciating effects of the 2005 reform as well as the compensation measures of the central government. As the former Premier Wen remarked publicly, the exchange rate reform in China must insist on three principles –initiative, controllability and gradual way (Zhao, 2005). Initiative means to determine the form, content and timing of the reform according to the needs of China's domestic development and taking into account its negative effects, especially on the stability of the macro economy, economic growth and employment. Controllability means that the reform process must be in control in terms of macro management and must avoid turbulence of the financial market and substantial fluctuation of the economy. Gradual way refers to the fact that the reform should be taken step by step considering both the short-time and long-time development. The three principles convey a message to the export sectors, the strongest lobbying group against the exchange reform, that RMB value would not be appreciated largely beyond most exporting companies' capability of adopting themselves to the change.

In the first two years after the 2005 reform (June 2005–June 2007) the RMB appreciated by around 7.8% from 8.28 to 7.63 RMB/US dollar (Fig. 1). Despite the appreciation, the RMB was still considered undervalued and the export sectors still had some comparative advantage. Looking into the textile industry in China, for example, Yang (2009, p. 188) observed 'export conditions for the Chinese textile industry were ideal for three straight years after 2005, with annual growth of around 20 percent'. In addition, compensation measures smoothed the 2005 reform by mitigating the negative effects of the reform on the export sectors. As Steinberg and Shih (2012, p. 1405) argued, 'tradable industries do not always demand

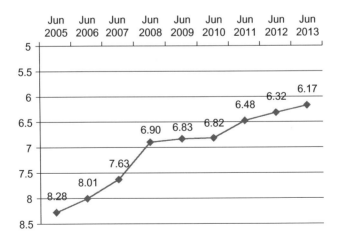

Fig. 1. China's Exchange Rates against US Dollar between 2005 and 2013.
Source: IMF Data and Statistics.

an undervalued exchange rate, but do so only when they are unable to receive other compensatory policies'. During the 2005 reform, tradable industries were compensated by favourable economic policies and, consequently, discouraged to lobby against the appreciation resulted in by the 2005 reform (Steinberg & Shih, 2012). Nonetheless, in the one-year period between June 2007 and June 2008, the RMB appreciated by about 9.6% from 1\$:7.63¥ to 1\$:6.9¥ (Fig. 1), which directly resulted in the stagnation of the 2005 reform.

Institutional conflicts regarding the 2005 reform, especially between the PBC and the MOFCOM, were evident but controllable and negotiable. The PBC and the MOFCOM are two major stakeholders in China's exchange rate policy. The PBC has been a strong backer and initiator of China's exchange reform, while the MOFCOM opposed the 2005 reform and the consequent appreciation of the RMB, concerned that the competitiveness of China's export sectors would be weakened. These competing stances stem from the different functions of the two government agencies. Among many others, the major functions of the PBC are to control inflation by formulating and implementing monetary policy, preventing and mitigating systemic financial risks to safeguard financial stability and maintaining the RMB exchange rate at an adaptive and equilibrium level (PBC, 2013). A more flexible exchange rate policy would be conducive to controlling inflation, handling the large amount of speculative capital inflows and maintaining China's financial and economic stability (Freeman III & Yuan, 2011). In contrast, the MOFCOM is mainly concerned with facilitating domestic and international trade. Obviously, the reform of China's exchange rate policy and the consequent RMB appreciation are harmful to China's export sectors and foreign trade in the short term. As for the 2005 reform, the institutional conflicts were negotiable and a weak reform consensus had been finally reached with the effort of the PBC. On the one hand, the compensation measures discussed above mitigated the export sectors' lobbying and, consequently, the external pressures of the MOFCOM to oppose the reform. On the other hand, the PBC carried out mass coordination and negotiations within the government, including extensive discussions and researches ranging from policy departments to academic research institutes, and finally obtained the support of the central government, domestic public opinion and mainstream media (He, 2011).

The externalities of the 2005 reform are not overly complex. The disputes between the PBC and the MOFCOM demonstrated clearly the major negative and positive effects of the 2005 reform. Therefore, decision makers can balance these effects before making a final decision. Although there are still some uncertain issues, such as the extent to which the RMB should appreciate and the fact that export sectors would be affected negatively, the general picture is clear that with the countering measures against the negative extremities of the 2005 reform the positive effects would outweigh the potential negative ones.

Short-time international pressure is another important factor that influenced the 2005 exchange reform. As discussed above, before and during the 2005 reform, China faced huge pressures from major Western countries, especially the United States, IOs like the IMF and international academia to reform its currency policy. Although, as emphasized before, external pressures are not the direct antecedent of the consequent 2005 reform, its influences on policy elites and finally on the policy-making process cannot be dismissed. These external pressures, in essence, are the interpretation and expectation of foreign actors, both countries and IOs, on China's currency policy. According to Constructivists' ideas, intersubjective understanding among social actors determines each actor's identities and interests, which will influence social actors' interpretation of the situation that they are facing and, consequently, their decisions (Wendt, 1992). This idea is still applicable to China's policy elites. Chinese policymakers' perspectives will be influenced, more or less, by the interpretation of foreign actors. Different from the influence of external pressures on *Guojia Liyi* formation in the medium or long term discussed above, the impact of external pressures on decision-making processes is short-term and relatively less evident, since the short-term pressures can be comparatively easily managed by the incumbent government through skilful diplomacy. Yet, in the long term, the Chinese government needs to take substantial actions rather than merely diplomatic tactics to alleviate external pressures. As such, in the highly globalized world, it is not sufficient for countries to make policies exclusively based on the domestic situation, even though the domestic environment is still the major source of national policies.

During the 2005 exchange reform, there was no emergent event that influenced the decision-making process. Emergent events always require immediate response in the short term and unconventional measures to cope with. Therefore, the more emergent the event is, the more cognitive the decision will likely be. In other words, when emergent events happen, the decision makers may consider more how to deal with these emergent crises in the short term, rather than comprehensively assess the long-term effects of these expedients.

Lastly, key policy elites and political leaders were motivated to launch the 2005 reform despite some potential risks including negative influence on China's export sectors, exchange rate fluctuation and some other unpredictable ones. Key policy elites, particularly Zhou Xiaochuan and his colleagues in the PBC, strongly advocate establishing a more free-floating and flexible exchange rate regime. Their efforts in both making a reform plan and persuading the central government to carry out the plan were remarkable particularly in the years before 2005. Therefore, in this period, although there were institutional conflicts, the voices of these policy elites advocating exchange rate reform were louder than the opposition, and the key exchange rate policy elites were more willing to take the potential risks of reforming China's exchange rate regime. An important reason for the relatively high risk appetite of the key policy elites is the stable international and domestic macro-economic situation in this period, which brought a relatively high risk resistance capability to the Chinese economy.

2008 Stagnation

In July 2008, China suspended the managed float exchange rate system and froze the RMB nominal value against the dollar at 6.83, which indicated that the 2005 reform had officially stagnated. In the following approximately two years (July 2008 to the first half of 2010) the exchange rate remained at a stable level around 6.83. This period is called here the '2008 stagnation'. The reason for the exchange rate policy transformation is not that the related *Guojia Liyi*, on which the policymaking is based, had been changed, but the decision-making process had been influenced by these factors mentioned above. In the long or medium term, China's *Guojia Liyi* related to the exchange rate policy is still to promote and maintain economic development by establishing and improving the socialist market economic system in China and enabling the market to fully play its role in resource allocation. However, the influences of these factors mentioned above had been substantially changed in the short term.

The lobbying of the export sectors against the exchange reform and the continuous appreciation of the RMB became far stronger in the run-up to the 2008 stagnation. The reasons for this increase lie in the following three aspects. First, the compensation policies to the export sectors implemented before and around 2005 had faded away. Following the 2005 reform, the Chinese government gradually transferred its focus to curbing trade surplus and upgrading industrial structure by cutting export tax rebates several times and coercing export industries out of low-cost and market-saturated product lines (He, 2011). The withdrawing of these compensatory policies forced the export sectors to lobby with more efforts for a favourable exchange rate policy. Second, the macro-economic environment, both international and domestic, was exacerbated, mainly by the eruption of the 2008 global financial crisis. Internationally, the 2008 global financial crisis depressed the world economy and, as a result, lowered the demand of the major exporting markets of China, especially the United States and the EU. Domestically, the tight monetary policy, the greater labour cost along with the new labour contract law and the declines of stock and property markets together reduced the profits of many export companies within few months (Steinberg & Shih, 2012). Third, the RMB value had been substantially appreciated since the 2005 reform, which directly shrank the profit margin of China's export sectors. The exchange rate against the US dollar experienced the fastest increase between June 2007 and June 2008 (Fig. 1).

The direct consequence of these three factors is a survival crisis of most exporting companies and, the subsequent lobbying blitz. Taking the textile industry as an example, in the first nine months of 2008 the growth rate of textile export decreased by 11.9% compared to a similar period in 2007, due to decreasing numbers of purchase orders, declining export rebate rate (from 13% in 2006 to 5% in middle 2007), increasing manufacturing costs and continued shrinking industry profits (Yang, 2009). Confronted with the worsening situation, the China Textile Industry Association (CTIA) set out a series of survey on the real condition of the China textile industry, mainly in provinces of Jiangsu, Zhejiang, Guangdong, Hebei, Shandong and Fujian, and concluded that China's textile industry was facing a survival crisis (Suo, 2008). Subsequently, the CTIA summarized the survey results and sent it to the MOFCOM for help. According to Steinberg and Shih's (2012) interviews, the growing hostility of the textile industry against exchange rate appreciation in 2008 transformed into lobbying efforts, especially in the governments of coastal provinces, which subsequently passed the pressures up to the central government and warned that more favourable exchange rate and rebate policies were required to prevent mass bankruptcies and social unrest.

As the major target of the lobbying of the export sectors, the MOFCOM's attitude against the exchange rate reform initiated in 2005 and the continuous appreciation of the RMB became much tougher. Consequently, the institutional conflicts between the PBC and the MOFCOM became intense in this period. The MOFCOM, which had long performed as an objector of fast exchange rate reform and appreciation, became more steadfast in opposing the exchange rate reform against the PBC, representing the interest groups of export companies and also on behalf of its own agency interests. In July 2008, the MOFCOM made a formal proposal to the State Council, pleading to slow the pace of yuan appreciation in order to give exporters more time to adjust (Chan, 2010).

The eruption of the 2008 global financial crisis was an emergent event that made assessing the extremities of China's exchange rate policy on domestic and international stakeholders much more opaque and complex. In the period before the initiation of the 2008 global financial crisis, as discussed before, the international and domestic effects of the exchange rate reform were comparatively easy to gauge. Yet during the economic depression, it became hard to discern what negative effects were caused by the crisis or by the exchange rate reform. Therefore, the exchange rate reform was often a scapegoat of the global financial crisis. In other words, many negative impacts of the global financial crisis were attributed to the exchange rate reform. For example, appreciation of the RMB and the sharp decline of the major Western market demand due to the weak economy in these economies both resulted in the decrease of Chinese export during the 2008 global financial crisis. Chinese export companies usually ascribe all the decline of export to the RMB appreciation or think that seeking to depreciate or slow the appreciation of RMB is the major way to regain their previous trade advantage. Under these conditions, on the one hand, the export sectors lobbied the related government agencies for slowing the RMB appreciation and/or gaining more other favourable policies sparing no efforts; on the other hand, the Chinese government, facing the complicated domestic and international environments, tended to stall the previous exchange rate reform waiting for a clearer international and domestic economic situation.

Short-time international pressure in this period was not as huge as around the 2005 reform, although China's exchange rate policy has always faced international pressures. The major reasons for the less international attention to China's exchange rate policy in this period lie in mainly two respects. First, major Western countries, especially the United States and the EU, had troubles sustaining their own economies due to the eruption of the crisis. Second, major international financial governance organizations were hard pressed to fix the problematic international financial governance system and rushed off their feet in rebuilding a new system.

Unlike during the 2005 reform, in 2008 the turbulence of international and domestic economy and the complexity of the effects of continuous exchange rate reform made the key policy elites who advocated exchange reform and RMB appreciation more cautious and risk-averse. In the midst of the financial crisis, the first task of the Chinese government was to maintain economic growth. Therefore, "*Bao Ba*" (ensuring 8% GDP growth) became the mantra among Chinese officials of all ranks in 2009. Against this background, all other issues, including the exchange rate reform, had to give way to this target.

2010 Relaunch

On June 19 2010, the PBC announced 'to proceed further with reform of the RMB exchange rate regime and to enhance the RMB exchange rate flexibility' (PBC, 2010), which indicates that the nearly two-year (July 2008–Jun 2010) dollar-pegged exchange rate policy came to an end and the currency reform initiated in 2005 was relaunched. The international community praised this move, although it was far from their expectation. For example, right after the PBC's announcement, the former IMF chief Dominique Strauss-Kahn said this move was 'a very welcomed development' that 'will help increase Chinese household income and provide the incentives necessary to reorient investment toward industries that serve the Chinese consumer' (People's Daily, 2010). Moreover, as mentioned before, since 2010, the Fund changed its assessment on China's exchange rate from 'substantially undervalued' to 'undervalued' and recently to 'moderately undervalued'. Although China's exchange rate policy has still been criticized by major Western countries and IOs, the 2010 relaunch of the exchange rate reform revealed China's stance in reforming its currency policy. Therefore, generally, in this period, China can be treated as a status-quo power in terms of its willingness in reforming its exchange rate policy toward the expectation of the international community. However, the 2010 exchange policy change is driven by the national interests or *Guojia Liyi* rather than by the external expectation. Exchange reform, in the long run, conforms to China's *Guojia Liyi*. The re-peg to the US dollar between 2008 and 2010 is only a temporary policy, while establishing a more flexible RMB exchange rate is China's fundamental economic policy (BBC Monitoring Asia Pacific [London], 2010). The temporary policy is a result of the perturbing influences of several key factors on the decision-making process. The relaunch of the exchange rate reform reveals that, first, from a long-term perspective, China's policies must be in accordance to its *Guojia Liyi*, and, second, in terms of the 2010 relaunch these perturbing factors failed to bound the decision-making process as they did in the 2008 stagnation.

The export sectors continued to lobby against the RMB appreciation and called for maintaining exchange rate stability, but the lobbying was not influential enough to change the final decision on the exchange rate policy for two reasons. First, since 2008 the Chinese government had made many favourable policies for the export industry. In the 10 months from August 2008 to June 2009, the export rebate rate policy was adjusted seven times and the export rebate rates of textile, some labour-intensive products and some mechanical and electrical products had been increased. These compensation measures mitigated the opposition against and transferred temporarily the focus of the export industry away from the exchange rate reform. Second, the PBC's attitude on continuing the exchange rate reform in this period was much more steadfast, as to be shown subsequently.

Second, the major defender of the export sector, the MOFCOM, lost its battle with the PBC in convincing the central leadership to stop or at least slow the exchange rate reform. In April 2010, under the guidance of the MOFCOM, local Chambers of Commerce launched an RMB exchange rate stress test and consequently concluded that Chinese export companies are highly vulnerable to RMB appreciation, saying for many industries, such as home appliances, autos and cell phones, a 3% appreciation in RMB would drive down their profits by 30−50% (Zhang, Liu, & Lei, 2010). During the 2010 annual meetings of the National People's Congress and Chinese People's Political Consultative Conference, Zhou Xiaochuan indicated that the re-pegged exchange rate to the US dollar is an unconventional measure in response to the 2008 global financial crisis and will exit sooner or later. Subsequently, the former vice Minister of Commerce Wei Jianguo pointed out that the current exchange rate policy is a corollary of China's opening-up policy and, therefore, is reasonable. He further explained that the foreign trade situation in 2010 would not be better than expectation and suggested the central government to maintain stable RMB value and increase support for the exporting sectors (Xu & Wu, 2010). The then Minister of Commerce Chen Deming also expressed his concern that China's export industry needs another 2 or 3 years to restore to the pre-crisis level and, therefore, any exchange rate policy change before that must be gradual and controllable (Xu & Wu, 2010). However, these voices on maintaining a stable RMB value and slowing exchange rate reform did not weaken the PBC's determination to restore the 2005 reform, mainly because of the domestic and international pressures that the PBC was facing. The international pressures will be dwelled on latter. The domestic pressures of the PBC in this period mainly include economic structure adjustment and inflation. Adjusting economic structure and upgrading

industrial structure have been a crucible for China's sustainable development. The eruption of the 2008 global financial crisis highlights the importance of accelerating the transforming process from an export-oriented to a
demand-oriented economy and from a labour- and resource-intensive to a
capital- and tech-intensive industrial structure. Restoring the reform of
RMB exchange rate formation mechanism is conducive to this transformation. As the former President of World Bank Group Robert Zoellick
remarked, 'as export-driven China remakes its society to depend more
on consumer spending, it could become an opportunity to revalue the
currency' (Agence France-Presse, 2010).

Fighting against inflation is another key battlefield of the PBC. Since
November 2009 Consumer Price Index (CPI) figures have entered into positive territory and have been rising, standing at 3.5% in August 2010 (Feng,
2010). In addition to quantitative instruments, a flexible exchange rate
policy is another effective way to curb inflation. The PBC held that a more
flexible exchange rate policy and the gradual appreciation of the RMB
would not only protect against short-term inflation, but also be conducive
to the long-term sustainable growth. In addition, the PBC insisted that the
negative impact of the exchange rate reform has been overestimated mainly
by the MOFCOM. Hu Xiaolian, the Deputy Governor of the PBC, for
example, said in an interview (Feng, 2010):

> Between 2006 and 2008 [after the 2005 revaluation], China's exports increased by
> 23.4% annually, while imports increased by 19.7%, representing a golden age of foreign
> trade development. Looking back, we can say that some have overestimated the nega-
> tive impact of foreign exchange reform whilst underestimated the adaptive capacities of
> Chinese enterprises.

Finally, the central leadership was more convinced by the PBC and reached
a consensus to restore the 2005 reform.

China's exchange rate has been a hot issue in the global financial governance and faced exceptionally high pressures in the post-2008 crisis era, for
it was blamed for resulting in the crisis. The basic logic of the criticism is
that the manipulated exchange rate has brought significant advantages to
China's export industries and, therefore, led to the imbalanced trade surplus and the accumulation of a huge amount of foreign reserve, which
partly caused the 2008 global financial crisis (Obstfeld & Rogoff, 2009).
Holding this view, the major Western countries have exerted unparalleled
pressure on China's exchange rate policy. For example, in early 2010 five
US senators introduced a bill to compel the US government to identify
'fundamentally misaligned currencies' based on specific criteria, in response

to 'the longstanding frustration over the Treasury Department's refusal under successive administrations to cite China formally for manipulating its currency' (Chan, 2010). Moreover, in March 2010 130 House members sent a letter to require the Treasury to issue a finding of manipulation and the Commerce Department to impose countervailing duties to protect American manufacturers (Chan, 2010). Although the US government delayed its decision on China currency manipulation many times and finally declined to name China as a currency manipulator, this is the first time that such a provocative declaration since President Obama's administration has been made (Schneider, 2010).

As the gradual recovery of the world economy from and the fade-away of the fear of governments on the 2008 global financial crisis, exchange rate reform, replacing the target of ensuring 8% economic growth, has been put forward again by major policy elites whose personal academic or political views advocate reforming China's exchange rate regime in the long term. In addition, the domestic and international economic situations become easier to observe and assess as the world and China's economy come back to the normal track. The effects of the exchange rate reform are consequently easier to gauge under a comparatively stable economic environment. Therefore, key policy elites were encouraged to resume the 2005 reform and take more risks in this reinvigorated reform. Lastly, no analogous emergent event to the 2008 global financial crisis has happened since 2010. To sum, the decision-making environment in this period has been comparatively sable and the *Guojia Liyi* is transformed into China's national policies and behaviours in this stable policy-making environment.

CONCLUSION

The examination on China's exchange rate policy in the past decade leads to several conclusions. First, external pressure on reforming China's exchange rate regime, especially from the United States and major IOs, is only one factor among many influencing the formation of China's national interests (or *Guojia Liyi* in Chinese) and the decision-making process on exchange rate policy to a limited extent. Second, *Guojia Liyi* is the fundamental driving force and substratum for making China's exchange rate policy. From a long-term perspective, China's *Guojia Liyi* is to promote and maintain economic development by establishing and improving the socialist market economic system in China and enabling the market to fully play its role in resource allocation. In this sense, China's exchange rate reform initiated in 2005 is a reflection of the *Guojia Liyi*. Third, in the short term, the specific exchange rate policies in different periods were not always in accordance to the *Guojia Liyi*, due to the influences of several factors on the decision-making environment. Table 1 summarizes the influence of these six key factors on China's exchange rate policymaking in the three stages. In the 2005 reform and 2010 relaunch, the weak lobbying and institutional conflicts, the low complexity of domestic and international economic situations, the high risk appetite and external pressures propelling exchange rate reform and the absence of emergent events together formed a comparatively stable decision-making environment, in which the *Guojia Liyi* has been obeyed in making decisions. On the contrary, in the 2008 stagnation, the indexes of these factors are in an opposite direction, which created a complicated decision-making environment and, therefore, bounded the rationality of decision makers. As a result, the exchange rate policy in this period (2008–2010) violated the long-term *Guojia Liyi* or national interests.

In a word, the formation of *Guojia Liyi* and decision-making process and environment both matter in explaining China's foreign and domestic policies, particularly in exchange rate policy. Analogously, the former can be compared to navigators and engines of planes, which guide the direction and provide driving forces, while the latter can be compared to the specific air routes to destination, which may be changed by the external factors such as airflow, heavy weather, wars and even emergent situation of passengers. Despite detours, delays or even temporary cancellation, planes aim to arrive at their destinations under the guidance of the navigators and the motivation of the powerful engines. China's exchange rate policy in the

Table 1. Influence of Key Factors on the Exchange Policy-Making Process.

Factors	2005 Reform	2008 Stagnation	2010 Relaunch
Lobbying	Weak	Strong	Weak
Institutional conflicts	Weak	Strong	Weak
Complexity of issues in point	Low	High	Low
Short-time pressures from IOs and Western countries	High	Low	High
Emergent events	No	Yes	No
Risk appetite of decision makers	High	Low	High

past decade is the same story. Under the guidance and motivation of China's *Guojia Liyi* (or national interests), China strives to arrive at its destination along the route of reforming its exchange rate regime, where a more free-float, flexible and healthy exchange rate regime based on market supply and demand will finally be established.

NOTE

1. The Chinese term *Guojia Liyi* means interests and preferences of China, interchangeably used with national interests here.

REFERENCES

Agence France-Presse. (2010). *Time is ripe for China to revalue yuan: World Bank chief*. Retrieved from http://www.lbr.lk/fullstory.php?nid=201003300941465654

Asia Pulse (Rhodes). (2010, September 17). *US lawmakers slam China for rigid yuan exchange rate policy*. Retrieved from ProQuest Database.

BBC Monitoring Asia Pacific [London]. (2010, June 23). *Economist says flexible yuan exchange rate China's fundamental economic policy*. Retrieved from ProQuest Database.

Beattie, A. (2009). IMF in discord over Renminbi. *Financial Times*, January 26. Retrieved from http://www.ft.com/intl/cms/s/0/b876fafc-eb18-11dd-bb6e-0000779fd2ac.html#axzz3HZv0GbKp

Bernanke, B. (2005). Monetary policy in a world of mobile capital. *Cato Journal*, 25(1), 1−12.

Broz, L., & Frieden, J. (2008). The political economy of exchange rates. In B. R. Weingast & D. A. Wittman (Eds.), *Oxford handbook of political economy* (pp. 587−600). Oxford: Oxford University Press.

Buckley, L. T. (2012). China's response to US pressure to revalue the RMB. *China Currents*, 11(1). Retrieved from http://www.chinacenter.net/chinas-response-to-u-s-pressure-to-revalue-the-rmb/

Chan, S. (2010). Pressure grows in US over China's currency. *New York Times*, March 16. Retrieved from http://www.nytimes.com/2010/03/17/business/17yuan.html?_r=0

Congressional Documents and Publications. (2010). *China's undervalued exchange rate hurts the US economy*. Lanham: Federal Information & News Dispatch, Inc.

Eichengreen, B. (2004). *Chinese currency controversies*. CEPR Discussion Paper No. 4375.

Feng, H. (2010). The People's Bank of China's battle on two fronts. *Central Banking*, 21(2), 18−22.

Frankel, J. (2005). *On the Renminbi: The choice between adjustment under a fixed exchange rate and adjustment under a flexible rate*. NBER Working Paper No. 11274.

Freeman III, C. W., & Yuan, W. (2011). *China's exchange rate politics − Decoding the cleavage between the Chinese Ministry of Commerce and the People's Bank of China*. A report of the CSIS Freeman Chair in China Studies. Retrieved from http://csis.org/files/publication/110615_Freeman_ChinaExchangeRatePolitics_Web.pdf

Goujon, M., & Guérineau, S. (2005). The modification of the Chinese exchange rate policy. *China Perspectives, 64.* Retrieved from http://chinaperspectives.revues.org/607

He, J. (2011). *"Zhongguo Ban Basaier Xieyi III" Dui Yinhangye de Yingxiang Fenxi* [The influence of Basel III of Chinese version on the banking sector]. *Finance Forum, 8,* 25−32.

Hersh, A. S. (2014). *China's path to financial reform: Looking beyond the market.* Washington, DC: Center for American Progress. Retrieved from https://www.americanprogress.org/issues/economy/report/2014/10/08/98477/chinas-path-to-financial-reform/

Hu, J. (2012). Full text of Hu Jintao's report at 18th party congress. *Xinhua News.* Retrieved from http://news.xinhuanet.com/english/special/18cpcnc/2012-11/17/c_131981259_5.htm

Huang, W. (2006). *Renmingbi Huilv Xingchen Jizhi Gaige Zhengdangshi* [Right time for reforming the formation mechanism of RMB exchange rate]. *Economic and Trade Update, 1−2,* 34−37.

IMF. (2003). *IMF concludes 2003 article IV consultation with the People's Republic of China.* Retrieved from https://www.imf.org/external/np/sec/pn/2003/pn03136.htm. Accessed on November 18.

IMF. (2009). 2009 Article IV consultation with the People's Republic of China. Public Information Notice (PIN) No. 09/87. Retrieved from https://www.imf.org/external/np/sec/pn/2009/pn0987.htm

IMF. (2012). 2012 Article IV consultation with the People's Republic of China. Public Information Notice (PIN) No. 12/195. Retrieved from http://www.imf.org/external/pubs/ft/scr/2012/cr12195.pdf

Kennedy, S. (2009). Comparing formal and informal lobbying practices in China: The capital's ambivalent embrace of capitalists. *China Information, 23*(2), 195−222.

Laurenceson, J., & Qin, F. (2006). The exchange rate debate. In Y. Wu (Ed.), *Economic transition, growth and globalization in China* (pp. 199−213). Cheltenham: Edward Elgar Publishing.

Li, Z., & Shi, M. (2013). A roadmap for China's foreign exchange reforms. *The Diplomat,* November 28. Retrieved from http://thediplomat.com/2013/11/a-roadmap-for-chinas-foreign-exchange-reforms/

Liao, K. (2011). *Deguo Huilvzhidu Gaige de Jingyan* [The experience of Germany's exchange rate reform]. *China Market, 35,* 38−39.

Liew, L. H. (2004). Policy elites in the political economy of China's exchange rate policymaking. *Journal of Contemporary China, 13*(38), 21−51.

Lu, Q., & Cha, T. (2011). *Yindu Huilvzhidu de Gaige ji dui zhongguo de Qishi* [India's exchange rate reform and its inspiration for China]. *Studies of International Finance, 5,* 13−22.

Mundell, R. A. (1963). Capital mobility and stabilization policy under fixed and flexible exchange rates. *Canadian Journal of Economics and Political, 29*(4), 475−485.

Obstfeld, M., & Rogoff, K. (2009). Global imbalances and the financial crisis: Products of common causes. Paper presented in the Federal Reserve Bank of San Francisco Asia Economic Policy Conference, Santa Barbara, CA, October 18−20, 2009.

PBC. (2010). Further reform the RMB exchange rate regime and enhance the RMB exchange rate flexibility. People's Bank of China. Retrieved from http://www.pbc.gov.cn/publish/english/955/2010/20100622144059351137121/20100622144059351137121_.html

PBC. (2013). *About PBC.* Retrieved from http://www.pbc.gov.cn/publish/english/952/index.html

People's Daily. (2010, June 20). *IMF welcomes China's decision on further exchange rate reform.* Retrieved from http://english.people.com.cn/90001/90778/7031380.html

People's Daily. (2012, February 03). *"Market fundamentalism" is unpractical.* Retrieved from http://english.people.com.cn/90780/7719657.html

SAFE. (2015). 2014 China international balance of payments report. State Administration of Foreign Exchange.

Schneider, H. (2010). Obama urged to act on China's currency manipulation. *The Washington Post*, March 26. Retrieved from http://www.washingtonpost.com/wp-dyn/content/article/2010/03/25/AR2010032503772.html

Steinberg, D. A., & Shih, V. C. (2012). Interest group influence in authoritarian states: The political determinants of Chinese exchange rate policy. *Comparative Political Studies*, *45*(11), 1405–1434.

Steinberg, D., & Walter, S. (2013). The political economy of exchange rate policy. In G. Caprio (Ed.), *Handbook of safeguarding financial stability* (pp. 27–36). London: Elsevier Academic Press.

Suo, H. (2008). Gao Yong: Zuizao de Qiujiuzhe [Gao Yong: The first to call help]. *China Business*, December 27. Retrieved from http://finance.jrj.com.cn/people/2008/12/2707273181146.shtml

Tang, W. (2005). *Aodaliya Huilv Zhidu de Yanbian ji dui Zhongguo Huobi Zhengce de Jiejian* [The evolution of Australian exchange rate regime and its implication on China]. *Journal of ABC Wuhan Training College, 2*, 49–52.

Wendt, A. (1992). Anarchy is what states make of it: The social construction of power politics. *International Organization, 46*(2), 391–425.

Xia, Y. (2004). Zhouxiaochuan: Qiangying de Gaigepai [Zhou Xiaochuan: An "arc-reformer"]. *Southern Weekly*, January 9. Retrieved from http://www.southcn.com/weekend/top/200401090012.htm

Xinhua. (2003). Decision of the central committee of the communist party of China on some issues concerning the improvement of the socialist market economy. *Xinhua News Online*, October 21. Retrieved from http://news.xinhuanet.com/newscenter/2003-10/21/content_1135402.htm

Xinhua. (2005). Renmin Yinhang Hangzhang Zhouxiaochuan jiu Huilvxingchengjizhi Giage Dajizhewen [Governor of People's Bank of China meets press]. *Xinhua News Online*, September 11. Retrieved from http://www.gov.cn/jrzg/2005-09/11/content_30807.htm

Xinhua. (2010). Zhou Xiaochuan: Guonei Yinsu shi Zhongguo Zhiding Huobizhengce de Zhongdian [Zhou Xiaochuan: Domestic factors are more important in making China's currency policy]. *Xinhua News Online*, May 24. Retrieved from http://www.gov.cn/jrzg/2010-05/24/content_1612608.htm

Xu, Y., & Wu, L. (2010). Renminbi Shengzhi Yuqi Jiqiang, Yanghang ShangwubuWeimiao Fenqi [The enhanced expectation for RMB appreciation and the subtle dispute between PBC and MOFCOM]. *China Times*, March 12. Retrieved from http://www.chinatimes.cc/pages/12139/moreInfo.htm

Yang, M. (2009). Hanging by a thread. *Caijing annual edition 2009: Forecasts and strategies* (pp. 188–190). Beijing: Acer-CN-Beijing Caijing Magazine Co. Ltd.

Yi, J. (2007). *China's exchange rate policymaking in the Hu-Wen era*. Nottingham: The University of Nottingham, China Policy Institute. Briefing Series – 29.

Yu, D. (2006). China's "twin surpluses": Causes and remedies. EAI Background Brief No. 283. Singapore: East Asian Institute, National University of Singapore.

Yuan, W. (2012). *China's export lobbying groups and the politics of the Renminbi.* A Freeman Briefing Report. Washington, DC: Center for Strategic & International Studies.

Zhang, M., Liu, L., & Lei, M. (2010). Duogehangye Renminbi Yaliceshi Jieguo Buleguan [The results of RMB stress test in many industries are not optimistic]. *Economic Information Daily*, April 2. Retrieved from http://money.163.com/10/0424/00/650C030N00253B0H.html

Zhang, Y. (2005). Huilv Gaige de Guoji Jingyan he Jiaoxun [Lessons and experience of international exchange rate reform]. *China Economic Times*, June 10. Retrieved from http://finance.sina.com.cn/g/20050610/00041672675.shtml

Zhao, J. (2005). *Zhongguo Guojia Zongli Wen Jiabao Chanshu Renminbi Huilvgaige Sanyuanze* [Chinese Premier Wen Jiabao explicates the three principles of China's exchange rate reform]. *Southern New*, June 27. Retrieved from http://www.southcn.com/news/china/zgkx/200506270008.htm

Zhu, D. (2006). Jingji Zhuanxing Guojia Huigai de Pouxi he Jiejian [Analysis on exchange rate reform in the economy transformation nations and their implication for China]. *Technology Economics*, 6, 62–66.

Zhu, D. (2007). *Huilv Gaige Anli ji dui Woguo de Qishi* [The inspiration of international exchange rate reform for China]. *China Collective Economy*, 9, 66–67.

EFFICIENCY OF REGULATED AND UNREGULATED FOREX MARKETS: AN ANALYSIS OF ONSHORE AND OFFSHORE RENMINBI FORWARD MARKETS

Zsuzsa R. Huszár, Ruth S. K. Tan and Weina Zhang

ABSTRACT

Purpose — *This study seeks to explore the presence and the relative strength of market efficiency in the onshore and offshore Renminbi (RMB) forward markets.*

Methodology/approach — *In the onshore and offshore foreign exchange markets, the RMB forward contracts are designed in similar ways. However, the underlying economic forces and regulatory frameworks are very different in these two markets. We first analyze the functioning of each market, by examining the covered interest rate parity (CIRP) conditions. Second, we explore the CIRP deviations in the two markets and quantify the role of market frictions and government interventions.*

The Political Economy of Chinese Finance
International Finance Review, Volume 17, 371–392
Copyright © 2016 by Emerald Group Publishing Limited
All rights of reproduction in any form reserved
ISSN: 1569-3767/doi:10.1108/S1569-376720160000017019

Findings — *We find that the CIRP condition does not hold in either the onshore or the offshore RMB forward markets. We also find that the offshore market is more efficient than the onshore market in conveying private information about investors' expectation.*

Originality/value — *Our results reveal that the onshore RMB forward market provides an imperfect platform for investors to manage their currency exposures. We suggest that by opening the offshore market to domestic participants and the onshore market to more foreigners, the forward rates may become more informative with a greater investor mix. These liberalization efforts are important steps in the right directions to improve market efficiency in the Chinese FOREX market.*

Keywords: Interest rate parity; market efficiency; onshore and offshore Renminbi forward markets; Chinese Renminbi

INTRODUCTION

In recent years, China has gained significant economic power and become the largest trading partner of the United States of America and the European Community. Its meteoric rise is the result of carefully planned economic and political reforms and the gradual opening up of its economy. However, despite its growing importance in global trade, its financial markets, including the Chinese foreign exchange (FOREX) market is still under development. In the relatively closed FOREX market, with limited foreign participants, the active government interventions could adversely influence the informativeness of the FOREX market prices.

While floating exchange rates regimes are dominant in the global economy, a large number of countries still manage or peg their exchange rates against some other currency or a basket of currencies. Thus, a careful analysis of a FOREX market for a managed currency such as the Chinese currency, the Yuan or Renminbi (RMB), is of major economic interest. Since its inception in the 1970s, the RMB has been pegged and closely managed by the Chinese government through controlled swap centers (Guo & Han, 2004). These swap arrangements have lost some importance since July 21, 2005, when the RMB transitioned into a managed float currency against a basket of currencies based on trade flows. However, the RMB, as a managed currency, is still inaccessible to most foreign participants who do not have access to the onshore RMB market. Hence, an offshore market was started by foreign financial institutions and multinational corporations to hedge their RMB exposures. Gradually, its role shifted toward facilitating speculation (Fung, Leung, & Zhu, 2004). As such, the offshore market is primarily market driven and is considered to be a better reflection of the market sentiment about RMB. While the offshore forward market has been active for a number of years, the onshore forward market was officially established only after 2005 and is primarily accessible to domestic market participants and government entities.

To the best of our knowledge, there is no extant research that examines the relative market efficiency of the regulated onshore versus offshore RMB forward markets. In this study, we conduct market efficiency tests and find that the offshore market is more efficient in pricing forward RMB (particularly at shorter maturities). Moreover, we find that the offshore forward market conveys more private information while the onshore market reflects more government related information.

This paper is organized as follows. "Literature Review on Interest Rate Parity Conditions" provides a review of the extant literature on interest rate parity condition in relation to economic development (in both developed and emerging markets). "Chinese Institutional Setting and Hypothesis Development" includes a discussion of the history of the RMB, the exchange rate policy, market development, and testable empirical hypotheses. "Data and Empirical Results" presents the data and empirical findings. "Conclusion" section concludes.

LITERATURE REVIEW ON INTEREST RATE PARITY CONDITIONS

The covered interest rate parity (CIRP) condition states that a currency's forward premium/discount should be equivalent to the interest rate differentials between two countries based on the assumption of the law of one price and the purchasing power parity principles. Under such circumstances, the CIRP condition can be written as follows:

$$(1+i) = \frac{F}{S}(1+i^*) \tag{1}$$

where i and i^* refer to the domestic and foreign interest rates respectively, and F and S refer to forward and spot exchange rates, respectively (Eun & Resnick, 2004).[1]

The uncovered interest rate parity (UIRP) condition defines interest rate differentials as the expected rate of change of the spot rate as follows:

$$(i - i^*) \approx \frac{E(S_{t+1}) - S_t}{S_t} \qquad (2)$$

Under the UIRP condition, the future spot rates are based on investor's expectation and are subject to fluctuations, unlike the CIRP condition where future spot rates are locked in by the commitment of a forward contract. As the UIRP condition utilizes the expected future spot rate (and is usually unknown at time t), the deviations of UIRP do not necessarily imply arbitrage opportunities (Sarno, 2005).

In the literature, the CIRP is a widely accepted condition for testing market efficiency in the FOREX market (e.g., Lipscomb, 2005). Ideally, the forward premiums should compensate for the lower interest rates (or vice versa), but this condition often does not hold in emerging markets where market frictions and capital controls hinder arbitrageurs from correcting mispricing. For example, Alper, Ardic, and Fendoglu (2009) suggest that the lower GDP levels, higher inflation rates, higher nominal interest rates, and higher interest rate volatility may explain the deviation of interest rate parity conditions in the emerging market context. The effect of time is especially relevant in the emerging market context where the financial instruments tend to have shorter maturities, higher volatilities, and greater inflationary pressures. Indeed, Ferreira and León-Ledesma (2007) find significant variation in interest rate differentials across developed and emerging markets. They can only reject the unit-root null hypothesis for all the emerging markets, but not for all developed economies. Francis, Hasan, and Hunter (2002) try to explain these differences across developed and less developed markets using financial liberalization and restrictions on capital mobility.

CHINESE INSTITUTIONAL SETTING AND HYPOTHESIS DEVELOPMENT

Review of the Chinese Interest Rate and Exchange Rate Policy Development

In the case of China, one of the most important factors in determining interest rate expectations is the relatively fixed exchange rate regime which requires substantial government intervention to manage the demand and supply of the domestic currency. Although China's de jure exchange rate regime is classified as a managed float since July 21, 2005, its de facto movements have been relatively tight (PBOC, 2008). This can also be verified by the time-paths of the RMB against other managed currencies, like the Singapore dollar (Ma & McCauley, 2010).

The Chinese economy started a major government initiated transformation in the 1970s, with the introduction of the "open-door trade policy" by establishing Special Economic Zones (Zhang, 2004). Since then, the Chinese FOREX market has undergone an extensive series of reforms which can be categorized into three eras, namely the "dual track" regime from the 1970s to 1994, the "unified pegged" regime from 1994 to July 21, 2005, and the "managed floating" regime post July 21, 2005.

The "dual track" regime was by and large a controlled regime where the RMB exchange rate was segregated into two distinct markets: one for international trading activity (i.e., the swap market, where foreign currency earnings from trade-related activities were exchanged at "swap rates" for foreign exchange share certificates), and the other for nontrading activities under official exchange rate.[2] The RMB swap arrangements were coordinated through centralized swap centers, and the FX certificate swap arrangements were gradually centralized and finally replaced by a centralized RMB rate (the "unified pegged" regime). Gradually, capital movement was relaxed with the centrally controlled liberalization of the financial markets, and some investors could gain access to the market through a special license (i.e., investors can apply for a special license under the Qualified Domestic Institutional Investor (QDII) and Qualified Foreign Institutional Investor (QFII) schemes for permission to trade up to a limit in the Chinese A-share and domestic bond markets; An, 2008).

The offshore market started in the 1990s to meet the demand of foreign investors, traders, and multinational corporations who needed to hedge their RMB exposure since they were prohibited from trading in the domestic market (Gang, 2008). A large part of the offshore market, outside of the jurisdiction of the Chinese government, exists in the form of nondeliverable forwards (NDFs). Being cash settled forward contracts, NDFs are essentially forward contracts of an unconvertible currency (i.e., the RMB) that are settled in a convertible currency (i.e., the USD), and do not require either party to deliver or take delivery of the underlying notional amount — as the value differences are netted and settled at maturity. Fig. 1 shows the time series of the number of QFII quotas.

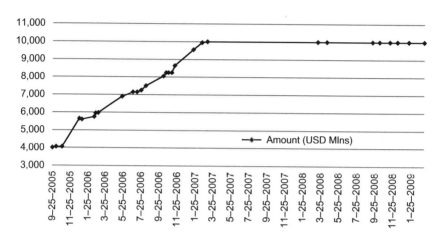

Fig. 1. Time Trend of QFII Quotas over Time. *Notes*: This figure shows the times series of qualified foreign institutional investors (QFII) quotas over time as a proxy for market liberalization. The data is collected from various news articles from Bloomberg.

China took a major step toward financial market liberalization on July 21, 2005 with the "managed floating" of the RMB, where the exchange rate was determined through the demand and supply mechanism. Since then, there have been extensive development of the onshore market, notably the introduction of derivative instruments (e.g., currency forwards and swaps) to provide market-driven pricing mechanisms for the RMB.

Research Hypotheses

The basic premise of weak and semistrong form market efficiency is that financial instruments fully incorporate all ex-post market and public information so that investors are unable to exploit the information to earn excess returns. In our context, past market and public information include historical spot rates, forward rates, ex-post realized forward biases, government policies in the forms of capital restrictions, floor limits on interest rates, and guidance policies.

Moreover, given that the offshore RMB forward is nondeliverable, we need to consider additional factors. For example, Higgins and Humpage (2005) suggest that NDF markets should ideally be "accurate estimators of future spot rates, with errors that are very small and symmetrically distributed around zero," through the law of large numbers (as NDFs are frequently traded on the markets). They argue that any systematic CIRP bias in the NDF biases is likely due to the incorporation of a risk premium during thin or volatile markets, or for underlying currencies with significant policy or country risk.[3] Lipscomb (2005) examines the CIRP conditions using NDFs and suggests a list of other factors that can influence NDF pricing besides interest rate expectations, such as trading flows, liquidity and counterparty risk, the perceived probability of changes in foreign exchange regime, speculative positioning, the integration between the onshore and offshore markets, and policy risk.

In this study, we hypothesize that in an efficient forward market: (1) forward rates should be unbiased estimators of future spot rates; and (2) market and public information should not result in any future forward biases. Thus, our first testable hypothesis aims to verify market efficiency of the onshore and the offshore RMB forward markets as follows:

H1. *The CIRP condition does not hold in the onshore and the offshore forward RMB markets, due to market frictions (e.g., capital controls, government interventions, etc.)*

Since extensive evidence suggests that CIRP deviations exist in emerging markets, our main focus is not about the existence of the deviation per se, but the magnitude of the deviation in the onshore and the offshore forward markets. These markets exist independently by serving different groups of investors under different jurisdictions. They face the same amount of exchange rate risk, as the financial instruments are comparable and therefore equally impacted by changes in RMB spot rate over time (as the profit and loss of both onshore and forward contracts depend on the future spot rate at time $t + k$). However, the two markets differ in the amount of political risk as they operate under different legal and economic jurisdictions. We postulate that the onshore market has more political risk, while the offshore market has more private unobservable information about the Chinese FOREX market as market participation is less likely influenced by government entities. This conjecture leads to our second hypothesis:

H2A. *The onshore CIRP deviations (DCIRP) contain a higher proportion of political risk premiums and can be explained to a greater extent by public information.*

H2B. *The offshore CIRP deviations (DCIRP) are larger and can be explained to a smaller extent by observables and contain more private information.*

DATA AND EMPIRICAL RESULTS

Data

Our data are from both Chinese onshore and offshore RMB markets from July 21, 2005 to February 27, 2009.[4] Unlike prior studies, we undertake a more comprehensive analysis of forwards across the entire term structure, for both onshore and offshore markets. For the CIRP tests, we obtain daily observations for US-China interest-rates of various maturities, from Bloomberg. Although we want to include the entire term structure of the interest rates to derive US-China interest rate differentials at all maturities, we can only obtain interest rate differentials for the 3- to 12-month horizons given the available Chinese interest rates. Consistent with the literature, we find strong evidence of stationarity for such interest-differential time series.

Table 1 panel A and B provide summary statistics of the forward contracts traded on the onshore and offshore Renminbi markets, respectively. We find that the onshore forwards are more volatile between 4- and 11-month maturity, while the NDFs are volatile only at 8- and 11-month maturity. This may be representative of a thin market. For the onshore market, the forwards tend to be stable for 1, 6, and 12 months, where the volatilities are relatively constant for the NDF markets.

Following the literature, we collect relevant macroeconomic information to explain potential DCIRP. Specifically, we consider a number of proxies for exchange rate and political risks. Table 2 provides the relevant summary statistics of these variables. Specifically we use four alternative political risk measures: (p1) change in foreign reserve (ΔNFA/RM), (p2) change in bank reserve ratios (ΔReserveratio), (p3) Change in 13-month moving-average variability of RMB rate (Δ13_Spotvolatility), and (p4) change in QFII quotas (ΔQFII).

These variables aim to capture the extent of government intervention (and therefore, political risk), and are expected to have greater explanatory power for the onshore DCIRP. The change in foreign reserves (p1 measure) is an important measure of China's sterilization efforts but it may be a poor proxy if used in isolation. Therefore, we scale the change in net foreign assets (NFA) by the prior month's reserve money stock (RM) as suggested by Glick and Hutchison (2008). Positive (negative) NFAs indicate foreign reserve inflows (outflows), which represent foreign asset accumulation (reductions) by the central bank. The change in bank reserve ratios (p2 measure) is a direct indicator of the government's monetary policy, as it is directly linked to the money supply in the Chinese banking system and it

Table 1. Summary Statistics of Chinese Renminbi Forward Contracts.

Variable	N	Min	Max	Mean	Std	Data Since
Panel A: RMB onshore forwards						
Spot rate	942	6.811	8.113	7.551	0.470	19/12/2003
1 Month	469	4.255	7.429	6.772	0.322	15/5/2007
2 Month	713	5.956	7.850	6.991	0.452	7/6/2006
3 Month	878	6.794	8.042	7.454	0.452	19/10/2005
4 Month	713	5.107	7.850	6.817	0.535	7/6/2006
5 Month	878	0.069	8.007	7.405	0.515	19/10/2005
6 Month	878	6.652	7.976	7.389	0.450	19/10/2005
7 Month	878	0.070	7.955	7.364	0.514	19/10/2005
8 Month	878	0.070	7.934	7.342	0.515	19/10/2005
9 Month	878	0.002	7.913	7.321	0.517	19/10/2005
10 Month	878	0.070	7.890	7.301	0.517	19/10/2005
11 Month	878	0.070	7.869	7.282	0.519	19/10/2005
12 Month	878	6.399	7.848	7.272	0.460	19/10/2005

Variable	N	Min	Max	Mean	Std	Data since
Panel B: RMB offshore forwards						
Spot rate	942	6.811	8.113	7.551	0.470	19/12/2003
1 Month	942	6.788	8.100	7.527	0.460	19/12/2003
2 Month	942	6.753	8.147	7.500	0.456	19/12/2003
3 Month	942	6.713	8.069	7.473	0.453	19/12/2003
4 Month	942	6.667	8.277	7.535	0.459	19/12/2003
5 Month	942	6.631	8.098	7.423	0.454	19/12/2003
6 Month	942	6.538	7.995	7.392	0.452	19/12/2003
7 Month	930	6.524	8.000	7.394	0.490	2/8/2005
8 Month	878	3.000	7.921	6.797	1.393	13/10/2005
9 Month	942	6.409	7.928	7.315	0.457	19/12/2003
10 Month	878	5.000	7.869	6.966	0.813	13/10/2005
11 Month	882	6.328	7.842	7.262	0.494	13/10/2005
12 Month	942	6.275	7.865	7.238	0.466	19/12/2003

Notes: This table presents the summary statistics of Chinese Renminbi forward contracts from July 21, 2006 to February 27, 2009. Panel A presents the statistics from the onshore forwards. Panel B presents the offshore forwards. We report the number of observations (N), minimum value (min), maximum value (max), mean, standard deviation (Std), and the earliest data available date (data since).

may have a positive relationship with DCIRP as higher reserve ratios may result in limited capital flows in the economy. The change in the 13-month moving-average volatility in the RMB rate (p3 measure) is expected to capture the market uncertainty and market dynamics. We posit that higher

Table 2. Summary Statistics of Macroeconomic Variables.

Variable	N	Min	Max	Mean	Std	Data Since
Panel A: Summary statistics for Chinese macroeconomic variables						
ΔNFA/RM	942	−0.367	0.410	0.032	0.085	May-05
ΔReserveratio	942	−1.500	1.000	0.182	0.407	May-05
Δ13m_Spotvolatility	942	0.002	0.080	0.025	0.024	May-05
ΔQFII	870	−0.004	0.144	0.000	0.006	Oct-05
91DRepo	608	2.000	5.400	3.566	0.787	Nov-06
182DRepo	740	2.500	2.700	2.511	0.046	May-06
ΔImports	942	−0.134	0.213	0.003	0.067	May-05
ΔExports	942	−0.167	0.172	−0.001	0.051	May-05
ΔCapitalFlow	942	−1.072	0.996	0.008	0.221	May-05

Variable	N	Min	Max	Mean	Std	Data Since
Panel B: Chinese interest rates						
1 Yr benchmark rate	882	5.310	7.470	6.402	0.758	21/7/2005
3 Mth SHIBOR	583	1.275	4.507	3.504	0.910	9/10/2006
6 Mth SHIBOR	583	1.549	4.597	3.612	0.893	9/10/2006
9 Mth SHIBOR	625	1.706	4.652	3.687	0.877	9/10/2006
12 Mth SHIBOR	583	1.928	4.716	3.806	0.837	9/10/2006
3 Mth deposit rate	899	1.710	3.330	2.274	0.668	21/7/2005
6 Mth deposit rate	899	1.980	3.780	2.695	0.706	21/7/2005
12 Mth deposit rate	942	2.250	4.140	3.006	0.784	21/7/2005

Variable	N	Min	Max	Mean	Std	Data Since
Panel C: Summary statistics for U.S. interest rates						
U.S. discount rate	938	0.500	6.250	4.208	2.050	21/7/2005
3 Mth LIBOR	942	1.083	5.725	4.279	1.272	21/7/2005
6 Mth LIBOR	942	1.465	5.640	4.369	1.169	21/7/2005
9 Mth LIBOR	942	1.624	5.711	4.381	1.142	21/7/2005
12 Mth LIBOR	942	1.738	5.766	4.394	1.115	21/7/2005
3 Mth deposit rate	942	0.850	6.130	4.302	1.230	21/7/2005
6 Mth deposit rate	942	1.100	5.770	4.380	1.120	21/7/2005
12 Mth deposit rate	942	1.870	5.725	4.458	0.996	21/7/2005

Notes: This table presents the summary statistics of macroeconomic variables and interest rates. Panel A shows the Chinese macroeconomic variables. Exchange rate risk and political risk measures are: the change in capital flows (ΔNFA/RM); the change in bank reserve ratios (ΔReserveratio); the change in 13-month moving-average variability of RMB rate (Δ13m_Spotvolatility); the change in QFII quotas (ΔQFII); the repo rate differentials at different maturities (e.g., 91DRepo and 182DRepo); the change in imports (ΔImports), the change in exports (ΔExports) from/to United States; and the change in the residual component of Balance of Payments (ΔCapitalFlow). Panel B reports the benchmark interest rates in China. Panel C reports the benchmark interest rates in the United States. We report the number of observations (N), minimum value (min), maximum value (max), mean, standard deviation (Std), and the earliest data available date (Data since).

volatility is associated with lower DCIRP because higher volatility is generally expected to capture greater exchange rate flexibility and informativeness (Bahmani-Oskooee & Malixi, 1987). Lastly, the change in QFII and QDII quotas (p4 measure) is used as a proxy for the opening of the capital market. This latter measure is expected to have a negative relation with DCIRP, as the greater foreign participation (with higher QFII) is likely to alleviate the onshore DCIRP by facilitating external capital flows.

To capture political risk, we adopt two alternative repo market measures and three trade and capital market flow measures. The two repo measures are the 91-day repo differential (91DRepo) and the 182-day repo (182DRepo) differential. We posit that these measures will have a positive relation with the deviations, as a higher repo rate is an indication of lower liquidity and reflects increased sterilization activity (Cao, 2009). In addition, we include measures for the annual change in exports and imports from the United States (ΔExport and ΔImport). Our last macro measure is the change in the Residual Component of Balance of Payments (BOP) which is denoted as ΔCapitalFlow. As China's capital account transactions are currently nonconvertible, we utilize residual components of the BOP to estimate the "hot money" flows that move between China's capital borders.

Since the macro variables are strongly related, we conduct Pearson correlation tests to check for possible collinearity issues in the regressions (see Appendix A). We find that all correlations are within reasonable limits allowing us to include all variables contemporaneously in a regression without multicollinearity problems.

We provide summary statistics on the relevant interest rates for the Chinese and the US markets in Table 2 panel B and C. We find that, on average, the Chinese interest rates are lower during our sample period with lower volatilities. This supports earlier arguments that the Chinese interest rates tend to be utilized as exchange-rate control measures (resulting in more "sticky rates") while the US rates tend to be more market-driven. In our sample, the US discount rate is the most volatile interest rate measure. This measure exhibits large swings because the US central bank (the Fed) frequently intervenes by adjusting the discount rate, especially during the 2008 financial crisis when it was abruptly reduced to 0.5%.

Empirical Analyses of Market Efficiency

To test for market efficiency, we can use either expectations-based survey data (as a market-driven expectation of the future spot rate) or observed ex-post forward rate deviations (as an unbiased predictor of future ex-ante deviations). As survey-based expectations data is unavailable for China, we will use the latter method to explore the forward rate bias in the Chinese currency market. For our first hypothesis on whether the RMB forward markets are efficient (both offshore and onshore), we test whether the CIRP conditions hold. Specifically we examine whether there is a persistent deviation from CIRP in these markets by adopting the following regression model from Alper et al. (2009):

$$f_{t,k} - S_t = \alpha_1 + \beta_{\text{interestdiff}}\left(i_{t,k} - i_{t,k}^*\right) + \beta_{\text{offbreak}}\text{offbreak} + \mu_t \qquad (3)$$

where, $i_{t,k}$ and $i_{t,k}^*$ refer to the domestic and foreign interest rates respectively with maturity k, the dummy variable offbreak, capturing a structural break, equals one after October 2006 when SAFE bans domestic individuals and institutions from participating in the offshore market. Similar to Fama (1984)'s work, we formulate the market efficiency CIRP condition with the null hypothesis: $H_0 : \alpha_1 = 0$, $\beta_{\text{interstdiff}} = 1$. This H_0 condition reflects that any gains in interest differentials should be equivalent to the forward discount (and vice versa).

Table 3 shows that, in general, the CIRP condition does not hold for the forward RMB market. In all regression models in Table 3, the intercepts (α_1) are statistically significant at the 1% significance level, suggesting that the CIRP conditions do not hold in either forward markets. Some coefficient estimates on the interest rate differentials have negative signs (i.e., a higher interest rate translates into an expected appreciation of the RMB) in the onshore market, which is against economic intuition. However, as these regressions are associated with low adjusted R-square values, the coefficient estimates should be interpreted with caution.

Overall, the results from Table 3 support our first hypothesis that the CIRP condition does not hold in either the onshore or offshore forward markets. The persistent deviation from the CIRP condition may be due to market imperfections (such as capital controls) or behavioral bias. To explain the deviation, we systematically analyze the CIRP deviation using a number of macro risk, political risk, and exchange rate risk measures. In addition, we compare the deviation and the fraction of explainable deviation across the two markets and consider whether investor composition may also play a role in the different price setting. For example, it is plausible that in the offshore market, the political risk effect is more pronounced because the foreign individuals and institutions overestimate or overprice political risk. Alternatively, the foreign investors in the offshore market

Table 3. GMM Regression of CIRP Condition.

The Relevant Interest Diff Measures	Onshore					Offshore				
	N	α_1	$\beta_{interestdiff}$	$\beta_{offbreak}$	Adj. R^2	N	α_1	$\beta_{interestdiff}$	$\beta_{offbreak}$	Adj. R^2
Metary policy rate	822	-0.0136 (0.0002)***	-0.0266 (0.0176)	0.0003 (0.0005)	0.001	881	-0.0162 (0.0002)***	0.1097 (0.0253)***	-0.0069 (0.0006)***	0.033
3 mth LIBOR differ	583	-0.0030 (0.0003)***	-0.0017 (0.0081)	-0.0002 (0.0002)*	-0.003	583	-0.0028 (0.0004)***	0.0291 (0.0117)**	-0.0016 (0.0002)***	0.006
6 mth LIBOR differ	583	-0.0069 (0.0005)***	-0.0423 (0.0149)***	-0.0004 (0.0003)*	0.009	583	-0.0065 (0.0006)***	0.0162 (0.0213)	-0.0031 (0.0004)***	-0.001
9 mth LIBOR differ	625	-0.0115 (0.0006)***	-0.1162 (0.0202)***	0.0004 (0.0003)	0.042	625	-0.0103 (0.0008)***	0.0040 (0.0277)	-0.0042 (0.0005)***	-0.001
12 mth LIBOR differ	583	-0.0160 (0.0007)***	-0.1792 (0.0267)***	0.0012 (0.0004)***	0.060	583	-0.0147 (0.001)***	-0.0261 (0.0372)	-0.0051 (0.0006)***	0.000
3 mth deposit rate differ	835	-0.0028 (0.0004)***	0.0175 (0.0094)*	-0.0001 (0.0002)	0.005	899	-0.0024 (0.0004)***	0.0600 (0.0122)***	-0.0011 (0.0002)***	0.033
6 mth deposit rate differ	835	-0.0082 (0.0006)***	-0.0390 (0.0169)**	0.0007 (0.0003)***	0.006	899	-0.0077 (0.0007)***	0.0249 (0.0227)	-0.0014 (0.0003)***	0.003
12 mth deposit rate differ	878	-0.0215 (0.0007)***	-0.2767 (0.0267)***	0.0050 (0.0004)***	0.122	942	-0.0196 (0.001)***	-0.1270 (0.0362)***	-0.0009 (0.0007)	0.024

Notes: This table reports the GMM regression on covered interest rate parity (CIRP) conditions using benchmark interest rates. The sample period is from July 21, 2005 to February 27, 2009, based on daily observational data. The $\beta_{interestdiff}$ coefficient represents the impact of interest rate differentials on the forward premium (discount) while $\beta_{offbreak}$ is a dummy that takes on the value of 1 after October 2006 where the ban on domestic individual and institution participation in the offshore market has been implemented. The LIBOR differentials are between the Shanghai Board Offer Rate (SHIBOR) and British Bankers Association LIBOR, the deposit rate differentials are between the Chinese household savings deposit rates and its US equivalent, the Treasury differentials are between the Chinese Inter-Bank Treasury bills and the US Treasury bills, and the policy rate differential is between the 1-year Chinese benchmark rate and the US discount rate. N represents the number of observations utilized. Probability values are computed using two-tailed t-tests and the Newey-West standard errors are represented in parentheses. The *, **, *** represent statistical significance at 10%, 5%, and 1% respectively.

may consider the Chinese political risk from a different angle, in conjunction with their own countries' economic objectives and potentials.

Analyses of CIRP Deviations: Onshore versus Offshore Markets

For this part of our study, we incorporate both approaches by Cheung, Chinn, and Fujii (2005) and Liu and Otani (2005) to test the CIRP deviations (which is DCIRP), and we replace the ex-post realized spot rate with both onshore and offshore forward rates.[5] We determine the DCIRP for both onshore and offshore forward markets, as follows:

$$\text{DCIRP}_{\text{on}} = \left(i_t^k - i_t^{k*}\right) - \left(f_{t\,\text{on}}^k - S_t\right) \tag{4A}$$

$$\text{DCIRP}_{\text{off}} = \left(i_t^k - i_t^{k*}\right) - \left(f_{t\,\text{off}}^k - S_t\right) \tag{4B}$$

where, Eqs. (4A) and (4B) describe the DCIRP for the onshore and the offshore forward markets, and $f_{t\,\text{on}}^k$ represents onshore forwards while $f_{t\,\text{off}}^k$ represents NDFs in the offshore market.

To shed more light on the differences in the two markets, we regress DCIRP against the same macroeconomic measures to uncover the impact of these determinants on DCIRP in the onshore Eq. (5A) and offshore Eq. (5B) markets:

$$\text{DCIRP}_{\text{on},k} = \alpha_0 + \beta_1 \left(\frac{\Delta\text{NFA}}{\text{RM}}\right) + \beta_2(\Delta\text{Reserveratio}) + \beta_3(\Delta 13m\_\text{Spot\_volatility})$$

$$+ \beta_4(\Delta\text{QFII}) + \beta_5\text{Repo\_rate}_k + \beta_6(\Delta\text{Import}_{\text{US}})$$

$$+ \beta_7\left(\Delta\text{Export}_{\text{US}}\right) + \beta_8(\Delta\text{Capitalflow})$$

$$\tag{5A}$$

$$\text{DCIRP}_{\text{off},k} = \alpha_0 + \beta_1 \left(\frac{\Delta\text{NFA}}{\text{RM}}\right) + \beta_2(\Delta\text{Reserveratio}) + \beta_3(\Delta 13m\_\text{Spot\_volatility})$$

$$+ \beta_4(\Delta\text{QFII}) + \beta_5\text{Repo\_rate}_k + \beta_6(\Delta\text{Import}_{\text{US}})$$

$$+ \beta_7\left(\Delta\text{Export}_{\text{US}}\right) + \beta_8(\Delta\text{Capitalflow})$$

$$\tag{5B}$$

where k refers to the maturity of the interest rate differential. In the regression analyses, we use Newey-West adjusted standard errors.

The eight β coefficients reflect the explanatory power of the macroeconomic variables that are used to capture political risk and exchange rate risk. As we use the same set of independent variables for both markets, we are able to compare the strength of the β coefficients and the relative importance of political versus exchange rate risk measures in explaining DCIRP in each market. If the β coefficients for the political risk determinants (ΔNFA, ΔReserveratio, Δ13m_Spot_volatility, ΔQFII) are greater than the coefficients on the exchange rate measures, then we can infer that the major driver of market inefficiency in the RMB forward market is political risk. Table 4 panel A and B present the results for the DCIRP regressions for the onshore and offshore markets, respectively.

Table 4 shows that most of the coefficient estimates are statistically significant, with the exception of the ΔQFII and ΔImports variables. Interestingly, the ΔCapitalFlow variable seems to be more relevant for the offshore markets than the onshore markets, although the values are economically small. In terms of all other explanatory macro variables, we find similar coefficient signs and most of them are in line with the extant literature. However, the ΔQFII and Repo_rates variables (i.e., 91DRepo is used in the 3-month regression and 182DRepo is used in the 6-, 9-, and 12-month regressions as there is no longer maturity Chinese repo rates) have coefficient signs that go against our predictions. One possible reason could be the stickiness of these variables, as the data series have remained unchanged over the recent years.[6] As such, these variables might be poor determinants in uncovering the risk premiums behind DCIRP.

By looking at Table 4 panel A and B individually, we see that in both markets, the Δ13m_Spotvolatility measure provides the highest explanatory power, followed by ΔExports, Repo_rates and ΔQFII (even though the latter two determinants have weak statistical significance). These findings suggest that exchange rate policy measures (i.e., the Chinese government's active intervention) are the key determinants of DCIRP during our sample period.

Comparing the adjusted R-squares across the onshore and the offshore market, we find that the political and exchange-rate risk measures have greater explanatory power in the onshore market. This suggests that the offshore market contains additional private information that are not captured by the macro measures used in Table 4 panel A and B. This means that the offshore market is more efficient in revealing private information while the onshore market, by and large, aggregates the observable macro information and political and exchange rate risk measures

Table 4. GMM Regression of DCIRP.

The Relevant Interest Diff Measures	N	α_1	β_1	β_2	β_3	β_4	β_5	β_6	β_7	β_8	Adj. R^2
			Exchange rate risk measures						Political risk measures		
		$\frac{\Delta NFA}{RM}$	ΔReserve Ratio	Δ13m_SpotVolatility	ΔQFII	Repo_Rates	ΔImports	ΔExports	ΔCapitalFlow		
Panel A: Onshore RMB market											
Monetary policy rate	690	0.009	0.016	0.014	−0.856	0.268	0.000	C.001	0.168	−0.010	0.85
		(0.001)***	(0.0025)***	(0.0006)***	(0.0129)***	(0.0625)***	(0.0001)***	(C.01)	(0.0152)***	(0.0014)***	
3 mth LIBOR	565	0.043	−0.019	0.003	−0.640	−0.012	−0.003	C.000	0.134	−0.001	0.89
		(0.001)***	(0.0029)***	(0.0007)***	(0.0102)***	(0.0416)	(0.0004)***	(0.0065)	(0.0084)***	(0.0007)	
6 mth LIBOR	582	0.243	−0.011	0.006	−0.659	0.018	−0.083	−0.002	0.077	0.001	0.93
		(0.0149)***	(0.0027)***	(0.0005)***	(0.0079)***	(0.0371)	(0.006)***	(0.0033)	(0.0071)***	(0.0007)*	
9 mth LIBOR	624	0.265	−0.006	0.010	−0.599	0.038	−0.092	0.002	0.074	0.000	0.90
		(0.013)***	(0.0027)**	(0.0005)***	(0.0087)***	(0.0505)	(0.0052)***	(0.0033)	(0.0077)***	(0.0009)	
12 mth LIBOR	582	0.268	−0.001	0.013	−0.550	0.046	−0.093	0.007	0.072	−0.001	0.88
		(0.0164)***	(0.0027)	(0.0004)***	(0.0105)***	(0.0694)	(0.0066)***	(0.003)**	(0.0098)***	(0.0008)	
3 mth deposit	567	0.047	−0.016	0.005	−0.551	0.061	−0.003	0.004	0.159	−0.003	0.77
		(0.0014)***	(0.0029)***	(0.001)***	(0.0154)***	(0.0655)	(0.0005)***	(0.0095)	(0.0115)***	(0.0009)***	
6 mth deposit	698	0.384	−0.013	0.005	−0.573	0.054	−0.138	−0.009	0.061	0.001	0.91
		(0.0141)***	(0.0026)***	(0.0008)***	(0.0074)***	(0.0289)*	(0.0056)***	(0.0037)**	(0.0059)***	(0.0007)	
12 mth deposit	739	0.388	−0.005	0.009	−0.491	0.090	−0.139	−0.006	0.057	0.000	0.89
		(0.0095)***	(0.0026)*	(0.0006)***	(0.008)***	(0.0476)*	(0.0038)***	(0.0027)**	(0.0055)***	(0.0008)	

Onshore

The Relevant Interest Diff Measures

				Offshore							
			Exchange rate risk measures					Political risk measures			
Interest Diff Measures	N	α_1	β_1	β_2	β_3	β_4	β_5	β_6	β_7	β_8	Adj. R^2
		$\frac{\Delta NFA}{RM}$	ΔReserveRatio	Δ13m_SpotVolatility	ΔQFII	Repo_Rates	ΔImports	ΔExports	ΔCapitalFlow		
Panel B: Offshore RMB market											
Monetary policy rate	690	0.012 (0.0012)***	0.022 (0.0024)***	0.022 (0.0008)***	-0.884 (0.0176)***	0.320 (0.0815)***	0.000 (0.0002)	0.022 (0.0127)*	0.203 (0.0182)***	-0.010 (0.0012)***	0.81
3 mth LIBOR	565	0.046 (0.0011)***	-0.014 (0.0025)***	0.007 (0.0007)***	-0.638 (0.0113)***	-0.010 (0.0649)	-0.004 (0.0004)***	0.011 (0.0069)	0.142 (0.0072)***	0.000 (0.0007)	0.89
6 mth LIBOR	582	0.291 (0.0182)***	-0.006 (0.0031)*	0.012 (0.0007)***	-0.679 (0.0119)***	0.039 (0.063)	-0.102 (0.0073)***	0.013 (0.0041)***	0.083 (0.0094)***	0.004 (0.001)***	0.90
9 mth LIBOR	624	0.363 (0.0172)***	-0.001 (0.0033)	0.016 (0.0007)***	-0.657 (0.0136)***	0.019 (0.0708)	-0.130 (0.0069)***	0.016 (0.0044)***	0.082 (0.0104)***	0.003 (0.0011)***	0.88
12 mth LIBOR	582	0.392 (0.0253)***	0.002 (0.0033)	0.021 (0.0007)***	-0.617 (0.0165)***	0.049 (0.0921)	-0.141 (0.0101)***	0.026 (0.0053)***	0.095 (0.0143)***	0.002 (0.0011)	0.85
3 mth deposit	567	0.050 (0.0015)***	-0.012 (0.0027)***	0.009 (0.001)***	-0.550 (0.0158)***	0.062 (0.0879)	-0.004 (0.0005)***	0.016 (0.01)	0.167 (0.0106)***	-0.002 (0.0009)***	0.78
6 mth deposit	698	0.437 (0.015)***	-0.007 (0.0031)**	0.011 (0.0009)***	-0.583 (0.0096)***	0.079 (0.0396)**	-0.159 (0.006)***	0.005 (0.0043)	0.061 (0.0075)***	0.003 (0.001)***	0.89
12 mth deposit	739	0.526 (0.0153)***	0.001 (0.0034)	0.017 (0.0007)***	-0.527 (0.0129)***	0.104 (0.0614)*	-0.193 (0.0061)***	0.011 (0.005)**	0.060 (0.0089)***	0.002 (0.0011)*	0.86

Notes: This table presents the GMM regression of the deviation of the CIRP (DCIRP) against all explanatory variables. The sample period is from July 21, 2005 to Feb 27, 2009, based on daily observational data. Panel A reports the results from the onshore market. Panel B reports the results from the offshore market. The β coefficients report the explanatory power for the DCIRP for the various interest rate pairs. N represents the number of observations utilized. Probability values are computed using two-tailed t tests. The Newey-West standard errors are displayed in parentheses and *, **, *** represent the statistical significance at 10%, 5%, and 1% respectively.

(Li, Morck, Yang, & Yeung, 2004; Morck, Yeung, & Yu, 2013). Thus, the additional information in the onshore forward market is limited while the offshore market conveys more private new information that can be useful for all market participants.

In a frictionless market setting, any deviations in interest rate differentials should be short-lived (given the sensitivity of capital flows toward these differentials). However, in China, the controlled interest rates may hinder effective capital flows across the border. As such, our findings of strong inefficiency (persistent DCIRP) in the onshore forward markets suggest that the government interventions such as interest rate management and RMB "boundary markers" inhibit the pricing in of private information from market participants, especially that of foreign investors.

On the other hand, the key factor that links up both markets is the RMB spot rate, which is actively influenced by frequent revaluations and reflects a certain level of political risk.[7] As such, through the RMB spot rate, the offshore market is exposed to a certain level of political risk as well (although not as much as the onshore markets), which is effectively priced into the forward premiums.

Overall, our findings document new insights about the onshore and offshore RMB forward markets and suggest that *further* research may be warranted to better understand the functioning and informativeness of these markets.

CONCLUSION

This study seeks to explore the presence and the relative strength of market efficiency in the onshore and offshore RMB forward markets. The results reveal that the CIRP conditions do not hold in either market. Hence, we conclude that both the onshore and offshore RMB forward markets are inefficient as we document significant deviation from CIRP conditions (i.e., systemic DCIRP).

As we examine the underlying dynamics behind the DCIRP for both markets, we find that on average, the unexplained portion of the offshore DCIRP tend to be greater, suggesting that more private information is revealed in this market. One possible reason is the extensive government control on interest rates and currency flows, resulting in the onshore forwards having little room to incorporate additional risk premiums. In the offshore market, foreign participants may be more sensitive to unobservable political risk from China or may exhibit more behavioral bias in their trading.

Overall, we find that the onshore RMB forward market provides an imperfect solution for investors seeking to manage their currency exposures. We suggest that greater investor mix with the opening of the offshore market to domestic participants and the onshore market to more foreigners are likely to improve the informativeness of the RMB forward rates. These liberalization efforts are important steps to modernize the RMB forward markets and to facilitate market efficiency in the Chinese FOREX market. As China is the major trading partner of many developed economies, the economic benefits will be realized not only by the Chinese domestic economy but also by many other countries worldwide.

NOTES

1. Using such notations, it is understood that the quotation convention for foreign exchange would be the amount of domestic currency per foreign currency. In our context, this would mean that quotes are in the RMB/USD notation.
2. Despite the apparent distortions between the RMB swap rates and the official rates, some argue that this "parallel market structure" was an essential step toward China's RMB market reforms.
3. The peso problem was in relation to the currency crisis that Mexico faced in the 1970s, where the peso (pegged to the USD) was under massive selling pressure. Most market participants believed that the peso would be forced to devalue (which resulted in peso forwards being priced at a discount), but the Mexican government had propped up interest rates to prevent capital flight − which was unsustainable in the long run. Eventually, the government had to relent and devalue the peso in 1976. (Krasker, 1980) provides an in-depth discussion on the peso problem.
4. As forward contracts are OTC products, there are no standardized quotes for forward rates. However, Bloomberg attempts to determine a composite quote by incorporating the quotes provided by a list of approved market makers, and then averaging them based on a quality score (i.e., accuracy of price feeds, update frequency, etc.). The interested reader can refer to the <QFX> function in Bloomberg for more explanations.
5. In fact, one of the main reasons why Cheung et al. (2005) used ex-post data was because of the lack of forward rate data at that time.
6. For instance, the QFII quotas have remained unchanged since Jan 07, and the 182 day repo rates have only changed once (in Jan 09) since its inception in May 06.
7. Defining political risk and exchange-rate risk can be a gray area, as elements that are driven by political risk (i.e., a fixed exchange rate regime) can be a risk factor that affects future spot rates.

ACKNOWLEDGMENT

The authors would like to thank Ong Choon Keong for his research assistance. All errors are our own.

REFERENCES

Alper, C. E., Ardic, O. P., & Fendoglu, S. (2009). The economics of the uncovered interest parity condition for emerging markets. *Journal of Economic Surveys, 23*, 115–138.

An, L. (2008). *Securities regulator says no massive stock selling and fleeing by QFII funds.* Retrieved from http://english.gov.cn/2008-10/18/content_1124365.htm. Accessed on March 01, 2009.

Bahmani-Oskooee, M., & Malixi, M. (1987). Effects of exchange rate flexibility on the demand for international reserves. *Economics Letters, 23*(1), 89–93.

Cao, B. (2009). China's interbank rates climb as PBOC drains cash; Yuan stable. *Bloomberg News, 2.* Retrieved from http://www.bloomberg.com/apps/news?pid=20601089&sid=apM_7XYr9EfU&refer=china#

Cheung, Y. W., Chinn, M. D., & Fujii, E. (2005). Dimensions of financial integration in greater China: Money markets, banks and policy effects. *International Journal of Finance and Economics, 10*(2), 117–132.

Eun, C. S., & Resnick, B. G. (2004). *International finance management* (4th ed., pp. 133–142). New York, NY: McGraw Hill International.

Fama, E. F. (1984). Forward and spot exchange rates. *Journal of Monetary Economics, 14*, 319–338.

Ferreira, A. L., & León-Ledesma, M. A. (2007). Does the real interest parity hypothesis hold? Evidence for developed and emerging markets. *Journal of International Money and Finance, 26*(3), 364–382.

Francis, B. B., Hasan, I., & Hunter, D. M. (2002). Emerging market liberalization and the impact on uncovered interest rate parity. *Journal of International Money and Finance, 21*(6), 931–956.

Fung, H. G., Leung, W. K., & Zhu, J. (2004). Nondeliverable forward market for Chinese RMB: A first look. *China Economic Review (1043951X), 15*, 348–352.

Gang, Y. (2008). Renminbi exchange rates and relevant institutional factors. *CATO Journal, 28*(2), 187–196.

Glick, R., & Hutchison, M. (2008). *Navigating the trilemma: Capital flows and monetary policy in China.* Federal Reserve Bank of San Francisco Papers, Dec 2008.

Guo, J., & Han, S. (2004). Reforms of China's foreign exchange regime and RMB exchange-rate behavior. *Chinese Economy, 37*(2), 76–101.

Higgins, P., & Humpage, O. F. (2005). Nondeliverable forwards: Can we tell where the Renminbi is headed? *Economic Commentary: Federal Reserve Bank of Cleveland, September 1.*

Krasker, W. S. (1980). The "Peso Problem" in testing the efficiency of forward exchange markets. *Journal of Monetary Economics, 6*(2), 269–276.

Li, K., Morck, R., Yang, F., & Yeung, B. (2004). Firm-specific variation and openness in emerging markets. *Review of Economics and Statistics, 86*(3), 658–669.

Lipscomb, L. (2005). *An overview of non-deliverable foreign exchange forward markets.* Bank of International Settlements Publications.

Liu, L.-G., & Otani, I. (2005). *Capital controls and interest rate parity: Evidences from China, 1999–2004.* Research Institute of Economy, Trade and Industry (RIETI) Working Papers.

Ma, G., & McCauley, R. N. (2010). *The evolving Renminbi regime and implications for Asian currency stability.* BIS Working Papers No 321.

Morck, R., Yeung, B., & Yu, W. (2013). R-squared and the economy. *Annual Review of Financial Economics, 5,* 143–166.

PBOC (2008). China: The evolution of foreign exchange controls and the consequences of capital flows. *BIS Papers, 44*(153), 143–153.

Sarno, L. (2005). Viewpoint: Towards a solution to the puzzles in exchange rate economics: Where do we stand? *Canadian Journal of Economics, 38,* 673–708.

Zhang, P. G. (2004). *Chinese Yuan Renminbi derivative products.* Singapore: World Scientific Publishing Co. Pte. Ltd.

APPENDIX

Table A1. Pearson Correlation Statistics on DCIRP Macro Determinant Variables.

	ΔNFA/RM	ΔReserveratio	Δ13m_Spotvol	ΔQFII	Δ91DRepo	Δ182DRepo	ΔImport	ΔExport	ΔCapitalflow
ΔNFA/RM	1								
ΔReserveratio	-0.083 *-0.012*	1							
Δ13m_Spotvolatility	0.028 *-0.393*	0.009 *-0.776*	1						
ΔQFII	0.001 *-0.977*	-0.012 *-0.717*	-0.059 *-0.082*	1					
Δ91DRepo	-0.347 *-0.001*	0.164 *-0.001*	0.325 *-0.001*	-0.094 *-0.021*	1				
Δ182DRepo	-0.085 *-0.022*	-0.127 *-0.001*	-0.107 *-0.004*	-0.023 *-0.54*	-0.206 *-0.001*	1			
ΔImports	0.108 *-0.001*	-0.075 *-0.021*	-0.049 *-0.136*	-0.004 *-0.9*	0.13 *-0.002*	-0.204 *-0.001*	1		
ΔExports	0.073 *-0.026*	0.162 *-0.001*	0.053 *-0.103*	-0.011 *-0.743*	0.297 *-0.001*	-0.544 *-0.001*	0.477 *-0.001*	1	
ΔCapitalFlow	0.500 *-0.001*	-0.019 *-0.566*	0.189 *-0.001*	0.019 *-0.571*	-0.264 *-0.001*	-0.005 *-0.902*	0.013 *-0.687*	0.098 *-0.003*	1

Notes: Exchange rate risk and political risk measures are: the change in capital flows (ΔNFA/RM); the change in bank reserve ratios (ΔReserveratio); the change in 13-month moving-average variability of RMB rate (Δ13m_Spotvolatility); the change in QFII quotas (ΔQFII); the repo rate differential at different maturities (Δ91DRepo and Δ182DRepo); the change in imports and exports from/to the United States (ΔImports and ΔExports); and the change in the residual component of Balance of Payments (ΔCapitalFlow). The coefficient estimates are shown with the corresponding *p*-values in italic.

DO SECTORAL AND LOCATIONAL FACTORS OF FOREIGN DIRECT INVESTMENT FROM EMERGING COUNTRIES MATTER FOR FIRM PERFORMANCE? THE CASE OF KOREAN FIRMS' FDI IN CHINA'S SERVICE SECTOR

Seong-Bong Lee, Masaaki Kotabe, Doohoi Heo, Byung Jin Kang and Albert H. Yoon

ABSTRACT

Purpose − *This paper examines the statistical relationship between outbound Foreign Direct Investment (FDI) and firm performance. We focus on how the link is influenced by sector-specific differences and geographical factors.*

Methodology − *We compile a time-series cross-sectional dataset that includes financial variables and FDI activities of South Korean firms*

The Political Economy of Chinese Finance
International Finance Review, Volume 17, 393−411
Copyright © 2016 by Emerald Group Publishing Limited
All rights of reproduction in any form reserved
ISSN: 1569-3767/doi:10.1108/S1569-376720160000017020

between 2005 and 2008 from the DART, a financial statement database. Then, we fit our data against the linear regression models that we designed to identify FDI-performance relationship in different subsamples. Our measurement of firm performance is specifically constructed to reflect excess returns in the stock market.

Findings — *We found compelling differences in the degree of FDI-performance relationships across different industries. In manufacturing sectors, the flow of direct investment is more heavily associated with firm performances than accumulated stock of direct investment, and vice versa in the service sector. The impact of China factors toward performance aspects of Korea's outbound FDI which also differs across sectors as well.*

Value — *Although there have been extensive research efforts on this subject in general, our paper addresses an increasingly significant class of FDIs that have received relatively less attention, that is, direct investment originating from developing economies. Also, our analysis adds a sectoral dimension that contributes to more comprehensive understanding of a multinational-performance relationship.*

Keywords: Foreign Direct Investment (FDI); emerging market; China market; South Korean firms; internationalization; sectoral differences

INTRODUCTION

Over the last two decades a new pattern of worldwide foreign direct investment (FDI) has emerged in which multinational enterprises (MNEs) from growing economies are actively seeking investment opportunities abroad. Investments from developing countries accounted for 20.8% of the world's total FDIs made in 2009, marking the highest number in modern world economy history (UNCTAD, 2010). This noticeable increase in outward FDI from developing countries received attention from the international investment literature (Buckley et al., 2007; UNCTAD, 2006). In particular, roughly 80% of the developing-country-initiated FDIs are from MNEs based in emerging Asian economies. This pattern posed new academic questions and spawned various studies trying to give explanations on the matter.

Alongside the new trend of worldwide FDI, Korea's outward FDI has also increased rapidly over the last ten years, from $5.2 billion in 2000 to $23.2 billion in 2010. This has been due to Korean companies making strategic moves to seek new overseas markets and low-cost manufacturing locations. Furthermore, Korea has seen an increase in the number of investments into new, emerging destinations such as China, Vietnam, Indonesia, and Brazil. According to Korea Eximbank (2011), FDIs in financial services, and technical services in particular, have been growing significantly as well as in manufacturing sectors. By considering the aforementioned aspects, Korean FDI arguably qualifies for an exemplary case insofar as one desires to examine the growing presence of emerging economy FDIs.

For a typical enterprise, the most immediate and important question regarding FDI is whether it helps to improve the parent company's performance, and if so, by how much (UNCTAD, 2006). This question relates to the competitiveness of a firm when internationalized. Many of the existing empirical studies that assessed the relationship between FDI and firm performance are focused on multinationals headquartered in developed countries. Results commonly suggest that FDIs help utilize firm-specific advantages in foreign locations (Hennart, 1982; Rugman, 1982). On the other hand, it creates synergy by enabling access to manpower, core technology, and resources in different geographic locations (Kogut, 1985; Porter, 1990). Although such earlier studies conjectured a positive linear relationship between internationalization and firm performance, it was seldom apparent in empirical tests. It was largely the consequence of cost-side variables being ignored or excluded (Gomes & Ramaswamy, 1999; Ruigrok & Wagner, 2003; Sullivan, 1994). Some of the later studies documented a nonlinear-shaped relationship between the two and attribute it to the influence of firms' maturity stage and differences in size (Geringer, Beamish, & Dacosta, 1989; Hitt, Hoskisson, & Kim, 1997; Lu & Beamish, 2001; Tallman & Li, 1996).

However, there are only a limited number of empirical studies that analyzed the FDI of MNEs from developing countries (Lecraw, 1993; Pangarkar, 2003). They mostly rely on limited datasets due to the difficulty involved in data access to MNEs of developing countries (UNCTAD, 2006). On a related note, many of the research papers on MNEs of developing countries are basically case studies of Asia-based multinationals (Hobday, 1997; Hoesel, 1999; Li, 2003; Mathews, 2002; Oh, Choi, & Choi, 1998; Sachwald, 2001; Sims & Pandian, 2002). These studies consistently find that multinationals which engage in FDIs in developing countries tend to improve the performance of parent firms. Nevertheless, a comprehensive examination of large panel datasets is necessary for a deeper understanding of the relationship, which would allow an effective control of industry- and destination-specific factors.

In this study, we examine the statistical relationship between FDI and the shareholder value (or annualized equity return) that exists among Korean companies listed on the Korea Exchange (KRX). We quantify FDI levels using investment data of foreign affiliates that are recorded in annual reports of all KRX-listed companies dated 2005–2008. This study differs from existing studies that had to deal with limited samples of data, as the data comprises virtually all publicly listed companies in Korea.

Due to the extensiveness of the data, we were able to further our research and conduct a more detailed analysis looking at the industry effect. Since the existing literature has been focused solely on manufacturing firms and its effect on performances, we believe that our analysis shows a comparison between the manufacturing and the service sector.

This study identifies the effect of China as a modifier and suggests that it is also an important addition to the literature. As posited at the beginning, outward direct investment from newly emerging economies largely concentrates into other emerging economies (UNCTAD, 2006), thus the so-called South-South FDI is a growing subject of interest. It is notable that intra-Asia FDI accounts for more than 80% of FDI flows between developing countries around the world. We are firmly convinced that studying FDI initiated by Korean firms toward Asian developing countries, especially China, will enable us to take an in-depth look at the ongoing phenomena. Roughly, 50% of the total FDI initiated by Korean firms was focused in Asian locations as of 2008, with half of the total resulting in direct investment in China.

In "Data Sources and Sample Description," the data and the methodology used are explained; and in "Empirical Results," we present and interpret the results of our empirical analyses. Lastly, in "Interpretation of Empirical Results," we will outline the findings and discuss the implications.

DATA SOURCES AND SAMPLE DESCRIPTION

The sample used in this study covered all the companies listed on the Korea Exchange in the month of November 2009. The details for the FDI sample of the Korean companies are extracted from the annual reports during the past four years, from 2005 to 2008. The annual reports are accessible on the DART (Data Analysis, Retrieval, and Transfer System), provided by the Korea Financial Supervisory Service.[1] We can find the total investments of overseas affiliated companies in the clause investments in other companies of the annual reports. As a matter of a fact, the reported figures in the clause above include not only the amount of new FDI outflows during a fiscal year, but also the net income of overseas affiliated companies reflected by the equity method during that year. This shows an increase (or decrease) of these values, which means either that the FDI flows increase (or decrease) for the year, or that overseas affiliated companies have positive net income for the year. In this aspect, the "outward FDI flows for the year shown," terms used in the study, cover both the amount of actual FDI outflows and the performance of overseas affiliated companies. Although it would be more desirable to separate the amount of actual FDI flows from the net income of overseas affiliated companies, the separation is practically not feasible as they are not reported separately within the clause of "investments in other companies" of the annual reports.

Tables 1 and 4 provide a summary of statistics of the sample data in various aspects. The reported figures in the tables are the total investments of overseas affiliated companies in the clause of "investments in other companies" of the annual reports. As our sample covers all the companies listed on the Korea Exchange, 599–689 companies are included in the sample each year.

Table 2 shows that 51.7% of the companies in the sample carried out FDI in the 2008 fiscal year. Compared to 58.9% of the manufacturing companies that had FDI outstanding, a smaller percentage of firms in the service sector (43.1% of the sample) and in financial industry (10.7%) carried out FDI. Average sample characteristics of the companies that engage in FDI are found in Table 3. On average, firms with foreign assets

Table 1. Overall Companies Listed on the Korea Exchange.

Year	Manufacturing Sector	Service Sector	Financial Sector[a]	Others	Total
2005	401	102	47	49	599
2006	409	128	48	50	635
2007	423	139	51	52	665
2008	431	144	56	58	689

[a]The financial companies can be classified into the service group, but we treated them separately from any other service companies, as the characteristics of the financial companies are quite different from those of other service companies.

Table 2. FDI Activities of the Sample Companies in the Fiscal Year 2008.

Industry	Companies with FDI		Companies without FDI		Total
	Number of companies	Ratio (percentage)	Number of companies	Ratio (percentage)	
Manufacturing	254	58.9%	177	41.1%	431
Service	62	43.1%	82	56.9%	144
Financial	6	10.7%	50	89.3%	56
Others	34	58.6%	24	41.4%	58
Total	356	51.7%	333	48.3%	689

Table 3. Mean Characteristics of the Companies with FDI.

Year	Sector	Total Asset (Million Korean Won)	Total Sales (Million Korean Won)	Return on Assets (%)	Return on Sales (%)	Stock Market Return (%)[a]
2005	Overall	1,918.8	1,770.4	5.3	5.6	119.4
	Nonfinance	1,850.9	1,767.6	5.4	5.7	119.3
	Manufacturing	1,528.7	1,563.4	5.2	5.1	121.9
	Service	2,065.6	2,158.6	6.8	8.5	105.7
2006	Overall	1,988.5	1,786.7	4.9	2.6	6.8
	Nonfinance	1,903.9	1,778.1	4.9	2.6	6.9
	Manufacturing	1,612.0	1,605.4	4.8	1.0	4.4
	Service	2,177.8	2,198.9	5.5	8.7	15.7
2007	Overall	1,972.5	1,738.3	6.1	10.0	46.1
	Nonfinance	1,972.5	1,769.0	6.1	10.0	45.8
	Manufacturing	1,653.1	1,519.2	5.9	10.1	46.5
	Service	2,256.1	2,335.3	7.1	11.5	33.5
2008	Overall	2,423.5	2,266.3	3.3	5.9	−40.5
	Nonfinance	2,423.5	2,266.3	3.3	5.9	−40.6
	Manufacturing	2,000.3	1,808.0	3.1	5.0	−39.5
	Service	2,604.8	2,879.3	3.9	10.1	−40.4

[a]Stock market return is calculated based on year-end closing prices at Korea Exchange (KRX).

in service industries are bigger in size than manufacturing firms. Note that the dominant year-specific effect on the stock market returns across sectors (i.e., large and negative average returns in 2008) are eventually controlled in our model by the stock market index.

Table 4 provides a more detailed look at the FDI originating from South Korea towards China, including the yearly trend of Korea-to-China FDI

Table 4. Amount of FDI into China by Year: 1 Million Korean Won, %.

Year	Total Assets of Parent Companies	Total FDI from Parent Companies	FDI/Total Assets	FDI Stock in China	Proportion of FDI Stock in China
2005	1,218,718	53,600	4.4%	23,901	41.6%
2006	1,290,360	81,488	6.3%	27,364	39.7%
2007	1,313,509	106,987	8.1%	43,661	37.2%
2008	1,583,593	155,123	9.8%	61,441	36.9%

and its relative weight within those parent firms. From our sample, the FDI stock in China reaches 36.9% of the total FDI stock at the end of 2008. This ratio is 25% higher than the proportion of FDI stock in China to the overall FDI reported by the Korea Eximbank in 2008. This difference can be due to the fact that the size of the sample companies in this study is larger than the average size of the overall companies in Korea, and thus they are more likely to carry out FDI than average-sized Korean firms. From our sample, we also find that the ratio of outward FDI to the total asset of parent companies increases from 4.3% in 2005 to 9.8% in 2008.

ANALYSIS MODEL

In this paper, we use the following linear regression model to verify the relationships between the performances of Korean parent companies and their FDI activities.

$$R_{jt} = \alpha + \beta_M R_{Mt} + \beta_1 X_{jt}^1 + \beta_2 X_{jt}^2 + \varepsilon_{jt} \tag{1}$$

where, R_{jt} is the rate of return of the common stock of j-th firm on year t, R_{Mt} is the rate of return of the KOSPI (Korea Composite Stock Price Index) on year t, X_{jt}^1 denotes the level of j-th firm's internationalization by FDI by the year t (which is calculated by dividing the FDI stock at the end of year t by the total asset at the end of year t), X_{jt}^2 denotes the degree of the j-th firm's effort to internationalize by FDI on the year t (which is calculated by dividing the change in the FDI stock during the year by the total asset at the end of the year t).

In our regression model presented above, we treat the rates of return of the common stock of parent companies as dependent variables. This treatment is based on the belief that if a parent company is a listed company, then the stock price would be the most reliable indicator reflecting all of the impact of FDI on the competitiveness, profitability, growth, and credibility of the parent company. In other words, this means that we assume the informational efficiency of stock markets to verify the impact of FDI on the performances of parent companies. As independent variables, we select the rate of return of market-wide stock index, the level of a firm's internationalization by FDI, and the degree of a firm's efforts to internationalize by FDI.

We use the stock index return as an instrumental variable to control the reward for bearing systematic risk of stock markets. We acknowledge that the market-wide stock index would not completely capture all the systematic risk as suggested by Fama and French (1993), but in this study we adopt the single factor model (i.e., market index model), most widely used in the conventional approach, to control the effect of systematic risk.

The level of a firm's internationalization by FDI, the second independent variable used in Eq. (1), is the ratio of FDI stock to total assets at the end of the year shown. It captures the effect of a firm's cumulative efforts to internationalize by FDI on the performances of the firms. The degree of a firm's efforts to internationalize by FDI, the third independent variable used in Eq. (1), is the ratio of FDI flows to total assets. It captures the effect of a firm's incremental efforts to internationalize by FDI during the year shown on the performances of the firms.

From Eq. (1), if the performances of parent companies can be improved by increasing the FDI flows, then the estimate of regression coefficient β_2 would be a positive value. In addition, if the continuous expansion of FDI, that is, the cumulative FDI stock, can contribute to the improvement of the performances of parent companies, then the estimate of regression coefficient β_1 would be a positive value.

We also find that the FDI in China could be strategically important for the Korean firms in our sample. Table 1 shows that almost 40% of the total Korean FDI has been concentrated in China. In addition, the economic growth rate of China is still as high as emerging economies despite the fact that the economic size of China already surpasses that of most developed economies. As China becomes a very important FDI destination for Korean firms, we need to separate the FDI into China from the FDI in the other markets for our analysis. The following regression model is designed to verify the "China effect" in this study.

$$R_{jt} = \alpha + \beta_M R_{Mt} + \beta_{C1} X_{jt}^{C1} + \beta_1 X_{jt}^1 + \varepsilon_{jt} \tag{2}$$

$$R_{jt} = \alpha + \beta_M R_{Mt} + \beta_2 X_{jt}^2 + \beta_{C2} X_{jt}^{C2} + \varepsilon_{jt} \tag{3}$$

where, R_{jt}, R_{Mt}, X_{jt}^1, and X_{jt}^2 are defined the same as in Eq. (1), X_{jt}^{C1} denotes the proportion of the FDI stock in China, which is calculated by dividing the FDI stock in China by the overall FDI stock at the end of the year t, X_{jt}^{C2} denotes the proportion of the FDI flow into China, which is calculated by dividing the change in the FDI stock in China during the year t by the change in the overall FDI stock during the year t.

If the FDI in China creates a pronounced positive impact on the performance of parent companies, then the estimate of regression coefficients β_{C1} and β_{C2} in Eqs. (2) and (3) would obviously be a positive value.

EMPIRICAL RESULTS

Relationship between FDI and Firm Performance

The second column of Table 5 shows the empirical results from our entire sample including all the firms regardless of industry sector, using the regression model in Eq. (1).[2] From this we find that the estimate of the regression coefficient for the stock market index, capturing the systematic risk, is

Table 5.   Empirical Results from the Regression Analysis.

Coefficient Estimates	All Industries	All Except Finance and Insurances	Manufacturing Sector	Service Sector
Intercept $\hat{\alpha}$	5.99***	5.25***	5.75***	−1.06
	(1.36)	(1.32)	(1.65)	(2.45)
Market effect $\hat{\beta}_M$	1.18***	1.13**	1.18***	0.81***
	(0.04)	(0.04)	(0.05)	(0.08)
FDI $\hat{\beta}_1$	−11.44	−11.26	−11.95	379.00**
	(7.70)	(7.24)	(7.24)	(160.17)
FDI^2 $\hat{\beta}_2$	6.35**	6.31**	6.43*	19.69
	(2.77)	(2.60)	(2.60)	(51.68)
Adj. R^2	0.36	0.36	0.37	0.31

Note: Numbers in parentheses are standard errors. Asterisks, *, **, and *** indicate that the coefficient estimate is statistically significant at the 10%, 5%, 1% level, respectively.

1.1849 with a great statistical significance. This result is consistent with the earlier findings, from most previous studies in the field of investment or empirical asset pricing, that the reward for systematic risk or market risk is the most important key factor in explaining the individual stock return.

The estimated regression coefficient $\hat{\beta}_1$, measuring the effect of the level of a firm's internationalization by FDI is negative, but is statistically insignificant, even at a level of 10%. This means that there is no clear evidence to support the relationship between the cumulative FDI stock and the performance of parent companies.

Contrastingly, the estimate of regression coefficient $\hat{\beta}_2$, measuring the effect of the degree of a firm's efforts to internationalize by FDI, is positive, which is statistically significant at a level of 5%. This suggests that increasing the FDI flows for the year shown results in a significant positive impact on the stock returns of the parent companies for the year. This is consistent with the several previous studies, which reported the relationship between the FDI of multinational corporations of developing countries and the firm performances.

Next, the adjusted R-square of the regression model from Eq. (1) is 0.36. This means that while 35.68% of the total variations in the stock return of the parent's companies is explained by the dynamics of the market-wide stock index (i.e., KOSPI), the remaining 64.32% of the variations can be explained by other factors, such as firm-specific factors. This adjusted R-square is much smaller than that of most previous studies in the literatures of finance, such as Davis, Fama, and French (2000), which reported that about 70% of the total variations in stock returns is explained by the dynamics of market-wide stock index, and the remaining 10−20% of the variations is further explained by the SMB factor (the stock return of small firms minus the return of big firms) and the HML factor (the stock return of firms with high book-to-market ratios minus the stock return of firms with low book-to-market ratios). This difference can be mainly caused by the fact that while the individual stock returns were used as dependent variables in the regression model of this study, the diversified portfolio's returns were used as dependent variables in the previous literature on empirical asset pricing.

Furthermore, in order to assess the possible differences of the empirical results across industries, we divided the total sample into three groups: nonfinancial companies, manufacturing companies, and service companies. Table 5 also presents the empirical results based on these three subsamples. By looking at the second and third column of Table 5, we find that the empirical results from the group of nonfinancial companies and from the group of manufacturing companies are not essentially different compared to those from the original whole sample, which are presented in the first column of Table 5. That is, while we cannot find any statistical evidence supporting the relationship between the cumulative FDI stocks and the performances of parent companies, we do find the statistics significant showing a positive relationship between the FDI flows for the year and the performances of parent companies. These findings may be due to the fact that more than two-thirds of whole companies belong to the manufacturing group (or the nonfinancial group).

However, the group of service companies in the fourth column of the Table 5 provides results that contrast with the previous ones. In the case of the group of service companies, as the estimate of regression coefficient $\hat{\beta}_2$ is statistically insignificant even at 10%, we found that increasing the FDI flows for the current year cannot raise the stock price of parent companies for the year. On the contrary, as the estimate of regression coefficient $\hat{\beta}_1$, denoting the level of a firm's internationalization by FDI, is statistically significant at 5%, we found that the service companies, who continued to try to internationalize by FDI, can increase their shareholder value.

To sum up, mutual relations between the FDI activities and the performances of parent companies were found to be different across industry sectors, at least among companies listed in the Korea Exchange. In the case of nonfinancial and manufacturing companies, the FDI flows for the current year rather than the cumulative FDI stock for the past years have a positive influence on the stock price of parent companies. That is, as the degree of a firm's efforts to internationalize by FDI increases, the performances of parent companies in manufacturing or the nonfinancial sector can be improved. On the other hand, in the case of service companies, the cumulative FDI stocks rather than the FDI flows for the current year have a positive influence on the stock price of parent companies. Therefore, as the level of a firm's internationalization by FDI increases, the performances of parent companies in the service sector can be improved.

China Effects

Table 6 presents the regression results from Eqs. (2) and (3), which selects the proportion of FDI stock in China as an explanatory variable. In the section "Introduction," it showed that the FDI flows have a significant effect on the performances of the parent companies in the case of manufacturing companies, they, together with the proportion of the FDI stock in China, are selected as explanatory variables in the regression model of Eq. (2). Additionally, the results display that the cumulative FDI stocks have a great influence on the performances of the parent companies in the

Table 6.   Empirical Results on China Effect.

Coefficient Estimates	Manufacturing Sector	Service Sector
Intercept $\hat{\alpha}$	5.47***(1.64)	4.56(1550)
Market effect $\hat{\beta}_M$	1.18***(0.05)	1.32***(0.11)
FDI $\hat{\beta}_1$	−9.55e-07(2.86e-06)	−464.65**(226.34)
FDI^2 $\hat{\beta}_2$	4.96*(2.54)	0.42(0.28)
Adj. R^2	0.37	0.30

Note: Numbers in parentheses are standard errors. Asterisks, *, **, and *** indicate that the coefficient estimate is statistically significant at the 10%, 5%, 1% level, respectively.

case of service companies; we select them and the proportion of the FDI stock in China as explanatory variables in the regression model of Eq. (3).

Column 2 of Table 6 presents the results for the case of manufacturing companies. It shows that the estimate of regression coefficient $\hat{\beta}_{C1}$ in Eq. (2) is positive, but not statistically significant even at any reasonable significance level. This means that the performances of parent companies in manufacturing sectors are not improved by increasing the FDI stocks in China.

On the other hand, in the service sector's case (column 3), we find that the estimate of regression coefficient $\hat{\beta}_{C2}$ in Eq. (3), measuring the China effect, is positive and the *p*-value of the estimate is relatively small, that is, 0.12. Although this *p*-value may not be enough for us to confirm the statistical significance of the China effect, it still entails informational content that should not be ignored. In addition, by comparing the estimated $\hat{\beta}_1$ from the fourth column of Table 5 with the estimated $\hat{\beta}_1$ from the second column of Table 6, it seems that the China effect would replace the effect of the cumulative FDI stock in explaining the performances of parent companies. Although we are not able to confirm the strong statistical significance of the China effect in the case of Korean service companies, it is fairly probable from an empirical point of view that the China effect (higher proportion of FDI stock in China) is one of the most important factors that improve the performance of parent companies in service sectors.

INTERPRETATION OF EMPIRICAL RESULTS

Interpreting the Contrast between Results from Manufacturing and Service Sector

The difference found between the manufacturing sector and the service sector can be attributed primarily to the historical characteristics of

Korean FDI. This requires a prior understanding of how the sectoral composition of Korean FDI has evolved over time. For the past two or three decades, Korean FDI has been heavily concentrated in manufacturing industries with a low fraction taking place in services. As UNCTAD (2006) documented, out of the total outward FDI stock from developing and transitional economies, FDI in service sectors accounts for 81% (71% with Hong Kong excluded) in 2004 with a considerable portion explained by merger and acquisition in telecom and transportation. In contrast, in Korea's case, the industrial composition of foreign affiliates' investments look quite different: Based on stock (54.8 million USD), manufacturing accounts for 52%, trade 20%, mining 6%, services 21% (excluding trade), and agriculture 1%. As of 2008, the most recent observation point of our study (total outward FDI stock amounts to 116.3 billion USD), the share of manufacturing and trade decreased to 45% and 16%, respectively, but the mining and nontrade services increased in shares to 9% and 29%, respectively. Although it has seen a significant growth of investment in services, but the relative proportion still remains low against other developing countries.

Since a country's sectoral composition of outward FDI basically reflects the country's own pattern of competitive advantages – the capacity to transform any given inputs into products and services at maximum profit (Kogut, 1985) – we can cautiously conjecture that the pattern found in Korean FDI may be an angiogram of its competitive advantages. The outward investment of Korean companies started to surge in the mid-1990s when manufacturers were gaining global competitiveness in electronic and electrical equipment. On the other hand, FDI in service sectors was relatively small except in trade-related ones. In fact, more than half of FDIs in trade services have been due to establishments of Korean manufacturing firms for the purpose of serving local markets (Lee, 2007). In fact, Korean FDIs in service sectors have remained largely insignificant until the mid-2000s. However, as Korea's advanced IT infrastructure found a way to improve competitiveness of Korean companies' services (Korea Eximbank, 2007), Korea's FDIs in the service sector took off. Also, it coincides with increases in financial services and real estate that were prompted by huge deregulating acts of the Korean government on capital outflows.

As discussed, the cross-sector difference in the empirical results can be explained by the historical trend in Korean industrial structure, and in addition, assessing the difference in motives of investment can also help explain it. The Korea Eximbank (2007) surveyed 2,000 foreign establishments out of total 4,670 establishments with direct investment of more than one million US dollars. It approached the motives in two different aspects: the target market focus and the production input focus.

First, for manufacturing sectors, 47.8% of them had foreign local market focus and the remaining 52.2% on the rest of the world markets (Korean market 20.6%, remaining world markets 31.7%). However, in service sectors, 77.4% had focused on local markets. This result suggests that FDIs in services tend to have strong local markets seeking characteristics, while Korean manufacturers rather find their establishments as production bases for other world markets, either Korea or remaining world markets. Thus, the local-market-dependent nature of the FDI in service sectors highlights the relative importance of long-term commitments and plans to expand the local presence and strengthen relationships. It can allow a weaker relationship between equity returns and the investment implemented in corresponding years.

Korean FDI in the manufacturing sector, on the other hand, seemingly focusing on the cost-side advantages of the locations, would generally require relatively little long-term approach. This is because the local input costs are not strongly tied to individual foreign affiliates strategies. Therefore, one can expect a tighter association between each year's direct investment and the shareholder value.

Furthermore, the Korea Eximbank's survey (2007) looks at production input focus, and it is very suggestive in understanding the difference between sectors as well. As expected, most Korean manufacturers (71.7%) responded that their FDI is intended for cost-saving. 18.8% were aimed at securing raw materials or resources, and 9.5% of them for technology and know-how concerns. In contrast, 49.7% of the service FDIs were for technology and know-how concerns, 42.1% for cost-saving, and the remaining 8.3% for resources. One observation that can be drawn from this is that Korean outward manufacturing FDIs show typical asset exploiting (or efficiency-seeking) characteristics while FDI in service sectors display asset augmentation (or created-asset seeking).

Nevertheless, the unique source of advantages that the majority of Korean manufacturers have is mostly production process capabilities obtained through specialization within specific intraindustry value chains, unlike few exceptionally competitive companies such as Samsung and Hyundai Motors with expertise and technology-based ownership advantages (UNCTAD, 2006). These process capabilities yield predictable successes from FDI when combined with inexpensive labor in the host countries, mostly developing countries in Asia. However, there are two main reasons why this advantage based on process capabilities is unlikely to be sustainable. One is the possibility that the input cost in host countries will rise in the foreseeable future. Another possibility is that local companies can become competitors by catching up with the production process capabilities, which could be easily followed or imitated. So an efficiency-seeking FDI based on technology with a moderate level of sophistication will tend to benefit more in the short-term from the firm's internationalization efforts by FDI as opposed to long-run internationalization levels. In services, since the created-asset seeking motive is generally more pronounced than cost reduction focus, long-term deliberated efforts is likely to be favored concerning firms' performances.

Interpreting China Effects

While little evidence for FDIs in manufacturing sectors was found to substantiate that the China effects on performance aspects of Korean outward FDI, a meaningful result for service sectors was obtained suggesting that a higher investment share in China is associated with higher equity returns. This empirical pattern can be understood in light of the relation-specificity between the two countries (Korea and China) and operational performances of Korean companies' subsidiaries in China as well.

According to the geographical breakdown of Korea Eximbank's extensive annual surveys,[3] the share of the Chinese market in total sales from Korean manufacturing FDI in 2008 was 48.9% with the rest of the world accounting for 51.1% (Korean market 28.0%, remaining world markets 23.1%). This largely resembles the composition (local market focus against the rest of the world) documented in the Korea Eximbank's (2007) survey regarding the motives of FDI (Korea Eximbank, 2007). One noticeable difference is that the share of sales in the Korean market out of total sales made by affiliates in China is higher than the overall sales share of the Korean market among all foreign affiliates around the world (28.0% compared to 20.6%). This seems to be the consequence of geographical proximity between Korea and China. It also implies that the Korean manufacturing FDI in China has relatively more focus on establishment of production bases since the labor and land usage costs are inexpensive in China. However, the rapid rise of input costs in China makes it difficult for expanding direct investment to guarantee a long-term sustainable improvement in the parent firm value.

Meanwhile, service-related FDI in China yields 95.2% of its total sales from the local market whereas 4.8% comes from Korea and remaining world markets. These types of investments are mostly aimed at serving the Chinese market, so more intensive investment in China may indicate a higher likelihood that the firm will establish its presence in the huge and rapidly expanding market. In particular, the fact that performance figures are much better for service establishments than for manufacturing establishments in China (Korea Eximbank, 2009) might be consistent with the China effect noticeable especially in FDIs in service sectors.

CONCLUSION

This study empirically analyzes the relationship between outward FDI and performances of investing Korean firms. By examining large panel datasets of outward FDI activities done by all publicly listed companies in Korea, this study extracted an in-depth understanding of the relationship, considering industry- and destination-specific factors. Empirical findings from this study in general show a positive relationship between outward FDI and investing Korean firms' performances. These results agree with the findings of previous studies, most of them case studies, on the relationship between FDIs and performance when parent firms are multinationals headquartered in developing countries.

One important contribution from this study is that it revealed compelling differences in the degree of relationships between FDI and firm performance across different industries. We can confirm that in manufacturing sectors, each year's flow of direct investment is more heavily associated with firm performance than accumulated stock of direct investment. While in the service sector, it is opposite. The reader should be cautioned before generalizing these findings due to the fact that we empirically analyzed the relationship using corporate dataset confined within a single country's economic boundary. Nevertheless, this study offers a constructive perspective as to why FDI-performance relationships are significantly different between manufacturing and service sectors.

This study also provides reasonable evidence for these cross-sector differences by analyzing FDI motives of Korean manufacturing and service firms in two different aspects; that is, the target market focus and the production (or service) input focus. In terms of target market focus, foreign affiliates of Korean manufacturers focus more on world markets than local foreign markets, where they have production establishments, while FDIs in service sectors have a stronger local market focus. These cross-sector differences in target market focus might influence the relative level of long-term commitments, which could lead to different (stronger or weaker) levels of relationships between direct investment and the shareholder value of an investing Korean firm. Furthermore, from the production input focus, the Korean outward manufacturing FDI shows typical asset exploiting (efficiency seeking) characteristics while FDI in service sectors presents the characteristics of asset augmentation (created-asset seeking) FDI. These cross-sector differences in FDI characteristics of Korean firms might lead to different time span of the firm's internationalization efforts by FDI, and result in different cross-sector relationships between FDI and firm performance.

Another important contribution of this study is the recognition of the China effect. We found from the analysis that the impact of China impacts on the performance aspects of Korea's FDI and differs between manufacturing sectors and service sectors. That is, our results suggest a tight relationship between the investment shares of China-bound FDI and the corresponding equity returns in service sectors, but little in manufacturing sectors. Careful inspection of the characteristics of Korea-China direct investment provides one plausible explanation for the difference across sectors. Korean manufacturing FDI in China has been focused on establishing production bases for global markets, but the rapid increase in input costs in China makes it difficult to expand direct investment for the long-run prospect of improvement in competitiveness of parent firms. Meanwhile, in service sectors, Korean FDI in China has been mostly aimed at serving China's domestic market so that a protracted economic growth of China can propagate to a sustained improvement in the parent firm value.

Despite our contributions to the aforementioned literature, we acknowledge a notable limitation in our analysis. The issues of endogeneity in our empirical model are not adequately addressed and may remain unresolved, even though an intuitive explanation for the results is provided based on the general properties of Korean FDI from previous surveys. For more elaborate and conclusive discussion of our empirical results, we need to examine a comprehensive relationship among FDI, firm's motivation, firm characteristics, and performance of the firm. Our future research directions would be to identify primary business motives for FDI at the individual firm level using the panel datasets that we have complied.

NOTES

1. Although the annual business reports are accessible on the DART provided by Korea Financial Supervisory Service since 1998, we did not use the earlier data

before 2004, as the methods of reporting and evaluating were absolutely different between the firms.

2. The original data is not a balanced panel because of the missing data and the entrance and exit of firms. It is usual that this type of the unbalanced panel data is reconstructed as a balanced panel data, and then used in an empirical analysis. We used, however, the original data rather than the reconstructed data, as we thought that losses or distortions of the information are likely to happen in the process of reconstructing the data. In addition, as the unbalance of the original data in this paper is not severe, and is not caused by endogenous factors, it is unlikely that using the original data is problematic.

3. The survey is for all foreign affiliates with more than one million US dollar worth of direct investments.

ACKNOWLEDGMENTS

This work was supported by the National Research Foundation of Korea Grant funded by the Korean Government (NRF-2013S1A2A1A01034104). The views expressed in this paper are solely those of the authors and not necessarily those of the U.S. Bureau of Economic Analysis or the U.S. Department of Commerce.

REFERENCES

Buckley, P. J., Clegg, L. J., Cross, A. R., Liu, X., Voss, H., & Zheng, P. (2007). The determinants of Chinese outward foreign direct investment. *Journal of International Business Studies*, *38*(4), 499−518.

Davis, J., Fama, E. F., & French, K. R. (2000). Characteristics, covariances, and average returns: 1929–1997. *Journal of Finance*, *55*(1), 389–406.

Fama, E. F., & French, K. R. (1993). Common risk factors in the returns on stocks and bonds. *Journal of Financial Economics*, *33*(1), 3−56.

Geringer, M. J., Beamish, P. W., & Dacosta, R. C. (1989). Diversification strategy and internationalization: Implications for MNE performance. *Strategic Management Journal*, *10*(1), 109−119.

Gomes, L., & Ramaswamy, K. (1999). An empirical examination of the form of the relationship between multinationality and performance. *Journal of International Business Studies*, *30*(1), 173−187.

Hennart, J.−F. (1982). *A theory of multinational enterprise*. Ann Arbor, MI: University of Michigan Press.

Hitt, M. A., Hoskisson, R. E., & Kim, H. (1997). International diversification: Effects on innovation and firm performance in product-diversified firms. *Academy of Management Journal*, *40*(4), 767−798.

Hobday, M. (1997). Latecomer catch-up strategies in electronics: Samsung of Korea and acer of Taiwan. *Asia Pacific Business Review, 4*(2/3), 48–83.

Hoesel, R. V. (1999). *New multinational enterprises from Korea and Taiwan.* London: Routledge.

Kogut, B. (1985). Designing global strategies: Profiting from operation flexibility. *Sloan Management Review, 27*(1), 27–38.

Korea Eximbank. (2007). *Performance analysis of Korean outward FDI for the accounting year 2006.* Seoul: Korea Eximbank (Korean).

Korea Eximbank. (2009). *Performance analysis of Korean outward FDI for the accounting year 2008.* Seoul: Korea Eximbank (Korean).

Korea Eximbank. (2011). *Analysis of trade effects of Korean outward FDI and policy implications.* Seoul: Korea Eximbank (Korean).

Lecraw, D. J. (1993). Outward direct investment by Indonesian firms: Motivation and effects. *Journal of International Business Studies, 24*(3), 589–600.

Lee, S.-B. (2007). New trends and performances of Korean outward FDI after the financial crisis. *International Finance Review, 7*, 75–96.

Li, P. P. (2003). Toward a geocentric theory of multinational evolution: The implications from the Asian MNEs as latecomers. *Asian Pacific Journal of Management, 20*(2), 217–243.

Lu, J. W., & Beamish, P. W. (2001). The internationalization and performance of SMEs. *Strategic Management Journal, 22*, 565–586.

Mathews, J. A. (2002). *Dragon multinationals: A New model of global growth.* New York, NY: Oxford University Press.

Oh, D., Choi, C. J., & Choi, E. (1998). The globalization strategy of Daewoo motor company. *Asia Pacific Journal of Management, 15*(2), 185–203.

Pangarkar, N. (2003). Determinants of alliance duration in uncertain environments: The case of the biotechnology sector. *Long Range Planning, 36*(3), 269–284.

Porter, M. E. (1990). *The competitive advantage of nations.* New York, NY: Free Press.

Rugman, A. M. (1982). *New theories of the multinational enterprise.* New York, NY: St. Martin's Press.

Ruigrok, W., & Wagner, H. (2003). Internationalization and performance: An organizational learning perspective. *Management International Review, 43*(1), 63–83.

Sachwald, F. (2001). *Going multinational: The Korean experience of direct investment.* London: Routledge.

Sim, A. B., & Pandian, R. (2002). Internationalization strategies of emerging Asian MNEs: Case study evidence on Taiwanese firms. *Journal of Asian Business, 18*(1), 67–80.

Sullivan, D. (1994). The 'threshold of internationalization': Replication, extension & reinterpretation. *Management International Review, 34*(2), 165–186.

Tallman, S., & Li, J. (1996). Effects of international diversity and product diversity on the performance of multinational firms. *Academy of Management Journal, 39*(1), 179–196.

UNCTAD. (2006). *FDI from developing and transition economies: Implication for development, world investment report.* Geneva: UNCTAD.

UNCTAD. (2010). *Investing in a low-carbon economy, world investment report.* Geneva: UNCTAD.